Directory of the City of Raleigh, N.C., 1896-'97

Containing the names of all the residents, together with a complete classified business directory of the city

Charles A. Separk

Alpha Editions

This edition published in 2020

ISBN : 9789354042836

Design and Setting By
Alpha Editions
www.alphaedis.com
email - alphaedis@gmail.com

As per information held with us this book is in Public Domain.
This book is a reproduction of an important historical work. Alpha Editions uses the best technology to reproduce historical work in the same manner it was first published to preserve its original nature. Any marks or number seen are left intentionally to preserve its true form.

DIRECTORY

OF THE

CITY OF RALEIGH, N. C.,

1896='97,

CONTAINING THE NAMES OF ALL THE RESIDENTS,
TOGETHER WITH A COMPLETE

CLASSIFIED BUSINESS DIRECTORY
OF THE CITY.

ALSO GIVING THE STATE, COUNTY AND CITY GOVERNMENTS,
AND AN AMOUNT OF VALUABLE INFORMATION CON-
CERNING CORPORATIONS, SOCIETIES, ETC.

Compiled by CHARLES A. SEPARK.

PUBLISHED BY
THE RALEIGH STATIONERY COMPANY.

PRICE, $2.00.

INTRODUCTORY.

In the publication of the Directory for 1896–'97, we offer no apology, firmly believing that a careful and unbiased examination must and will convince our subscribers that the work will speak for itself. In obtaining correct information in regard to Raleigh, we have spared neither labor nor expense, and have made a house-to-house canvass in gathering information; and though the labor has been both tedious and expensive, it has been greatly facilitated by the courtesy of our citizens, whose generous support and cooperation have enabled us to present so full and complete a publication.

In presenting to you this, our first effort at Directory-making, we desire to express our thanks for the assistance and information so cheerfully given, and at the same time claim a just appreciation of our own efforts to place before the public and into the hands of every merchant and professional man in Raleigh a Directory worthy of the Capital City of the grand old Commonwealth of North Carolina.

RALEIGH STATIONERY COMPANY.

August 1, 1896.

INDEX TO ADVERTISEMENTS.

	PAGE
Allen & Cram Machine Co.,	VIII
Agricultural & Mechanical College,	158
Andrews, A. B. Jr.	55
Ashe, S. A. & Son	V
Ayer, Dr. J. M.	58
Baptist Book Store,	61
Batchelor, Jos. B.	64
Bauer, A. G.	65
Betts Bros,	68
Blake, T. W.	IV
Blake, Jos. Manager,	70
Briggs, Thomas H. & Sons	112 A
Brown, Jno. W.	81
Broughton, J. M. & Co.	112 A
Bullock, Chas. F.	264 B
Burwell, J. B.	87
Cameron & Batchelor,	192 B
Capital Printing Co.,	89
Carroll, Dr. N. G.	91
Carroll, J. D.	90
Carpenter & Peebles,	VIII
Clark, M. S.	46
Commercial & Farmers Bank,	III
Cooper Bros.,	II
Crawford, Dr. J. H.	101
Douglass, W. C.	111
Drewry, Jno. C.	III
Dughi, A.	45
Eberhardt & Baker,	VIII
Fasnach, Ed.	46
Faust, E. G.	73
Ferrall, J. R. & Co.	VII
Folsom, Finger & Co.,	281
Fleming, Dr. J. Martin	VI
Gill, J. H.	VIII
Gray, R. T.	II
Hay, T. T. & Bro.	145
Hermann, F.	147
Hicks & Rogers,	149
Hinsdale, Jno. W.	153
House, S. V.	163
Hughes, W. H.	IV
Hunter, Carey J.	166
Johnson, Jas. I.	VI
Johnson, T. B.	173
Jolly, B. R.	192 B
Jones, W. N.	VII
Jones & Powell,	VI
Kenny, Jno. B.	45
King, W. H. & Co.	185
Linnell Steam Laundry, outside back cover.	
Lewis, Julius Hardware Co.	193
MacRae, Jno. Y., inside back cover.	
Macy, W. R.	197
Massey, A. P.	201
McDonald, C. C.	203
Mechanics & Investors Union,	I
Mills Manufacturing Co.,	V
Montague, B. F.	45
National Bank of Raleigh,	VII
N. C. Book Co.,	364
N. C. Building and Supply Co.,	219
N. C. Car Co.,	220
N. C. Home Insurance Co.,	218
Oak City Steam Laundry,	II
Occoneechee Farm, outside back cover.	
Otey, W. G.	222
Park Hotel,	III
Peace Institute,	322
Pearson, Chas., outside back cover.	
Pescud, Thos.	231
Physioc, J. E.	233
Press Visitor.	362
Raleigh Savings Bank,	240
Raleigh Stationery Co., second page cover.	
Roberts, H. H.	247
Royal & Borden,	V and 363
Seaboard Air-Line R. R.,	264 A
Shaw University,	364
Simpson, Wm.	46
Southern Building & Loan Asso'n,	IV
Southern Railway Co., outside front.	
Southern Railway Co.,	192 A
Spence Plumbing Co., outside back cover.	
Stedman, J. P., top inside back cover.	
St. Augustine School, second page cover and	112 B
St. Mary's School,	VI
Staunton Life Ins. Co.,	I
Steinmetz, H.	269
Stevens & Son.	V
Stevenson, T. S.	270
Sun Life Assurance Co.,	264 B
Taylor, W. A.	III
Temple, A. H.	277
Thomas, Maxwell & Co.,	284
University Publishing Co.,	291
Upchurch, B. W.	112 A
Uzzell, E. M.	293
Walters, Geo. N.	VII
Watson, F. A.	II
Weikel, C.	301
Wharton, C. P.	IV
Whitelaw, John	112 A
Woollcott & Son,	315
Woollcott, Fred.	316
Wynne & Birdsong,	192 B
Yarborough House,	283

CITY OF RALEIGH.

The beautiful "City of Oaks," capital of the Commonwealth of North Carolina, was laid out from a piece of land purchased from Colonel Joel Lane, by commissioners appointed by the General Assembly for that purpose, on the 4th day of April, 1792. It is situate upon the rise that begins to mark the lower from the upper portion of the State, upon easy undulations, only three hundred feet above the sea, surrounded by lands in high state of cultivation, with a most equable climate, and withal presents as many attractions for all that constitutes a desirable home as any city upon the Atlantic slope.

While lacking in some of the advantages alike of the sea-coast and the mountain, it possesses many not common to either. No disease has ever appeared here in its most virulent form, and its rate of mortality is far below the average. Together with Aiken, S. C., Raleigh was recommended by a commission of army surgeons as a proper and suitable point for the establishment of a Government sanitarium.

The population of Raleigh has always been one of remarkable culture, chivalrous but conservative and law-abiding; and though the centre of all political excitement, and enjoying the utmost freedom of discussion and expression of opinion, it is its proud boast that it has never had a riot. "A beautiful and appropriate monument erected by the new to one of the most illustrious political martyrs of the old world, and by North Carolina to the author of the first attempt at colonization within her borders," Raleigh has always maintained an enviable reputation as the home of brave action and refined culture.

From a village of some four or five thousand in 1865, Raleigh has steadily grown into a respectable city of about eighteen thousand, including the population upon its outskirts not strictly within its sharply-defined limits. Its city government is of the best, order strictly but mildly enforced; it has an efficient system of street railway; a thorough and satisfactory water supply; a well-equipped fire department; is beautifully lighted by electricity; has its main thoroughfares paved; has a well-conducted telephone system; is adorned with a number of magnificent public buildings and private residences; its population is employed by many and varied industries; has churches of all the leading denominations; its public and private school facilities are most excellent; its debt is small and its credit is high. In a word, we have a city of which we speak with pride and to which we cordially invite the industrious and honest home-seeker.

Raleigh Police Census, 1896.

In the census recently taken by this department, the enumerators received and conscientiously followed instructions, putting the name of no one on their books who lived outside the corporate limits. This showed a population of 13,081. When we recall the fact that the corporate limits have not been extended since 1856, that a large number of our citizens who are essentially of the city have built up homes just outside, that the increase by reason of establishment of factories and manufacturing plants is all on the outside, amounting in round numbers to not less than 4,500, we can reasonably claim a population incident to and being a part of our city of not less than 17,500, showing a gratifying increase since the census taken in 1890. The following shows the result by wards and sex:

	WHITE.	COLORED.
First Ward,	2,255	749
Second Ward,	1,996	705
Third Ward,	1,776	2,238
Fourth Ward,	1,092	2,160
	7,119	5,962

BY SEX.

	MALE.	FEMALE.
First Ward,	1,401	1,602
Second Ward,	1,233	1,468
Third Ward,	1,920	2,204
Fourth Ward,	1,494	1,758
	6,048	7,033

Total,	13,081
Excess of whites over colored,	1,157
Excess of females over males,	985

CITY HALL.
Fronting on Fayetteville street, running back to Wilmington street.

W. M. Russ, Mayor; Ham. F. Smith, City Clerk; W. B. Hutchings, Tax Collector; J. N. Holding, City Attorney; Chas. D. Heartt, Chief of Police.

Street Directory.

The State Capitol is the meeting-point for the streets which divide the city on the North, South, East and West. Fayetteville and Halifax streets separate the city East and West, Fayetteville street running South and Halifax street running North. The other streets running North and South are in the following order:

EAST SIDE.	WEST SIDE.
Wilmington,	Salisbury,
Blount,	McDowell and Manly,
Person,	Dawson,
Bloodworth,	Harrington,
East,	West,
Swain and Haywood.	Saunders.

Newbern avenue and Hillsboro' street separate the city North and South. From the Capitol, Newbern avenue runs East and Hillsboro' street runs West. The other streets running East and West are as follows:

NORTH SIDE.	SOUTH SIDE.
Edenton,	Morgan,
Jones,	Hargett,
Lane,	Martin,
North and Oakwood ave.,	Davie,
Johnson and Polk,	Cabarrus,
Peace,	Lenoir,
Firwood ave.	South,
	Smithfield and Cannon.

The buildings are numbered on the Philadelphia plan, 100 to a block, beginning at the State Capitol.

THE STATE CAPITOL, Union Square.

GOVERNMENT OF NORTH CAROLINA.

Executive Department.

Elias Carr, Edgecombe county, Governor; salary $3,000, and furnished house, fuel and lights.

R. A. Doughton, Alleghany county, Lieutenant-Governor and President of Senate.

S. F. Telfair, Beaufort county, Private Secretary to the Governor; salary $1,200.

Charles M. Cooke, Franklin county, Secretary of State; salary $2,000, and $1,000 extra for clerical assistance.

Robert M. Furman, Buncombe county, Auditor; salary $1,500, and $1,000 extra for clerical assistance.

William H. Worth, Lenoir county, Treasurer; salary $3,000.

John C. Scarborough, Johnston county, Superintendent of Public Instruction; salary $1,500, and $500 per annum for traveling expenses.

Frank I. Osborne, Mecklenburg county, Attorney-General; salary $2,000, and $600 for clerical assistance.

Francis H. Cameron, Wake county, Adjutant-General; salary $600.

J. C. Ellington, Johnston county, State Librarian; salary $1,000.

Charles L. Hinton, Wake county, Executive Clerk; salary $600.

W. P. Batchelor, Wake county, Chief Clerk to Secretary of State; salary $1,000.

F. S. Saunders, Orange county, Clerk.
T. P. Jerman, Jr., Warren county, Chief Clerk to Auditor; salary $1,000.
J. J. Dunn, Wake county, Pension Clerk Auditor's Department.
J. W. Denmark, Wake county, Chief Clerk to Treasurer; salary $1,500.
Stephen L. Crowder, Guilford county, Teller of the Treasury Department; salary $750.
W. H. Martin, Wake county, Clerk for Charitable and Penal Institutions; salary $1,000.
C. M. Roberts, Vance county, Superintendent of Public Buildings and Grounds; salary $850.
J. C. S. Lumsden, State Standard Keeper; salary $100.

GOVERNOR'S COUNCIL.

The Secretary of State, Treasurer, Auditor and Superintendent of Public Instruction.

STATE BOARD OF EDUCATION.

The Governor, Lieutenant-Governor, Secretary of State, Treasurer, Auditor, Superintendent of Public Instruction and Attorney-General constitute the State Board of Education.

BOARD OF PUBLIC BUILDINGS AND GROUNDS.

The Governor, Secretary of State, Treasurer and Attorney-General.

BOARD OF INTERNAL IMPROVEMENTS.

The Governor (chairman *ex officio*), Hon. Ed. Chambers Smith and Hon. H. E. Norris.

PUBLIC WORKS AND INSTITUTIONS IN N. C.

North Carolina Department of Agriculture.

Located at Raleigh, in a building especially arranged for the purpose, immediately north of Capitol Square.

STATE BOARD OF AGRICULTURE.—Colonel W. F. Green, chairman, Fourth District; J. B. Coffield, First District; Dr. W. R. Capehart, Second District; H. E. King, Third District; J. H. Gilmer, Fifth District; D. A. Tompkins, Sixth District; Dr. J. R. McLelland, Seventh District; H. E. Fries, Eighth District; E. A. Aiken, Ninth District.

STATE AT LARGE.—W. S. Primrose, R. W. Wharton, N. B. Broughton, J. L. Nelson, Frank Wood.

AND EX OFFICIO.—Dr. Cyrus Thompson, President State Farmers' Alliance.

EXECUTIVE COMMITTEE.—Colonel W. F. Green, Dr. W R. Capehart, Colonel R. W. Wharton, J. L. Nelson.

FINANCE COMMITTEE.—J. B. Coffield, J. H. Gilmer, E. A. Aiken.

OFFICERS.—S. L. Patterson, Commissioner, salary $1,800; T. K. Bruner, Secretary, salary $1,500; H. B. Battle, Ph. D., Chemist and Director of the Experiment Station, salary $2,500 from the Hatch Fund.

North Carolina Agricultural Society.

OFFICERS.—Bennehan Cameron, President, Stagville; John Nichols, Secretary and Treasurer, Raleigh.

VICE-PRESIDENTS (Permanent).—Hon. Kemp. P. Battle, Orange; R. H. Battle, Wake.

The salaries of the officers of the State Fair are not fixed. Fairs are held in October of each year.

North Carolina Agricultural Experiment Station, including the Fertilizer Control Station and State Weather Service, Raleigh, N. C.

The officers of the Station are: H. B. Battle, Ph. D., Director and State Chemist; F. E. Emery, B. S., Agriculturist; Gerald McCarthy, B. Sc., Botanist and Entomologist; W. F. Massey, C. E., Horticulturist; C. F. von Hermann, U. S. Weather Bureau, Meteorologist; F. P. Williamson, D. V. S., Consulting Veterinarian; B. W. Kilgore, M. S., Assistant Chemist; F. B. Carpenter, B. S., Assistant Chemist; W. M. Allen, Assistant Chemist; C. B.

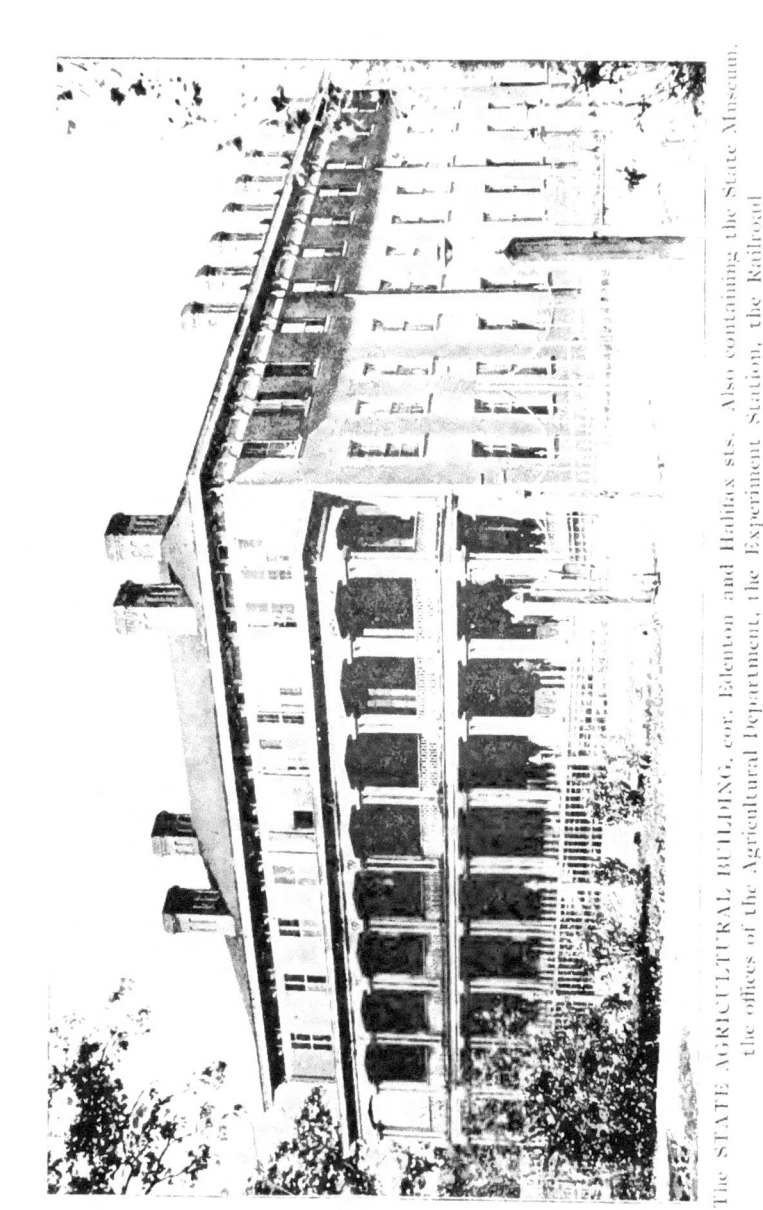

The STATE AGRICULTURAL BUILDING, cor. Edenton and Halifax sts. Also containing the State Museum, the offices of the Agricultural Department, the Experiment Station, the Railroad Commission and Weather Bureau.

Williams, B. S., Assistant Chemist; Roscoe Nunn, U. S. Weather Bureau, Assistant Meteorologist; Alexander Rhodes, Assistant Horticulturist; F. E. Hege, Poultry Manager; A. F. Bowen, Secretary.

Offices and Laboratories in Agricultural Building, Raleigh. Farm, Stable, Plant Houses and Dairy adjoin State Fair Grounds. Visitors cordially welcomed. Correspondence on all agricultural subjects invited. The Station prints many valuable and timely publications, which are free to those applying for them.

North Carolina College of Agriculture and Mechanic Arts.

FACULTY AND OFFICERS.—Alexander Q. Holladay, President and Professor of History; W. F. Massey, C. E., Professor of Horticulture, Arboriculture and Botany; W. A. Withers, A. M., Professor of Pure and Agricultural Chemistry, and Secretary; D. H. Hill, A. M., Professor of English; B. Irby, M. S., Professor of Agriculture; W. C. Riddick, A. B., C. E., Professor of Mathematics and Civil Engineering; N. R. Craighill, M. E., Professor of Mechanics; Richard Henderson, Lieutenant U. S. N., Professor of Military Tactics and Physics; R. E. L. Yates, A. M., Adjunct Professor of Mathematics; F. E. Emery, B. S., Assistant Professor of Agriculture; Charles M. Pritchett, B. S., Instructor in Mechanics; Charles B. Park, Superintendent of Shops; B. S. Skinner, Assistant in Farm Practice and Farm Superintendent; F. P. Williamson, D. V. S., Instructor in Veterinary Science; S. E. Asbury, B. S., Instructor in Chemistry; L. T. Yarborough, B. E., Assistant in Shops; Charles Pearson, B. E., Assistant in Shops; B. F. Walton, B. S., Dairyman; C. D. Francks, B. E., Tutor of the Sub-Freshman Class; Mrs. Sue C. Carroll, Matron; J. R. Rogers, M. D., Physician.

Bureau of Labor Statistics.

B. R. Lacy, of Wake county, Commissioner, salary $1,500; W. E. Faison, Wake county, Clerk, salary $900.

North Carolina Board of Railroad Commissioners

COMMISSIONERS.—J. W. Wilson, Burke county (chairman), term expires April, 1899; E. C. Beddingfield, Wake county, term expires April, 1897; S. Otho Wilson, Wake county, term expires April, 1901—salary $2,000 each; Henry C. Brown, Surry county, regular clerk, salary $1,200.

Regular sessions of the court are held at Raleigh; special sessions are also held at other places, under such regulations as made by the Commission.

Office of the Commissioners is located in the Agricultural building.

North Carolina Geological Survey.

Prof. J. A. Holmes, State Geologist; H. B. C. Nitze, Assistant Geologist, in charge of iron and gold investigations; J. V. Lewis, Assistant Geologist, in charge of corundum and building-stone investigations; W. W. Ashe, Forester. Other assistants are employed for special investigation of mineral products and water powers at irregular intervals, and still other investigations are being carried on by geologists and topographers of the United States Geological Survey. The general office of the Survey is in the Agricultural building, Raleigh.

State Museum.

In the Agricultural building, Raleigh, embracing geology, mineralogy, forestry, agriculture, fishes and mammalia, and is under the control of the Board of Agriculture—J. A. Holmes and T. K. Bruner Directors, H. H. Brimley Curator. There are no fixed salaries and no fixed terms of office.

North Carolina Institution for the Blind.

The North Carolina Institution for the Blind is located at Raleigh.

OFFICERS.—F. R. Place, Principal, salary $1,800—term expires 1896; Dr. Hubert Haywood, Physician, salary $500—term expires 1897; W. H. Rand, Steward, salary $750—term expires 1897; W. H. Worth, Treasurer *ex officio*.

BOARD OF TRUSTEES.—B. F. Montague, President, term expires 1897; C. F. Meserve, term expires 1901; Hugh Morson, term expires 1899; J. R. Williams, term expires 1899; Dr. H. C. Herring, term expires 1899; Ivan M. Proctor, term expires 1901; James A. Briggs, term expires 1897.

North Carolina Insane Asylum.

Situated in the vicinity of Raleigh, and will accommodate 300 patients.

OFFICERS.—W. H. Worth, Treasurer *ex officio*; W. T. Smith, Esq., Keeper of Records, salary $100.

RESIDENT OFFICERS.—Dr. George L. Kirby, Superintendent, salary $2,800; term six years from June 1, 1894. J. A. Faison, First Assistant Physician, salary $1,200; term two years from March 1, 1895. Dr. R. S. McGeachey, Second Assistant Physician, salary $1,200; term two years from March 1, 1895. W. R. Crawford, Jr., Steward, salary $1,200; term one year from March

1, 1895. Mrs. M. A. Whitaker, Matron, salary $600; term one year from March 1, 1895.

BOARD OF DIRECTORS.—Major John B. Broadfoot, Cumberland county, President; J. W. Bellamy, New Hanover county; B. F. Boykin, New Hanover county; J. D. Biggs, Martin county; G. M. Curtis, Halifax county; R. S. Cotten, Esq., Pitt county; Dr. R. H. Speight, Edgecombe county; John R. Smith, Wayne county; J. W. Sanders, Carteret county.

The Executive Committee receive $4 per day for one day, and mileage to and from their homes.

Officers North Carolina State Penitentiary.

A. Leazar, General Manager, salary $2,500; John M. Fleming, Warden, salary $900; Wm. Ledbetter, Deputy Warden, salary $750; J. W. McGee, Physician, salary $500; J. J. Bernard, Clerk, salary $900.

DIRECTORS.—A. B. Young, Concord, President; Dr. I. E. Green, Weldon; T. J. Armstrong, Rocky Point; D. N. Bennett, Norwood; S. C. Rankin, Fayetteville; B. W. Ballard, Franklinton; R. L. Ryburn, Cleveland county; W. H. Smith, Wayne county; W. A. Warden, Snow Hill; W. J. White, Warrenton; R. H. Ricks, Rocky Mount; T. S. Dale, Davidson county. Salaries $4 per diem and five cents per mile

There are four farms cultivated by the convicts, under State authority, viz.: Halifax farm and Northampton farm, near and below Weldon; the Caledonia farm, near Tillery, Halifax county; the Castle Hayne farm, near Wilmington.

Supreme Court.

William T. Faircloth, of Wayne, Chief Justice; Alphonso C. Avery, of Burke county; Walter Clark, of Wake county; David M. Furches, of Iredell county; and Walter A. Montgomery, of Wake county, Associate Justices. Salary $2,500 each.

Thos. S. Kenan, Clerk, salary 300 and fees.

Robert T. Gray, Reporter, salary $750.

Robert H. Bradley, Marshal and Librarian, salary $1,000.

J. L. Seawell, Office Clerk.

The Court meets in Raleigh on the first Monday in February and the last Monday in September of each year.

Spring Term.—1st Judicial District, February 3d; 2d District, February 10th; 3d District, February 17th; 4th District, February 24th; 5th District, March 2d; 6th District, March 9th; 7th District, March 16th; 8th District, March 23d; 9th District, March 30th; 10th District, April 6th; 11th District, April 13th; 12th District, April 20th.

Fall Term.—1st District, September 28th; 2d District, October 5th; 3d District, October 12th; 4th District, October 19th; 5th District, October 26th; 6th District, November 2d; 7th District, November 9th; 8th District, November 16th; 9th District, November 23d; 10th District, November 30th; 11th District, December 7th; 12th District, December 14th.

Applicants for license to practice law are examined on Monday (the first day of each term).

United States Courts.

United States Circuit Court—Eastern District of North Carolina—Held at Raleigh on the fourth Monday in May and first Monday in December, and at Wilmington the first Monday after the fourth Monday in April and October.

Charles H. Simonton, Circuit Judge; residence Charleston, S. C.; salary $6,000.

Augustus S. Seymour, District Judge; residence Newbern, N. C.; salary $5,000.

Charles B. Aycock, United States Attorney; office Raleigh, N. C.; residence Goldsboro'.

Solomon C. Weill, Assistant United States Attorney; residence Wilmington, N. C.

Owen J. Carroll, United States Marshal; office Raleigh, N. C.

N. J. Riddick, Clerk Circuit Court, Raleigh and Wilmington; residence Raleigh; offices at Raleigh and Wilmington.

Vitruvius Royster, Deputy Clerk, Raleigh, N. C.

W. H. Shaw, Deputy Clerk, Wilmington, N. C.

North Carolina Facts and Statistics.

Number of counties, 96.

State area, 52,286 square miles.

Extreme length is 503¼ miles.

Extreme breadth is 187½ miles.

Number of electoral votes, 11.

Length of coast line is 314 miles.

Land surface, 48,666 square miles.

Water surface, 3,620 square miles.

Area Dismal Swamp, 150,000 acres.

Number of miles of railroad, 3,579.

Indian population (census 1890), 1,571.

Inland steamboat navigation, 900 miles.

The N. C. SUPREME COURT BUILDING, cor. Edenton and Salisbury sts.
Also containing the State Library and Bureau of Labor Statistics.

Total population (census 1890), 1,617,947.
Average mean annual rainfall, 52 inches.
White population (census 1890), 1,049,191.
Colored population (census 1890), 567,170.
Total water-power, 3,500,000 horse-power.
Western boundary—longitude 84°, 42', 20".
Average winter temperature, 43° Fahrenheit.
The highest point is Mitchell's Peak, 6,888 feet.
Average area of counties is 507 square miles.
Number of varieties of minerals discovered, 180.
Average summer temperature, 75 degrees Fahrenheit.
Average elevation of State above sea level is 640 feet.
Average mean annual temperature, 59° Fahrenheit.
Area of largest county (Brunswick) is 950 square miles.
Number of towns with a population of over 2,000, 23.
Area of smallest county (New Hanover) is 80 square miles.
Highest towns—Boone, 3,250 feet; Highlands, 4,000 feet.
Legal rate of interest six per cent.; usury forfeits interest.
Deaths by consumption, 1.05 per 1,000 of State population.
Limit to State and County taxes, 66¾ cents. Limit to poll-tax, $2.
Highest point of Smoky Mountain range is Clingman's Dome, 6,660 feet.
Mean annual summer temperature of Raleigh, 76 degrees; Florence, Italy, 75 degrees.
Mean annual temperature at Raleigh, 60 degrees; Florence, Italy, 59 degrees.
State, Congressional and Presidental elections, Tuesday after first Monday in November.
Mean annual winter temperature of Raleigh, 44 degrees; Florence, Italy, 44 degrees.
The highest point of Blue Ridge mountains in the State is Grandfather Mountain, 5,897 feet.
The average date of first killing frost is October 10th, and the last killing frost in spring is in April.
The largest drainage area of the State is that of the Cape Fear river, aggregating over 8,000 square miles.
Asheville is 2,250 feet above sea level. Mean annual temperature, 54.20°—summer, 71.70°; winter, 38.02°.
Mean annual rainfall at Raleigh, 48 inches; Florence, Italy, 27 inches. Altitude above sea level of Raleigh, 365 feet.

Position of Raleigh—State capital—is latitude 35 degrees, 47 minutes; longitude, 78 degrees, 38 minutes, 5 seconds.

The death penalty is only inflicted for murder, arson, burglary and rape. The General Assembly have power to abolish it in all cases if deemed advisable.

Married women retain all their real and personal property, exempt from the debts of their husbands. Liens of mechanics and laborers, for their work, are required.

Legislature, biennial in odd-numbered years, meeting Wednesday after the first Monday in January. Limit of session 60 days. Terms of Senators and Representatives two years each. Pay, $4 per day.

Homesteads are allowed to the amount of $1,000 value, and personal property to the amount of $500. The homestead is not only exempt during the life of owner, but after death during the minority of any of his children, and also during the widowhood of his wife.

Wake County Government.

Sheriff, M W Page
Deputy Sheriffs Raleigh Township, C M Walters, R H Brooks and J T Rowland
Clerk of Superior Court, Dan H Young
Deputy Clerk Superior Court, A W Moye
Register of Deeds, J J Rogers
Deputy Register of Deeds, J Q Williams
Treasurer, H H Knight
Deputy Treasurer, R H Rigsbee
Surveyor, Pittman Stell
Coroner, Dr R B Ellis
Superintendent of Health, Dr P E Hines
Examiner of Teachers, J P Goodwin
Superintendent of Poor, W G Allen
Supervisor of Roads, W C McMackin
Constable of Raleigh Township, John R Upchurch
Janitor of Court-House, A B Booker
County Commissioners, W C Stronach (chairman, Raleigh), R H Jones, W H Hood, J D Allen and W H H Jones
Offices in Wake county court-house bldg, Fayetteville st, opp Yarborough House

City Government.

Mayor, W M Russ
Clerk, Ham F Smith
Tax Collector, W B Hutchings

WAKE COUNTY COURT-HOUSE, Fayetteville st., bet. Martin and Davie, containing the offices of the County and County Court-Room.

M. W. PAGE, Sheriff.
J. J. ROGERS, Register of Deeds.
R. B. ELLIS, M. D., Coroner.
D. H. YOUNG, Clerk of Superior Court.
H. H. KNIGHT, Treasurer.
PITTMAN STELL, Surveyor.

Chief of Police, C D Heartt
Treasurer, Joseph G Brown
Commissioner Sinking Fund, B S Jerman
Auditor, W W Willson
City Attorney, J N Holding
Street Commissioner, W Z Blake
Chief of Fire Department, L A Mahler
Superintendent of Health, Dr James McKee
Health Inspector and Clerk to Board of Health, T P Sale
City Physicians, Drs G A Renn and J W McGee Jr
Keeper of Market, J T Nottingham
Janitor City Building, J H Marshall
Keeper of Clock, T W Blake
Sexton City Cemetery, S A Jones
Sexton Mt Hope Cemetery (col), Sampson Aaderson (col)

ALDERMEN.

First Ward—Chas E Johnson, J R Ferrall, H M Ivey
Second Ward—J C Drewry, J D Bushall, Frank Stronach
Third Ward—F W Hunnicutt, L N White, C W Hoover (col)
Fourth Ward—Jno A Mills, James Baker (col), B J Robinson (col)

The Board of Aldermen, in regular session, meets in City Hall the first Friday night in each month

COMMITTEES.

Finance—Bushall chairman, Johnson, Ivey
Street—Drewry chairman, Ferrall, Bushall
Police—Ferrall chairman, Johnson, Drewry
Light—Bushall chairman, Mills, Hoover
Market—Johnson chairman, Hunnicut, White
Building—Mills chairman, Hunnicut, Baker
Schools—Ivey chairman, Mills, Baker
Park—Ferrall chairman, Drewry, Bushall
Water—Ivey chairman, Ferrall, Johnson
Sewer—Drewry chairman, Ferrall, Bushall
Fire—Johnson chairman, Ferrall, Baker
Cemetery—Mills chairman, Hunnicut, Baker

BOARD OF CHARITIES.

Mayor W M Russ chairman, Aldermen Drewry, Ivey, White and Baker

BOARD OF HEALTH.

James McKee, M D, President; W M Russ Mayor, J R Ferrall Alderman, C D Heartt Chief of Police, J C Drewry Alderman, J N Holding City Attorney, T P Sale Clerk

RALEIGH SCHOOL COMMITTEE.

Mayor W M Russ chairman, Needham B Broughton, T H Briggs, Dr R H Lewis, R O Burton, Alf A Thompson, G Rosenthall secretary

CITY POLICE.

Alderson, T B	Conrad, R J	Mullen, J H
Andrews, Melvin	Creighton, Chas	Thompson, Mart
Beasley, J W	Ellison, L S	Upchurch, G C
Belvin, F A	Haynes, A H	Woodall, W A
Cates, J A	Jones, G M	

POLICE TURNKEYS.

Hardie, P C   Johnson, Marion

CITY LAMP-LIGHTER.

Weatherspoon, W H

Raleigh Water Supply.

The Raleigh Water-Works was constructed by the National Water-Works Construction Company, of Dayton, Ohio, in 1887, Mr. M. M. Moore, C. E., engineer in charge. The supply is taken from Walnut creek, two miles from the city. Water is pumped through the filters into the reservoir; from reservoir pumped to tower, on west Morgan street, holding 101,516 gallons. When installed there were two compound duplex steam-pumping engines, of one million gallons each, and two compound power pumps, of one million gallons each, connecting with turbine wheels. Power was obtained from the pond, covering about 60 acres. An order of court compelled the abatement of the pond in 1895. The Raleigh Water Company, with the indomitable push that has characterized all of their actions, accepted the situation and at once made arrangements to give the citizens of Raleigh the same ample fire protection.

This necessitated the purchase of a new pump and boiler. At great expense they purchased from Henry R. Worthington the first triple expansion compound-condenser engine ever shipped to this State, with a daily capacity of two million gallons, with the two Smith-Vaile one million gallons each. This gives to our citizens a pumping capacity of four million gallons per day.

At this time a new 100-horse-power boiler was purchased, of the latest type. There are 125 public fire-hydrants and twenty-five private fire hydrants, making 150, which gives ample fire protection.

Domestic pressure is from fifty to seventy-five pounds, according to the location; fire pressure, from seventy-five to 100 pounds.

The pipe is R. D. Wood & Company's, guaranteed to stand 300 pounds to the square inch; hydrants, Mathew's; valves, Eddy.

The Pump-House, Engineer's house, office and Superintendent's house are connected with the fire-alarm system.

Every citizen of the city is justly proud of the efficient service rendered, which is fully shown by the fact that no controversy has ever taken place between the city and the Raleigh Water Company.

The officers of the Company are Julius Lewis, President; A. A. Thompson, Vice-President; F. H. Briggs, Treasurer; A. M. McPheeters, Jr., Superintendent and Secretary; J. E. Underwood, Engineer.

Raleigh Fire-Alarm Telegraph System.

For a number of years Raleigh has been equipped with the fire-alarm telegraph, but the Gamewell Fire-Alarm Telegraph Company, of New York, have just completed the instalment of a storage-battery system, together with a switchboard, for the regulation of the same in the new fire department building. This storage battery is made by the well known Storage Battery Company, of Philadelphia, for the special purpose of telegraph.

Raleigh is the first city in America to put in a new complete storage-battery system in connection with the fire-alarm department. It is in keeping with the progress and advancement in her fire department that this should be the case. The system has just been completed by the inventors, and it is known to be far in advance of the old system employed. The new system alone saves 80 per cent. in the cost of maintaining batteries for the fire-alarm system, and in three years it is calculated that it will pay for itself.

It is a matter of pride to every citizen that we have such an excellent fire department, and with the addition of the new storage-battery system the department is more fully equipped to fight the flames.

All the fire-alarm wires that radiate over the city lead directly to to the new building on Morgan street, where the battery system is located.

The switchboard is made of slate, and is arranged with a lamp rheostat, an automatic cut-out, a polarized relay or switch, an ammeter and voltmeter, and a switch for the changing from one set of batteries to the other with just one move.

It is stated that on a fire-alarm circuit or line the batteries duplicate, so that while one set is being charged the others are discharging on to the lines.

The object of the lamp rheostat is to govern the rate of discharging the batteries. The automatic cut-out is used in case the charging current stops at any time. The switch falls and prevents a back charge of the batteries, and when the power returns the switch is again drawn up into its place and the batteries again charged. The polarized switch is used in case the poles of the charging currents are reversed; in this case it would ring a bell and so notify the operator of the change of poles. The ammeter and voltmeter are cut in by the use of plug, and in this way we are enabled to read at what rate and at what voltage we are discharging or charging, as the case may be.

If we should insert a plug in discharging the circuit and find we are discharging too rapidly, we could, by the moving of a switch, throw in more resistance into the line and thereby reduce the current until it reaches the proper rate of discharge. In case the discharge is not high enough, the operation is reversed.

Number and Location of Fire-Alarm Boxes.

Box No. 12—S W corner Polk and East streets
" 13—S E corner Johnson and Halifax streets
" 14—S W corner North and Person streets
" 15—N W corner Edenton and East streets
" 16—N W corner Polk and Blount streets
" 21—N E corner Morgan and Blount streets
" 23—N W corner Wilmington and Martin streets
" 24—N E corner Davie and Bloodworth streets
" 25—S W corner Wilmington and South streets
" 26—N E corner Hargett and Swain streets
" 27—S W corner Blount and Cabarrus streets
" 212—N E corner Fayetteville and Hargett streets
" 214—N E corner Hargett and Bloodworth streets

The UNITED STATES BUILDING, cor. Fayetteville and Martin streets, containing the Post-Office, the Internal Revenue Department of 4th N. C. District, and the U. S. Marshal's office; also the U. S. District Court-Room.

CHAS. M. BUSBEE, P. M.   F. M. SIMMONS, Collector.
O. J. CARROLL, U. S. Marshal.

Box No. 31—S W corner Davie and Dawson streets
" 32—S W corner Hillsboro' and West streets
" 34—S E corner Lenoir and McDowell streets
" 35—N E corner Hargett and Dawson streets
" 36—N E corner South and Harrington streets
" 37—N W corner West and Hargett streets
" 4—Morgan street, between Salisbury and McDowell. Box in Water Tower. Key at Capital Hose House
" 41—Dawson street (w side), bet Jones and Lane streets
" 42—N W corner Halifax and Edenton streets
" 43—N E corner Jones and Saunders streets
" 47—North street, west of Salisbury, near car shed
" 321—N W corner Railroad and Fayetteville streets
" 45—Raleigh Cotton Mills
" 52—Insane Asylum

TO GIVE AN ALARM.

Break the glass front to key-box, unlock the fire-box, pull lever down once, and let go. You cannot release the key from the lock
If the small bell in the box is ringing, do not pull the hook, as this indicates that an alarm has already been sent in from another box. Key to all boxes will be in lock
Be particular to remain at the box until some officer of the fire department or some piece of apparatus arrives
Always send in the alarm from the box nearest the fire

SIGNALS.

One blow—Test of Line. Any policeman or other officer of the city, on hearing this signal, is instructed to report it at once to the Superintendent of Fire Alarm
Two blows, repeated two (2) times—Call for Direct Pressure
Two blows, repeated three (3) times—Call for Increased Pressure
Three blows—Fire Under Control
Four blows—Direct Pressure on
Ten blows—Call for Police

Raleigh Fire Department

Capital Hose, w Morgan st, W A Linehan, Foreman; F Woollcott, Assistant Foreman; William Allcott, Secretary
Walter R Womble Hook and Ladder Co, w Morgan st, W W Parish, Foreman; Jos S Correll, Secretary
Rescue Hose and Fire-Engine Co, Fayetteville st, R E Lumsden, Foreman; W A Faucett, Secretary
Victor Hose Co (col), cor Davie and Salisbury sts, T B Burgess, Foreman; John Taylor, Secretary

Military.

Governor's Guard, Armory Briggs bldg, Fred Woollcott, Captain; J F Jordan, First Lieutenant; A J Crawford, Second Lieutenant

Public Buildings.

Agricultural and Mechanical College, West Raleigh
City Hall and Market, Fayetteville
Colored Deaf, Dumb and Blind Institution, cor South and Bloodworth
County Court-House, Fayetteville
County Jail, rear of county court-house
Executive Mansion (Governor's residence), Burke Square, n Blount
N C Insane Asylum, South-west Raleigh
N C State Penitentiary, on Southern R R, o s w
N C Institution for the Blind, cor Jones and Dawson
N C Agricultural Building, cor Edenton and Halifax
N C Experimental Buildings, Hillsboro' rd, o s w
N C Exposition and Agricultural Society Buildings, Hillsboro', o s w
State Capitol (Executive Building), Union Square, centre of city
State Arsenal, Union Square
Soldiers' Home Buildings, Newbern ave, o s e
Supreme Court Building, cor Edenton and Salisbury
U S Court-House and Post-Office, Fayetteville

Public Monuments.

Confederate Soldiers' Monument, Union Square
Washington's Monument, Union Square

Public School Buildings.

(IN CHARGE OF RALEIGH SCHOOL COMMITTEE.)

Centennial Graded School, foot of Fayetteville
Garfield Graded School (col), s Swain
Murphy Graded School, cor Person and Polk
Washington Graded School, w South

Schools and Academies.

Raleigh is well equipped in schools, and her citizens point with pride to the advantages here offered. Under the careful and efficient management of Professor L D Howell, Superintendent of the Raleigh graded schools, the public-school system in Raleigh compares very favorably with any city in the South. The private schools are a source of gratification to the citizens of Raleigh. The following is a list of the schools and their location:

WHITE.

Centennial Graded School, Fayetteville, Prof L D Howell supt, Miss Mabel Hale prin
Murphy Graded School, cor n Person and Polk, Prof L D Howell supt, Miss Eliza Pool prin
Institution for the Blind, square bet Jones, Lane, Dawson and McDowell, F R Place prin
Peace Institute, Peace, Prof James Dinwiddie pres and prin
Raleigh Male Academy, 120 n Bloodworth, Morson & Denson prins
St Mary's School, 784 Hillsboro', Rev Bennett Smedes, A M, prin and rector
The N C College of Agriculture and Mechanic Arts, Hillsboro' rd, Alex Q Holladay pres

COLORED.

Estey Seminary, 128 e South, Charles F Meserve, A M, pres
Garfield Graded School, Swain, Charles N Hunter (col) principal
Institution for the Deaf, Dumb and Blind, corner e Lenoir and s Bloodworth, F R Place principal, Prof A W Pegues (col) supervisor
Leonard Medical School, 750 s Wilmington, Charles F Meserve, A M, president, Dr James McKee dean; consulting physicians—Drs A W Knox, W I Royster, K P Battle, R H Lewis, H B Battle and A W Goodwin
Shaw University, 118 e South, Charles F Meserve, A M, president
St Augustine Normal School and Collegiate Institute, Oakwood avenue, Rev A B Hunter principal
Washington Graded School, w South, H S Christmas (col) principal

Raleigh Public School Teachers.

CENTENNIAL GRADED SCHOOL—WHITE.

Bailey, Miss Cornelia
Bellamy, Miss Lizzie
Fleming, Miss Belle
Hale, Miss Mabel (Principal)
Lawrence, Miss Kate
Mills, Miss Mary P
Patterson, Mrs P C
Redford, Miss Minnie
Riddle, Miss Loula
Royster, Miss Edith
Terrell, Mrs M B
Williams, Mrs Sarah

MURPHY GRADED SCHOOL—WHITE.

Barbee, Mrs J M
Bates, Miss Grace
Devereux, Miss Laura M
Hicks, Miss Lillie
Marsh, Miss Mary
Pool, Miss Eliza (Principal)
Sherwood, Mrs Frank
Strong, Miss Carrie
Williamson, Mrs C M
Womble, Miss Ada

WASHINGTON GRADED SCHOOL—COLORED.

Branch, Mrs John H
Cardwell, Mary
Christmas, H S (Principal)
Hackney, Ella B
Hamlin, Annie
Hunter, L M
King, Ella M
Lane, P M
Mitchell, Ida

GARFIELD GRADED SCHOOL—COLORED.

Burwell, M T
Gary, Florence
Hunter, C N (Principal)
Love, M A
Nichols, Tena
Rogers, N D
Thornton, Emma

All under the supervision of Professor Logan D Howell, Superintendent of Raleigh Public Schools

THE UNION STATION, cor. Dawson and Martin streets.

Raleigh Church Directory.

Raleigh is abundantly supplied in churches, and has gained for herself the name of the City of Churches. Below is the list:

WHITE.

Brooklyn Methodist, n w city limit, Rev R H Whitaker pastor
Central M E Church, cor Morgan and Person sts, Rev D H Tuttle pastor
Christ Episcopal Church, cor Wilmington st and Newbern ave, Rev Dr M M Mashall rector
Christian Church, cor Hillsboro' and Dawson sts, Rev J L Foster pastor
Church of the Good Shepherd, Hillsboro' st, Rev Dr I McK Pittinger rector
Church of the Sacred Heart, cor Hillsboro' and McDowell sts, Rev Father J M Prendergast
Edenton-Street Methodist Episcopal Church, cor Edenton and Dawson sts, Rev Dr W C Norman pastor
Epworth Chapel (Methodist), cor Halifax and Franklin sts, Rev R H Whitaker pastor
First Baptist Church, cor Edenton and Salisbury sts, Rev Dr J W Carter pastor
Presbyterian Church, cor Salisbury and Morgan sts, Rev Eugene Daniel pastor
Jewish Synagogue, Fayetteville st
McDowell-Street Mission (Presbyterian), under care of Presbyterian Church
Primitive Baptist Church, cor Morgan and Dawson sts; no regular pastor
Raleigh Baptist Tabernacle, cor Hargett and Person sts, Rev Dr A M Simms pastor
St Mary's Episcopal Chapel, at St Mary's School, Rev Bennett Smedes, A M, rector
Swain-Street Baptist Mission, Rev A L Betts in charge
St Saviour Episcopal Church, cor Johnson and West sts, Rev Isaac A Canfield rector
Third Baptist Church, cor Fayetteville and South sts; no regular pastor; Jno T Pullen supt
West-End Baptist Church, Hillsboro' st, Rev A L Betts pastor

COLORED.

Christian Church, Manly st, Rev A A Bright pastor
Cox Memorial M E Church, cor Newbern ave and East sts, Rev L A Humphries pastor

THE CHRISTIAN CHURCH, cor. Hillsboro' and Dawson streets.
REV. JAS. L. FOSTER, PASTOR.
Pasor's Study at the Church. Services: Sunday Morning and Evening;
Sunday-school 9:30 A. M.; Wednesday night, Prayer-Meeting.

Davie-Street Presbyterian Church, cor Davie and Person sts, Rev A G Davis pastor
East Martin Baptist Church, Rev A R Price pastor
First Baptist Church, n Salisbury st, Rev J J Worlds pastor
First Congregational Church, cor South and Manly sts, Rev A W Curtis, D D, pastor
Second Baptist Church, cor Cabarrus and Blount sts, Rev Freeman Howell pastor
St Augustine Episcopal Church, cor Dawson and Lane sts, Rev A B Hunter pastor
St Paul's M E Church, cor Harrington and Edenton sts, Rev R H W Leak pastor
The Dawson-Street Baptist Church, s Dawson st, Deacon William Atwater in charge
The Zion Methodist Church, Rev H P Walker pastor

RALEIGH BAPTIST TABERNACLE, cor. Hargett and Person sts.,
REV. A. M. SIMMS, D. D., PASTOR.
Services, Sunday Morning and Evening; Sunday-school 9:30 A. M.

The North Carolina Soldiers' Home.

NEWBERN AVENUE, OUTSIDE EAST.

Colonel A B Andrews president, William C Stronach business manager, Capt J H Fuller superintendent

INMATES.

Abbott, Elias
Adams, Meredith
Aldridge, W R
Bagwell, J B
Baird, Thomas
Banks, Harrison
Benoish, J J
Bennett, J E
Benton, Edward
Bowen, Richard
Brown, A J
Brown, Peter A
Brown, Wm J
Browning, L R
Buck, T W
Buis, W A
Capps, H H
Carter, Owen
Chistenall, James
Collins, David
Cushing, J F
Dancy, William
Easom, John M
Foy, Marcus M
Francis, Samuel
Gathings, S H
Gay, Solomon
Goodwin, Geo T
Goodwin, I M
Gooch, W L
Haithcock, Jesse
Hamilton, Wesley
Hancock, J R
Harris, W T
Harris, Jesse
Harris, J T

Hart, John
Hill, A D
Horne, Jesse
Houch, Solomon
Joiner, Robt W
Justice, J W
Lancaster, G W
Landis, C E
Lee, Henry
Lippard, Marcus
Mahoney, J R
Noland, Patrick
Olive, Anderson
Parker, W H
Parker, W B
Parker, W Howell
Peebles, W F
Pool, J M
Puryear, J R
Pugh, David
Robbins, Starkie
Sprinkle, John
Stancil, E S
Stevens, Festus
Street, W D
Strickland, Lemuel
Sutton, J D
Thain, A
Thomas, Ether
Thompson, William
Waddell, E M
Walker, W A
Walker, Carter
Watkins, David
Watson, Isaac
Williams, James

Whitaker, W S

Cemeteries.

WHITE.

City Cemetery, e of East st bet e Hargett st and Newbern ave, S A Jones keeper
Catholic Cemetery, Tarboro' road, outside east
Confederate Cemetery, adjoining Oakwood
Hebrew Cemetery, in Oakwood
National Cemetery, Rock Quarry road, W J Elgie superintendent
Oakwood Cemetery, Oakwood avenue, A B Forrest superintendent

COLORED.

Mt Hope Cemetery, Fayetteville road, outside south, Sampson Anderson (col) sexton

SECRET AND BENEVOLENT SOCIETIES.

Masonic.

WHITE.

Grand Lodge A F & A M: Francis M Moye G M, W H Summerell Dep G M, Walter E Moore Sr G W, B S Royster Jr G W, William Simpson G Treas, J C Drewry G Sec. Meets in Raleigh on the second Tuesday in January of each year, in Masonic Hall
Hiram Lodge No 40: W W Willson W M, Augustus Bradley S W, W N Snelling J W, T W Blake Treas, E B Thomas Sec. Meets third Monday night of each month, in Masonic Hall
Wm G Hill Lodge No 218: B R Lacy W M, W E Faison S W, R B DeVault J W, J A Briggs Treas, Z P Smith Sec. Meets second and fourth Monday nights of each month, in Masonic Hall
Raleigh Chapter No 10: John C Drewry H P, Chas Kleuppelberg K, Z P Smith S, T W Blake Treas, John Nichols Sec. Meets first Tuesday after third Monday night of each month, in Masonic Hall
Enoch Council No 5: John Nichols G M, M Bowes H T, Chas Kleuppelberg P C W, William Simpson M E, B R Lacy Rec. Meets at close of Chapter meeting

Raleigh Commandery, Knights Templar, No 4: Z P Smith Em Com, W E Faison Generalissimo, R B DeVault Capt-Gen, B R Lacy Prelate, M Bowes S W, W R Blake J W, William Simpson Treas. Meets first Thursday in each month, in Masonic Hall

Independent Order of Odd Fellows.

Grand Lodge I O O F: W T Dortch G M, J P Sawyer Dep G M, R W Murray G W, B H Woodell G Sec, R J Jones G Treas, C F Lumsden and W C Douglass Grand Representatives. Meets annually at different places in the State

Manteo Lodge No 8: J J Harris N G, A E Glenn V G, George L Tonnoffski R S, C H Beine F S, T W Blake Treas. Meets every Tuesday evening in Odd Fellows' Hall

Seaton Gales Lodge No 64: A M Powell N G, H J Young V G, Phil Thiem R S, Phil J Thiem F S, William Woollcott Treas. Meets every Thursday night in Odd Fellows' Hall

Capital Lodge No 147: Z P Smith N G, W W Willson V G, J J Bernard R S, W C Lindsey F S, K P Merritt Treas. Meets every Tuesday night in hall over J Lewis Hardware Co

McKee Encampment No 15: T W Adams C P, W R Blake S W, T W Blake H P, George L Tonnoffski Scribe, W C McMackin R S, C H Beine Treas. Meets second and fourth Friday nights of each month in Odd Fellows' Hall

Litchford Encampment No 26: A F Bowen C P, J M Lindsey S W, L A Kuester H P, J S Keith Scribe, W P Betts F S, Philip Thiem Treas. Meets every Monday night in Odd Fellows' Hall

Ruth Lodge No 4, Daughters of Rebecca: Miss Nannie Edwards N G, J S Keith R S, Miss Barbara Adams Treas, Miss Nellie Weddon F S. Meets first and third Friday nights in each month in I O O F Hall, Pullen bldg

Knights of Pythias.

Phalanx Lodge No 34: A M McPheeters Jr C C, W E Ashley V C, C R Lee Prelate, Z P Smith M at A, I T Jones M of F, F P Haywood Jr M of E, J J Bernard K of R and S, William Ledbetter M of W. Meets every Thursday night in hall over J Lewis Hardware Co

Centre Lodge No 3: J H Raby C C, R C Rivers V C, P H Denton Prelate, W T Maynard M at A, C H Beine M of W, T P Sale M of F, J L Foster M of E, W W Willson K of R and S. Meets every Monday night in Castle Hall

Sir Walter Raleigh Division No 3, Uniform Rank K of P: W W Willson Sir Knight Capt, A M McPheeters Sir Knight First

Lieut, W G Separk Sir Knight Second Lieut, C B Hart Sir
Knight Recorder, John Ward Sir Knight Treas. Meets second
Wednesday night in each month in Castle Hall

Knights of Honor.

Oak City Lodge No 419: A M Powell Dictator, R H Bradley
Reporter, C C McDonald Fin Rep, J A Jones Treas

Knights and Ladies of Honor.

Carolina Lodge: B F Faison Protector, L C Bagwell Vice-Pro,
Rev L Branson Sec, W N Snelling Treas
Pullen Lodge: Mrs E S Cheek Protector, A J Jackson Vice-Pro,
A M Hanff Fin Sec, L W Smith Rec Sec, John F Smith
Treas. Meets first and Third Thursday nights in each month
in Pullen bldg

American Legion of Honor.

Raleigh Council No 1118: J A Jones Commander, J S Keith Sec,
H Heller Collector, A M Powell Treas

Royal Arcanum.

Grand Council: E L Harris Regent, A M Scales Vice-Regent, Dr
J Howell Wray Sec, A M Powell Treas
Raleigh Council No 551: W C McMackin Regent, T W Blake
Vice-Regent, W A Faucett Orator, W H Dodd Sec, J C Marcom Collector, J G Brown Treas. Meets second and fourth
Monday nights in each month in Pullen bldg

Junior Order United American Mechanics.

Raleigh Council No 1: Z P Smith Councilor, W W Andrews
Warden, T P Sale Fin Sec, M R Haynes Rec Sec, W L Davis
Treas. Meets every Wednesday night in Pullen bldg

Fraternal Mystic Circle.

Raleigh Ruling No 324: E C Smith Worthy Ruler, M Rosenthal
W Rec, D T Johnson W Collector, H Heller W Treas. Meets
in Pullen bldg

Improved Order of Heptasophs.

Raleigh Order No 399: W N Snelling Archon, Dr G A Renn
Provost, W E Foster Secretary, Dr J W McGee Jr Financial

Secretary, Frank P Haywood Treasurer, Henry Matthews Inspector, L H Woodall Prelate, W T Maynard Warden. Meets in Pullen building

Order of Railway Conductors.

Raleigh Division No 264: H M Faucette Chief Conductor, F F Brown Assistant C C, G M Lasater Sr C, J F Weaver Jr C, W W Newman Secretary and Treasurer. Meets first and fourth Sundays in each month in Pullen building

Brotherhood of Locomotive Engineers.

C H Beckham Chief Engineer, D K Wright 1st Engineer, W H Fetner 2d Engineer, B R Lacy 1st Assistant Engineer, W A Faison 2d Assistant Engineer, C R Hunnicutt 3d Assistant Engineer, T S Stove Guide, T B Terrell Chaplain

Typographical Union.

Raleigh Union No 54: John Cheek President, C F Cooke Vice-President, E C Owens Secretary, C D Christophers Treasurer, Simeon Smith Sergeant-at-Arms. Meets every month in Pullen building

Carpenters' Union.

Raleigh Union: M F Ruth President, J W Hunt Recording Secretary, J L Cross Financial Secretary, W L Riddle Treasurer. Meets in Pullen building

Raleigh and Gaston R. R. Workingmen's Relief Association.

J S Bland President, W D Jordan Vice-President, W H Cole Recording Secretary, E R Pace Financial Secretary, J S Riddle Treasurer

Confederate Veterans' Camp.

Junius Daniel Camp No 515: Dr P E Hines Commander, W H Hughes 1st Lieut Commander, J T Watts 2d Lieut Commander, J C Birdsong Adjutant

Ancient Order United Workingmen.

Murphy Lodge No 3: W W Parish M W, J R Norman Foreman, J H Crawford Overseer, L W Smith Recorder, T J Bashford

A. DUGHI,

DEALER IN
CONFECTIONS
—AND—
Foreign and Domestic
FRUITS.

PROPRIETOR OF
JUNALUSKA WINE CO.

Cakes for Parties and Weddings
Made to Order.

Ice-Cream Manufactured by Steam.

Raleigh, N. C.

"I feast on Dughi's delicious Fruits and Creams and Ices."

"Dughi is a stranger to me. Oh, that I knew his whereabouts."

B. F. MONTAGUE,
Attorney at Law.

Money to Loan on first-class Security,
either Real or Personal.

Notes, Bonds, &c., &c., Bought and Sold.

Room 2, Commercial and Farmers Bank.

JOHN B. KENNEY,
General Insurance Agent,

No. 2 Pullen Building,   RALEIGH, N. C.

Represents first-class Foreign and American Companies.

Solicits a share of your patronage. Prompt attention given to business.

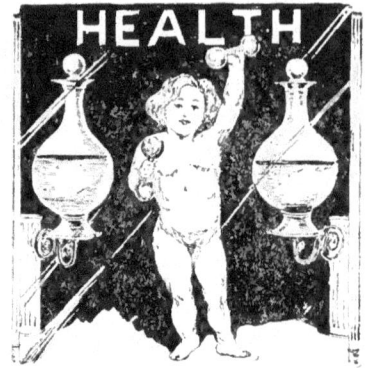

TO KEEP THE SYSTEM
IN A HEALTHY CONDITION, USE

SIMPSON'S
KIDNEY AND LIVER PILLS

FOR

Jaundice, Dyspepsia, Biliousness, and all Diseases of the Stomach and Liver.

IS BETTER THAN WEALTH.

SIMPSON'S ECZEMA OINTMENT
CURES ECZEMA, MILK CRUST, OLD SORES, ITCHING PILES, NASAL CATARRH, AND ALL SKIN DISEASES.

Either Sent by Mail, on Receipt of Twenty-five Cents.

SIMPSON'S PHARMACY,
Pullen Building, - - - - - **Raleigh, N. C.**
WILLIAM SIMPSON, Manager.

M. S. CLARK,
Slate Roofer,
RALEIGH, N. C.

P. O. Box 132.

Residence: 319 E. Jones St.

EDWARD FASNACH,
RALEIGH, N. C.

DIAMONDS,
Fine Jewelry,
Sterling Silverware,
18-Karat Plain Gold Rings

Repairs carefully attended to.
Optical Department.
Artificial Eyes inserted.

Financial Secretary, John W Brown Receiver. Meets second and fourth Thursday nights in each month in hall, Pullen building

Young Men's Christian Association.

Corner Fayetteville and Morgan sts, W H Overton Secretary

Raleigh Academy of Medicine.

Dr W I Royster President, Dr Hubert Royster Secretary. Meets second and fourth Wednesday nights in each month in the Academy, rooms at Drs Lewis & Battle's

Colored Societies.

MASONIC.

Widow's Son Lodge No 4: W F Debnam W M, Moses Thompson S W, Joseph B Mills J W, S J Hawkins Sec, James Baker Treas. Hall over Raleigh Savings Bank

Excelsior Lodge No 21: Charles Higgs W M, Samuel Hayes S W, H J Dunn J W, Abram Bryant Sec, Caesar Johnson Treas. Hall over Raleigh Savings Bank

ODD FELLOWS.

Hope-for-All Lodge No 2645: Burton Perry N G, J J Jones Sec, George Alston Treas. Meets first and third Friday nights in each month in hall over Raleigh Savings Bank

Virtue Lodge: Frank Phillips N G, J H Rhodes Sec, Fred Yeargan Treas. Meets first and third Tuesday nights in each month in hall over Raleigh Savings Bank

ROYAL KNIGHTS OF KING DAVID.

W H Holder W M, S A Drake W C, G W Fleming W S, W M Williams Treas, J T Anderson Sec. Meets first and second Tuesday nights in each month in hall e Cabarrus st

GRAND FOUNTAIN, UNITED ORDER TRUE REFORMERS.

Raleigh Division: Robert Evans Chief, Mary A Stanley Sec and Treas, Dr L A Scruggs Medical Director, J J Jones State Organizer. Meets first Friday night in each month in hall over Raleigh Savings Bank

Raleigh Fountain No 341: M G Gilliam Mess, J B Cook W M, Laura Freeman W Mrs, Lewis Bembry Treas. Hall over 135 Fayetteville st

True Workers No 356: Bettie Taylor Mess, Bettie Taylor W M, Caroline Taylor W Mrs, Luvenia Taylor Sec, Nancy Hunter Treas. Hall over 135 Fayetteville st

Raleigh Sons No 509: Annie E Powell Mess, Wm Wimbush W M, Nancy Dunston W Mrs, Wm Atwater Sec, George Montgomery Treas

North Carolina No 515: J T Freeman Mess, W M Graves W M, Dallie Barber W Mrs, Della Conyard Sec, James Richardson Treas. Hall over 135 Fayetteville st

Wise Plan No 516: Mary A Stanly Mess, James H Young W M, Mary Ellis W Mrs, Lula S Hines Sec, Emily Yarboro Treas. Hall over 135 Fayetteville st

Queen of Honor No 567: Thos Hayes Mess, Rhoda McSwain W M, Candace Smith W Mrs, Chas Hunter Sec, Clara McCloud Treas. Hall over 135 Fayetteville st

Sons of King Solomon No 779: W H Faucette Mess, H G Hunter W M, Wm Plummer V M, J H Yeargan Sec, David Curtis Treas. Hall over 135 Fayetteville st

Light and Life No 805: W H Patterson Mess, Gideon Alston W M, Sallie Drake W Mrs, Hayes Drake Sec, Wm Ashe Treas. Hall over 135 Fayetteville st

Energetic Lodge No 529: Dr L A Scruggs Mess, E A Johnson W M, Hattie Davies W Mrs, Thos Davies Sec, Cornelia Gary Treas. Hall over 135 Fayetteville st

RALEIGH STATIONERY COMPANY'S

RESIDENT AND CLASSIFIED

BUSINESS DIRECTORY OF RALEIGH, N. C.,

1896-'97.

ABBREVIATIONS USED IN THIS WORK.

ab..........above.	frt..........freight.	prin..........principal.
adv..........advertisement.	gen..........general.	pubr..........publisher.
agt..........agent.	g-d..........grand-daughter	r. or res..........residence.
al..........alley.	g-s..........grand-son.	Rai..........Raleigh.
app..........apprentice.	hkpr..........housekeeper.	rd..........road.
asst..........assistant.	ins..........insurance.	r. r..........railroad.
ave..........avenue.	lab..........laborer.	Rev..........Reverend.
bds..........boards.	mfg..........manufacturing.	s..........south.
bet..........between.	mfr..........manufacturer.	S. A. L..Seaboard Air Line.
bkkpr..........book-keeper.	mgr..........manager.	s. e..........south-east.
bldg..........building.	n..........north.	sec..........secretary.
bus..........business.	n. e..........north-east.	st..........streets.
carp..........carpenter.	n. w..........north-west.	supt..........superintendent.
clk..........clerk.	o. s. e..........outside east.	tel. opr..telegraph operator.
co..........county.	o. s. w..........outside west.	trav..........traveling.
cor..........corner.	o. s. s..........outside south.	treas..........treasurer.
cot..........cotton.	o. s. n..........outside north.	w..........west.
d..........daughter.	opp..........opposite.	wid..........widow.
dept..........department.	p. o..........post-office.	wks..........works.
e..........east.	pres..........president.	*..........colored.
eng..........engineer.		

ABBOTT Elias, inmate Soldier's Home
Abel Thos,* wks S A L shops, res 120 w Peace
Abernathy W R, attendent at Insane Asylum, res same
Abrams W J, harness maker, res n Saunders
Abrams Mrs Jennie, wife W J
Abrams Charles, shoemaker, res Brooklyn o s w
Abrams Frank, carp, res Brooklyn o s w
Abrams Edward, son Chas, res same
Adams Len H & Co, grocers and com mer, 310 s Wilmington
Adams L H, (L H Adams & Co) merchant, r 227 e Edenton
Adams Mrs Sarah, wife L H
Adams Miss Annie S, d L H, res same, student
Adams Jack L, son L H, res same, huckster city market
Adams G N, son L H, res same, clerk
Adams S J, son L H, res same, student
Adams D T, chief letter-carrier, res 520 S Bloodworth
Adams Mrs Nettie, wife D T
Adams Thos N, son D T, res same, student

Adams Jas McK, son D T, res same, student
Adams Miss Maud T, d D T, res same, student
Adams Alonzo L, son D T, res same
Adams Miss Nellie, d D T, res same
Adams Warren,* whitewasher, res Freeman, o s e
Adams Mary,* wife Warren, washerwoman
Adams Walter,* son Warren, res same, butcher
Adams Martha,* d Warren, res same, washerwoman
Adams Mamie,* d Warren, res same, washerwoman
Adams Augusta,* d Warren, res same, nurse
Adams Julia,* d Warren, res same, servant
Adams Warren Jr,* son Warren, res same, lab
Adams Charles, city hand, res 523 e Davie
Adams Mrs Victoria, wife Charles, house work
Adams J G, grocer, 201 n Harrington, res same
Adams Mrs Julia, wife J G
Adams Arthur, son J G, res same
Adams Mrs Maggie M, wid, dressmaker, res 414 w Jones
Adams Thos W, son Mrs Maggie M, res same, printer
Adams Miss Barbara, d Mrs Maggie M, res same
Adams Miss Mary, d Mrs Maggie M, res same
Adams John, city hand, res 549 e Lenoir
Adams Mrs Docile, wife John
Adams Miss Bessie, d John, res same, student
Adams Hubert, son John, res same, student
Adams Alex, city hand, bds 581 e Cabarrus
Adams Ed A, saloon, 221 s Wilmington, res 423 s Wilmington
Adams Mrs Nannie, wife Ed A
Adams Miss Bessie, d Ed A, res same, student
Adams Miss Alma, d Ed A, res same, student
Adams Thomas,* painter, res 10 Hunter
Adams Minerva,* wife Thomas
Adams Herbert,* son Thomas, res same, student
Adams Thomas*, student, res 10 Hunter
Adams James, city hand, res 593 e Cabarrus
Adams Miss Elizabeth, d James, res same, student
Adams M J, engineer S A L R R, res 526 Hillsboro'
Adams Mrs Emma, wife M J
Adams Mrs Francis, wid, mother of Mrs Annie Woods, res same
Adams Mary,* washerwoman, res e Davie
Adams Creasy,* washerwoman, res 508 e Davie
Adams Troy,* lab, res rear 125 e Hargett
Adams Mrs Mary, wid, res 818 s Wilmington
Adams Miss Leona, student, lives with J E Potter
Adams Lonnie, student, lives with J E Potter
Adams Miss Mamie, student, lives with J E Potter
Adams Meridith, inmate Soldier's Home
Adams James H, bkkpr, res 520 s Bloodworth

Adams Jesse E, clk Thomas & Maxwell, res 563 Newbern ave
Adams Mrs Anna, wife Jesse E, dressmaker
Adkins Syree,* lab, res 110 e Lenoir
Adkins Frances,* wife Syree, dressmaker
Adkins Mrs Susan, wid, dressmaker, res 625 e Hargett
Akins Rev Sandy,* Methodist minister, res 506 w South
Akins Nancy,* wife Rev Sandy, house work
Akins Etta J,* d Rev Sandy, washerwoman
Akins Benj,* son Rev Sandy, res same, farm hand
Akins James,* son Rev Sandy, res same, lab.
Akins Estelle,* d Rev Sandy, res same, house work
Akins Cornie,* d Rev Sandy, res same, house work
Akins Julia,* d Rev Sandy, res same, house work
Akins Mack,* son Rev Sandy, res same, student
Albright Miss Sallie, bkpr for Mrs Addie Woods, res same
Alderman J T, conductor S A L R R, bds 204 Halifax
Alderson T B, city policeman, res 212 n Harrington
Alderson Mrs Agnes V, wife T B
Alderson Eddie H, son T B, res same, clk J McKimmon & Co
Alderson Miss Mamie, d T B, res same, stenographer and type-
    writer at telephone office
Aldridge W R, inmate Soldier's Home
Allcott Wayne, book and machinery agt, office in Academy of
    Music bldg, res cor Polk and East
Allcott Mrs Ernestine T, wife Wayne
Alexander Millie,* washerwoman, res 116 n West
Alford W H, carp, res 213 n West
Alford Mrs Helen, wife W H
Alford Miss Bertha, d W H, res same, student
Alford Alonzo, son W H, res same, student
Alford James H, pri'r at Edwards & Broughton, r 113 n Salisbury
Alford Mrs Susan V, wife James H
Alford Nick,* lab, res rear e Davie
Alford Mary,* wife Nick, restaurant cook
Alford Julia,* d Nick, res same, cook for J W McGee Jr
Alford Leroy, foreman of type-setting machines News and Obser-
    ver office, bds 125 e South
Allen Jacob S, builder and contractor, res 515 n Person
Allen Mrs Mattie O, wife Jacob S
Allen Thos Camden, son Jacob S, student
Allen Miss Nella Ada, d Jacob S, student
Allen Jos W, loco eng S A L R R, res 118 n Dawson
Allen Mrs Emma W, wife Jos W
Allen Wm M, son Jos W, res same, clk J C S Lumsden
Allen Claude, son Jos W, r same, wks Julius Lewis Hardware Co
Allen Archie, son Jos W, res same, student
Allen Miss Jessie L, d Jos W, res same, student
Allen Leroy, son Jos W, res same, student

Allen Miss Hallie H, d Jos W, res same, student
Allen Paul D, clk S A L frt depot, res 213 n Saunders
Allen Mrs Mary, wife Paul D
Allen Mrs Ira N, wid, res 304 n Dawson
Allen Oscar, son Mrs Ira N, res same, clk J G Ball & Co
Allen Fred, son Mrs Ira N, res same, student
Allen Miss Ira E, d Mrs Ira N, res same, student
Allen G M, office mgr The Allen & Cram Co, res 116 s West
Allen Mrs Helen, wife G M
Allen Miss Helen P, d G M, res same, student
Allen George, sec of Mechanics and Investors Union, office Pullen bld, bds cor Newbern ave and Person
Allen Mrs Leah, wife Geo
Allen Alex,* whitewasher, res Martin, o s e
Allen Lucinda,* wife Alex, washerwoman
Allen Bud,* son Alex, res same, whitewasher
Allen David,* son Alex, res same, student
Allen Charles,* son Alex, res same, student
Allen Mary,* d Alex, res same, student
Allen Mrs M J, wid, res with Rev Alvin Betts
Allen D H, clk for Myatt & Hunter, res 306 Newbern ave
Allen Mrs Virginia F, wife D H
Allen Miss Maria, d D H, res same, student
Allen Miss Katie, d D H, res same, student
Allen D H Jr, son D H, res same
Allen & Boyden, real estate, office Pullen bldg
Allen Thos W, eng S A L R R, res 203 n Saunders
Allen Mrs Bettie A, wife Thos W
Allen Miss Maggie, d Thos W, res same, student
Allen J E, brick mason and plasterer, res 300 n Saunders
Allen Mrs B J, wife J E
Allen Marvin M, son J E, res same, student
Allen Edward, son J E, res same, student
Allen David R, son J E, res same
Allen Bettie,* cook for W J Ellington, res 118 n Dawson
Allen Bettie,* cook for G A Strickland, res 3 Stronach ave
Allen Norman,* carp, res Smithfield al
Allen Catherine,* wife Norman, washerwoman
Allen Minerva,* d Norman, res same, washerwoman
Allen William, lab, res 536 e Davie
Allen Roxie,* cook, res old Fair Ground, o s e
Allen Susie,* sister of Roxie, res same, nurse
Allen Frank, bkkpr for A B Stronach, bds 321 e Lane
Allen James, lab, res 228 s Bloodworth
Allen Mrs Annie, wife Jas Allen
Allen Anthony,* cook at Park Hotel, res 720 s McDowell
Allen Louisa,* wife Anthony
Allen Lettie,* d Anthony, res same, student

Allen Maggie,* d Anthony, res same, student
Allen Wesley,* lab, res Pugh
Allen J A,* shoemaker, res 207 w South
Allen Belle,* wife J A, washerwoman
Allen Mrs L F, seamstress, res 114 w South
Allen Wm H, son Mrs L F, res same, painter
Allen Miss Mary A, d Mrs L F, res same, student
Allen Anna,* washerwoman, res rear 508 s West
Allen Nick,* lab, res 243 s Harrington
Allen Chas S, frt agt S A L, res cor Hargett and Harrington
Allen Mrs Annie E, wife C S
Allen Chas S Jr, son C S, res same, student
Allen Talbot M, son C S, res same, student
Allen Miss Mariam B, d C S, res same, student
Allen Daniel B, son C S, res same, student
Allen James,* lab, res 202 w Lenoir
Allen Sarah J,* wife James, housework
Allen Nick,* driver for A D Royster & Bro, res 202 w Lenoir
Allen Arthur,* porter at A V Emery, res 202 w Lenoir
Allen Archie,* porter J J Wright, res 202 w Lenoir
Allison Robert, supt Postal telegraph repair, res 305 w Jones
Allison Mrs Belle, wife Robert
Allison James W, tel opr, bds 305 w Jones
Allison Mrs Nannie, wife James W
Alston Thomas,* lab, res 325 s Bloodworth
Alston Amanda,* cook for V C Royster, res on lot
Alston Ellis,* driver, res 219 s Bloodworth
Alston Mattie,* wife Ellis, laundress
Alston Annie,* cook for Thos F Wilson, res on lot
Alston Eliza,* cook, res Newbern ave, o s e
Alston Madison,* gardener, res 550 e Martin
Alston Martha,* wife Madison, washerwoman
Alston Warren,* lab, res e Lane
Alston Susan,* wife Warren, washerwoman
Alston Jos,* driver for city, res 106 Smithfield
Alston Adeline,* wife Jos
Alston Mary E,* d Jos, res same, student
Alston Sarah V,* d Jos, res same, student
Alston Anderson,* driver for Dr Hubert Haywood, r 413 n West
Alston Henry,* carp, res 402 s Blount
Alston Sol,* whitewasher, res 815 Manly
Alston Josephine,* wife Sol, cook
Alston Clarence,* musician, res 118 w Lenoir
Alston Sallie E,* wife Clarence
Alston Mary,* cook, res Railroad
Alston Ernest,* cook at Park Hotel, res 39 Railroad
Alston Jordan,* farm hand, res 209 w Lenoir
Alston Lizzie,* wife Jordan, washerwoman

Alston Jennie,* d Jordan, res same, washerwoman
Alston Richard,* son Jordan, res same, student
Alston Emma,* d Jordan, res same, student
Alston Gid,* office boy at Dr D E Everett, res 19 McKee
Alston Virginia,* grocer, 760 Fayetteville, res 19 McKee
Alston Chaney,* mother of Virginia Alston, res same
Alston Robert,* wks ice factory, res 516 s McDowell
Alston Alice,* wife Robert, house work
Alston George,* porter at Supreme Court bldg, res 14 Railroad
Alston Julia,* wife George, housework
Alston Henry,* son Geo, res same, porter at Agricultural bldg
Alston William,* son Geo, res same, lab
Alston Rachel,* d Geo, res same, housework
Alston Susan,* d Geo, res same, student
Alston J L,* grocer, cor McDowell and South, res same
Alston Eliza,* cook, res 409 w Martin
Alston John,* carp, res Avent Ferry rd, o s w
Alston Jane,* wife John
Alston Lizzie,* seamstress, res Avent Ferry rd, o s w
Alston Moses,* son John, res same, lab
Alston Gertrude,* d John, res same, nurse
Alston Janet,* d John, res same
Alston Rosa Belle,* d John, res same
Alston Eustice,* son John, res same
Amis M N, lawyer, office Central Hotel, res same
Anderson Chas H & Co, grocers, 8 and 10 e Hargett
Anderson C H (C H Anderson & Co), grocer, res 114 s Person
Anderson Mrs Luta E, wife C H
Anderson Miss Lucile, d C H, res same
Anderson Jas H, clk Lyon Racket store, res 222 s Blount
Anderson Mrs Melissa, wife Jas H
Anderson Paul N, son Jas H, res same
Anderson Virgil,* carp, res e Martin, o s e
Anderson Bessie,* wife Virgil
Anderson Turner,* teacher, res e Martin, o s e
Anderson Laura,* wife Turner, washerwoman
Anderson Rosa L,* d Turner, res same, student
Anderson Mrs M E, wid, res 516 e Jones
Anderson R F, clk So Express Co, bds 108 Fayetteville
Anderson Chas K, Broom dept Blind Institution, res same
Anderson Ellen,* dressmaker, res 744 s Wilmington
Anderson Martha,* washerwoman, res 211 w Lenoir
Anderson J A, photographer, bds 515 s Harrington
Anderson Fannie E,* house work, res 709 Manly
Andrews Col A B, first vice-president Southern Railway Co, office Yarborough House bldg, res 407 n Blount
Andrews Mrs Julia M, wife A B
Andrews Wm J, son A B, res same, mechanical engineer

ANDREWS A B Jr, son A B, res same, lawyer, office upstairs 303 Fayetteville
Andrews John H, son A B, res same, student
Andrews Graham H, son A B, res same, student
Andrews Miss Jane H, d A B, res same
Andrews Phil H, chief clk U S post-office, res 128 n Wilmington
Andrews Mrs Margaret, wife Phil H
Andrews Miss Mary H, d P H, res same
Andrews Miss Lucy C, d P H, res same
Andrews Miss Belle A, d P H, res same
Andrews R M, blacksmith, shop s McDowell, res 216 e Davie
Andrews Mrs Mary, wife R M
Andrews W E, son R M, res same, blacksmith
Andrews Miss Emma L, d R M, res same
Andrews Miss Maggie L, d R M, res same
Andrews Zeb V, son R M, res same, boiler maker
Andrews Melvin, city policeman, res 410 w Hargett
Andrews Mrs Collie V, wife Melvin
Andrews Floyd, son Melvin, res same
Andrews Joseph,* porter for M Rosenthal, res 420 s Swain
Andrews Silvia,* washerwoman, res 420 s Swain
Andrews George,* lab, res 420 s Swain
Andrews Walter,* brother Jos, res same, student
Andrews Ella,* sister Jos, res same, student
Andrews Greek O, editor of Press-Visitor, bds Yarboro' House
Andrews Mrs Harriet, companion to Mrs V B Swepson, res same
Andrews Mrs Viser C, wid, res with John Kelly
Andrews W H, eng U S bldg, res 120 w Lane
Andrews Mrs Elizabeth, wife W H
Andrews D H, son W H, res same, printer
Anticephalalgine Factory, 301 Fayetteville, Jas I Johnson, proprietor
Applewhite Henry,* lab, res Manly
Applewhite Mary,* wife Henry, house work
Applewhite Lou,* cook, res 719 s McDowell
Arendell F B, bus mgr of News and Observer, r 425 n Bloodworth

A. B. ANDREWS, Jr.,
Attorney and Counsellor at Law,
303 Fayetteville Street, Raleigh, N. C.

Does a general Law business. Will practice in State and Federal Courts. Special attention paid to collections. Local Counsel for Southern Railway Company. Prompt attention given all correspondence.

Arendell Mrs Bessie E, wife F B
Arendell Holmes, son F B, res same, student
Arendell Mrs P A, wid mother F B, res same
Arendell B J, flagman S A L, bds 425 n Bloodworth
Argo & Snow, attorneys-at-law, office law bldg, 333 Fayetteville
Argo Thos M (Argo & Snow), lawyer, 12 n Person
Argo Mrs Ernest, wife Thos M
Arnold T A, carp, res 520 n West
Arnold Mrs Nannie, wife T A
Arnold Alley, son T A, res same, student
Arnold Mrs Dora L, wid Jas E, res 211 Smithfield
Arnold Miss Florence B, d Jas E, res same, student
Arnold Miss Carrie, d Jas E, res same, student
Arnold Hubert D, son Jas E, res same, student
Arnold Mrs M J, wid, res 304 n Dawson
Armistead David,* gas maker, res 718 s Dawson
Armistead Minta,* wife David, sick nurse
Arrington T G, clk Yarboro' House, res same
Arrington Mrs P D B, bds Branson House
Arrington Bryan, son Mrs P D B, res same, clk
Arrington Miss Hattie, d Mrs P D B, res same
Arrington Nancy,* laundress, res 525 e Cabarrus
Arrington John,* son Nancy, res same, lab
Arrington Minnie,* cook for Mrs A E Macy, res on lot
Arrington Lillie,* house work, res 326 s East
Arrington Erasmus,* lab, res 234 e South
Arrington Rachel,* wife Erasmus, wks col Deaf & Dumb Asylum
Arrington Erasmus,* son Erasmus, res same, student
Arrington Catherine,* d Erasmus, res same, student
Arrington Jno M,* son Erasmus, res same
Arthur Chas D, fish dealer city market, bds Exchange Hotel
ASHE S A & SON, ins agts, office 240 Fayetteville, up-stairs
Ashe S A, lawyer and ins agt, res 628 Hillsboro'
Ashe Mrs Thos H, wid, res 628 Hillsboro'
Ashe Miss Sarah W, res with S A Ashe
Ashe W W, son S A, res same, forester N C Geological Survey
Ashe S A Jr, son S A, res same, cotton-mill bus
Ashe Thos M, son S A, res same, architect and ins agt, office cor Martin and Fayetteville, up-stairs
Ashe Miss Elizabeth E, d S A, res same
Ashe Miss Mary P, d S A, res same, student
Ashe Miss Josephine, d S A, res same, student
Ashe Jno G, son S A, res same, student
Ashe Miss Hannah W, d S A, res same, student
Ashe Geo B, son S A, res same
Ashe John,* lab, res rear 516 s Salisbury
Ashe Malvina,* cook, res rear 516 s Salisbury
Ashley Wm E, supt N C Car Co, res Firwood ave

Ashley Mrs Mary E, wife W E
Ashley Miss Mabel E, d W E, res same
Ashley Miss Alma A, d W E, res same
Ashley Louis H, son W E, res same, student
Ashley William, son W E, res same, student
Askew Mrs H J, wid, res with J N Holding, 528 s Salisbury
Atkins John, cotton-mill opr, res 517 s Bloodworth
Atkins Miss Lovie, sister of John, res same, student
Atkinson J C, carp, res 228 e Cabarrus
Atkinson Mrs Ellen, wife J C
Atkinson Chas J, son J C, res same, guard penitentiary
Atkinson Miss Cora, d J C, res same
Atkinson Henry A, son J C, res same, huckster
Atkinson Miss Alma E, d J C, res same, student
Atwater Charles,* lab, res 560 e Cabarrus
Atwater Eliza,* wife Chas, washerwoman
Atwater Hattie,* d Chas, res same, cook
Atwater Lula,* d Chas, res same, nurse
Atwater Gertrude,* d Chas, res same, nurse
Atwater Ella,* d Chas, res same, student
Atwater Cabe,* son Chas, res same, lab
Atwater Clarence,* son Chas, res same, lab
Atwater William,* porter at Stronach & Sons, res old Fair
    Ground, o s e
Atwater Emma,* wife Wm
Atwater William Jr,* son Wm, res same, student
Atwater Alex,* son Wm, res same, student
Atwood A G, eng S A L R R, res n Saunders
Atwood Mrs Ida, wife A G
Austin Wm H, farmer, res 211 Bledsoe ave
Austin Sarah A, wife Wm H
Austin Robert E, son Wm H, res same, wks Caraleigh mill
Austin Jos F, son Wm H, res same, wks Caraleigh mill
Austin C T, son Wm H, res same
Austin Jno L, son Wm H, res same
Austin Elizabeth,* laundress, res 550 e Cabarrus
Austin Walter,* son Elizabeth, res same, tobacco worker
Austin Joseph,* son Elizabeth, res same, student
Austin Harry,* son Elizabeth, res same, lab
Austin Mariah,* servant at Mrs R C Badger's, res 209 w Morgan
Austin Chaney,* cook for Jas A Briggs, res on lot
Austin Silvia,* cook for W M Russ, res 525 e Edenton
Austin Emma,* cook for Mrs W H Pace, res on lot
Austin Geneva,* cook for Mrs R W Smith, res same
Austin John,* farm hand, res 322 e Martin
Austin Maggie,* wife John, washerwoman
Austin Pattie,* d Emma Jones, res same, student
Austin Bessie,* d Emma Jones, res same, nurse Mrs Stanback

Austin Haywood,* lineman Telephone Co, res 206 w South
Austin Mary,* wife Haywood, cook
Austin W E, attendant at Insane Asylum, res same
Austin Lottie,* washerwoman, res 409 w Martin
Austin Granville D, horse-trainer, res Hillsboro' rd, o s w
Austin Mrs J Etta, wife G D
Austin Miss Ruth L, d G D, res same
Austin Roy O, son G D, res same
Austin A Carter, son G D, res same
Austin Wiley C, son G D, res same
Avera David S, planter, res Newbern ave, o s e
Avera Mrs Charlotte A, wife David S
Avera Wm S, son David S, res same
AVERA A C, Asst Justice of Supreme Court, bds 611 Fayetteville
Avery Susan,* washerwoman, res 118 w Cabarrus
Avery Jane,* house servant, res 525 s McDowell
Avery Charles,* son Jane, res same, student
Avery Joseph,* son Jane, res same, student
Avery Effie,* d Jane, res same, student
Aydlett Charles, carp S A L, res 709 n Salisbury, o s n
Aydlett Mrs Carrie, wife of Charles
Ayer Mrs V C, wid, res cor Hargett and s Salisbury
Ayer H W, editor Weekly Caucasian, r cor Salisbury and Hargett
AYER Dr J M, surgeon dentist, 208 Fayetteville, res cor s Salisbury and Hargett

BADGER Thomas, ex-mayor, res 218 Halifax
Badger Mrs Eleanor H, wife Thomas
Badger Thomas Jr, son Thomas, res same
Badger Miss Catherine, d Thomas, res same
Badger Miss Janet, d Thomas, res same
Badger George, son Thomas, res same, student
Badger Mrs R C, wid, res 103 s McDowell
Bagley Mrs W H, wid, res 125 e South

Dr. J. M. Ayer,

Dentist,

208 Fayetteville Street,

Raleigh, N. C.

Bagley Mrs Ethel, d Mrs W H
Bagley David, son Mrs W H
Bagley Worth, son Mrs W H, in U S Navy
Bagley Wm Henry, son Mrs W H, student
Bagley Miss Belle, d Mrs W H, in U S employ
Bagley Mrs Minnie, wid, res with Mrs R C Badger
Bagwell L C, traveling salesman, res 704 s Blount
Bagwell Mrs Adilia W, wife L C, dressmaker
Bagwell Miss Mary, d L C, r same, stock clk W H & R S Tucker & Co
Bagwell Miss Minnie, d L C, res same, student
Bagwell Eugene, son L C, res same, student
Bagwell Charles, son L C, res same, student
Bagwell Garland, son L C, res same, student
Bagwell George, son L C, res same, student
Bagwell J B, inmate Soldiers' Home
Bailey Frank L, saloon and grocer, 233 s Wilmington, res 303 e Hargett
Bailey Mrs Mollie, wife F L
Bailey Miss Lillie, d F L, res same, student
Bailey Joseph, son F L, res same, student
Bailey Mrs Martha, mother of F L, res same
Bailey Mrs Julia A, wid, res 213 n Dawson
Bailey Miss Cornelia, d Mrs Julia A, r same, teacher Cen Graded School
Bailey Oscar L, son Mrs Julia A, res same, printer
Bailey Mrs C T, wid, res 513 n Blount
Bailey C Tom, son Mrs C T, res same, trav salesman
Bailey J W, son Mrs C T, res same, editor of Biblical Recorder
Bailey Pete, son Mrs C T, res same
Bailey W E, bookbinder, bds 305 s Person
Bailey A L, clk, res 113 s Blount
Bailey Mrs Bettie, wife A L
Bain Mrs Adelaide V, wid, res 414 Hillsboro'
Bain Wm H, son Mrs Adelaide V, res same, accountant
Bain Mrs Margaret C, wife Wm H
Bain Ernest B, son Mrs Adelaide V, res same, accountant
Bain Miss Adelaide V, d Mrs Adelaide V, res same
Bain Miss Julia G, res with Mrs E F Partin
Bain Joe,* waiter for Mrs Emma Myatt, res on lot
Baird Thomas, inmate Soldiers' Home
Baker Needham, wks S A L, res 536 w Peace
Baker Mrs Addie, wife Needham
Baker Nathan T, son Needham, res same, wks Ral cot mill
Baker Walter, son Needham, res same, wks Ral cot mill
Baker Miss Hattie, d Needham, res same, wks Ral cot mill
Baker Mrs Lucy A, wid, res Fayetteville below Railroad
Baker Atlas, son Mrs Lucy A, res same, lab

Baker James,* hostler for Dr Harvey Upchurch, r 719 s McDowell
Baker Rhina,* wife James, house work
Baker Chas C, traveling salesman, res 529 s Salisbury
Baker Mrs Lois C, wife C C
Baker Aubrey L, son C C, res same, student
Baker James,* wood dealer, res 736 Fayetteville
Baker Jennie,* wife James
Baker A L, pres Va Cotton Mills, office 126 Fayetteville, res Halifax st and Firwood ave
Baker B W (Eberhardt & Baker), coal and wood, res Halifax st and Firwood ave
Baker Peter,* driver for J R Ferrall & Co, res 115 w Lenoir
Baker Hollie,* wife Peter, washerwoman
Baker Hattie,* d Peter, res same, student
Baker J T,* teacher, res 223 Cannon
Baker Lizzie,* wife J T
Baker L A, weaver Caraleigh mill, res 426 Cannon
Baker Mrs L V, wife L A
Baker James & Co, grocers, 301 w South
Baker Nancy,* servant, res 748 s Person
Baker Fannie,* d Nancy, res same, cook
Baker Nellie,* d Nancy, res same, cook
Baker Ella,* d Nancy, res same, washerwoman
Baker Macon, son Mrs Mollie Lowery, res same, student
Baker Joseph, son Mrs Mollie Lowery, res same, student
Baker Miss Dora, res with L B Phillips
Baker John, lab, res 802 s Wilmington
Baker Mrs Susan, wife John, washerwoman
Baker Miss Jane G, res with Mrs Samuel Ruffin
Baker J H, mechanic S A L, bds 122 w Jones
Baker Tempie,* washerwoman, res Martin, o s e
Baker Sylvester,* son Tempie, res same, lab
Baker Cora,* washerwoman, res 212 Blount-st al
Baker Dr Wm, physician, res 813 s Blount
Baker Mrs Mary, wife Dr Wm
Baker Hester,* house work, res 330 s East
Baker Cora,* cook, res old fair ground, o s e
Baker Mary,* teacher, bds 16 Matthew's lane
Ball Jos R, salesman for Barbee & Co, res 312 s Person
Ball Mrs Lida R, wife Jos R
Ball Miss Jessie B, d Jos R, res same, student
Ball Dallas B, son Jos R, res same, student
Ball Miss Mildred M, d Jos R, res same, student
BALL JESSE G, grocer and smoking tobacco mfr, 7 e Hargett, res 117 n Bloodworth
Ball Mrs Luvenia, wife Jesse G
Ball Miss Helen, d Jesse G, res same, student
Ball Richard, son Jesse G, res same, student

Ball C O, merchant, res 215 e Morgan
Ball Mrs Annie, wife C O
Ball Jno G, mgr Jesse G Ball's tobacco factory, res 215 e Morgan
Ball Mrs Laura, wife John G
Ball George F, merchant, res 204 Smithfield
Ball Mrs Nellie, wife Geo F
Ball Miss Gracie, d Geo F, res same, student
Ball Miss Bessie O, d Geo F, res same, student
Ball W T, clk J G Ball, bds Central Hotel
Baldwin James,* lab, res 917 Manly
Ballard David, bds 549 n Person
Banks Harrison, inmate Soldiers' Home
Banks Jno R, collector for Thomas & Maxwell, bds at Mansion House
Banks Mrs Dora, wife Jno R
Banks Mrs M E, boarding-house, 508 Fayetteville
Banks Miss Stella H, d Mrs M E, saleslady for C A Sherwood & Co
Banks T G, attendant at Insane Asylum, res same
Banks Wilson,* driver for Wm Grimes, res 816 s Blount
Banks Mary,* wife Wilson
Banks Mattie,* d Wilson, res same, student
Banks William,* son Wilson, res same, student
BAPTIST SUPPLY STORE, 113 Fayetteville
Barbee J M (Barbee & Pope), confectioner, res 317 s Dawson
Barbee Mrs Jennie M, wife J M, teacher
Barbee Robt J, son J M, res same
Barbee & Pope, candy mfrs, 105 Fayetteville
Barbee Miss Virginia, dressmaker, res 212 n Harrington
Barbee & Co, cot brokers, 305 s Wilmington
Barbee E B (Barbee & Co), cot broker, bds Yarboro' House
Barbee Miss Fannie, saleslady Woollcott & Son, r 411 e Morgan
Barbee Miss Alma, res 411 e Morgan
Barbee Claude B, cot broker, res 507 Fayetteville
Barbee Mrs Nannie W, wife Claude B
Barbee Miss Katie W, d Claude B, res same, student

BAPTIST BOOK STORE, 113 Fayetteville Street,

OWNED BY BAPTIST STATE CONVENTION,
——DEALERS IN——

Bibles,
   Testaments,
      Sunday School Quarterlies,
         Papers,
            Bible Lesson Pictures,
Reward Cards,
   Banners,
      Roll-Books,
         Class Books,
            Collection Envelopes and

SUPPLIES OF ALL KINDS FOR CHURCH OR SUNDAY-SCHOOLS.

Religious and Standard Books.

Barbee M B, Justice of the Peace, office and r 418 s Wilmington
Barbee Mrs Mary A E, wife M B
Barbee Miss Marie E, g-d M B, saleslady
Barbee Miss Florence C, g-d M B
Barbee Jos V, stenographer and typewriter, res 418 s Wilmington
Barbee Thomas P, son M B, res same, marble cutter
Barber Miss Jennie, dressmaker, res 212 n Harrington
Barber S B,* shoemaker, 135 s Wilmington, res same
Barber Miss Ellie, hkpr for Mrs R S Tucker, res same
Barber Rev S S,* minister A M E church, res 618 e Cabarrus
Barber Mary E,* wife Rev S S
Barber Carrie,* d Rev S S, res same, student
Barber James,* son Rev S S, res same, student
Barber J W & Son, grocers, furniture dealers and wagon and buggy dealers, 110 and 112 e Martin
Barber J W (J W Barber & Son), merchant, res 212 Newbern ave
Barber Mrs Emma, wife J W
Barber Marshall (J W Barber & Son), merchant, r 212 Newbern ave
Barber Miss Minnie, d J W, res same
Barbour David,* lab, res 514 Smith
Barbour Emma,* wife David, laundress
Barbour Elizabeth,* d David, res same, student
Barbour Hubert,* son David, res same, student
Barefoot Edward S, watchman, res 226 s Swain
Barefoot Mrs Cornelia, wife Ed S
Barefoot Miss Susan, d E S, res same, seamstress
Barefoot Jesse P, son E S, res same, wks Ral cot mill
Barefoot Hubert H, son E S, res same, wks Ral cot mill
Barefoot Miss Emily D, d E S, res same, student
Barefoot Thos L, son Ed S, res same, student
Barham G S, cotton-mill opr, res 512 n Salisbury
Barham Mrs L T, wife G S, boarding-house
Barham C B, son G S, res same, book agt
Barham A A, son G S, res same, livery stable
Barham Mark, son G S, res same, cotton-mill opr
Barham John, son G S, res same, cotton-mill opr
Barham Miss Lucy, d G S, res same, wks Christian Sun
Barham A A, grocer and livery stable, 121 and 123 e Martin
Barham Betsy,* cook for S C Pool, res on lot
Barker Corrine,* washerwoman, res 404 Cannon
Barker Mary,* cook, res 732 Fayetteville
Barkley J R, traveling salesman, res n Person
Barkley Mrs M E, wife J R, boarding-house
Barkley Miss O G
Barkley Miss Ida B, niece of J R Barkley, res same
Barnes Guy V, printer and binder, res 518 n East
Barnes Mrs Mary E, wife Guy V
Barnes R E, stenographer and typewriter for R B Raney, bds 518 n East

Barnes William,* restaurant cook, res 108 Newbern ave
Barnes Hattie,* wife Wm, washerwoman
Barnes Lucinda,* sick nurse, res 111 w Lenoir
Barnes Lila,* house servant, res 111 w Lenoir
Barnes Willis,* hackman, res 724 Manly
Barnes Lizzie,* wife Willis, house work
Barnes Sandy,* driver for N T Norris, res 554 e Edenton
Barnes Alice,* wife Sandy, cook
Barnes Ralph I, printer, res n Bloodworth
Barnes, Mrs Nellie L, wife R I
Barnes Col N H, U S Navy, Professor of Military Tactics and Physics A & M College, bds Prof B Irby
Barron Chas E, flagman S A L, res Johnson
Barron Mrs Linda M, wife Chas E
Barron Miss Rosa E, d Chas E, res same, student
Barron Miss Lena R, d Chas E, r same, student
Barton Mrs Jane, cook at Rex Hospital, res same
Bashford Mrs Sarah, wid, res Cox ave, o s w
Bashford Miss Annie, d Mrs Sarah, res same
Bashford Alonzo, son Mrs Sarah, res same, conductor
Bashford & Godwin, horseshoers and repairers, shop s Wilmington, near Central Hotel
Bashford Thos J, bkkpr for Edwards & Broughton, res 516 Polk
Bashford Mrs Fannie, wife T J
Bashford Ernest, son T J, res same
Bashford Arthur, son T J, res same, bookbinder
Bashford Walter R, tinner, res 618 e Davie
Bashford Mrs Isadore, wife W R
Bashford Miss Nellie, d W R, res same, student
Bashford Miss Susie, d W R, res same, student
Bashford Jno A, blacksmith, res 603 Polk
Bashford Mrs Mary A, wife J A
Bashford Lewis G, son J A, res same, student
Bashford Edward, son J A, res same, student
Bashford Miss Martha, d J A, res same
Baskerville Wm,* porter S A L R R, res 575 e Lenoir
Baskerville Sarah,* wife Wm, washerwoman
Baskerville Wm,* porter for O G King, res 575 e Lenoir
Baskerville Mary,* d Wm, res same, student
Baskerville Charles,* son Wm, res same, student
Batchelor W P, chief clk to Sec of State, res 753 Hillsboro'
Batchelor Mrs D, wife W P
BATCHELOR J B, lawyer, office cor Fayetville and Davie, res 213 w Martin
Batchelor Mrs Mary C, wife J B
BATCHELOR S S (Cameron & Batchelor), ins agt, bds Park Hotel
Bates Fleming, bkkpr for T T Hay, res 214 e Morgan

Bates Mrs Hannah, wife Fleming
Bates Miss Bessie, d Fleming, res same
Bates Miss Grace, d Fleming, res same, teacher in Murphy School
Bates Henry, son Fleming, bkkpr for J R Ferrall & Co, res 214 e Morgan
Bates Robert,* lab, res 517 e Davie
Bates Hannah,* washerwoman, res 201 w Morgan
Battle & Mordecai, lawyers, up-stairs, cor Martin and Fayetteville
Battle Richard H (Battle & Mordecai) lawyer, office cor w Martin and Fayetteville, up-stairs, res 11 e Lane
Battle Miss L P, d R H, res same, student
Battle Miss Caroline B, d R H, res same, student
Battle E S, son R H, res same, lawyer
Battle Miss Rosa A, d R H, res same, student
Battle Wm K, son R H, res same, student
Battle Dr K P Jr (Lewis & Battle), eye, ear, throat and nose specialist, res cor e Lane and n Wilmington
Battle Mrs Eliza, wife Dr K P Jr
Battle Dr H B, Director N C Experimental Station and State Chemist, res cor n Wilmington and Edenton
Battle Mrs A W, wife Dr H B
Battle Miss Nellie, d Dr H B, res same, student
Baucom Adolphus,* driver for city, res 425 s McDowell
Baucom Joanna,* wife A, washerwoman
Baucom Dilly,* washerwoman, res 306 s East
Baucom Sophronia,* d Dilly, res same, cook
Baucom Geo T,* son Dilly, r same, wks for W M Sawyer
Baucom W D, wks Ral cot mill, res 526 n West
Baucom Mrs Lola, wife W D, res same, wks Ral cot mill
Baucom Miss Rena, d W D, res same, wks Ral cot mill
Baucom Miss Mary I, d W D, res same, wks Ral cot mill
Baucom Miss Laura, dressmaker, res with Mrs W R Eatman
BAUER A G, architect, office 212 Fayetteville, up-stairs, res 13 w Cabarrus
Bauer Mrs Rachel, wife A G
Baugh Miss Grizzie, aunt Miss Dixie Steine, res same

Joseph B. Batchelor,

Attorney at Law,

No. 331 Fayetteville Street,

Raleigh, N. C.

Bauman, Mrs M P, wid, res 614 Halifax, o s n
Bauman Albert, son Mrs M P, res same
Baxter Mrs T H, wid, res 411 n Saunders
Beale Jesse, carp, res 224 w Lane
Beale Mrs Mary, wife Jesse
Beale Miss Rebecca, d Jesse, res same, seamstress
Beale Miss Cornelia, d Jesse, res same, seamstress
Beale Tony, son Jesse, res same, carp
Beale Nathaniel, son Jesse, res same, wks Ral cot mill
Beale Samuel, son Jesse, res same, student
Beale Charles, carp, res 409 s Person
Beale Mrs Dora E, wife Chas
Beale Joseph,* wks Peace Institute, res Yearby's lane
Beale Maggie,* wife Joseph
Beasley Thomas, res 827 Fayetteville, farmer
Beasley Elizabeth, wife Thomas
Beasley Geo T, son Thomas, res same, farm hand
Beasley Archie, son Thomas, res same, lab
Beasley Miss Della, d Thomas, res same, house work
Beasley Miss Susan, d Thomas, r same, spinner Caraleigh cot mill
Beasley Miss Lenora, d Thomas, r same, spinner Caraleigh cot mill
Beasley Josh,* waiter at Yarboro' House, res 410 s Blount
Beasley Mary,* wife Josh
Beasley Sam,* son Josh, res same, student
Beasley Herman,* son Josh, res same, student
Beasley J W, city policeman, res 309 e Cabarrus
Beasley Mrs Carrie, wife J W
Beasley Jane,* laundress, res Rock Quarry rd
Beasley Jasper J, grocer, 518 Newbern ave, res same
Beasley Mrs Elizabeth, wife J J
Beasley Celia,* washerwoman, res 116 w Peace
Beasley Clara,* washerwoman, res 116 w Peace
Beckham J H, stationary eng S A L, res 239 n Dawson
Beckham Mrs M E, wife J H
Beckham C H, locomotive eng S A L R R, res 239 n Dawson
Beckham Mrs E A, wife C H

ADOLPH G. BAUER,
Architect and Superintendent,
HOLLEMAN BUILDING, - RALEIGH, N. C.

PLANS, ELEVATIONS, DETAILS, WORKING DRAWINGS AND SPECIFICATIONS FURNISHED FOR BUILDINGS OF EVERY DESCRIPTION.

Beckham John,* carp, res 521 s McDowell
Beckwith B C, lawyer, office over Commercial and Farmers bank, bds 118 n Wilmington
Beckwith Mrs Iola, wife B C
Beeton Harriet,* laundress, res Manly
Beddingfield E C, R R Commissioner, office Agr bldg
Beebe Miss Dee, teacher in Peace Institute, res same
Beebe Sam,* brick mason, res 125 e Cabarrus
Beemer J W, carp, res 311 n Dawson
Beemer Mrs S A, wife J W
Beine Chas H & Co, auction and commission house, 108 and 110 e Hargett
Beine C H (C H Beine & Co), merchant, res cor Swain and e Hargett
Beine Mrs Maud A, wife C H
Beine Miss Maggie, d C H, res same, student
Bell Hilliard, lock and gunsmith, res 703 n Bloodworth, o s n
Bell Mrs Nannie, wife Hilliard
Bell Henry, son Hilliard, res same
Bell Miss Nannie, d Hilliard, res same, student
Bell W B, merchant, bds 411 n Saunders
Bell Alonzo,* brakeman S A L R R, bds 320 w North
Bell Fannie,* house servant, res 814 Manly
Bell Charles, attendant at Insane Asylum, res same
Bell Haywood, attendant at Insane Asylum, res same
Bell Lewis C,* lab, res 310 Manly
Bell Mary,* wife L C, cook
Bell Eliza,* d L C, res same, house servant
Bellamy Mrs Joe, wid, res 329 Hillsboro'
Bellamy Miss Lizzie, d Mrs Joe, res same, teacher in Centennial Graded School
Belvin C H, Pres National Bank of Ral, res Hillsboro' rd, o s w
Belvin Mrs Lizzie L, wife C H
Belvin Miss Katie B, d C H, res same
Belvin Miss Bessie, d C H, res same
Belvin Miss Nannie, d C H, res same, student
Belvin Mrs Lacy, wid, res e Martin
Belvin Mrs Connie, mother of Mrs Geo P Young, res same
Belvin Thos J, carp, r 635 e Hargett
Belvin Mrs Sallie, wife Thos J
Belvin Miss Nora, d T J, res same, student
Belvin F A, city policeman, res 221 s Swain
Belvin Mrs Lillie V, wife F A
Belvin Arthur P, son F A, res same, student
Belvin Wm H, son F A, res same, student
Belvin Peyton C, son F A, res same, student
Belvin Norman McKee, son F A, res same, student
Belvin Orrin W, salesman, res 418 s Person

Belvin Mrs Jackie H, wife Orrin W
Belvin Chas H, son Orrin W, res same, plumber
Belvin Miss Myrtle I, d Orrin W, res same, student
Bembry Lewis,* porter Agricultural bldg, res 130 w Lenoir
Bembry Martha,* wife Lewis, house work
Bembry Cam,* drayman, res Hargett, o s e
Bembry Ida,* wife Cam, washerwoman
Bembry Wilson,* gardener and wood-cutter, res Hargett, o s e
Bembry Annie,* wife Wilson, washerwoman
Bemery Wm,* lab, res 717 s McDowell
Bemery Julia G,* wife Wm, laundress
Bemery Pauline,* d Wm, res same, nurse
Bemery Mary L,* d Wm, res same, nurse
Bemery Susan O,* d Wm, res same, student
Bemery Willie B,* d Wm, res same, student
Bemery Novella,* d Wm, res same, student
Bemery Jennie V,* d Wm, res same, student
Bennett Mary, seamstress, res 525 s Dawson
Bennett J E, inmate Soldiers' Home
Benoish J J, inmate Soldiers' Home
Benton Edward, inmate Soldiers' Home
Benton Gertrude,* cook, res rear 420 s Salisbury
Bernard Jos J, bkkpr N C Penitentiary, res 413 Hillsboro'
Bernard Mrs Ella M, wife Jos J
Bernard Miss Katherine, d Jos J, res same
Berwanger S & D, clothiers, 219 Fayetteville
Berwanger Sam (Berwanger Bros), merchant, r 211 n Wilmington
Berwanger Mrs R, wife Sam
Berwanger Dave (Berwanger Bros), mercht, bds 211 n Wilmington
Besson Madame E, millinery, notions, etc, Fayetteville, res West Edenton, bet Dawson and McDowell
Besson Miss Caroline, d Madame E, res same, milliner
Besson Miss Mamie, d Madame E, res same, milliner
Besson Miss Jennette, d Madame E, res same, milliner
Besson Miss Lucy, d Madame E, res same, milliner
Bethel Priscilla,* washerwoman, res 512 w Morgan
Bethel Mary,* d Priscilla, res same, nurse
Bethel John,* son Priscilla, res same, laborer
Bethel William,* son Priscilla, res same, laborer
Betts C J, printer, res 406 w Lane
Betts Mrs Sallie, wife C J
Betts Miss Mamie, d C J, res same
Betts Miss Annie, d C J, res same, student
Betts Ovey, son C J, res same, clk for W A Betts & Co
Betts Leland, son C J, res same, student
Betts Raymond, son C J, res same, student
Betts Rev Alvin, Baptist minister, res cor s Person and Morgan
Betts Mrs Lucy J, wife Rev Alvin

Betts W F (Betts Bros), merchant, res cor Person and Morgan
Betts Everett A, son Rev Alvin, res same, druggist
Betts Mrs Mary L, wid, dressmaker, Firwood ave, o s n
Betts Miss Bettie H, step-d Mrs Mary L, res same
Betts Miss Janet, d Mrs Mary L, res same, student
Betts Willie N, son Mrs Mary L, res same, mail-boy Ral cot mills
Betts Chas H, bkkpr for Allen & Cram, res 215 s Bloodworth
Betts Mrs Roxie, wife Chas H,
Betts Miss Vivian G, d Chas H, res same, student
Betts D S, copyist, res 115 w Cabarrus
Betts Mrs Maria, wife D S
Betts Rev A L, Baptist city missionary, bds 514 s Harrington
BETTS BROS, grocers, 12 e Hargett
Betts Anderson, mechanic, res 516 s West
Betts Mrs Elizabeth, wife A
Betts W A, grocer, res 516 s West
Betts Mrs Annie L, wife W A
Betts Nancy H,* seamstress, res 222 w Lenoir
Betts Wiley P, clk at E F Wyatt & Son, res n Saunders
Betts Mrs Rosa, wife Wiley P
Betts Oscar L, bkkpr Ral oil mill, bds J R Barkley
Betts Mrs Addie R, wife J R
Betts Mrs Sallie, wid J M, res 213 n Harrington
Betts W A & Co, grocers, 14 e Hargett
Bevers Chas W, wks for city, res 605 e Hargett
Bevers Mrs Eliza, wife Chas W
Bevers Wm R, son Chas W, res same, bkkpr Royall & Borden
Bevers Chas L, son Chas W, res same, asst pressman News and Observer
Bevers Miss Lillian M, d Chas W, res same, student
Bevers Miss Katie A, d Chas W, res same, student
Bevers J C, chief attendant at Insane Asylum, res same
Biggs Henry,* janitor for News and Observer office, res 107 e Cabarrus
Biggs Ann,* wife Henry, washerwoman
Biggs Hattie,* d Henry, res same, washerwoman

BETTS BROS.,
Staple and Fancy Groceries,
Country Produce, Etc.,

Nos. 12 and 14 Hargett Street. - RALEIGH, N. C.

'Phone 144.

Biggs Queen,* d Henry, res same, washerwoman
Biggs Maud,* d Henry, res same, washerwoman
Biggs Richard,* son Henry, res same, lab
Bilyeu Henry, grape vineyard, res Avent Ferry rd, o s w
Bilyeu Miss Sadie, sister of H, res same
Birdsall Aaron S, lab, res Womble lane
Birdsall Mary,* wife A S, washerwoman
Birdsall Alex,* son A S, res same, lab
Birdsall Nancy,* d A S, res same, cook
Birdsall Samuel, son A S, r same, lab
Birdsall David,* lab, res old fair ground, o s e
Birdsall Julia,* wife David, house work
Birdsall Daisy,* student, res Cotton lane, o s e
Birdsall Turner,* student, res Cotton lane, o s e
Birdsong James C, printer, res 306 e Hargett
Birdsong Mrs O C, wife Jas C
Birdsong Ed G (Wynne & Birdsong), druggist, rooms 115 Halifax
Birdsong Miles B, son Jas C, res same, clk for J D Turner
Birdsong Miss Mamie, d Jas C, res same, stenographer and typewriter
Birdsong Jno H, son Jas C, res same, student
Birdsong Ludlow, son Jas C, res same, student
Birdsong Miss Heber, d Jas C, res same, student
Bishop R T, mechanic, res 221 n Salisbury
Bishop Mrs Virginia, wife R T
Bishop W R, son R T, eng S A L, bds 221 n Salisbury
Bishop Mrs Margaret, wife W R
Bishop Walter T, son R T, trav salesman
Bishop E B, son R T, res same
Bishop Miss Ella, d R T, res same
Bishop Miss Laura, d R T, res same
Bishop Mrs Polly A, wid, res 517 s Bloodworth
Bishop Hilliard, lab, res o s e
Bissett R O, bkkpr, res 312 e Jones
Bissett Miss Laura, wks Caraleigh mill, bds 514 s Harrington
Bivins J A, builder and contractor, res 317 w Morgan
Bivins Mrs Sarah E, wife J A
Bivins Miss Lillie, d J A, res same, student
Bivins Oder, son J A, res same, student
Bivins Edgar, son J A, res same, student
Bivins Grover, son J A, res same, student
Bivins Claude, son J A, res same, student
Bivins Hubert, son J A, res same, student
Bizzell J A, Asst Professor of Chemistry A & M College, bds A J Ellis
Blackledge Miss Addie, seamstress, bds 311 w Morgan
Blackman Phillis,* washerwoman, res old Fair Ground, o s e
Blackman Janie,* d Phillis, res same, cook

Blackman Viola,* d Phillis, res same, nurse
Blackman Ethel,* d Phillis, res same, nurse
Blackman Charles,* son Phillis, res same, servant
Blackman Edward,* musician, res 13 w Worth
Blackman Mamie,* d Ed, res same, student
Blackman Frank,* brick-mason, res 110 w Cabarrus
Blacknall Randolph,* drayman, res s e Davie
Blacknall Julia,* wife Randolph, washerwoman
Blacknall Dr George W, U S Internal Revenue Service, res 130 Hillsboro'
Blacknall Mrs M T, wife Dr G W
Blacknall Louis,* lab, res old Fair Ground, o s e
Blacknall Belle,* wife Louis, washerwoman
Blacknall William, train dispatcher S A L R R, bds 104 n McDowell
Blacknall Julia,* washerwoman, res 217 w South
Blacknall Carrie,* cook, res 715 s Dawson
Blacknall Maggie,* d Carrie, res same, student
Blacknall Flora,* house servant, res 522 s McDowell
Blacknall Geo,* son Flora, res same, student
Blacknall Mollie,* cook, res 522 s McDowell
Blair I C, teacher at N C Institution for the Blind, res 123 n Saunders
Blair Mrs D N, wife I C
Blake Wm R, machinist and eng, res 330 e Hargett
Blake Mrs Susan T, wife Wm R
Blake Miss Birdie, d Wm R, res same
Blake Albert, clk Wm Rogers, res 211 n West
Blake Mrs Cora, wife Albert
Blake Tilden, son Albert, res same, wks Ral cot mill
Blake Edward, son Albert, res same, wks Ral cot mill
Blake Miss Beulah, d Albert, res same, student
BLAKE'S LIVERY STABLES, cor s Blount and e Martin, Jos Blake, mgr
Blake John, carp, res 30 Hunter
Blake Gilly, wife John
Blake Alfred, son John, wks Caraleigh mill, res 30 Hunter

BLAKE'S Livery and Sale Stables,

No. 129 Martin Street,
RALEIGH, N. C.

Carriages furnished with reliable and polite drivers. Gentle Teams night or day meet all trains. A good line of Light Livery. Drummers' and Picnic Wagons on reasonable terms.

JOS. BLAKE, Manager.

Blake Julius, son John, res same, wks Mills mfg co
Blake Miss Rebecca, d John, res same, student
Blake Rev E B,* Baptist minister, res 524 s Dawson
Blake Nancy,* wife Rev E B
Blake Ardelia,* servant at Rex Hospital, res 524 s Dawson
Blake W Z, street commissioner, res 414 s Salisbury
Blake Joseph, livery stable, res 231 w Morgan
Blake Mrs L C, wife Joseph
Blake H D, traveling salesman, bds 231 w Morgan
Blake Mrs Fannie, wife H D
Blake Miss Julia Miller, d H D, res same, student
Blake Mrs M L, stamping, res 328 s McDowell
BLAKE T W, jeweler and watchmaker, 109 Fayetteville, res 328 s McDowell
Blake N A, res 328 s McDowell
BLAKE D C, carp, res 413 w Lane
Blake Mrs Lucy, wife D C
Blake Miss Blanche A, res with Mrs H Mahler
Blake Robert,* teacher, res 10 e Worth
Blake Ella,* wife Robert
Blalock Mrs Tabitha, wid, boarding-house, 224 e Martin
Blalock Miss Delia F, d Mrs Tabitha, res same, dressmaker
Blalock Miss Alice, d Mrs Tabitha, res same
Blalock Chas C, son Mrs Tabitha, res same, carp
Blalock Hugh H, son Mrs Tabitha, res same, clk
Blalock Miss Mattie, d Mrs Tabitha, res same, student
Blalock Miss Rena, d Mrs Tabitha, res same, student
Blalock Susan,* house work, res Rock Quarry rd
Blalock Mary,* d Susan, res same, servant
Blalock Franklin,* son Susan, res same, farm hand
Blalock Annie,* cook, res Tarboro' rd
Blalock Oscar,* son Susan, res same, farm hand
Blalock Alma,* washerwoman, res 812 s Wilmington
Blalock Lovie,* washerwoman, res 533 s Harrington
Blalock Mack, wks Insane Asylum, res Cannon
Blalock Mrs Emma, wife Mack, ironer at Insane Asylum
Blalock W H, miller, res 738 Fayetteville
Blalock Mrs Bessie E, wife W H
Bland J S, carp, res 509 n West
Bland Mrs Isabella, wife J S
Bland Miss Enolia, gen delivery clk at p o, res 509 n West
Bland Miss Isabella, d J S, res same, student
Bledsoe Rosa,* washerwoman, res s Swain
Bledsoe Eliza,* washerwoman, res 562 e Cabarrus
Bledsoe Chas,* son Eliza, res same, errand boy
Bledsoe N H, guard at workhouse, res e Hargett, o s e
Bledsoe Mrs G F, wife N H
Bledsoe Miss Mona M, d N H, res same, student

Bledsoe Owen H, son N H, res same, student
Bledsoe Moses A, lawyer, res cor South and Salisbury
Bledsoe Mrs D M, wife Moses A
Bledsoe Miss Minnie, d Moses A, res same
Bledsoe Miss Annie, d Moses A, res same
Bledsoe Moses A Jr, grocer, 401 Fayetteville, res cor South and Salisbury
Blount H L, eng Pilot cot mill, res n Blount, o s n
Blount Mrs Mary, wife H L
Blount Miss Katie, d H L, res same, student
Blount Fortune,* lab, res 225 s Bloodworth
Blount Lucy,* servant, res 554 e Martin
Blount William,* lab, res Martin, o s e
Blount Claude,* lab, res Martin, o s e
Blount Henry,* servant for Sam Woods, res same
Blount Mrs Matilda, wid, res 524 n West
Blount N B,* lab, res 22 w Worth
Blount M A V,* wife N B, house servant
Blount Emma,* washerwoman, res 126 w South
Blount Sadie,* d Emma, res same, cook
Blount Geo H,* son Emma, res same, house servant
Bobbitt Dr Wm H, physician and surgeon, office 222 w Hargett, res same
Bobbitt Mrs Laura, wife Dr Wm H
Bobbitt Benjamin, son Dr Wm H, res same
Bobbitt Miss Laura Miller, d Dr Wm H, res same
Bobbitt Rev Dr J B, minister and farmer, res 129 s Dawson
Bobbitt Mrs Hattie M, wife Dr J B
Bobbitt A M, son Dr J B, res same, medical student
Bobbitt J Hal, druggist, 233 Fayetteville, res 123 s Dawson
Bobbitt Mrs May, wife of J Hal
Bobbitt L B, son J Hal, res same
Bobbitt Mary D, d J Hal, res same
Bobbitt Miss Susie May, d J Hal, res same
Bobbitt J Hal Jr, son J Hal Sr, res same
Bobbitt Chas T, fireman S A L, bds 508 Halifax
Bobbitt Clayton,* driver for Pool & Moring, res 312 w South
Bobbitt Maria,* wife Clayton, washerwoman
Bobbitt Henry,* lab, res 303 w Lenoir
Bobbitt Clara,* wife Henry, washerwoman
Bobbitt Robt E,* son Henry, res same, driver
Bobbitt Estelle,* d Henry, res same, nurse
Bobbitt Rosa,* d Henry, res same, washerwoman
Bobbitt John,* son Henry, res same, student
Bobbitt Dexter,* lab, res rear 405 s Dawson
Bobbitt Martha,* cook, res 408 w Jones
Bobbitt Stephen,* porter Jas McKimmon & Co, res 729 s Blount
Bobbitt Maria,* wife Stephen, seamstress

Bobbitt Victoria,* d Stephen, res same, student
Bogan Walter,* brakeman S A L, res 137 n Salisbury
Bogasse Sam, foreman at News and Observer, res 315 e Martin
Bogasse Mrs Rosa, wife Sam
Bogasse Miss Bettie, d Sam, res same
Bogasse Sam Jr, son Sam, res same
Booker P A, night-watchman, res 117 s Dawson
Booker Mrs Mattie V, wife P A
Booker Miss Floy L, d P A, res same, wks Caraleigh mill
Booker Ardenna P, son P A, res same, wks Caraleigh mill
Booker Robt L, son P A, res same, student
Booker Miss Maggie O, d P A, res same, student
Booker Leroy G, son P A, res same
Bookram Susie A R,* seamstress, res 615 s McDowell
Bookram Ellen A,* d Susie, res same, student
Bookram Jas M,c son Susie, res same, student
Boler Mrs Harriet, wid, res 523 s Person
Bolton S M, carp, res 505 n Wilmington
Bolton Mrs Blanche, wife S M
Bolton E, machinist, bds 112 Halifax
Bolyn Mrs Clara, wid, dressmaker, res 108 w Jones
Bolyn William H, harness maker E F Wyatt & Co, r 108 w Jones
Bolyn Fred, son Mrs Clara, res same, student
Bonner Wm E, lineman for Ral Gas Co, res 421 s Dawson
Bonner Mrs Florence M, wife W E
Bonner Peter,* whitewasher, res 829 Mandy
Bonner Mrs Elizabeth, wid, res 118 s Dawson
Bonner Miss Virginia E, d Mrs Elizabeth, res same
BON TON SHAVING AND HAIR DRESSING SALOON.
    Park Hotel basement
Boone Wesley S, mechanic, res 217 s East
Boone Mrs Mary A, wife W S, dressmaker
Boone Miss Laura, bkkpr for Ruffin Roles, res same
Boone Martha, maid for Mrs W N H Smith, res on lot
Bost Jacob,* baker app, res 603 s McDowell

Bon Ton SHAVING AND HAIR-DRESSING PARLOR,

PARK HOTEL BASEMENT.

W. Martin Street,   **RALEIGH, N. C.**

Up-to-date service by white barbers who are skilled workmen and use the sharpest tools.

Hot and Cold Baths.   **E. G. FAUST, Prop'r.**

Bonshall J D, gen agt Ætna Life Ins Co, 113½ Fayetteville, res 401 e Jones
Bonshall Mrs Mattie H, wife J D
Bonshall John H, son J D, res same, student
Bowden Julia,* cook for Walter Harding, res 620 Elm
Bowen Richard, inmate Soldiers' Home
Bowen Dr M D,* physician, office and res Shaw Institute
Bowen Amy,* wife Dr M D, house work
Bowen Thos A, wagon maker and repairer, 132 e Morgan, res cor Oakwood ave and Elm
Bowen A F, son T A, res same, sec of the N C Agricultural and Experiment Station
Bowen Miss Iphia G, d T A, res same
Bowen Wm F, son T A, res same, student
Bowen Harry M, son T A, res same, student
Bowen Andrew H, son T A, res same, student
Bowen Miss Annie L, d T A, res same, student
Bowen Richmond G, son T A, res same, student
Bowers Miss Annie, seamstress, res 403 s Blount
Bowes M, supt Ral gas wks, res 223 e Lenoir
Bowes Mrs L A, wife M
Boyd Miss Lucy, dressmaker, res 124 n Wilmington
Boyd Ellen,* washerwoman, res 550 e Cabarrus
Boyd Sandy,* lab, res 2001 Yearby lane
Boykins Harry,* wood-cutter, res 817 s Wilmington
Boykins Julia,* wife Harry, washerwoman
Boylan Adelaide,* second-hand clothes dealer, r rear 304 n Person
Boylan Virginia,* nurse, res 516 e Martin
Boylan Ailsey,* washerwoman, rear 616 e Cabarrus
Boylan Fannie,* d Ailsey, res same, cook
Boylan Wm M Sr, planter, res Boylan ave
Boylan Mrs Mary K, wife Wm M Sr
Boylan Wm M Jr (W H & R S Tucker & Co), merchant, res Boylan ave
Boylan Wm J, son Wm M Jr, res same, student
Boylan Miss Josephine E, d Wm M Jr, res same, student
Boylan Wheeler,* lab, res 729 s Blount
Boylan Rosa,* wife Wheeler, cook for Dr W A Lodge
Boylan Elizabeth,* d Wheeler, res same
Boylan Lula,* d Wheeler, res same, student
Boylan Isabelle,* d Wheeler, res same, student
Boylan Miss Adelaide, res with Mrs E McSnow, 30 Boylan ave
Boylan James (W H & R S Tucker), merchant, res Boylan ave
Boylan Mrs Margaret T, wife James
Boylan Miss Florence T, d James, res same
Boylan Miss Mary K, d James, res same, student
Boylan Miss Margaret J, d James, res same, student

Boylan Wm M, son James, res same, student
Boylan Miss Katherine, d James, res same, student
Boylan Rufus T, son James, res same
Braan Joseph,* grocer, e Hargett, o s e, res same
Braan Caroline,* wife Jos, restaurant, 116 e Hargett
Braan Catherine,* d Jos, res same, servant
Braan Jesse,* son Jos, res same, lab
Braan Isaac,* son Jos, res same, lab
Braan Joseph,* hackman, res Blake stable
Braan Jack,* lab, res 127 n Harrington
Bradford Sarah,* washerwoman, res 820 s Wilmington
Bradford Sarah,* d Sarah, res same, washerwoman
Bradley Robt H, librarian Supreme Court, res 309 e Morgan
Bradley Mrs Cynthia, wife R H
Bradley Fred, son R H, res same
Bradley Miss Laura, d R H, res same
Bradley Miss Lillie, d R H, res same
Brady Miss Katie, hkpr for Mrs Geo J Williams, res same
Brady Emery, flagman Southern R R, bds 407 Fayetteville
Bragassa Jno A, baker and confectioner, shop and res 306 s Salisbury
Bragassa Mrs F E, wife J A
Bragassa Jos B, son J A, res same
Bragassa L H, son J A, res same, student
Bragassa Aldert S, son J A, res same, student
Bragassa Miss Bessie A, d J A, res same, student
Bragassa Miss Katie, d J A, res same, student
Bragassa Wm N, son J A, res same, student
Bragg Mrs Eliza, wid, res with mother, Mrs Mary Pierce
Bragg Wm H, bkkpr, res 620 w Jones
Branch Frank,* blacksmith, cor Harrington and South, res 611 s Harrington
Branch Columbia,* wife Frank, washerwoman
Branch James,* son Frank, res same, waiter at Rex Hospital
Branch Guilford,* driver, res 324 w South
Branch Mary,* wife Guilford, nurse
Branch Silas,* lab, res 518 s Dawson
Branch Georgia,* wife Silas, cook
Branch Jno H,* lawyer and teacher, res 719 s Saunders
Branch Bettie E,* wife Jno H
Branch James, weaver Caraleigh mill, res 722 Fayetteville
Branch Gilbert,* lab, res 503½ w South
Branch Roney,* wife Gilbert, washerwoman
Branch Florida,* d Gilbert, res same, student
Branch Hubert,* son Gilbert, res same, student
Branch Adeline,* washerwoman, res 503 Cannon
Branch Quint,* musician, res 503 Cannon
Branch Ernest,* lab, res 503 Cannon

Branch Bessie,* student, 503 Cannon
Branch D M, grocer, 401 w South, res same
Branch Mrs Josephine, wife D M
Branch Miss Claudie, d D M, res same, student
Branch Miss Minnie, d D M, res same, student
Branch Miss Maud, d D M, res same, student
Branch Haywood, farmer, res 416 w South
Branch Mrs Mollie, wife Haywood
Branch Miss Mamie, d Haywood, res same, wks Caraleigh mill
Branch Miss Hattie, d Haywood, res same, wks Caraleigh mill
Branch Leon, son Haywood, res same, wks Caraleigh mill
Branch James, son Haywood, res same, student
Branch Miss Ora, d Haywood, res same, student
Branch Martha,* cook, res 549 e Martin
Branch Margaret,* washerwoman, res 549 e Martin
Branch Theodore,* son Martha, res same, lab
Branch James,* son Martha, res same, lab
Branch Nannie,* d Martha, res same, chambermaid
Branch Hattie,* d Martha, res same, nurse
Branch Martha,* d Martha, res same, student
Branch Annie,* washerwoman, res 436 s Blount
Branch Jennie,* d Annie, res same, washerwoman
Branch George,* son Annie, res same, laborer
Branch Hubert,* son Jennie, res same, student
Branch Mrs L O'B, wid, res 305 Hillsboro
Branch Dennis,* student, res 308 w South
Branch Mack N, carp, bds 407 Fayetteville
Brannan Mrs Penny, wid, tailoress, res 305 s Bloodworth
Branson Rev Levi, minister and publisher of N C Almanac, res Branson House, 103½ Fayetteville
Branson Mrs Edith C, wife Rev Levi
Branson Miss Daisy C, d Rev Levi, res same
Brasel Wright,* well-digger, res 106 n East
Brasel Jane,* sick-nurse, res 106 n East
Brasel Nancy,* d Wright, res same, washerwoman
Brasel Ada,* d Wright, res same, seamstress
Brasel Lillie,* d Wright, res same, washerwoman
Bray Mary,* cook for H C Brown, res on lot
Bretsch Chas M, bakery, 103 Fayetteville, bds 109½ Fayetteville
Bretsch Albert, son Chas M, res same, student
Bretsch Charlie, son Chas M, res same, student
Brewster Miss Helen, student, res 321 s Person
Brewster E J, clk, res 321 s Person
Brewer S W (J J Thomas & Co), cot broker, res 604 n Blount
Brewer Mrs Bessie, wife S W
Brewer Talcott, son S W, res same, student
Brewer Miss Lula, d S W, res same, student
Brewer William, carp, bds 324 w Lane

Brickhouse Thomas, nephew of J A Egerton, res same
Brickle Eddie,* tobacco worker, res 115 e Cabarrus
Brickle Henry,* student, res 115 e Cabarrus
Brickle Catherine,* washerwoman, res 115 e Cabarrus
Brickle William H,* gardener, res Cotton lane, o s e
Brickle Lucetta,* wife Wm H, cook J J Johnson
Bridgeford Ben T,* drayman, res 905 Manly
Bridgeford Phillis,* wife B T, house work
Bridgeford Lizzie,* d B T, res same, dressmaker
Bridgeford Elnora,* d B T, res same, student
Bridgeford Vernon,* son B T, res same, student
Bridgers Samuel, night-watchman at Blind Institution, res 528 n East
Bridgers Mrs Narcissa, wife Sam
Bridgers Miss Eugenia, d Sam, res same, dressmaker
Bridgers Miss Nannie, d Sam, res same
Bridgers Jno E, son Sam, res same, wks N C Trouser Co
Bridgers Miss Nellie, d Sam, res same
Bridgers Miss Ella, d Sam, r same, bkkpr for Singer Machine Co
Bridgers Miss Effie, d Sam, res same
Bridgers Arthur, son Sam, res same, student
Bridgers Edgar, son Sam, res same, student
Bridgers J A, plasterer, res 112 n East
Bridgers Mrs Mary, wife J A
Bridgers Ernest, son J A, res same, student
Bridgers Thomas, son J A, res same, student
Bridgers Charles, son J A, res same, plumber app
Bridgers Richard,* city hand, res rear 405 s Dawson
Bridgers Wm J, sewing machine agt, res 706 n Person
Bridgers Mrs Katie O, wife Wm J
Bridgers Bros, merchant tailors, 216½ Fayetteville
Bridgers Cherry,* laundress Peace Institute, res Cotton lane, o s e
Bridgers Andrew,* wks Allen & Cram, res old Fair Ground, o s e
Bridgers Sarah,* wife Andrew, washerwoman
Bridgers Minnie,* cook for W B Kendrick, res same
Brie Louie, salesman, bds 105½ Fayetteville
Brierley William, supt for J H Gill, res 325 s McDowell
Briggs Fab H, cashier of National Bank of Ral, res cor Bloodworth st and Oakdale ave
Briggs Mrs Cosey W, wife F H
Briggs Jno B, son Fab H, res same, student
Briggs Fab L, son Fab H, res same, student
Briggs Chas R, son Fab H, res same, student
Briggs Miss Mary L, d Fab H, res same
Briggs James A (T H Briggs & Sons), hardware merchant, res 322 Hillsboro
Briggs Mrs Lula H, wife Jas A
Briggs Miss Lula H, d Jas A, res same

Briggs James A Jr, son Jas A, res same, student
Briggs Everett, son Jas A, res same, student
Briggs Mrs T H, wid, lives with son James A Briggs
Briggs Jno D, builder and contractor, res 117 n Dawson
Briggs Mrs Florence, wife Jno D
Briggs Willie, son Jno D, res same, wks Telephone Exchange
Briggs Hubert, son Jno D, res same, student
Briggs Miss Helen, d Jno D, res same
Briggs Thos H (Thos H Briggs & Son), hardware merchant, res 116 n Dawson
Briggs Mrs Sarah G, wife Thos H
Briggs Willis G, son Thos H, res same, student
Briggs Miss Elizabeth N, d Thos H, res same, student
BRIGGS THOS H & SONS, wholesale and retail hardware dealers, 220 Fayetteville
Briggs Mrs M E, wid, res 317 s McDowell
Briggs B F, son Mrs M E, res same, machine hand
Briggs Mrs P H, wid, res 317 s McDowell
Briggs Hannah,* house work, res 728 Fayetteville
Bright Rev A A,* Christian minister, res 814 Manly
Bright Lucy R,* wife Rev A A
Bright Valina,* d Rev A A, res same, student
Brim John,* wks for W C Stronach, res Oakdale ave
Brim Fannie,* wife John, washerwoman
Brimley H H, curator at State Museum, res 316 s Person
Brimley Mrs Edith J, wife H H
Brimley Clem, taxidermist, res Rock Quarry rd
Brimley Miss Sophia, sister Clem, res same, taxidermist
Brinkley Geo W, eng S A L, res 114 Johnson
Brinkley Lawrence, son G W, res same, spinner Ral cot mill
Brinkley Miss Lessie, d G W, res same, student
Brinkley Mary,* washerwoman, res 818 Manly
Brinkley Edward,* son Mary, res same, farm hand
Brinkley Blake,* son Mary, res same, farm hand
Brinkley Delmer,* son Mary, res same, student
Briscoe Nettie,* cook, res 310 Manly
Britt Mrs Elizabeth, res 403 s Blount
Britt Charles, son Mrs Elizabeth, res same, student
Britt Gaston W, real estate agt, bds 117 Fayetteville
Broadhurst R D, attendant at Insane Asylum, res same
Broadnax Peter,* grocer, bds 434 s Blount
Broadwell D J, grocer, s Blount
Broadwell Mrs Annie, wife D J
Broadwell Miss Blanche, d D J, res same
Brockwell T F, lock and gunsmith, s Salisbury, r 322 s McDowell
Brockwell Mrs Kate M, wife T F
Brockwell Miss Laura E, d T F, res same, student
Brockwell Sherwood B, son T F, res same, student

Brockwell Miss Katie L, d T F, res same, student
Brockwell Edgar M, son T F, res same, student
Brockwell Robt L, son T F, res same
Brodie Martha,* cook for Dr A W Knox, res on lot
Brodie Henrietta,* washerwoman, res w Lenoir
Brodie Susanna,* d Henrietta, res same, student
Brodie James,* wood-cutter, res 225 e Lane
Brodie Edie,* wks tobacco factory, res 114 e Morgan
Brodie Richard,* wks tobacco factory, res 114 e Morgan
Brogden Mrs O H, mother Mrs Jas O Ruth, res same
Bromley Miss Maggie, music teacher at Blind Institution, r same
Bronson Miss Lillie, attendant at Insane Asylum, res same
Brooklyn Methodist Episcopal Church, Rev R H Whitaker, pastor
Brooks Robt H, deputy sheriff, res 558 e Hargett
Brooks Mrs Annie, wife Robt H
Brooks Buck, son Robt H, res same
Brooks Mrs Sarah, wid, seamstress, res in Prairie bldg
Brooks Amos,* hostler, res 516 e Edenton
Brooks Annie,* wife Amos, washerwoman
Brooks Bessie,* d Amos, res same, house servant
Brooks Henry,* son Amos, res same, lab
Brooks Birdie,* d Amos, res same, student
Brooks Minnie,* d Amos, res same, student
Brooks Louise,* d Amos, res same, student
Brooks Helen,* laundress, res 516 Smith
Brooks Edward,* son Helen, res same, porter for E M Uzzell
Brooks Lawrence,* drayman, res rear Catholic church
Brooks Nancy,* nurse for S F Mordecai, res on lot
Brooks Maggie,* washerwoman, res rear 517 s Dawson
Broughton Needham B (Edwards & Broughton), job printer, binder and pubr, res 426 n Person
Broughton Mrs Caroline R, wife N B
Broughton Edgar E, son N B, r same, clk at Edwards & Broughton
Broughton Miss Rosa C, d N B, res same
Broughton Miss Carrie L, d N B, res same, student
Broughton Miss Mary N, d N B, res same, student
Broughton N B Jr, son N B, res same
BROUGHTON J M & CO, fire ins and real estate agency, s w Martin
Broughton J M (J M Broughton & Co), notary public, s w Martin, res outside city
Broughton Gaston H, night-watchman, res 312 e Martin
Broughton Mrs Sarah C, wife Gaston H
Broughton Cecil, son Gaston H, res same, student
Broughton Wm H, saloon clk, bds 217 Linden ave
Broughton Zach T, printer, res 117 w Cabarrus
Broughton Mrs M J, wife Z T
Broughton Phil H, son Z T, res same, pressman Caucasian office

Broughton Miss Ida M, d Z T, res same, book binder
Broughton Miss Ella E, d Z T, res same, student
Broughton Zach T Jr, son Z T, res same
Broughton Miss Sadie A, d Z T, res same, student
Broughton Jack,* lab, res 403 w South
BROWN L T, proprietor Yarborough House and asst proprietor Park Hotel, res Yarborough House
Brown Mrs Josephine, wife L T
Brown Miss Eliza, d L T, res same
Brown Neville, son L T, res same
Brown W D, shoemaker, res 121 w Cabarrus
Brown Mrs Sallie A, wife W D, dressmaker
Brown Albert,* restaurant, r 305 s West
Brown Kate,* wife Albert
Brown Lillie,* waiter in restaurant, res 305 s West
Brown Angeline,* washerwoman, res 539 Newbern ave
Brown Mrs S E, wid, res 108 w Edenton
Brown James E, mgr cotton compress, res 320 w Jones
Brown Mrs Emma Y, wife James E
Brown Henry,* porter Capital club, res 523 Newbern ave
Brown Harriet,* wife Henry, washerwoman
Brown James,* son Henry, res same, student
Brown Henry,* elevator-boy W H & R S Tucker & Co, res 523 Newbern ave
Brown Hattie,* d Henry, res same, student
Brown F F, conductor Southern R R, bds 110 s McDowell
Brown Mrs Rena, wife F F
Brown Jos G, pres Citizens National Bank, res 227 w Morgan
Brown Mrs Alice B, wife Jos G
Brown Miss Josephine L, d Jos G, res same
Brown Robert A, son Jos G, res same
Brown Theo (Levine & Brown), merchant, bds 12 e Davie
Brown Melinda,* washerwoman, res 121 e Cabarrus
Brown Osborn,* lab, res Hood's al
Brown Mills H, res 603 s Wilmington
Brown Mrs Hattie L, wife Mills H
Brown M H Jr, son Mills H, res same
Brown Miss Joanna, hkpr for Green Maynard, res same
Brown William,* lab, res 217 w Lenoir
Brown Isaac,* lab, res 307 w South
Brown Fannie,* wife Isaac, house work
Brown S W,* carp, res 815 Manly
Brown Alice,* wife S W, house work
Brown Sarah L,* d S W, res same, student
Brown Shelly,* lab, res 815 Manly
Brown Addie,* student, res 815 Manly
Brown Miss Elizabeth, cook, res 821 Manly
Brown Henry,* gardener, res 330 Cannon

Brown Rebecca,* washerwoman, res 413 Cannon
Brown Maria,* house work, res 413 Cannon
BROWN JNO W, funeral director and embalmer, office s Salisbury near cor Hargett, res 101 w Hargett
Brown Mrs Elizabeth, wife Jno W
Brown Henry,* lab, res 715 s Dawson
Brown Annie,* cook, res 211 w Davie
Brown Fab P (Wynne, Ellington & Co), real estate and rental agt, res 412 Elm
Brown Mrs Lena, wife Fab P
Brown George,* wks frt depot S A L, res 622 Harp's lane
Brown Matilda,* wife George
Brown Thos,* lab, res 526 e Cabarrus
Brown Laura,* wife Thos, cook
Brown H C, clk to railroad commission, res 429 n Person
Brown Mrs Mollie M, wife H C
Brown Mary,* washerwoman, res Newbern ave, o s e
Brown Mrs H J, wid, res 413 s Dawson
Brown Miss Janie L, d Mrs H J, res same
Brown Miss Lucy L, g-d Mrs H J, res same
Brown Nellie,* servant at Mrs E E Moffitt, res same
Brown Fab,* farmer, res Fayetteville, o s s
Brown Susan,* wife Fab, washerwoman
Brown Gabriel,* blacksmith, res 807 Jenkins
Brown Polly,* wife Gabriel, washerwoman
Brown Kate,* washerwoman, res 807 Jenkins
Brown Ida,* washerwoman, res 807 Jenkins
Brown Nannie,* d Gabriel, res same, student
Brown Miss Pauline, d Peyton Brown, lives with Mrs Laura Watkins, 416 s Wilmington
Brown Wm M, printer, res 327 w Jones
Brown Mrs Frances, wife Wm M
Brown Miss Annie, d Wm M, res same, dressmaker
Brown Bedford, son Wm M, wks weather bureau
Brown Jacob,* wks S A L R R, res rear 305 Hillsboro'
Brown Nellie,* wife Jacob, washerwoman

ESTABLISHED 1836.

H. J. BROWN COFFIN HOUSE,
RALEIGH, N. C.,

Keeps the largest, finest and best selected stock of

Coffins and Caskets, in Cloth, Wood and Metal,

Burial Robes, Wrappers, Slippers for Ladies, Gents and Children; also
BURGLAR-PROOF GRAVE VAULTS.

JOHN W. BROWN, Prop.,
Funeral Director and Embalmer.

Brown Edward S, cabinet maker and coffin trimmer, with Jno W Brown, res 311 w Morgan
Brown Mrs Maggie A, wife Ed S
Brown Wm E, son Ed S, res same, student
Brown Russell E, son Ed S, res same
Brown Mollie,* cook for Dr Hubert Haywood, res 324 e Martin
Brown Ada,* d Mollie, res same
Brown A,* lunch house, 111 e Hargett
Brown Rhodia,* washerwoman, res 207 e South
Brown Nannie,* d Rhodia, res same, washerwoman
Brown Hilliard,* son Rhodia, res same, lab
Brown Nat L, bkkpr for Thos Pescud, res 609 Hillsboro'
Brown Mrs Sallie S, wife Nat L
Brown Miss Allie W, d Nat L, res same
Brown Henry J, son Nat L, res same, app at Allen & Cram
Brown Miss Katherine E, d Nat L, res same
Brown Miss Ray La Mont, d Nat L, res same, student
Brown Creacy,* house servant for Mrs J M Heck, res on lot
Brown B B, printer, res 118 s Person
Brown Mrs Sallie, wife B B
Brown Miss Bessie T, lives with Mrs T H Briggs
Brown Millie,* washerwoman, res e Martin, o s e
Brown Cora,* cook, res e Martin, o s e
Brown Omega,* d Cora, res same, student
Brown Katie,* d Cora, res same, student
Brown Bruce,* lab, res old Fair Ground, o s e
Brown Jennie,* wife Bruce, washerwoman
Brown Julia,* student, res with Robt Watson
Brown Chas A, printer, res 126 w Lane
Brown Mrs Ada J, wife C A, bkpr for Mrs Ann Perry
Brown A J, inmate Soldiers' Home
Brown Wm J, inmate Soldiers' Home
Brown Peter A, inmate Soldiers' Home
Brown Addie G,* student, res with Jeff Stanley
Brown Thomas,* hackman, res 717 s East
Brown Winnie,* wife Thos
Brown Joseph,* son Thos, res same, student
Brown John,* hotel waiter, res Martin, o s e
Brown Polly,* wife John, chamber-maid at Park Hotel
Brown Joanna,* washerwoman, res 403 w South
Brown Wm M Jr, letter carrier, res 304 e Morgan
Brown Mrs Kate, wife Wm M Jr
Brown Miss Fannie, d Wm M Jr, res same, student
Brown N A, clk in Revenue office, res 217 s Swain
Brown Mrs Annie K, wife N A
Brown Miss Nettie M, d N A, res same, student
Brown W H, res 312 Newbern ave
Brown Mrs Roxie, wife W H

Brown Mrs M J, wid, res 304 n Person
Brown Miss Maggie, d Mrs M J, res same, milliner
Brown Miss Minnie, d Mrs M J, saleslady at A B Stronach
Brown Frank, son Mrs M J, res same, student
Brown Miss Pattie, d Mrs M J, res same, student
Brown James,* eng Ral cot mill, res 513 w Lenoir
Brown Martha,* wife Jas, washerwoman
Brown Horace,* son Jas, res same, student
Brown Mary,* d Jas, res same, student
Brown George,* lab, bds 219 s Harrington
Brown Daniel,* lab, res room 1 R R al
Brown Agnes,* wife Daniel, washerwoman,
Brown Lucinda,* d Daniel, res same, student
Brown Bettie,* d Daniel, res same, washerwoman
Brown Judge,* son Daniel, res same, farm hand
Browning L R, inmate Soldiers' Home
Bryan Miss Mary, student, res with Mrs J C Winder
Bryan James, student, res with Mrs J C Winder
Bryan Winder, student, res with Mrs J C Winder
Bryan A P, agt So Express Co, res 119 n Person
Bryan Mrs Isabella, wife A P
Bryant Zilphia,* washerwoman, res 28 Fowle
Bryant Kate,* cook Seth Jones, res same
Bryant Abram,* shoemaker, res rear e Davie, o s e
Bryant Patsy,* wife Abram
Bryant Rosa,* d Abram, res same, servant
Bryant Aaron,* son Abram, res same, lab
Bryant Henry,* son Abram, res same, student
Bryant Richard,* brick-mason and grocer, res 505 Haywood
Bryant Mary,* wife Richard
Bryant Geo H,* son Richard, res same, clk for father
Bryant Rachel,* d Richard, res same, student
Bryant Prof Geo W, teacher instrumental music Peace Institute, res 605 Halifax
Bryant Mrs Maggie E, wife G W, teacher vocal music Peace Institute
Bryant Mrs J A, wid, res 605 Halifax
Bryant Amanda,* cook for F H Cameron, res on lot
Bryant Mary,* nurse, res 408 e Edenton
Bryant Thos N, butcher, res 516 n East
Bryant Mrs Martha B, wife Thos N
Bryant Miss Hattie N, d Thos N, res same
Bryant Ned,* shoemaker, res 321 w South
Bryant Birtie,* d Ned, res same, washerwoman
Bryant Frank V, tinner, res 544 s Bloodworth
Bryant Mrs Mary H, wife F V
Bryant J N, brick-mason, res 544 s Bloodworth
Bryant Mrs Melissa, wife J N

Bryant Miss Sallie M, seamstress, res 514 s Bloodworth
Bryant Mrs Jno H, wid, res 520 n Person
Bryant Miss Mary S, d Mrs Jno H, res same, teacher
Bryant Miss Margaret R, d Mrs Jno H, res same
Bryant Miss Mary S, res 520 n Person
Bryant Mrs Luvenia, wid J S, res 520 n West
Bryant Ernest, son Mrs Luvenia, res same, wks for Ruffin Roles
Bryant Mrs Emma, wid, seamstress, res 515 s Bloodworth
Bryant Sallie,* washerwoman, res 402 w North
Bryant Eliza,* washerwoman, res 402 w North
Bryant Ned,* driver for Jones & Powell, res 426 s Blount
Bryant Nellie,* d Ned, res same, student
Bryant Frances,* d Ned, res same, washerwoman
Bryant Helen,* wife Ned, cook for Wm Woollcott
Bryant Richard,* son Ned, res same, wks M Watt's barber shop
Bryant Dock,* drayman, res 35 Hunter
Bryant Louise,* wife Dock, washerwoman
Bryant Emma,* d Dock, res same, student
Bryant Isaac,* hostler, res Dodd
Bryant Nancy,* d Isaac, res same
Bryant Saxie,* son Isaac, res same, driver for W E Carter
Bryant Pauline,* d Isaac, res same, hkpr
Bryant Irene,* son Isaac, res same, wks Ice cellar
Bryant Mary,* d Isaac, res same, student
Bryant Julia,* d Isaac, res same
Bryant Joseph,* wood-cutter, res e Hargett, o s e
Bryant Emily,* wife John, washerwoman
Bryant Clara,* nurse for Ed H Lee, res same
Bryant Will,* brakeman S A L, res 113 w Peace
Bryant Nancy,* wife Will, washerwoman
Bryant Robert,* son Will, res same, student
Bryant Betsy,* house servant, res 526 s McDowell
Bruce N C, teacher in Shaw University, res same
Bruce John,* lab, res rear 517 s Dawson
Bruner T K, sec N C dept of agriculture, res 112 e Jones
Bruner Mrs Belle, wife T K
Buck F W, inmate Soldiers' Home
Budd Mrs Maggie, wid, res 519 n Person
Budd Miss Mary, d Mrs Maggie, res same, student
Buffaloe Sheppard,* porter for A B Stronach, res 508 e Edenton
Buffaloe Martha,* house work, res Martin, o s e
Buffaloe Dr A J, physician and surgeon, res 312 w Edenton, office same
Buffaloe Mrs Julia H, wife Dr A J
Buffaloe Miss Ethel H, d Dr A J, res same, student
Buffaloe Mrs Mary, seamstress, res 410 Haywood
Buggs Robert,* waiter, res 8 Matthews' lane
Buis W A, inmate Soldiers' Home

Bullard E L, loom fixer, res Cannon
Bullard Mrs Emma, wife E L
Bullock Mrs C W, wid, res 713 s Blount
Bullock Miss Mamie, d Mrs C W, res same, artist
Bullock James G, son Mrs C W, res same, app painter
Bullock Miss Margaret, d Mrs C W, res same
Bullock Miss Emma, d Mrs C W, res same, student
Bullock George R, son Mrs C W, res same, student
Bullock Everett, son Mrs C W, res same, student
BULLOCK CHAS F, sign writer, shop basement Central Hotel, res 713 s Blount
Bullock Francis,* cook for Sam T Smith, res same
Bullock Dolly,* washerwoman, res 215 w North
Bullock Susan,* student, res 603 s McDowell
Bullock Kate,* washerwoman, res 417 w South
Bullock Coleman C,* lab, res 304 w Lenoir
Bullock Martha A,* wife C C, cook
Bumpass Chas,* wks oil mill, res 404 Smithfield
Bumpass Martha,* wife Charles, cook
Buncombe Mary,* cook for Armistead Jones, res Townes al
Bunch T V, station master Union depot, res 508 s Harrington
Bunch Mrs Jane, wife T V
Bunch Burke H, son T V, r same, baggage master Southern R R
Bunch N N, carp, res 305 n West
Bunch Mrs Annie H, wife N N
Bunch Miss Dora, d N N, res same
Bunch Ivan, son N N, res same, lab
Bunch Bernard, son N N, res same, student
Bunch Wm H, clk for Fred Woollcott, res 514 n Bloodworth
Bunch Mrs Columbia H, wife Wm H
Bunch Henry D, son Wm H, res same, clk for J A Duncan
Bunch Chas C, son Wm H, res same, clk for W H King & Co
Bunch Miss Eva C, d Wm H, res same
Bunch Miss Nora, res with Mrs A L Watson
Bunch Mrs Mary A, sister of Mrs Wm M Utley, res same
Bunch D T, carp S A L, res 415 n Salisbury
Bunch Mrs M V, wife D T
Bunch Guy L, mailing clk p o, bds 123 w Martin
Bunch Mrs Flora M, wife Guy L
Bunn Riley, carp, res 715 n Person
Bunn Mrs Olivia, wife Riley
Bunn Edgar, son Riley, res same
Bunn Miss Dora, d Riley, res same
Bunn William, carp, res 715 n Person
Bunn Mrs Julia, wife Wm
Bunn Robt,* lab, res 526 e Cabarrus
Bunn Washington,* coachman, res 307 s East
Bunn Henrietta,* wife Wash, sick nurse

Bunn Lula E,* d Wash, res same, house-servant
Bunn Asa,* son Wash, res same, lab
Bunn Claude,* son Wash, res same, student
Burch Lillie,* cook, res 211 w Lenoir
Burch Jane,* cook for Mrs C H Smith, res 128 n Wilmington
Burch Harriet,* washerwoman, res 407 w Edenton
Burch Cora,* d Harriet, res same, washerwoman
Burch Charles,* son Harriet, res same, lab
Burch Otey,* son Harriet, res same, lab
Burch John,* son Harriet, res same, lab
Burch George,* son Harriet, res same, lab
Burden Ada,* cook for Mrs M L Blake, res on lot
Burdick R A, book agt, res 115 s Harrington
Burdick Silvia, wife R A, teacher
Burdick Daniel R, son R A, res same, student
Burdick Miss Henrietta, d R A, res same, student
Burgess Thos,* lab, res 219 e South
Burgess Stella,* wife Thos, washerwoman
Burgess Albert,* carp, res 107 n Harrington
Burkhead Robt L, ins agt, bds 104 n McDowell
Burkhead Mrs Mary, wife Robt L
Burkhead & Farwell, life ins, 4 Pullen bldg
Burkhead & Lindsey, life ins, 4 Pullen bldg
Burkhead L L, clk, bds 123 s Dawson
Burney Silas,* porter at J I Johnson, res 214 w Lenoir
Burney Onia,* house-servant, res 513 s McDowell
Burnett Lucy,* cook for Mrs Andrew Syme, room 221 s Blount
Burnett Charles,* son Lucy, res same, wks in barber shop
Burnett Ephraim,* well-digger, res 318 e Davie
Burnett Clarissa,* wife Ephraim, cook
Burnett George,* wks S A L, res 104 w Edenton
Burns Alfred,* carp, res 723 Manly
Burns Virginia,* wife Alfred, washerwoman
Burns John,* son Alfred, res same, carp
Burns Emma,* d Alfred, res same, laundress
Burns Lydia,* d Alfred, res same, cook
Burns Annie E,* d Alfred, res same, laundress
Burns James M, d Alfred, res same, student
Burns Matthew,* son Alfred, res same
Burns Robert,* carp, res 313 w Lenoir
Burns Mary,* wife Robt, washerwoman
Burns Lula,* d Robt, res same, student
Burns Mamie,* d Robt, res same
Burns Tony,* restaurant, up-stairs 205 s Wilmington, res 504 Haywood
Burns Eliza,* wife Tony, cook in restaurant
Burns Miss Helen, house-girl for A J Floyd, res same
Burns Mrs Lydia, wid, mother of Mrs J W Cole, res same

Burroughs Chaplin, wks Ral cotton mill, bds R T Winston
Burroughs William, conductor S A L R R, bds 105½ Fayetteville
Burroughs James M, car inspector S A L, bds 508 Halifax
Burroughs Luther,* lab, res 511 s Dawson
Burroughs Ellen,* wife Luther, washerwoman
Burroughs George,* son Luther, res same, student
Burt Thomas,* lab, res Cannon
Burt Mary,* wife Thos, house work
Burt Edie,* d Thos, res same, cook
Burt Lillie,* d Thos, res same, cook
Burt Lee,* son Thos, res same, farm hand
Burt Jane,* cook for Mrs C H Smith, res on lot
Burt James G, grocer, 16 s Bloodworth, res same
Burt Mrs Zipporah, wife Jas G
Burton Robt O, lawyer, office Pullen bldg, res cor Peace and n Person
Burton Mrs Virginia, wife Robt O
Burton Miss Mary, d Robt O, res same, student
Burton Miss Lizzie, d Robt O, res same, student
Burton Charles, son Robt O, res same
Burton William,* lab, res 710 s McDowell
Burton Iola,* nurse, res 710 s McDowell
Burwell J B, Teachers' Agency, res with B R Lacy
BURWELL TEACHERS' AGENCY AND EDUCATIONAL BUREAU, 16 w Martin
Burwell Michael,* carp, res 510 n Bloodworth
Burwell Panthia,* housekeeper for M Burwell, res same
Burwell Mary,* teacher in Garfield Graded School, res 510 n Bloodworth
Burwell Willie,* student, res with M Burwell
Busbee F H, lawyer, office 217 Fayetteville, res 204 n Person
Busbee Mrs Sally H, wife F H
Busbee Miss Annie T, d F H, res same
Busbee Richard S, son F H, res same, student
Busbee Miss Eliza T, d F H, res same, student
Busbee Philip H, son F H, res same, student

Teachers' Agency and Educational Bureau,

JNO. B. BURWELL, formerly Principal Peace Institute, Manager.

Supplies Schools, Colleges and Families with Teachers without charge. Secures positions for Teachers at moderate cost. Deals in School Furniture and Supplies of all kinds, also Church Furniture. Sells and Rents School Property. Have on file large number of first-class Teachers in all branches. Correspondence solicited, and all business entrusted to Agency promptly attended to.

Address **JNO. B. BURWELL,**
Corner Martin and Salisbury Sts., RALEIGH, N. C.

Busbee Chas M, lawyer and postmaster, res n w cor Salisbury and Hargett
Busbee Mrs Florence C, wife Chas M
Busbee Perrin, son Chas M, res same, lawyer
Busbee Jaques, son Chas M, res same, registry clk post-office
Busbee Miss Louisa T, d Chas M, res same
Busbee Miss Sophia D, d Chas M, res same
Busbee Miss Isabelle B, d Chas M, res same, student
Busbee Miss Christiana, d Chas M, res same
Busbee Mrs Lizzie, dressmaker, 226 w Hargett
Busbee Miss May, student, res 603 Hillsboro'
Busbee Mamie,* student, res with Jane Jones
Busbee Johnston, res with Mrs C H Jordan, 565 e Hargett
Busbee Miss Sophia P, student, res with Mrs C H Jordan, 565 e Hargett
Busbee Johnston T, Train Dispatcher, S A L R R, bds Charles M Busbee
Busbee Frank M, carp, bds 522 n Person
Bush Mrs F L, wid, res cor Blount and Polk
Bush Thos F, clk at C E Johnson & Co, res cor Blount and Polk
Bush Miss C F, d Mrs F L, res same
Bush Miss G L, d Mrs F L, res same
Bush S D, son Mrs F L, res same, student
Butler Henry, bkkpr at Weekly Caucasian, rooms at H W Ayer's
Butler Henry C, supt Caraleigh cotton mill, res 503 e Jones
Butler Mrs Lucy J, wife H C
Butler Miss Edith M, d H C, res same, student
Butler Mrs Athia, hkpr for J J Hayes, res same
Butler Miss Estelle, d Mrs Athia, res same
Butner Hattie, seamstress, res 535 e Lenoir
Bynum Robert,* fireman S A L, res 21 Hayti
Bynum Bettie,* wife Robert, laundress
Bynum Alvis, clk at Julius Lewis Hardware Co, bds 508 Fayetteville
Bynum Annie,* cook, res 321 s Bloodworth
Bynum Raymond D, printer, res 13 s East
Bynum Mrs Emma A, wife Raymond D
Byrd Adora,* house-servant, res w Lenoir

CAIN Ida,* hkpr, 116 w South
Calvert John, cot buyer, res 504 n Blount
Calvert John Jr, son John, res same, student
Cameron & Batchelor, gen ins and real estate agents, 238 Fayetteville
Cameron Francis H (Cameron & Batchelor), gen ins agt, res 504 e Jones
Cameron Mrs Eugenia L, wife F H

Cameron Duncan H, son F H, res same, fire ins agt
Cameron Miss Fannie H, d F H, res same, student
Cameron Miss Le Grand, d F H, res same, student
Cameron Miss Natalie, d F H, res same, student
Cameron Miss Eugenia, d F H, res same, student
Campbell Mrs Laura E, wid, res 119 w Martin
Cannady Daniel,* grocer, res 317 Cannon
Cannady Bettie,* wife Daniel, washerwoman
Cannady Burke,* son Daniel, res same, lab
Cannady Esther,* d Daniel, res same, nurse
Cannady Belle,* nurse for C C McDonald, res on lot
Canady Minerva,* cook, res 323 w South
Canfield Rev I A, pastor St Saviour Episcopal church, res 113 s McDowell
Capehart L B,* teacher at Shaw University, res 310 e Davie
Capehart Maggie,* wife L B
CAPITAL PRINTING CO, Academy of Music bldg
Capps William, lab, res 19 Hayti
Capps Mrs Elizabeth, wife Wm
Capps Miss Eader L, d Wm, res same
Capps Harold, son Wm, res same
Capps Miss Bertha, d Wm, res same
Capps H H, inmate Soldiers' Home
Card C O, wks on air-brakes S A L R R, res 527 Hicks' lane
Card Mrs Ellen, wife C O
Cardwell Mary,* d Charles Cardwell, school-teacher, res 519 s Wilmington
Cardwell Chas,* butler for Mrs V B Swepson and sexton First Baptist church, res 421 s Blount
Cardwell Joanna,* wife Chas, dressmaker
Cargille Jno A, wks Peter Stumpf bottling wks, bds 215 s Person
Carleton Miss Kate, teacher at St Mary's, res same
Carmingie Citie,* washerwoman, res north end Dawson
Carmingie Annie,* d Citie, res same, student
Carmingie Cassie,* d Citie, res same, servant at Mrs Dr Perry
Carmingie Henry,* son Citie, res same, wks for Jno White

BARNES BROS., Established 1892.   SMITH, FAISON & CO., Established 1895.

Capital Printing Company, (Incorpor'd 1895. Capital Stock $10,000.) Raleigh, N. C.,

Correspondence solicited. Mail orders will receive prompt and careful attention. **Will do your Job Printing.**

CAPITAL PRINTING COMPANY, RALEIGH, N. C.

Carmingie James,* son Citie, res same, driver for Dr G A Renn
Carnley William,* wks Park Hotel, room 421 s Blount
CARPENTER & PEEBLES, architects, cor Martin and Fayetteville, up-stairs
Carpenter J C S, ins agt, office Pullen bldg, bds Park Hotel
Carpenter Mrs Pattie, wife J C S
Carpenter Miss Katherine, d J C S, res same, student
CARR Hon ELIAS, Governor of the State of N C, res Executive Mansion, Burke Square
Carr Mrs Eleanor, wife Gov Elias
Carr Miss Annie B, d Gov Elias, res same
Carr Miss Eleanor, d Gov Elias, res same
Carr Dr J B, druggist N C Insane Asylum, res same
CARROLL JAS D, saloon and groceries, 225 s Wilmington, res 513 s Bloodworth
Carroll Mrs Ella T, wife Jas D
Carroll Robt G, clk for J D Carroll, bds 513 s Bloodworth
Carroll John, carp, res 223 w Jones
Carroll Mrs Emma, wife John
Carroll James, carp, res 207 n Harrington
Carroll Mrs Bettie, wife James
Carroll Miss Ella, d James, res same
Carroll William, son James, res same, carp
Carroll George, son James, res same, wks Royster's candy factory
Carroll Miss Mattie, d James, res same
Carroll Robert, son James, res same, student
Carroll James R, son James, res same, student
Carroll O J, U S Marshal Eastern District of N C, office in p o bldg, res 513 Fayetteville
Carroll Mrs Mary A, wife O J
CARROLL Dr N G, surgeon dentist, office cor Fayetteville and Hargett, up-stairs, bds at O J Carroll
Carroll J C, son O J, res same, chief clk to U S Marshal
Carroll Miss Jessie, d O J, res same
Carroll Miss Pattie, d O J, res same
Carroll Herbert, son O J, res same, student

J. D. CARROLL,
Merchandise Broker and General Commission Merchant.
A COMPLETE LINE OF
STAPLE AND FANCY **GROCERIES**, WHOLESALE AND RETAIL.
CHOICEST WINES, LIQUORS AND CIGARS.
225 S. Wilmington Street.   -   -   RALEIGH, N. C.
TELEPHONE 186.

Carroll Mrs Sue, matron A and M College, res same
Carter Clem W, trav salesman, bds Exchange Hotel
Carter Mrs Irene, wife Clem W
Carter Mary Helen, d Clem W, res same
Carter W E, grocer and oyster dealer, 120 Fayetteville, res same
Carter Mrs Kate C, wife W E
CARTER Rev Dr J W, pastor First Baptist church, res 104 w Edenton
Carter Mrs Elizabeth J, wife Rev Dr J W
Carter Wm J, son Rev Dr J W, res same, wks Ral Electric Co
Carter Miss Martha E, d Rev Dr J W, res same
Carter Miss Mary G, d Rev Dr J W, res same
Carter Miss Mary (deaf mute), cook for T H Tillinghast, res same
Carter Mrs Salina, hkpr for Mrs Emma Myatt, res same
Carter Owen, inmate Soldiers' Home
Carter Edward H, tailor, res 341 n East
Carter Mrs Sallie A, mother of E H, res same
Carver Mrs Nellie, wid, saleslady at W H & R S Tucker & Co, res 318 Newbern ave
Carver Henry, son Mrs Nellie, res same student
Carver Lewis C,* contractor and builder, res Fayetteville near Centennial Graded School
Carver Cora M,* wife Lewis C
Carver Cora A,* d Lewis C, res same, student
Carver Lewis D,* son Lewis C, res same, student
Carver Mrs E A, wid, res Newbern ave, o s e
Carver Miss Nellie, d Mrs E A, res same, student
Carver James, son Mrs E A, res same, student
Cary Alex, cotton broker, bds 118 n Wilmington
Caspari Miss V, teacher in Peace Institute, res same
Castlebury F D, grocer, 508 Hillsboro', res same
Caswell Joanna,* nurse for W T McGee, res same
Cater Ben, grocer, e Hargett, o s e, res same
Cates J A, city policeman, res 17 McKee
Cates Mrs Laura L, wife J A
Cates J E, son J A, res same, student

Dr. Norwood G. Carroll.

Dentist,

Raleigh, N. C.

Office:
Over W. H. King & Co.'s Drug Store.

Cates Miss Iola, d J A, res same, student
Cates Miss Ida, d J A, res same, student
Cates James, salesman, bds 323 s Person
Caudle W H T, grocer, e Martin, res same
Caudle Mrs Loretta A, wife W H T
Caudle Archie H, son W H T, res same
Caudle Miss Lydia A, d W H T, res same
Caudle Miss Lucy A, d W H T, res same, student
Caudle Miss Minnie L, d W H T, res same, student
Caudle Miss Bessie E, d W H T, res same, student
Caudle Henry E, saloon kpr for Sam T Smith, res 502 w Morgan
Caudle Mrs Alice, wife Henry E
Caudle Wm H (Caudle & Ruth), grocer, bds 502 w Morgan
Caudle Mrs Mollie, wife Wm H
Caudle & Ruth, grocers, 501 Hillsboro'
Caulk Miss Elizabeth, wks dress dept W H & R S Tucker & Co, bds Park Hotel
Cawthorne Mrs A W, wks dress dept W H & R S Tucker & Co, bds Park Hotel
Cawthorne Miss Eula Y, wks dress dept W H & R S Tucker & Co, bds Park Hotel
Cawthorne Charles, carp, rooms cor e Davie and Haywood
Caynon Mary E,* washerwoman, res Newbern ave
Caynon Thomas,* son Mary E, res same, lab
Chamberlain J R, pres Caraleigh phosphate wks, res Hillsboro' rd, o s w
Chamberlain Mrs Hope S, wife J R
Chamberlain A L, sec and treas Caraleigh phosphate wks, res Hillsboro' rd, o s w
Chamberlain Mrs Nellie, wife A L
Chamblee Lillie,* washerwoman, res e Davie
Chamblee Miss Eleanor, g-d Jno Whitley, res same
Chamblee Cornelia,* washerwoman, res 832 s Wilmington
Chamblee Charles,* son Cornelia, res same, hotel servant
Chamblee Britt,* son Cornelia, res same, servant
Chamblee Abe,* son Cornelia, res same, porter J E Duke
Chamblee Kitty,* d Cornelia, res same, house-servant
Chamblee Viney,* d Cornelia, res same, student
Chamblee Millie,* d Cornelia, res same
Chamblee Maud,* d Cornelia, res same
Chamblee Peter,* carp, res Cotton lane, o s e
Chamblee Hettie,* wife Peter, laundress at Peace Institute
Chamblee Miley,* son Peter, res same, student
Chamblee Elbert,* son Peter, res same, porter for L D Womble
Chamblee Melvin,* son Peter, res same, porter for David Taylor
Chamblee Ernest,* son Peter, res same, farm hand
Chamblee Charles,* wks Park Hotel, res 9 Stronach ave
Chamblee Hattie,* wife Chas

Chamblee Kitty,* cook, res 720 Fayetteville
Champion Miss Mary, res with Mrs Bettie Worlds
Champion Emma,* cook for Mrs J M Heck, r rear 205 e Hargett
Champion William, wks Caraleigh mill, res 414 w South
Champion Mrs Mary, wife Wm
Champion Miss Lula, d Wm, res same, wks Caraleigh mill
Champion William Jr, son Wm, res same, wks Caraleigh mill
Chapman Rosetta,* washerwoman, res 310 Manly
Chapman Mrs S, wid, res with Mrs Wm Moncure
Chapman James, blacksmith S A L, res 602 n Salisbury
Chavasse Thos H, conductor S A L R R, bds Yarboro' House
Chavasse Mrs Lizzie, wife Thos H
Chavasse Miss Mary, d Thos H, res same
Chavis Nora,* laundress, res 712 s Saunders
Chavis Francis,* washerwoman, res 316 s Harrington
Chavis George,* lab, res 317 e Lenoir
Chavis Julia,* wife George
Chavis Wm E,* son George, res same, lab
Chavis Lenora,* d George, res same, student
Chavis Mark,* lab, res old Fair Ground, o s e
Chavis Dicey,* wife Mark, chambermaid at Yarboro' House
Chavis Emma,* d Mark, res same, farm hand
Chavis Ed,* hackman, res Martin, o s e
Chavis Mary,* wife Ed, washerwoman
Chavis Mamie,* d Ed, res same, student
Chavis Lucy,* house work, res 556 e Martin
Chavis Cora,* washerwoman, res 523 e Davie
Chavis Stella,* d Cora, res same, student
Chavis Melissa,* cook, res 523 e Davie
Chavis Dan,* hackman, res 548 e Cabarrus
Chavis Fannie,* wife Dan, washerwoman
Chavis Melvin,* son Dan, res same, student
Chavis Nora,* d Dan, res same, student
Chavis Walter,* son Dan, res same, student
Chavis Dora,* cook for Wm S Primrose, res on lot
Chavis Kate,* cook, res Hood's al
Chavis Mary,* servant, res o s e
Chavis Eliza,* laundress, Yarboro' House, res 430 s Blount
Chavis Chas,* son Eliza, res same, wks city market
Chavis Lula,* d Eliza, res same, wks Miss Sarah King
Chavis Wm B,* junk shop, 132 s Wilmington, res o s e
Chavis Alfonzo, watchman for Potter & Scott, res same
Cheatham C Y, train master S A L R R, res 123 Polk
Cheatham Mrs G C, wife C Y
Cheatham Howard, tel opr S A L R R, res 123 Polk
Cheatham R H, tel opr S A L R R, res 313 Halifax
Cheek J W, printer, foreman at Edwards & Broughton, res 325 e Edenton

Cheek Mrs Nannie, wife J W
Cheek Irvin, son J W, res same, student
Cheek Miss Sallie M, d J W, res same, student
Cheek Miss Ida, seamstress, res 114 n Dawson
Cheek E S, foreman at Edwards & Broughton, res 114 n Dawson
Cheek Mrs Adeline P, wife E S
Cheek Miss Julia, d E S, res same, student
Cheek Miss Emma, d E S, res same, student
Cheek John, son E S, res same, student
Cheek Charles, son E S, res same
Cheek Mrs Emeline, mother E S, res same
Cheek Lithia,* cook for Walter A Montgomery, res on lot
Cheshire Rt Rev Dr J B, Bishop of the Episcopal diocese of N C, res 105 e North
Cheshire Mrs Annie, wife Rev J B
Cheshire Miss Annie, d Rev J B, res same
Cheshire Miss Sarah, d Rev J B, res same
Cheshire Miss Elizabeth, d Rev J B, res same
Cheshire J B Jr, son Rev J B, res same
Childress Thos W, grocer, 115 e Hargett, res o s w
Chisenhall Jas R, asst agt Peter Stumpf beer-house, r 117 e Davie
Chisenhall Mrs Georgia, wife Jas R
Chisenhall Miss Omega, d Jas R, r same, student
Chistenall James, inmate Soldiers' Home
Christain W E, traveling correspondent for News and Observer
Christian Lee,* fireman p o, res 18 Matthews' lane
Christian Patsy,* wife Lee, washerwoman
Christian John,* son Lee, res same, wks Insane Asylum
Christian James,* son Lee, res same, student
Christian Daisy,* d Lee, res same, student
Christmas John,* lab, res 405 s Dawson
Christmas Nellie,* wife John, washerwoman
Christmas Aaron,* porter Union depot, res 405 s Dawson
Christmas Emma,* d John, res same, student
Christmas Millie,* d John, res same, student
Christmas H S, prin Garfield Graded School
Christmas Lula,* wife H S
Christmas James,* fireman at Insane Asylum, res Manly
Christmas Nellie,* wife James, house work
Christmas Pattie,* house-servant, res 531 e Edenton
Christmas Ida,* nurse, res 531 e Edenton
Christmas Seth,* carp, res 118 Smithfield
Christmas Susan,* wife Seth, washerwoman
Christmas Helen,* res 528 Newbern ave
Christmas James,* son Helen, res same, student
Christmas Grover,* son Helen, res same, student
Christmas Roscoe,* son Helen, res same, student
Christophers Chas D, printer, res 309 e Morgan

Christophers Mrs Valeria K, wife C D
Christophers Miss Valeria, d C D, res same
Christophers Miss Hattie, d C D, res same
Churchill Charles, wks Caraleigh mill, res Cannon
Churchill Mrs Elizabeth, wife Charles
Civiles E E, res with Mrs M V Lowe
Clanton Stephen,* lab, res 315 Cannon
Clanton Lizzie,* wife Stephen, washerwoman
Clanton Annette,* d Stephen, res same, student
Clanton Rufus,* son Stephen, res same, student
Clanton Annette,* mother of Stephen, res same
Clanton William,* porter S A L, res 120 w Peace
Clanton Mary,* wife William, washerwoman
Clark Galvin, salesman Lyon Racket Store, bds 209 w Morgan
Clark Helen,* washerwoman, res S Matthews' lane
Clark Ernest,* son Helen, res same, blacksmith
Clark Mrs A M, wid, mother of Judge Walter Clark, res 549 n Person
Clark Miss Lucy, d Mrs A M, res same
Clark Miss Sallie, d Mrs A M, res same
CLARK M S, house slater, res 319 e Jones
Clark Mrs Frankie, wife M S
Clark Miss Annie, d M S, res same, student
Clark Miss Mamie, d M S, res same, student
Clark Heber, son M S, res same, student
Clark Maggie,* washerwoman, res 116 e Lenoir
Clark Maggie,* cook, res 31 McKee
Clark Haynes,* porter U S p o, res s Saunders
Clark Janie,* wife Haynes, house work
CLARK WALTER, Associate Justice of Supreme Court of North Carolina, office Supreme Court bldg, res 440 Halifax
Clark Mrs Susan W, wife Walter
Clark David, son Walter, res same, teacher A & M College
Clark Wm A G, son Walter, res same, student
Clark Walter Jr, son Walter, res same, student
Clark John W, son Walter, res same, student
Clark Thorne M, son Walter, res same
Clark Miss Eugenia G, d Walter, res same
Clark Millie,* washerwoman, res 423 n Salisbury
Clark E J, mechanic, res Hillsboro' rd, o s n
Clark Mrs Sarah E, wife E J
Clark Mrs Gertrude H, d E J, res same, student
Clements W P, conductor S A L R R, bds 408 w Morgan
Clements William, son W P, res same
Clements Feagan,* driver for T R Jones, res rear 508 s West
Clements Isaac,* painter, res Cotton lane, o s e
Clements Amanda,* wife Isaac, washerwoman
Clifton Mourning,* cook for J P Gulley, res same

Clifton Wiley V, contractor and bridge builder, res 538 n Person
Clifton Mrs Mary, wife W V
Clifton Miss Lelia, d W V, res same
Clifton James S, farmer, res 714 n Person, o s n
Clifton Mrs Lucy, wife J S, dressmaker
Clifton Miss Annie, d J S, res same, dressmaker
Clifton Miss Ida, daughter J S, res same, dressmaker
Clifton John H, son J S, res same, printer
Clifton Robert, son J S, res same, machinist
Clifton Mrs Delia, wife Robert, dressmaker
Clifton Lonnie, son Robt, res same, weaver at Pilot mill
Cobb Maggie,* nurse, res 305 w Lenoir
Cobb Rev Dr N B, Baptist minister, res 526 Polk
Cobb Mrs De Lisle, wife Dr N B
Cobb Whitfield, son Dr N B, res same, student
Cobb Miss Nell, d Dr N B, res same, student
Cobb N T, stenographer and typewriter for A B Andrews, res 607 n Person
Cobb Mrs E H, wife N T
Cobb Miss Lucy, d N T, res same, student
Cobb Monroe,* wood-cutter, res Cotton lane, o s e
Cobb Lizzie,* wife Monroe, washerwoman
Cobb Peter,* stone-mason, res 7 Stronach ave
Cobb Alice,* wife Peter, washerwoman
Cobb Carrie,* d Peter, res same, student
Cobb Joseph,* son Peter, res same, student
Coffee George, lab, res 515 e Cabarrus
Coffee Mrs Susan, wife George
Coffee Miss Gussie, d Geo, res same, student
Coffin Mrs Laura, wid, res 423 Fayetteville
Coffin Miss Jennie, d Mrs Laura, res same, professional nurse
Cohen Joseph, clk, bds 114 s Blount
Coke Mrs Kate F, wid, res 215 w Morgan
Coke Jeff F, son Mrs Kate F, res same, student
Coke Miss Kate F, d Mrs Kate F, res same, student
Coke Miss Julia F, d Mrs Kate F, res same, student
Coke Octavius, bds 404 Fayetteville
Cole Reuben,* grocer, 112 e Hargett, res 737 s Blount
Cole Ella,* wife Reuben
Cole W Henry, machinist S A L, res Firwood ave, o s n
Cole Mrs Laura A, wife W H
Cole Harry E, son W H, res same, machinist S A L
Cole Frank A, son W H, res same, wks Ral cot mill
Cole Wilmer, son W H, res same, student
Cole Rebecca,* washerwoman, res 121 n Harrington
Cole John W, watchmaker and jeweler, 13 w Hargett, res 716 n Person, o s n
Cole Mrs Sarah D, wife Jno W

Cole Miss Nellie, d J W, res same
Cole Miss Nora, d J W, res same
Cole Eugene C, son J W, res same, messenger Western Union Tel Co
Cole Chester, son J W, res same, student
Coley Mollie,* cook for C B Edwards, res 114 w Davie
Coley Mrs E S, wid, res 325 s McDowell
Coley Miss Hannah L, d Mrs E S, res same, bookbinder
Coley Caleb H, eng S A L, res 523 Hicks' lane
Coley Mrs Cora M, wife C H
Coley Clarence, son C H, res same, wks Ral cot mill
Coley Stuart, son C H, res same
Coley Miss Maud, d C H, res same
Coleman Hardy,* lab, res Smith
Coleman Bettie,* wife Hardy, laundress
Coleman Emma,* d Hardy, res same, laundress
Collier J W, carp, res 516 w North
Collier Mrs Mary E, wife J W
Collier Stephen A, son J W, res same, lab
Collier Miss Effie, d J W, res same, student
Collier Jno A, carp, res 221 s West
Collier Mrs Fannie A, wife J A
Collier Miss Juanita, d J A, res same, cashier at W E Jones
Collier Annie,* washerwoman, res 26 Railroad
Collins David, inmate Soldiers' Home
Collins Joseph,* carp, res 329 Cannon
Collins Hattie,* house-servant, res 329 Cannon
Collins Bettie,* washerwoman, res old Fair Ground, o s e
Collins John B, printer, res 511 n Person
Collins Mrs Indiana G, wife Jno B
Collins Miss Ethel, d Jno B, res same
Collins Paul, son Jno B, res same, printer
Collins Miss Eunice, d Jno B, res same, student
Collins Hamp,* lab, res Martin, o s e
Collins Stuck,* lab, res Martin, o s e
Collins Celia,* farm hand, res old Fair Ground, o s e
Collins Julia,* nurse for W E Jones, res 622 Elm
Collins Amy,* washerwoman, res 121 n Harrington
Collins James, flagman S A L, res w Lane
Collins Mrs Stella, wife James
Collins Miss Mattie, seamstress, bds 701 s Blount
Collins Martha,* washerwoman, res 434 s Blount
Congleton Dr Jno R, patent medicines, res 105 s Bloodworth
Congleton Miss Kate, d Dr Jno R, res same
Congleton Miss Malina, d Dr Jno R, res same, saleslady at W H King & Co
Congleton Wm A, son Dr Jno R, res same, druggist
Conn Dixon G, grocer, 102 w Jones, res 106 w Jones

Conn Mrs E R, wife Dixon G
Conn Miss Lucy D, d D G, res same, teacher
Conn Miss Katie P, d D G, res same, teacher
Conn Miss Emma D, d D G, res same, student
Conn Dixon G Jr, son D G, res same, student
Conn Edward L, son D G, res same, student
Conn Miss Eleanor, d D G, res same, student
Conn Miss Corrina, seamstress, res 410 Haywood
Conn Miss Mary, seamstress, res 104 w Jones
Conrad Robt J, city policeman, res 231 e Lenoir
Conrad Mrs Cora V, wife Robt J
Conrad Robt J Jr, son Robt J, res same, student
Conrad Eugene, son Robt J, res same
Convers Della,* washerwoman, res e Edenton
Cook Hannah,* cook Mrs Hannah Bates, rooms 229 Blount st al
Cook Thomas,* driver for W E Jones, res 413 n Salisbury
Cook Sarah,* wife Thomas
Cook Silas,* fireman S A L R R, res Fleming's lane
Cook Chas F, printer, res 318 e Cabarrus
Cook Mrs Lizzie, wife Chas F
Cook Miss Maggie T, d Chas F, res same, student
Cook Miss Mattie L, d Chas F, res same, student
Cook Henrietta,* nurse for W R Tucker, res 511 e Davie
Cook Maggie,* d Henrietta, res same, student
Cook Ben,* son Henrietta, res same, student
Cook Martha,* washerwoman, res 511 e Davie
Cook Betsy,* laundress, res 419 Haywood
Cook W L, bkkpr for Standard Oil Co, res 411 Elm
Cook Henrietta,* cook for W R Tucker, res on lot
Cook Thomas,* driver for W E Jones, res 707 s East
Cook Sarah,* wife Thos
Cook Laura,* laundress, res 523 Haywood
Cook Fannie,* house-servant, res 715 Manly
Cook Richard,* student, res 714 s McDowell
Cook Nelia,* washerwoman, res 724 Fayetteville
Cook William,* carp, res 724 Fayetteville
Cook Rebecca,* washerwoman, res 714 s McDowell
Cooke Chas M, Sec of State of N C, bds Yarboro' House
Cooke A J, ins agt, bds cor McDowell and Hargett
Cooke Mrs Stella, wife A J
Cooper James W, farmer, res Hillsboro' rd, o s w
Cooper Mrs Martha H, wife J W
Cooper W E, son J W, res same

COOPER BROS (T R & W A), propr Ral marble wks, monuments, tombstones, curbing, &c; office and yard 417 and 419 Fayetteville

Cooper Thomas R (Cooper Bros), marble and granite worker, res Linden ave

Cooper Mrs Ella S, wife Thos R
Cooper Geo W, marble and granite worker, bds Thos R Cooper
Cooper Mrs Aryann, wid, res Fayetteville, o s s
Cooper James W, carp, res Fayetteville, o s s
Cooper Rufus A, salesman, bds 603 s Wilmington
Cooper Mrs Pattie M, wife Rufus A
Cooper J W, pattern-maker S A L, res 419 n Salisbury
Cooper Mrs Laura, wife J W
Cooper Willie Jr, son J W, student
Cooper Katie A, d J W, student
Cooper Lizzie,* house work, res 566 e Cabarrus
Cooper Edward,* son Lizzie, res same, hackman
Cooper Walter, painter, res 537 e Martin
Cooper Mrs Alice, wife Walter
Cooper W A (Cooper Bros), marble cutter, res 424 Fayetteville
Cooper Mrs Lula, wife W A
Cooper Green,* butler, res Fayetteville, below r r
Cooper Della,* wife Green, house work
Cooper Lat,* son Green, res same, student
Cooper Larry,* son Green, res same, student
Coppedge Greenbury, carder Pilot cot mill, res n Blount, o s n
Coppedge Mrs Annie, wife Greenbury
Coppedge Thomas, wks Ral cot mill, res 446 Halifax
Coppedge Mrs Julia, wife Thos
Coppedge Jesse H, son Thos, res same, clk
Coppedge Miss Jennie, d Thos, res same
Coppedge Miss Polly, d Thos, res same, seamstress
Cope Charlotte,* washerwoman, res 518 e Martin
Cope Mollie,* washerwoman, res 518 e martin
Cope Carrie,* d Charlotte, res same, house work
Cope Ella,* d Charlotte, res same house-servant
Cope Jos C, wks Caraleigh cot mill, res 739 Fayetteville
Cope Mrs Mary, wife Jos C
Cope Clarence, son Jos C, res same, student
Correll Jos S, clk at W H & R S Tucker & Co's, res 503 s Bloodworth
Correll Mrs Nellie G, wife Jos S
Correll Miss Annie R, d Jos S, res same, student
Correll Jos W, son Jos S, res same, student
Correll H A, shoemaker, res 503 s Bloodworth
Corney Julia,* washerwoman, res e Edenton
Cornish Fannie,* cook for A B Forrest, res on lot
Cosby Mrs L L, wid, res 216 s Dawson
Cosby Miss L F, teacher in N C Blind Institution, r 216 s Dawson
Costner Jonas M, teacher in Literary and Music Dept Colored Institution for the Blind, res at white Institution
Costner Mrs Carrie W, wife Jonas M, bkpr at Blind Institution
Cotten Cora,* cook, res 416 s Bloodworth

Cotten Emma,* seamstress, res 589 e Cabarrus
Cotten Rosa,* d Emma, res same, student
Cotten Vivian,* d Emma, res same, student
Cotten Malvina,* laundress, res 417 s East
Cotten Maggie,* laundress, res 417 s East
Cotten Miss Ag, attendant at Insane Asylum, res same
Cotton Platform and Compress, cor Halifax and Jones
Cotton Amanda,* washerwoman, res 417 s Person
Cotton Annie D,* d Amanda, res same, washerwoman
Cotton Nancy,* d Amanda, res same, washerwoman
Cotton Willie,* son Amanda, res same, porter for Heller Bros
Cotton Minnie,* washerwoman, res 318 s Bloodworth
Couch Charity,* washerwoman, res 320 w Lenoir
Couch Edward,* porter for E H Horton & Co, res 320 w Lenoir
Couch Martha,* house-servant, res 418 s McDowell
Couch Mary,* cook, res 418 s McDowell
Couch Miss M J, bkpr at J T Farmer, res same
Couch Nicey,* cook, res 25 w Worth
Council Henry,* hostler, res rear Catholic church
Council Adeline,* cook, res rear Catholic church
Council Wiley,* son Adeline, res same, servant
Council Monroe,* son Adeline, res same, servant
Council Maurice,* lab, res 513 Newbern ave
Council Margaret,* wife Maurice, washerwoman
Council Abram,* shoemaker, res 9 Johnson ave
Council Julia,* wife Abram, laundress
Council Marcellus,* drayman, res Gatling's lane
Council Mary,* wife Marcellus, washerwoman
Covington Jno M, clk in store-room S A L, res 216 Halifax
Covington Mrs G M, wife Jno M
Cowan Martha,* house-servant, res s West
Cowan Henry M, accountant, rooms over 127 Fayetteville
Cowand A J, cot buyer, bds Armistead Jones
Cowman Miss Rosa B, teacher in St Mary's school, res same
Cowper Pulaski, fire ins adjuster, res 514 Fayetteville
Cowper Mrs Mary B, wife P
Cowper Miss Meggie I, d P, res same
Cowper Miss Mary P, d P, res same
Cowper B G, gen ins agt, 240 Fayetteville, up-stairs, r 218 n East
Cowper Mrs Minnie H, wife B G
Cowper Miss Mary, d B G, res same, student
Cowper B G Jr, son B G, res same, student
Cox Sophia,* cook A E Glenn, res 804 s Wilmington
Cox Daniel,* son Sophia, wks cot compress, res same
Crabtree Otho, printer, res 221 n West
Crabtree Mrs Mollie, wife Otho
Crabtree Sidney, son Otho, res same, carp
Crabtree Miss Esther, d Otho, res same, wks Ral cot mill

Crabtree Miss Florence, d Otho, res same, wks Ral cot mill
Crabtree Miss Mary, d Otho, res same, wks Ral cot mill
Crabtree Thomas, son Otho, res same, wks Ral cot mill
Crabtree Richard, bookbinder, res 323 e Martin
Crabtree Mrs Susan, wife Richard, dressmaker
Crabtree Mollie, cook, res 213 e Cabarrus
Crabtree Mrs Amy, wid, seamstress, res 205 n Salisbury
Crabtree Walter, son Mrs Amy, res same, stenographer and typewriter for Ral water company
Crabtree Miss Lizzie, d Mrs Amy, res same
Crabtree Crossley, spinner Ral cot mill, res Firwood ave, o s n
Crabtree Thomas, spinner Ral cot mill, res Firwood ave, o s n
Crabtree Gilbert, son Crossley, res same, student
Crabtree Miss Alma, student, bds 321 e Lane
Craighill Nathaniel R, prof mechanical engineering at A and M College, res Maiden lane, o s w
Craighill Mrs Blanche M, wife Prof N R
Cram W C (Allen & Cram), machinist, bds Park Hotel
Crawford A J, clk for W R Crawford & Son, res 116 s McDowell
Crawford Mrs Bessie, wife A J
Crawford W R Jr, steward N C Insane Asylum, res same
Crawford R E, co-mgr Park Hotel, res same
Crawford W R & Son, butchers, 230 Fayetteville
CRAWFORD Dr J H, surgeon dentist, office 116 Fayetteville, res same
Crawford Mrs M B, wife Dr J H
Crawford Jno W, watchmaker and jeweler with B R Jolly, rooms 116 Fayetteville
Crawford D H, butcher, res 220 w Lane
Crawford Mrs N A, wife D H
Crawford Miss Hattie, d D H, res same, wks Ral cot mill
Crawford Miss Violet, d D H, res same, wks Ral cot mill
Crawford Miss Mamie, d D H, res same
Crawford Miss Hazel, d D H, res same, student
Crawford Miss Metta, d D H, res same, student
Crawford Miss Mattie, d D H, res same, student

J. H. CRAWFORD,
Dentist.

Office and Residence: 116 Fayetteville Street,
RALEIGH, N. C.
P. O. BOX 124.

Crawford W R (W R Crawford & Son), butcher, res Hillsboro' rd, o s w
Crawford Chas E (W R & Son), butcher, res Hillsboro' rd, o s w
Crawford Miss Lovie V, d W R, res same
Crawford Miss Lula A, d W R, res same
Crawford Miss May Hines, d W R, res same
Craven Delia,* sick nurse, res 829 Fayetteville
Craven Emma,* servant, res 402 w North
Creech J W, clk J G Adams, bds 122 n Harrington
Creech Jno D, clk for S A L R R, res 518 n Person
Creech Mrs Mamie, wife Jno D
Creech Alex, son Jno D, res same, student
Creech Miss Mamie, d Jno D, res same, student
Creech Jno A, son Jno D, res same, student
Creech Mrs A, wid, res 615 s Salisbury
Creech Joseph A, lawyer, res 615 s Salisbury
Creech Miss Flora E, d Mrs A, res same
Creel J R, lock and gunsmith, bds 514 s Harrington
Creel Mrs Ava M, wife J R
Creel Mrs Lydia, wid, res with Ed Vaughan
Creighton Jos, driver City Fire Dept, res 328 s Salisbury
Creighton Mrs Elizabeth, wife Jos
Creighton Martie, son Jos, res same, student
Creighton John, son Jos, res same, student
Creighton Charles, city policeman, res 510 Polk
Creighton Mrs Bettie L, wife Chas
Crenshaw Prince,* gardener, res 829 s Wilmington
Crenshaw Elizabeth,* wife Prince
Crew Miss A, teacher in Peace Institute, res same
Crews W J, mgr Postal Telegraph and Cable Co, r 44 Boylan ave
Crews Mrs Kate L, wife W J
Crews Miss Juliet S, d W J, res same
Crocker Mrs Maggie, wid, res cor Davie and East
Crocker Nathaniel, tel messenger, bds 311 s Dawson
Crocker H H, dry goods, &c, 9 e Hargett, res 304 e Hargett
Crocker Mrs Nellie, wife H H
Crone Wm H, loco eng S A L R R, res 214 n Harrington
Crone Mrs Sarah E, wife Wm H
Crone Richard T, son Wm H, res same
Crone Moses V, son Wm H, res same
Crone Miss Menvilie, d Wm H, res same, student
Crone Edwin, son Wm H, res same
Crone Miss Alice, d Wm H, res same
Crone Miss Lillie, d Wm H, res same
Crosby Mrs Georgia, wid, dressmaker, res 308 s Bloodworth
Cross John, carp, res Fayetteville below R R
Cross Mrs Caroline, wife John
Cross Miss Amanda, d Jno, res same, student

Cross Miss Maggie, d Jno, res same, student
Cross Jno Jr, son Jno, res same, student
Cross James,* lab, res s e Davie, o s e
Cross Henry C, clk Fred Woollcott, res 545 e Martin
Cross Mrs Caroline, wife Henry, seamstress
Cross Mattie,* cook for W W Wynne, res 622 Elm
Cross Mrs Sallie, wid, res 224 s Bloodworth
Cross Hardy,* carp, res 112 e Cabarrus
Cross Anna,* wife Hardy, washerwoman
Cross Emma,* d Hardy, res same, washerwoman
Cross Sarah,* d Hardy, res same, in charge linen room Yarboro' House
Cross & Lenehan, clothiers and haberdashers, 210 Fayetteville
Crossan Isaiah,* carp, res 102 Smithfield
Crossan Rosetta,* wife Isaiah, cook for N Deboy
Crossan Henderson, carp, res 214 e Cabarrus
Crosson Philip,* painter, res 403 Haywood
Crosson George,* son Philip, res same, lab
Crosson Philip Jr,* son Philip, res same, student
Crosson Caroline,* cook, res 205 w South
Crosson Florence E,* d Caroline, res same, chambermaid
Crosson Mary,* washerwoman, res 525 e Edenton
Crosson Emily,* d Mary, res same, cook Central Hotel
Crosson Olivia,* d Mary, res same, nurse
Crosson James,* son Mary, res same, student
Crosson Edward,* son Mary, res same, student
Crow Miss Elizabeth S, teacher kindergarten dept Blind Institution, res same
Crow C C, life ins agt, res 129 n Person
Crow Mrs Maria, wife C C
Crow Miss Elizabeth, d C C, res same, teacher
Crow Miss May, d C C, res same
Crow Miss Marguerite, d C C, res same
Crow Clinton C Jr, son C C, res same, student
Crow John, son C C, res same, student
Crow William, son C C, res same, student
Crow Miss Susan, d C C, res same
Crow Ed B, clk in Farmers & Commercial Bank, res 204 Halifax
Crow Miss Anna B, sister Ed B, res same
Crowder & Rand, wholesale grocers and commission merchants, 301 s Wilmington
Crowder Robert,* carp, res 721 s Dawson
Crowder Harriet,* wife Robt, house work
Crowder Maggie,* d Robt, res same, student
Crowder Edna,* washerwoman, res 225 e Lane
Crowder Rachel,* washerwoman, res 401 s Dawson
Crowder Ella,* cook, res 401 s Dawson
Crowder Mary,* nurse, res 401 s Dawson

Crowder Rev W J W, city missionary and colporter, res 115 s Harrington
Crowder Stephen L, teller Treasury dept, bds Branson House
Crowder Rena,* nurse, Mrs E C Smith, res on lot
Crowder Thos B (Crowder & Rand), merchant, res 523 Fayetteville
Crowder Mrs Maggie, wife Thos B
Crudup Byrd,* driver for J G Ball, res 112 n Swain
Crudup Delia,* wife Byrd, washerwoman
Crudup Mattie,* d Byrd, res same, student
Crudup Jordan,* sewing machine and organ repairer, room 519 s Wilmington
Crudup Condery,* section hand Southern R R, res 35 Hunter
Crump Avie,* washerwoman, res 408 w Jones
Crump Charity,* washerwoman, res 408 w Jones
Crump Lucinda,* cook, res 710 Manly
Crump Lucinda Jr, student, res 710 Manly
Crutchfield R B, cottin-gin maker, res 516 n West
Crutchfield Mrs Kate, wife R B, dressmaker
Crutchfield Miss Effie, d R B, student
Crutchfield W H, mechanic, bds 404 Fayetteville
Cully Mrs E A, wid, res 613 e Hargett
Cummings M C, tailor, bds 326 Newbern ave
Cummings Miss Katie, d M C, res same, student
Cunningham Herd, life ins agt, bds Park Place
Cunningham Mrs Janie, wife Herd
Cunningham Lucy,* washerwoman, res 531 s Dawson
Cunningham James, tel opr, bds 507 s West
Curtis David,* servant for Thos T Hay, res on lot
Curtis Rev Dr A W, minister of Congregational church and general missionary of Congregational churches, res 225 e Lenoir
Curtis Mrs Jennie L, wife Rev Dr A W, writer
Curtis Miss Minnie May, d Rev Dr A W, res same, artist
Curtis Lucinda,* laundress for Dr T D Hogg, res on lot
Curtis Hasty,* washerwoman, res 117 w North
Curtis Annie,* cook for T T Hay, res 117 w North
Cushing J F, inmate Soldiers' Home
Cuthbert E B & Co, brokers, 305 s Wilmington
Cuthrell James, machinist, bds 10 e North
Cutts William, lineman Ral Telephone Co

DANCY Mrs Julia, seamstress, res Smith
Dancy Katie, d Mrs Julia, res same, student
Dancy William, inmate Soldiers' Home
Dancy William, butcher, res e Cabarrus
DANIEL Rev Dr EUGENE, pastor Presbyterian church, res cor Hargett and Dawson

Daniel Mrs S T, wife Rev Eugene
Daniel Miss Mary, d Rev Eugene, res same, student
Daniel Miss Henrietta M, d Rev Eugene, res same, student
Daniel Jno W, son Rev Eugene, res same, student
Daniel Miss Roberta M, d Rev Eugene, res same, student
Daniel Miss Shannie W, d Rev Eugene, res same, student
Daniels Josephus, editor News and Observer, bds 125 e South
Daniels Mrs Addie, wife Josephus
Daniels Mrs M A, wid, dressmaker, res 625 e Hargett
Daniels Walter, son Mrs M A, res same, clk
Daniels Susie, d Mrs M A, res same, student
Dann David,* lab, res e Hargett, o s c
Dann Roxana,* wife David, washerwoman
Dann Willie,* son David, res same, porter Dr V E Turner
Dann David,* res same, student
Dann Early,* brakeman S A L R R, res e Hargett, o s c
Dann Nannie,* wife Early, washerwoman
Darnell & Thomas (A J Thomas, Lucy Darnell), pianos, organs and musical instruments, 114 Fayetteville
Darnell Miss Lucy (Darnell & Thomas), musical instruments, bds Branson House
Davie D G, train-hand S A L, bds 120 Johnson
Davie Charlie, train-hand S A L, bds 120 Johnson
Davis Robert,* grocer, e Hargett, o s c, res same
Davis Annie,* seamstress, res Cotton lane, o s c
Davis Grant,* train-hand S A L R R, res 437 Johnson
Davis Olivia,* wife Grant
Davis Henry Y,* shoemaker, res rear Exchange Hotel
Davis Lou,* servant, res rear 110 s McDowell
Davis John,* fireman S A L, bds 435 n Salisbury
Davis W L, tinner S A L, res 520 n Salisbury
Davis Mrs Emily, wife W L
Davis Miss Dixie, d W L, res same
Davis Miss Hattie, d W L, res same
Davis W T, son W L, res same, app tinner S A L
Davis Arthur,* fireman S A L, res 437 n Salisbury
Davis Edna,* cook, res rear First Baptist church
Davis Mary,* d Edna, res same, student
Davis Sam,* grocer, 837 Fayetteville
Davis Ellen,* cook for W H Day, res on lot
Davis Isaiah,* lab, res 518 w Lane
Davis Ellie,* wife Isaiah, washerwoman
Davis Jno C,* blacksmith, res 409 s Blount
Davis Edna,* wife Jno C
Davis Rev A G,* pastor of Davie-Street Presbyterian church, res 407 s Person
Davis Eva A,* wife Rev A G
Davis Lillie A,* d Rev A G, res same, student

Davis Riddick H, watchman, res 415 Elm
Davis Mrs Eupha A, wife R H
Davis Frank H, son R H, res same, painter
Davis Miss Mary G, d R H, stenographer and typewriter for R T Gray
Davis Miss Eula R, d R H, res same, student
Davis Julia,* washerwoman, res 113 n Harrington
Davis Miss Carrie, bkpr for W F McDowell, res same
Davis Annie,* washerwoman, res 550 e Cabarrus
Davis John,* son Annie, res same, student
Davis Mrs J D, res with father, J W Marcom
Davis Miss Ruby G, d Mrs J D, res same
Davis Mrs Mary A, wid, tailoress, res 412 e Hargett
Davis Miss Annie M, d Mrs Mary A, res same, book-binder
Davis Henry,* clk for Sam Davis, res 834 s Wilmington
Davis Helen,* laundress, res 752 e Davie, o s e
Davis Alice,* d Helen, res same, cook
Davis Kittie,* washerwoman, res 607 s East
Davis Annie,* washerwoman, res 601 s East
Davis Ben,* lab, res 529 s East
Davis Peter M, quiller at pilot mill, res s East
Davis Mrs Susie, wife P M
Davis Nellie,* cook for Mrs B E Williams, res 510 e Edenton
Davis Hattie,* washerwoman, res 525 e Edenton
Davis Lonnie,* driver for J G Ball, res e Edenton
Davis Ellen,* wife Lonnie, washerwoman
Davis & Dunston,* barbers, 202½ Fayetteville
Davis Della,* laundress, res 726 Manly
Davis Rebecca,* d Della, res same, student
Davis Georgia,* d Della, res same, student
Davis Harriet,* nurse, rooms 524 s Dawson
Davis Minerva,* cook, res old Fair Ground, o s e
Davis Lewis C,* barber, res 122 w Lenoir
Davis Jennie S,* wife L C, house work
Davis Jonah R* (Davis & Dunston), barber, res 111 w South
Davis Lucy M,* wife J R
Davis Annie C,* d J R, res same, student
Davis Katie T,* d J R, res same, student
Davis Jonah H V,* son J R, res same, student
Davis James McC,* son J R, res same
Davis George,* carp, res 309 w Lenoir
Davis Sarah,* wife Geo, washerwoman
Davis Carrie,* d Geo, res same, student
Davis Lizzie,* cook for J Schwartz, res same
Davis Ann,* washerwoman, res 715 s Dawson
Davis Andrew,* shoemaker, res 545 Newbern ave
Davis Penny,* wife Andrew
Day W H (McRae & Day), lawyer, res 120 Halifax

Day Mrs M G, wife W H
Day Rufus,* painter, res 604 e Cabarrus
Day Hattie,* wife Rufus
Day Thomas,* son Rufus, res same, shoemaker
Day Sadie,* nurse, res 208 w South
Day Annie,* washerwoman, res 111 w Lenoir
Day Robert, wks Caraleigh mill, res 722 Fayetteville
Day Mrs Ida, wife Robt
Day David, wks Caraleigh mill, res 722 Fayetteville
Day Charles, wks Caraleigh mill, res 722 Fayetteville
Dean John A, blacksmith, res Caswell lane
Dean Mrs Biddy J, wife Jno A
Dean Joseph, son Jno A, res same, wks Caraleigh cot mill
Dean Wm T, son Jno A, res same, lab
Dean Richard, wks Caraleigh mill, res 20 McKee
Dean Mrs Mary F, wife Richard
Dean Miss Marinda, d Richard, res same, weaver
Dean Miss Ella, d Richard, res same, spinner Caraleigh mill
Dean Arthur, son Richard, res same, wks Caraleigh mill
Dean J A, loom-fixer at Caraleigh mill, res 820 Fayetteville
Dean Mrs Ardelia, wife J A
Dean Dorcey, weaver at Caraleigh mill, bds 820 Fayetteville
Debnam Harry,* hackman, res 430 s Blount
Debnam Mattie,* wife Harry, house work
Debnam David,* son Harry, res same, student
Debnam Magnolia,* d Harry, res same, student
Debnam John,* driver for Dr A W Goodwin, res same
Debnam Jane,* house-servant for Dr A W Goodwin, res same
Debnam Cora,* house-servant for T T Hay, res on lot
Debnam Nona,* house servant, res 622 Elm
Debnam Emma,* farm hand, res old Fair Ground, o s e
Debnam Edward,* farm hand, res old Fair Ground, o s e
Debnam Elizabeth,* farm hand, res rear 554 e Hargett
Debnam Ada,* farm hand, res rear 554 e Hargett
Debnam Allison,* son Ada, res same, farm hand
Debnam C F, overseer, r 105 w Jones
Debnam Mrs M G, wife C F
Debnam Miss L J, d C F, res same, dressmaker
Debnam Miss M G, d C F, res same, dressmaker
Debnam Julia,* d Francis Jones, res same, student
Debnam Junius,* son Francis Jones, res same, student
Debnam Etta,* washerwoman, res o s e
Debnam James E,* lab, res 511 s Dawson
Debnam W F,* real estate, res 214 w Lenoir
Debnam Jas E,* son W F, res same, student
Debnam Irma P,* d W F, res same, student
Deboy N & Son, grocers, 15 Exchange Place
Deboy Nick Jr, saloon, 15 Exchange Place, res 110 s Blount

Deboy Mrs Mamie, wife Nick Jr
Deboy Nick (N Deboy & Son) grocer, res 109½ Fayetteville
Deboy Mrs Katherine, wife N, proprietress of Germania House, 109½ Fayetteville
Deboy Alfred, son Nick, res same
Deboy Miss Allie, d Nick, res same, saleslady
Deboy Miss Katie, d Nick, res same, student
Deboy Henry, son Nick, res same, traveling salesman
De Forest John, pressman at E M Uzzell, res 121 w Cabarrus
De Forest Mrs Daisy M, wife John
Dement A J, livery stable, res 215 e Davie
Dement Mrs Lucretia F, wife A J
Dement Robert L, son A J, res same, carriage painter
Dement Miss Martha F, d A J, res same, student
Dement Miss Lucretia F, d A J, res same, student
Dement Wm A, son A J, res same, student
Denmark Jas W, chief clk to State Treasurer, res 404 n East
Denmark Mrs Juanita, wife J W
Denmark Miss Leonita, d J W, res same
Denning Mrs Martha R, dressmaker, res 512 s Wilmington
Denning Miss Sinie B, d Mrs Martha R, res same, student
Denning Miss Mattie B, d Mrs Martha R, res same, student
Dennis C R, clk for Levine & Brown, res 505 n Wilmington
Dennis Mrs S M, wife C R
Denny Miss Addie, dressmaker, res 313 s Dawson
Denson Capt C B (Morson & Denson), teacher, r 403 Newbern ave
Denson Mrs Matilda, wife C B
Denson Miss Daisy, d C B, res same
Denson Miss Katherine, d C B, res same
Denson Miss Mary, d C B, res same
Denson Thos C, son C B, res same, clk W H & R S Tucker & Co
Denson Eugene, son C B, res same, medical student
Denson C B Jr, son C B, res same, student
Denton P H, clk W E Jones, bds Central Hotel
Denton Ed V, saloon and cafe, 311 and 313 Fayetteville, res 410 s Person
Denton Mrs Gussie, wife Ed V
Denton Edwin V Jr, son Ed V, res same
Denton Mrs J N, wid, res 117 s Bloodworth
Denton Miss Bessie, d Mrs J N, res same, student
Denton Willie, son Mrs J N, res same, student
Denton Miss Mabel, d Mrs J N, res same, student
Denton Mrs N V, wid, res 327 e Cabarrus
Denton Miss Lalla, d Mrs N V, res same, milliner at Woollcott & Son
Denton Miss Maud, d Mrs N V, res same, saleslady at Woollcott & Son
Denton Miss Florence, d Mrs N V, res same, student

Denton Miss Cleo, d Mrs N V, res same, student
Denton Burke, son Mrs N V, res same, student
Denton A G, clk for D C Mangum
Denton John,* porter at Yarboro' House, res 207 w Davie
Denton Mary,* wife John, washerwoman
De Vault R B, ins agt, bds 204 Halifax
Devereux Mrs John, wid, res with Col Jno W Hinsdale, 330 Hillsboro'
Devereux Austin,* gardener, res 812 s Wilmington
Devereux T P, lawyer, office over Commercial and Farmers Bank
Devereux Miss Laura, teacher in Murphy School, bds Park Place
Devine Becky,* farm hand, res e Davie
Devine Mary,* washerwoman, res 320 w South
Dewar W E (Dewar & Wilder), merchant, res 406 s Salisbury
Dewar Mrs Susan F, wife W E
Dewar Edwin S, son W E, res same, student
Dewar & Wilder, wholesale grocers and commission merchants, 13 e Martin and 14 Exchange Place
Dewey Guion, machinist, bds Park Place
Dewey Miss Mary, sister to Mrs R D Wildes, res 118 s Dawson
Dicks Wm R, bookbinder, res 425 n East
Dicks Mrs Bettie, wife W R
Dicks Miss Lilla, d W R, res same
Dicks Miss Ellee, d W R, res same, student
Dicks Arthur, son W R, res same, student
Dickins Gilbert,* carp, res 613 e Cabarrus
Dickinson Geo C, pressman Edwards & Broughton, bds 701 s Bloodworth
Dickinson George, printer, room 813 s Blount
Dickinson Miss Nannie, sister of Mrs Annie W Emery, res same
Dickson Miss Catherine, seamstress, res 519 s Bloodworth
Dickson Miss Melissa, sister of Miss Catherine, res same, student
Dickson Katie,* washerwoman, res 579 e Lenoir
Dickson Robt L, clk for Berwanger Bros, rooms 327 e Hargett
Dildy Hattie,* cook for W H Dodd, res 113 n Harrington
Dilliard James,* hotel waiter, res 27 McKee
Dilliard Bettie,* wife James, house work
Dinkins Thomas, wks for city, res Smithfield
Dinkins Susan, wife Thos
Dinkins Miss Ida, d Thos, res same, student
Dinkins W D, carp, res 612 e Hargett
Dinkins Mrs Susan, wife W D
Dinkins Miss Millie G, d W D, res same
Dinkins Wm E, son W D, res same, printer
Dinkins Mrs Martha J, wid, res 220 s East
DINWIDDIE JAMES, Prin of Peace Institute, res same
Dinwiddie Mrs Bettie, wife James, Lady Prin of Peace Institute
Dinwiddie Miss Nannie C, d James, teacher in Peace Institute, res same

Dinwiddie Miss Susan H, d James, teacher in Peace Institute, res same
Dinwiddie Miss Janet W, d James, teacher in Peace Institute, res same
Dinwiddie Miss Mary D, d James, res same, student
Dinwiddie Miss Bettie C, d James, res same, student
Dinwiddie Miss Maud T, d James, res same, student
Dishman Joshua,* lab, res 615 e Cabarrus
Dishman Margaret,* wife Joshua, washerwoman
Dishman Jennie,* d Joshua, res same, student
Dishman Florence,* d Joshua, res same, student
Dishman Cornelius,* wks cot compress, res 419 Haywood
Dishman Mary A,* wife Cornelius, washerwoman
Dixon Chas N, mechanic S A L R R, res Franklin, o s n
Dixon Mrs Estelle, wife Chas N
Dixon Mrs N A, wid, res with son C N
Dobbin Robert, shoemaker, res 220 w Davie
Dobbin Mrs Mary A, wife Robt
Dobbin Miss Emma, d Robt, res same
Dobbin Jas C, son Robt, res same, bkkpr
Dobbin Theo W (W H & R S Tucker & Co), buyer and gen mgr, res Hillsboro' near Capital
Dobbin Mrs Mary A, wife T W
Dockery A V, newspaper man, room 9 Frap's bldg
Dodd Wm H, bkkpr for J J Thomas, res 107 n McDowell
Dodd Mrs R M, wife Wm H
Doolittle Mrs Mary, wid, res 223 w Davie
Doolittle Archie, son Mrs Mary, res same, lab
Doolittle James O, wks at oil mill, res 130 w Cabarrus
Doolittle Mrs Rebecca, wife Jas O
Donaldson John,* lab, res 318 e Davie
Donaldson Thos,* butcher, city market
Donehoe Patrick, bkkpr, bds 211 Smithfield
Dorham Burton,* porter, res 321 w South
Dorham Jennie,* wife Burton, washerwoman
Dorkins Mamie,* house work, res 326 s East
Dorsett Bros, grocers, cor s Wilmington and e Hargett
Dortch Miss Sallie, g-d of Dr Thos D Hogg, res same, student
DOUGLASS W C, lawyer, office 301½ Fayetteville, res cor Bloodworth and Polk
Douglass Isaac,* fireman S A L, res 602 s McDowell
Douglass Alice,* wife Isaac, washerwoman
Douglass W C, lawyer, office Commercial and Farmers Bank bldg
Dowb W H,* artist and teacher, res 107 n Harrington
Dowb Patience,* wife W H
Dowd P W, cotton weigher, res Hillsboro' rd, o s w
Dowd Miss Martha A, d P W, res same, student
Dowd Miss Charity, d P W, res same, student

Dowd Wylie P, son P W, res same, student
Dowd Miss Nellie, niece of P W, res same, student
Dowd Henry A, res Hillsboro' rd, o s w
Dowd Mrs Laura B, wife Henry A
Dowd Miss Martha A, d Henry A, teacher in Peace Institute, res same
Dowd Wilson,* wks Ral Gas Co, res rear 305 Hillsboro'
Dowd Margaret,* wife Wilson
Dowd Squire,* driver, res 216 w South
Dowd Anna,* wife Squire, washerwoman
Dowd Belle,* d Squire, res same, student
Dowd Carson,* son Squire, res same, student
Dowd Ella,* d Squire, res same, student
Dowell Miss Emma J, sister Mrs D G Conn, res 106 w Jones
Dowell H J, prop Central Hotel, res same
Dowell Mrs Mattie, wife H J
Dowell Williard, son H J, res same, student
Dowell Paul, son H J, res same, student
Dowell Miss Lucy, d H J, res same, student
Dowden John,* lab S A L R R, res 534 Halifax
Dowden Almeta,* wife John, washerwoman
Doyle Fred C, student, res 16 s Salisbury
Doyle Miss Annette,* niece of Mrs C F Lodge, res same
Drake Caroline,* cook, res 512 e Davie
Drake Eaton,* lab, res Caswell lane
Drake Eliza,* wife Eaton, washerwoman
Drake Hayes,* son Eaton, res same, driver for Dewar & Wilder
Drake Solomon,* son Eaton, res same, student
Drake Samuel,* clk J E Hamlin, res Caswell lane
Drake Sallie,* wife Sam, res same, washerwoman
Drake Sam Jr,* son Sam, res same, student
Drake Pearl,* d Sam, res same, student
Drake William,* son Sam, res same, student
Draughan Penny,* washerwoman, res 118 e Cabarrus
Drew Thomas,* lab, res 302 w South
Drew Mary,* wife Thos, washerwoman

W. C. DOUGLASS,

ATTORNEY AT LAW,

RALEIGH, N. C.

Office: Corner Fayetteville and Martin Streets up-stairs.

Practices in all the Courts of the State.

Drew Arthur,* son Thos, res same, student
Drew Willie,* son Thos, res same, student
Drew John A, overseer at Caraleigh mill, res 111 Cabarrus
Drew Mrs Nannie H, wife Jno A
DREWRY JOHN C, gen agt Mutual Life Ins Co of N J, office in Holloman bldg, res 517 Oakwood ave
Drewry Miss Emma L, d J C, res same, student
Driver Ella, washerwoman, res Pugh
Driver Mrs Mollie, wid, res Pugh
Driver Miss Addie, d Mrs Mollie, res same, student
Driver Charles, son Mrs Mollie, res same, wks Ral cot mill
Driver James, son Mrs Mollie, res same, student
Dry Frank L,* student, res 322 Cannon
Dry James,* student, res 322 Cannon
Dudley E M, clk for W J Reavis, res same
Duffy Miss Nannie, d Mrs Eugene Schilling, student
Duffy Mrs Rosa, paper-folder, res 224 s Blount
Duffy Miss Katie, d Mrs Rosa, res same, paper-folder
Duffy Joseph, son Mrs Rosa, res same, student
Duffy Miss Rosa, d Mrs Rosa, res same, student
Duffy Miss Sarah, d Mrs Rosa, res same, student
Duffy John, son Mrs Rosa, res same, wks Ral cot mill
DUGHI ANTHONY L, confectioner, ice-cream parlor and oyster saloon, 235 Fayetteville, res 524 n Saunders
Dughi Mrs Elizabeth, wife A L
Dughi Jno J A, son A L, res same, clk for father
Dughi Miss Rosa, d A L, res same, student
Dughi Miss Annie, d A L, res same, student
Dughi Toney, son A L, res same, student
Dughi Miss Mary, d A L, res same, student
Dughi Miss Elizabeth, d A L, res same, student
Dughi Leo J, son A L, res same, student
Dughi Jos A, son A L, res same
Dughi Christian M, son A L, res same
Duke Jno A, eng S A L, res 508 Halifax
Duke Mrs Della A, wife Jno A, boarding-house
Duke Miss Laura, d Jno A, res same, student
Duke Otho, son Jno A, res same, student
Duke Fred, son Jno A, res same, student
Duke John E, grocer, cor e Davie and East, res 554 e Hargett
Duke Mrs Minnie, wife Jno E
Duke Miss Lora B, d Jno E, res same, student
Duke Miss Bessie, d Jno E, res same, student
Duke Jno E Jr, son Jno E, res same, student
Duke Willie, son Jno E, res same
Duke Nannie,* teacher, res 815 Manly
Duke Rebecca,* house-servant, res 815 Manly
Duke James B, watchman Mills Mfg Co, res 813 Jenkins

J. M. BROUGHTON.   T. B. MOSELEY.

City and Country Property Bought and Sold on Commission. Loans Negotiated. Investments Placed. Reliable Credit Information Furnished.

Real Estate, Rental and Collecting Agency.

J. M. BROUGHTON & CO.,

RALEIGH, N. C.,

Real Estate and Fire Insurance.

JOHN WHITELAW,

STONE CONTRACTOR.

ALL KINDS OF STONE WORK DONE ON SHORT NOTICE.

WORK GUARANTEED.

ALL WORK GIVEN PERSONAL ATTENTION.

YARD: -   Corner Martin and McDowell Streets.

THOMAS H. BRIGGS & SONS,

RALEIGH, N. C.,

DEALERS IN

General Hardware, Stoves, Paints, Oils, Glass, Lime and Cement, Sash, Doors and Blinds.

HEADQUARTERS FOR BICYCLES: "CRESCENTS," "RAMBLERS" and "SPECIALS."

Correspondence Solicited.

B. W. UPCHURCH,

GROCER,

15 EAST HARGETT STREET.

Best Groceries AT LOWEST PRICES.

All Goods Guaranteed and Promptly Delivered.

'Phone No. 238.

Best Oysters in season From Virginia Waters.

ST. AUGUSTINE SCHOOL, RALEIGH, N. C. Rev. A. B. HUNTER, Principal.

Duke Mrs Susie A, wife Jas B
Duke Willie E, son Jas B, res same, student
Duncan Jno A, merchandise broker, 240 Fayetteville, up-stairs, res 126 e Edenton
Duncan Miss Annie, d J A, res same, student
Duncan Miss Delia, d J A, res same, student
Duncan L P, yard foreman N C Car Co, cor Firwood and n Salisbury
Duncan Mrs Jannette, wife L P
Duncan Miss Sadie C, d L P, res same
Duncan Miss Mary H, d L P, res same, student
Dunn Ben,* carp, res 413 w Martin
Dunn Emily,* wife Ben, washerwoman
Dunn Helen,* d Ben, res same, cook
Dunn Mary,* d Ben, res same, laundress
Dunn Eliza,* d Ben, res same, laundress
Dunn John,* son Ben, res same, driver
Dunn James,* son Ben, res same, student
Dunn Katie,* cook, res e South
Dunn Julia,* washerwoman, res 432 s Blount
Dunn Susanna,* chambermaid at Yarboro' House, res 2 Stronach ave
Dunn Helen,* cook for Mrs D B Stith, res same
Dunn J J, pension clk, State Auditor's office, res 411 Elm
Dunn Mrs Dora V, wife J J
Dunn Rebecca,* washerwoman, res 401 s East
Dunn Ocety,* d Rebecca, res same, student
Dunn Luvenia,* d Rebecca, res same, student
Dunn Miss Lillie, saleslady at A B Stronach, bds 219 s Swain
Dunn Alice,* seamstress, res 213 s Harrington
Dunn Rufus G, cot weigher, office cot platform, res o s e
Dunn Mrs Minnie, wid, d Mrs J M Betts, res 213 n Harrington
Dunn Priscilla,* cook, 402 w North
Dunn Sidney,* farm hand, res room 2 R R al
Dunn Fannie,* cook for Chas Klueppelberg, res same
Dunn Lizzie,* nurse G E Hunter, res same
Dunn Howell,* cupalo tender N C Car Co Foundry
Dunn Silvia,* wife Howell, washerwoman
Dunston Cissie,* d Mary Miller, res same, student
Dunston Amanda,* d Mary Miller, res same, student
Dunston Betsy,* d Mary Miller, res same, student
Dunston Nelson* (Davis & Dunston), barber, res 225 e South
Dunston Ella,* wife Nelson
Dunston John T,* son Nelson, res same, student
Dunston Wm H,* son Nelson, res same, student
Dunston Mary A,* d Nelson, res same, student
Dunston Jos N,* son Nelson, res same
Dunston Amanda J,* d Nelson, res same

Dunston Albert,* lab, res 622 Harp's lane, o s n
Dunston Ada,* wife Albert
Dunston Bedie,* wid Anderson, res Blount-st al
Dunston H N,* barber, res 520 s Blount
Dunston Emma,* house-servant for Dr A W Goodwin, res on lot
Dunston Amanda, restaurant, 229 s Wilmington
Dunston Chas A,* barber, res 220 e Davie
Dunston Eliza T,* seamstress, res 220 e Davie
Dunston Hillery,* driver for S W Brewer, res East, o s n
Dunston Nellie,* wife Hillery, washerwoman
Dunston Jessie,* d Hillery, res same, student
Dunston Willie,* son Hillery, res same, student
Dunston Hattie, d Hillery, res same, student
Dunston Hillery Jr, son Hillery, res same, student
Dunston Julia,* washerwoman, res Martin, o s e
Dunston Ned,* lab, res e Hargett, o s e
Dunston Mary,* wife Ned, washerwoman
Dunston Sallie,* d Ned, res same, student
Dunston Annie,* d Ned, res same, student
Dunston Alex,* lab, res 20 Fowle
Dunston Annie,* nurse, res 20 Fowle
Dunston Margaret,* cook for W V Clifton, res on lot
Dunston M N,* shoemaker, 304 s Harrington, res o s e
Dunston Sylvester,* whitewasher, res 520 s McDowell
Dunston Harriet,* wife Sylvester, washerwoman
Dunston James,* son Sylvester, res same, student
Dunston Minnie,* d Sylvester, res same, student
Dunston Hubert,* son Sylvester, res same, whitewasher
Dunston Martha,* washerwoman, res 513 s Dawson
Dunston Mamie,* d Martha, res same, washerwoman
Dunston George,* son Martha, res same, student
Dunston Sylvester Jr,* whitewasher, res 520 s McDowell
Dunston Lillie,* wife Sylvester Jr, house work
Dunston Roy,* whitewasher, res 520 s McDowell
Dunston Anna,* wife Roy, house work
Dunston John,* barber, res 214 w Lenoir
Dunston Austin,* Governor's messenger, res 203 w South
Dunston L M,* wife Austin, house work
Dunston Robert,* student, res 203 w South
Dunston Charles,* porter at Mrs A S Merrimon, res on lot
Dunston Frances,* washerwoman, res 520 Newbern ave
Dunston Mamie,* d Frances, res same, washerwoman
Durham Edie,* washerwoman, res 412 w Edenton
Durham Mrs C, wid, res 112 w Edenton
Durham Walter, son Mrs C, res same, teller Mechanics Dime Savings Bank
Durham Baxter, son Mrs C, res same, clk M Rosenthal
Dupree Joseph, grocer, res 534 Cannon

Dupree Mrs Bettie, wife Jos
Dupree Adam,* lab, res 305 w Lenoir
Dupree Janie,* wife Adam, res same, laundress
Dupree T M, attendant at Insane Asylum, res same
Dupree Addie,* cook, rooms 229 Blount-st al
Dye A W, bkkpr frt office S A L, res 327 Oakwood ave
Dye Mrs Jennie, wife A W
Dye Miss Lelia, d A W, res same, student
Dye Miss Annie, d A W, res same, student

EAGLE Miss Annie, attendant at Insane Asylum, res same
Eakins Mrs Clelia, wid, res 307 Smithfield
Eakins Henry, son Mrs Clelia, res same
Eakins Burke, son Mrs Clelia, res same, app at J H Gill
Eakins Gottardo, son Mrs Clelia, res same, messenger Postal Tel office
Eakins Miss Helen, d Mrs Clelia, res same, student
Eakins Miss Katie, d Mrs Clelia, res same, student
Eakins Louis, son Mrs Clelia, res same, student
Earp H W, shoemaker, res 539 e Martin
Earp Mrs Bettie, wife H W
Earp Mrs Louisa, wid, res 514 s Bloodworth
Easom Wm H, beamer at Caraleigh cot mill, res 208 e Lenoir
Easom Mrs Rena B, wife Wm H
Easom Jno M, inmate Soldiers' Home
Eatman Hill,* lab, res 113 n Harrington
Eatman George,* lab, rooms 320 w Lenoir
Eatman Annie,* washerwoman for Mrs C R Lee, res on lot
Eatman Cherry,* sexton A M E church, res 107 n Harrington
Eatman W C, wks S A L R R, res w North
Eatman Mrs M A, wife W C
Eatman F R, beamer Pilot cot mill, res n Blount, o s n
Eatman Mrs Florence, wife F R
Eatman W R, mechanic, res 113 n Bloodworth
Eatman Mrs Annie, wife W R, dressmaker
Eaton Don,* gardener, res 618 Elm
Eaton Henrietta,* wife Don, dressmaker
Eaton Mary,* d Don, res same, dressmaker
Eaton Kate,* d Don, res same, dressmaker
Eaton Charles,* son Don, res same, lab
Eaton Lizzie,* d Don, res same, house-servant
Eaton Nannie,* d Don, res same, house-servant
Eaton Sarah,* d Don, res same, house-servant
Eaton James,* son Don, res same, errand-boy
Eaton John,* son Don, res same, student
Eaton Flossie,* d Don, res same student
Ebrom Frances,* washerwoman, res rear 605 Hillsboro'

Ebrom Randall,* servant at Mrs W H Holloman, res rear 605 Hillsboro'
EBERHARDT & BAKER, coal and wood dealers, office 126 Fayetteville
Eberhardt T L (Eberhardt & Baker), wood and coal, and pres of Ral Ice & Refrigerating Co, bds 6 Newbern ave
Eckman Edward, machinist, bds 112 Halifax
Eden Stephen,* carp, res 301 w Lenoir
Eden Malinda,* wife Stephen, washerwoman
Eden Mary,* d Stephen, res same, cook
Edens James, tel opr, bds 10 e North
Edmunds Miss Mamie, house work, res 317 s East
EDWARDS & BROUGHTON, printers, binders and publishers, cor w Hargett and Salisbury
Edwards Rev T B,* Baptist minister, res 821 s Wilmington
Edwards Charlotte C,* wife Rev T B
Edwards Laura L,* d Rev T B, res same, student
Edwards Peter A,* son Rev T B, res same, student
Edwards Solomon J,* son Rev T B, res same, student
Edwards Lucinda I,* d Rev T B, res same, student
Edwards Thos B G W,* son Rev T B, res same, student
Edwards Peggie,* washerwoman, res 322 Cannon
Edwards Delia,* washerwoman, res 610 s McDowell
Edwards E W, bookbinder, res 323 s McDowell
Edwards Mrs Delia C, wife E W
Edwards C B (Edwards & Broughton), printer and binder, res 123 w Martin
Edwards Mrs Alice R, wife C B
Edwards Miss Bettie C, d C B, res same
Edwards M J, boarding-house, 10 e North
Edwards Mrs M E, wife M J
Edwards Manly E, son M J, res same
Edwards Miss Alice, d M J, res same, student
Edwards Wm J, railroading, res 501 n Person
Edwards Mrs Katie E, wife Wm J
Edwards Harry P, son Wm J, res same, student
Edwards James,* butcher, res 410 w Edenton
Edwards Mary,* wife James
Edwards Mary,* cook, res 517 s Blount
Edwards Alice,* cook, res 517 s Blount
Edwards Julia,* cook, res rear 210 e Cabarrus
Edwards Lucinda, servant, res rear 210 e Cabarrus
Edward Mary,* cook W H Lyon, res same
Edwards Rosa,* washerwoman, rear 102 w Lane
Edwards Mrs W J, wid, res with daughter Mrs J W Phillips
Edwards Miss Mamie, d Mrs W J, res same, bookbinder
Edwards Miss Maud, dressmaker, res with Mrs W R Eatman
Edwards James, clk for Whiting Bros, rooms 327 e Hargett

Edwards Mrs M A, wid, res with J H Robbins
Edwards Thos,* student, res with Matilda Scott
Edwards Mrs Nancy, wid, res 527 s Person
Egerton Lina,* student, res 320 w South
Egerton J A, mgr of the Western Union tel office, res 212 Peace
Egerton Mrs A M, wife J A
Egerton Miss Virginia, d J A, res same
Ellen Mrs W H, wid, res 142 n East
Ellen Miss Cornelia, d Mrs W H, res same, dressmaker
Ellerbe Mrs E A, wid M F, boarding-house, 213 w Martin
Ellerbe A W, son Mrs E A, res same, bookbinder
Ellerbe Wm A, son Mrs E A, res same, student
Elgie Wm J, supt National cemetery, res at same
Elgie Mrs Julia, wid, mother of Wm J, res same
Ellington Jot,* lab, res Stronach ave
Ellington Mary,* wife Jot, washerwoman
Ellington Austin,* lab, res 322 w South
Ellington Eleander,* wife Austin, washerwoman
Ellington Cora,* d Austin, res same, washerwoman
Ellington Albert,* driver for Jones & Powell, res 609 s McDowell
Ellington Rena,* wife Albert, house work
Ellington Edgar E, bkkpr for N C Building & Supply Co, res s Blount
Ellington Mrs Mattie D, wife Edgar E
Ellington Edgar E Jr, son E E, res same
Ellington Ella,* cook for Mrs W W Holden, res 108 Newbern ave
Ellington John, carp, res 745 Fayetteville
Ellington Mrs Lula, wife John
Ellington Chas, son John, res same, student
Ellington Lonnie, son John, res same, student
Ellington John Jr, son Jno Sr, res same, student
Ellington Albert,* driver Jones & Powell, res s s Harrington
Ellington Raney,* wife Albert, washerwoman
Ellington W J (N C Building and Supply Co), builder and contractor, res 18 n Saunders
Ellington Mrs R S, wife W J
Ellington Miss Eula, d W J, res same
Ellington William, son W J, res same, student
Ellington Delmar, son W J, res same, student
Ellington Mart, son W J, res same, student
Ellington Frank K (Wynne, Ellington & Co), fire ins, real estate, &c, office 10 w Hargett, bds Jno W Thompson
Ellington J C, State librarian, res 326 Newbern ave
Ellington Mrs Bettie, wife J C
Ellington J C Jr, son J C, res same, bkkpr for W H & R S Tucker & Co
Ellington Miss Lizzie, d J C, res same
Ellington Miss Clyde, d J C, res same

Ellington Miss Bernice, d J C, res same
Ellington Miss Placide, d J C, res same, student
Ellington Miss Lalla, d J C, res same, student
Ellington R L, machinist, res 121 s West
Ellington Mrs Annie M, wife R L
Elliott Lula J,* cook, res 26 Fowle
Elliott Joanna,* nurse, res rear 309 s Bloodworth
Elliott Lula J,* servant for Dr W H Bobbitt, res same
Ellis A J, grocer, Hillsboro' rd, o s w, res same
Ellis Mrs Kate C, wife A J
Ellis Miss M M, d A J, res same
Ellis Miss M L, d A J, res same
Ellis Miss Alma E, d A J, res same
Ellis Mrs P A, mother A J, res same
Ellis Edwin R, mailing clk U S p o, res 119 s Harrington
Ellis Mrs Jane, wife Edwin R
Ellis Miss Mary, d Edwin R, res same
Ellis Miss Jennie, d Edwin R, res same, student
Ellis D J, miller, res 745 Hillsboro'
Ellis Mrs A J, wid, res 745 Hillsboro'
Ellis Charlie, student, res 745 Hillsboro'
Ellis Miss Gertrude, student, res 745 Hillsboro'
Ellis Benj, student, res 745 Hillsboro'
Ellis Raymond, student, res 745 Hillsboro'
Ellis Mary,* chambermaid for Mrs H Mahler, res 739 s Blount
Ellis John, night clk Yarboro' House, res same
Ellis Jno W, clk for E R Pace, res same
Ellis Dr R B, res 218 e Morgan
Ellis Mrs C E, wife Dr R B
Ellis Miss Evie S, d Dr R B, res same
Ellison Roger,* hackman, res 531 e Edenton
Ellison Stewart,* carp, res 24 Hayti
Ellison Narcissa,* wife Stewart
Ellison Mary A,* d Stewart, res same, student
Ellison L S, policeman, res 415 n Salisbury
Ellison Mrs Nannie, wife L S
Ellison Miss Nannie D, d L S, student
Ellison Miss Mary, d L S, student
Ellison Miss Musa, d L S, student
Ellsworth C B, machinist, bds 212 n Harrington
Ellsworth Mrs Emma, wife C B
Emmett L C, machinist, res 426 Halifax
Emmett Mrs Mary, wife L C
Emmett William, son L C, res same, machinist
Emmett Eugene, son L C, res same
Emmett Miss Julia, d L C, res same, student
Emery F E, agriculturist at Experiment Station, res same
Emery Mrs Laura, wid, boarding-house, 12 e Davie

Emery Miss Hattie, d Mrs Laura, res same
Emery Mrs Eliza, wid, res 418 s Salisbury
Emery Miss Cornelia, d Mrs Eliza, res same, dressmaker
Emery Geo E, son Mrs Eliza, res same, city hand
Emery Miss Oudie E, d Mrs Eliza, res same, student
Emery Fred, son Mrs Eliza, res same, student
Emery A V, grocer, cor Dawson and Cabarrus, res 304 w Cabarrus
Emery Mrs Mollie F, wife A V
Emery Edward, moulder, bds Walter Sadler
Emery Miss Emma, dressmaker, res 313 s Blount
Emery L A, carp, res e Hargett, o s e
Emery Annie W, wife L A
Englehard Frederick, machinist, res 313 e Martin
Englehard Mrs Augusta, wife Fred
Ennis P C, clk in agricultural department, res 112 n McDowell
Ennis Mrs Kate C, wife P C
Ennis Miss Virgie D, d P C, res same, student
Ennis Miss Estelle, d P C, res same, student
Ennis Peyton, son P C, res same, student
Ennis James H, publisher Turner's N C Almanac, office 119 n Salisbury, res 117 n Salisbury
Ennis Miss Mamie H, d James H, res same,
Ennis Thos C, son James H, res same, engineer S A L
Ennis Mrs H H, wid, r 110 n Person
Ennis Miss Eliza B, d Mrs H H, res same, student
Ennis Miss Katherine Y, d Mrs H H, res same, saleslady at Tucker & Co's
Ennis Miss Bettie, d Mrs H H, r same, saleslady at Tucker & Co's
Enoch George,* brakeman S A L, bds 435 n Salisbury
Epworth Methodist Episcopal church, Halifax, Rev R H Whitaker pastor
Evans Mrs Lucy B, wid, boarding-house, 104 n McDowell
Evans Edgar,* lab, res w South
Evans Robt,* carp, res w South, Rex Hospital property
Evans Mary A,* wife Robt, washerwoman
Evans Sallie,* d Robt, res same, cook
Evans Robert,* son Robt, res same, carp
Evans Polly,* d Robt, res same, nurse
Evans William,* son Robt, res same, lab
Evans Albert,* lab, res 721 Manly
Evans Willie,* wife Albert, washerwoman
Evans Edward,* son Albert, res same, student
Evans Lucinda,* d Albert, res same, student
Evans Oscar,* son Albert, res same, student
Evans Carrie,* d Albert, res same, student
Evans Turner,* shoemaker, res 219 s Harrington
Evans Alice,* wife Turner, washerwoman
Evans George,* son Turner, res same, student

Evans Jennie,* washerwoman, res 304 s Harrington
Evans James,* lab, res 304 s Harrington
Evans J W, carriage and buggy maker and repairer, shop cor s Blount and Morgan, res 120 Newbern ave
Evans Mrs Mary, wife J W
Evans John, son J W, res same, student
Evans Miss Mary, d J W, res same, student
Everett Dr D E, surgeon dentist, office over W H & R S Tucker & Co, rooms 322 Hillsboro'

FAIRCLOTH W T, Chief Justice Supreme Court of N C, bds Yarboro' House
Faison Mrs Annie H, wid, res 9 e Edenton
Faison Jno W, son Mrs A H, res same, wks S A L R R
Faison Stanley, son Mrs A H, res same, salesman
Faison Sherwood B, son Mrs A H, res same, electrician
Faison Duncan M, son Mrs A H, res same, student
Faison Paul F, son Mrs A H, res same, student
Faison F S, farmer, res cor Jones and McDowell
Faison Miss G, d F S, res same
Faison Miss Nannie, d F S, res same
Faison F S Jr, student, res cor Jones and McDowell
Faison Miss Grace, d F S, res same, student
Faison Miss Ellen, d F S, res same, student
Faison Miss Mary, d F S, res same, student
Faison Haywood R, student, bds 225 w Edenton
Faison Miss Margaret A, lives with Mrs M E Beckham
Faison Benj F, clk, res 8 s East
Faison Mrs Emaline, wife B F
Faison Wm E, chief clk to Commissioner Labor Statistics, res 8 s East
Faison Wm A, engineer S A L R R, res 617 w Jones
Faison Mrs Margaret A, wife Wm A
Faison Dr J A, First Asst Physician N C Insane Asylum, res same
Faison Maggie,* cook, res rear 548 e Hargett
Falcon J C,* lab, res 309 n West
Falcon Horace,* lab, res 309 n West
Falcon Ben,* lab, res 309 n West
Falkner William,* carp, res 9 Gatling's lane
Falkner Ida,* wife Wm, washerwoman
Falkner Miss Eliza, hkpr, res 214 w Cabarrus
Fann Miss R B, sister of Mrs L V Baker, res same
Fann D H, blacksmith, res 420 Cannon
Fann W E, brick-mason, res 419 Cannon
Fann Mrs Eleander, wife W E
Fann Walter, son W E, res same, plasterer
Fann Miss Katie, niece of W E, res same

Fann Mrs Caroline, mother of W E, res same
Fann W E Jr, brick-mason, res 419 Cannon
Fann Mrs Sallie, wife W E Jr
Farrar Lucy,* washerwoman, res 23 Fowle
Farrar Setha A,* student, res 729 Manly
Farrar Julia J,* student, res 729 Manly
Farrington Albert,* lab, res 32 Railroad
Farrington Jane,* wife Albert, cook
Farmer J T, letter-carrier, res 513 s West
Farmer Mrs A R, wife J T
Farmer F C, son J T, res same, wks Ral Gas Co
Farmer C D, son J T, res same, student
Farmer Miss Louise E, d J T, res same
Farmer Miss H L, d J T, res same, student
Farnsworth H M, house and sign painter, shop and res 112 w Jones
Farnsworth Mrs Sophia, wife H M
FASNACH EDWARD, jeweler and optician, 110 Fayetteville, res same
Fasnach Mrs S V, wife Edward
Faucette Bettie,* servant at Phil Theim's, res same
Faucette Capt Henry M, conductor S A L R R, r 223 n Harrington
Faucette Mrs E E, mother Henry M
Faucette Miss N M, d Mrs E E, res same
Faucette Mary S,* cook for J H Redford, res same
Faucette William,* invalid, res 703 e Davie
Faucette Mary,* wife Wm, washerwoman
Faucette William,* son Wm, res same, painter
Faucette Thos O, printer, res 510 s Salisbury
Faucette Mrs Leanora, wife Thos O
Faucette W A, printer for Edwards & Broughton, res 228 n Saunders
Faucette Mrs Amelia, wife W A, dressmaker
FAUST E G, propr Bon Ton Barber Saloon, res 514 Hillsboro'
Faust Mrs Lizzie, wife E G
Fayetteville-St Baptist church,* Rev Thomas Edwards pastor
Feagan Lon,* cook, res 529 s Dawson
Fellows Celia,* laundress for Judge Walter Clark, res 102 n East
Felton Adeline,* house work, res 16 w Worth
Felt Mrs O T, wid, res with S W Brewer
Fendt Henry L, res 308 e Martin
Fendt Mrs Mary H, wife H L
Fenner Miss Clara I, teacher in St Mary's, res same
Ferrall John R (J R Ferrall & Co), grocer, res 110 s Salisbury
Ferrall Miss Margaret E, d Jno R, res same, student
Ferrall Miss Lillian M, d Jno R, res same, student
Ferrall Miss Mary A, sister Jno R, res same
FERRALL J R & CO, wholesale and retail grocers, 222 Fayetteville

Ferrall W V, attendant at Insane Asylum, res same
Ferrall Jos F, bkkpr W H & R S Tucker & Co. res Hillsboro' near Capitol
Ferrall Mrs Annie, wife Jos F
Ferrell Thomas, lab, res 826 s Wilmington
Ferrell Mrs Lula, wife Thos, dressmaker
Ferrell Willie, son Thos, res same, student
Ferrell Miss Sarah, d Thos, res same, student
Ferrell Miss Katie, d Thos, res same, student
Ferrell John, watchman, r 122 n Harrington
Ferrell Mrs Bettie, wife John
Ferrell Miss Katie, d John, res same
Ferrell Wm W, laborer, r 215 s Blount
Ferrell Mrs Malinda, wife Wm W
Ferrell William F, son Wm W, res same
Ferrell Mrs A L, wid, res 517 Oakwood ave
Ferrell Miss Alice C, d Mrs A L, res same, teacher
Ferrell Miss Hattie, d Mrs A L, res same, dressmaker
Ferrell Miss Rosa, d Mrs A L, res same, bookbinder
Ferrell Wayland, son Mrs A L, res same, messenger-boy p o
Ferrell Ralph, son Mrs A L, res same
Ferrell Rev R H,* Christian minister, res 617 Elm
Ferrell Louise,* wife Rev R H, house work
Ferrell Henrietta,* washerwoman, res e Davie
Ferrell Miss Julia, res with C J Hunter
Fetner Frank, machinist, res 233 n Saunders
Fetner Mrs Blanche, wife Frank
Fetner W H, engineer S A L R R, res 313 w Jones
Fetner Mrs Mattie A, wife W H
Fetner Harris, son W H, res same, student
Fetner Miss Pansy E, d W H, res same
Fetner Willie B, son W H, res same, student
Fetner Ross H, son W H, res same, student
Fields Isham,* upholsterer and furniture repairer, 113 s Salisbury, res 408 e Edenton
Fields Callia,* wife Isham, house-servant
Fields Hessie,* d Isham, res same
Fields Victoria,* d Isham, res same, student
Fields William,* wks at gas-house, res 516 s McDowell
Fields Matilda,* wife Wm, house work
Fike Lucy,* house work, res s West
Fike George,* son Lucy, res same, student
Fike Carrie,* d Lucy, res same, student
Finch Morton, frt dept Southern depot, bds 305 Hillsboro'
Finch Edith,* washerwoman, res 424 s Swain
Finch Henry, lab, res 406 Haywood
Finch Mrs Cornelia, wife Henry
Finch Miss Lucy, d Henry, res same

Finch Miss Gertrude, d Henry, res same
Finch Mrs Metta, wid, res 225 w Davie
Finch Miss Lillian, d Mrs Metta, res same
Finger Louis, peddler, res 412 s Blount
Finger Esther, wife Louis
Finnell Albert, machinist, res 419 Cannon
Finnell Mrs Lena, wife Albert
Finnell Miss Blanche, d Albert, res same, student
Finlayson Miss Fanny, hkpr for Mrs Bettie Lockre, res same
Fisher Mrs Julia, wid mother of Mrs Kate F Coke, res same
Fitts Thomas,* leaf tobacco worker, res Idlewild
Fitts Lizzie C,* wife Thomas, washerwoman
Fitts John H,* son Thos, res same, student
Flannagan Annie,* cook, res Yearby's lane
Fleming & Hunter,* blacksmiths, cor s Blount and Hargett
Fleming J M, warden N C penitentiary, res 130 s Harrington
Fleming Mrs Nannie C, wife J M
FLEMING Dr J MARTIN, surgeon dentist, 132½ Fayetteville, res 130 s Harrington
Fleming Miss Nannie McK, d J M, res same, teacher
Fleming Miss Belle, d J M, res same, teacher in Centennial Graded School
Fleming Daniel,* blacksmith, res 417 s Blount
Fleming Bettie,* wife Daniel, cook
Fleming Octavia,* d Daniel, res same, washerwoman
Fleming & Moffit, lawyers, 13½ w Martin
Flemming Miss Maggie, seamstress, res 821 Manly
Flemming Thomas, student, res 821 Manly
Flemming George, student, res 821 Manly
Fleming Flora,* washerwoman, res 521 s McDowell
Fleming E L, tobacco broker, res 516 s Salisbury
Fleming Mrs Eugenia A, wife E L
Fleming M E, tobacco broker, bds 516 s Salisbury
Fleming Julia,* washerwoman, res 303 s West
Fleming Agnes,* cook, 708 s McDowell
Fleming Robert,* lab, res 708 s McDowell
Fleming John,* lab, res 407 s Dawson
Fleming Alice,* wife John, washerwoman
Fletcher Emma,* washerwoman, res 514 e Martin
Fletcher Minnie,* d Emma, res same, student
Flowers Georgiana,* washerwoman, res 119 e Cabarrus
Flowers James,* lab, res 119 e Cabarrus
Flowers Miss Mary, seamstress, res 718 Fayetteville
Flowers Mrs Elizabeth, wid, res 718 Fayetteville
Floyd Miss Fannie, music teacher at Blind Institution, res same
Floyd James,* gardener, res 6 s Harrington
Floyd Susan,* wife James, washerwoman
Floyd Esther,* d Jas, res same, student

Floyd Willie,* son Jas, res same, student
Floyd Thomas,* son Jas, res same, student
Floyd Alex,* son Jas, res same, student
Floyd Nellie,* d Jas, res same, student
Fogg Eliza,* cook for W F Wyatt, res on lot
Fogg Mary,* laundress, res 509 e Cabarrus
Fogg Annie,* d Mary, res same, laundress
Fogg Patrick,* son Mary, res same, wks Linnell Laundry
Fogg Carrie,* d Mary, res same, student
Fogg Bessie,* d Mary, res same, student
Fogg Lewis,* son Mary, res same, lab
Fogg Nancy,* washerwoman, res Cotton lane, o s e
Fordham C C, druggist, res 222 w Davie
Fordham Mrs Maggie S, wife C C
Ford Alonzo C, wks cot platform, res o s e
Ford R W, carriage trimmer, bds 112 Halifax
Ford Bros, wood shop, 136 e Morgan
Ford Chas T, carp, res w North
Ford Mrs Eliza, wife Chas T
Ford Robert J O, carp, res w North
Ford Mrs Matilda, wife Robert J O
Ford Emily,* cook, res 322 s East
Ford Susan,* washerwoman, res 415 Haywood
Ford Cenia,* d Susan, res same, washerwoman
Ford Susie,* d Susan, res same, washerwoman
Ford Austin,* son Susan, res same, painter
Ford Eleanor,* d Susan, res same, student
Ford Bessie,* nurse, res 9 Johnson ave
Ford Maggie,* farm hand, res 9 Johnson ave
Ford Robert,* student, res 9 Johnson ave
Ford R J, night watchman, res 521 s Person
Ford Mrs Arkansaw S, wife R J
Ford Miss Ella A, d R J, res same, student
Ford James B, son R J, res same, stenographer and typewriter
Ford Miss May, d R J, res same, student
Ford Mary,* laundress, res 727 Manly
Foote Jno W,* servant of Rev J B Cheshire, res on lot
Foote Daniel,* fireman, res rear 114 w Cabarrus
Forrest Asa B, supt Oakwood Cemetery, res 517 Polk
Forrest Mrs Bettie J, wife A B
Forrest Mortimer E, son A B, res same, student
Forsythe Wm G, merchant, res 222 e Lenoir
Forsythe Mrs Mary A, wife Wm G
Forsythe Edward E, book agt, res 606 s Person
Forsythe Mrs Clara, wife Ed E
Forsythe Mrs Sarah M, wid, seamstress, res 324 s Bloodworth
Fort David I, real estate, res 315 n Boundary
Fort Mrs Fannie, wife D I

Fort Miss Katie W, d D I, res same, stenographer and typewriter for W H & R S Tucker & Co
Fort Wm L, son D I, res same, messenger Western Union Tel Co
Fort Miss Sallie, d D I, res same, student
Fort Miss Fannie, d D I, res same, student
Fort Gaston W, son D I, res same, student
Fort Miss Nellie, d D I, res same, student
Fort David I Jr, son D I, res same, student
Foster W E, bkkpr for Myatt & Hunter, res 118 n McDowell
Foster Mrs Cora E, wife W E
Foster Miss M C, d W E, res same
Foster Miss Dora, d W E, res same
Foster Miss Susie, d W E, res same, student
Foster Dawson B, son W E, res same, clk for C A Sherwood & Co
Foster John W, son W E, res same, student
Foster Rev James L, pastor Christian church, res 318 w Edenton
Foster Mrs Myrtle W, wife Rev James L
Foster Margaret,* cook Spier Whitaker, res 220 e Cabarrus
Foster Nelson,* drayman, res 220 e Cabarrus
Foster Lucy,* washerwoman, res 220 e Cabarrus
Foster Etta,* d Margaret, res same, nurse
Foster Omega H, mfr, res 536 n Blount
Foster Mrs Ada, wife Omega H
Foster Mack,* lab, res 562 e Cabarrus
Foster Louise,* wife Mack, washerwoman
Foster Martha A,* dressmaker, res 510 e Edenton
Foster Grace,* house-servant, res 510 e Edenton
Foster Eliza,* washerwoman, res Hayti
Foster Willie,* son Eliza, res same, student
Foster Kate,* washerwoman, res 830 Manly
Foster Clayton,* waiter at Park Hotel, res 830 Manly
Foster Phillis,* cook, res 830 Manly
Foster Mary E,* d Phillis, res same, washerwoman
Foster Willie,* son Phillis, res same, student
Foster Chester L,* son Phillis, res same, student
Foster Vester L,* son Phillis, res same, student
Foster Harry,* brick-mason, res rear 311 w Cabarrus
Foster Alex,* son Harry, res same, student
Foster Mary J,* cook for J W Barber, res 402 s Blount
Foushee Ben,* lab, res 521 Haywood
Foushee Mary,* wife Ben, washerwoman
Foushee Daisy,* d Ben, res same, nurse
Foushee George,* son Ben, res same, lab
Foushee Robert,* son Ben, res same, student
Foushee Mrs Emeline, wid, bds 513 Hillsboro'
Fowler Walter W, collector for Press-Visitor, res 743 Fayetteville
Fowler Mrs Fannie, wife W W
Fowler Miss Maggie, d W W, res same

Fowler Geo W, farmer, res Fayetteville
Fowler Mrs Dora, wife Geo W, dressmaker
Fowler Harry, son Geo W, res same, student
Fowler Mrs Elizabeth, mother Mrs Dora Stokes, res same
Fowler Henry, lab, res rear e Davie
Fowler Mrs Narcissa, wife Henry, house work
Fowler Charles, son Henry, res at Blind Institution
Fowler Adolphus, locomotive eng, res 313 s Dawson
Fowler Mrs Fannie R, wife Adolphus
Fowler Jas T, son Adolphus, res same, student
Fowler Miss Myrtle D, d Adolphus, res same, student
Fowler Miss Nora B, d Adolphus, res same, student
Fowler Rev Fenner,* Christian minister, res 720 Fayetteville
Fowler Emerline,* wife Rev Fenner, washerwoman
Fowler Emma,* d Rev Fenner, res same, nurse
Fowler William,* son Rev Fenner, res same, lab
Fowler Rosana,* d Rev Fenner, res same, house work
Fowler Mrs Melissa, wid, res with D M Branch
Fowler Lucinda, washerwoman, res 429 s East
Fowler Willis N, blacksmith, res 309 s Blount
Fowler Hubert, son Willis N, res same
Fowler Rod, bill-poster, res 828 Fayetteville
Fowler Mrs Eva, wife Rod
Fowles Mrs M A, wid, res with J W Evans
Foy Marcus M, inmate Soldiers' Home
Foy James W, trav salesman
Franklin June, clk for F D Castlebury, res same
Francis Samuel, inmate Soldiers' Home
Francis Peter, shoemaker, res Prairie bldg
Francis Mrs Virginia, wife Peter
Francis Joseph, son Peter, res same, shoemaker
Francis Miss Annie, d Peter, res same, dressmaker
Francis Miss Jennie, d Peter, res same, seamstress
Francis J E, shoemaker, res 220 s East
Francis Mrs Fannie C, wife J E
Francis Miss Pearl, d J E, res same, student
Fraps A W, agt for German Electric Belts, room No. 1 Fraps bldg
Fraps Geo S, son A W, student A and M College, room No. 2 Fraps bldg
Freidman Sam, salesman, bds 12 e Davie
Freeman Mack,* barber, res 405 w South
Freeman Allie,* wife Mack, house work
Freeman Lillian M,* d Mack, res same, student
Freeman Maria,* cook, r 717 s Dawson
Freeman William,* house-servant, res 521 e Davie
Freeman Miss Susie B, saleslady at A B Stronach, res 324 s Salisbury
Freeman Jas T,* lab, bds 108 e Hargett

Freeman James, saloon, 13 e Hargett, res 13 s East
Freeman Mrs Mary A, wife James
Freeman Emily,* res 516 Newbern ave, washerwoman
Freeman Solomon,* wks for city, res 108 Smithfield
Freeman Sallie,* wife Solomon, washerwoman
Freeman Josephine,* d Solomon, res same
Freeman Ada,* d Solomon, res same, student
Freeman Solomon Jr,* son Solomon, res same, student
Freeman Tuney,* cook for Robt Dobbin, res 512 w Morgan
Freeman John,* porter T W Blake, res 600 s Person
Freeman Amanda,* cook for W H Lyon, res 600 s Person
Freeman Bertha,* d Amanda, res same, dressmaker
Freeman James,* lab, res 505 s Blount
Freeman Victoria,* wife James, washerwoman
Freeman Alex,* stationary eng for T L Eberhart, res 121 n Harrington
Freeman Nortleet,* janitor Garfield School, res 554 e Martin
Freeman Clara,* washerwoman, res 414 e Martin
Freeman Cornelius,* son Clara, res same, lab
Freeman Mort,* son Clara, res same, student
Freeman Roden,* drayman, res old Fair Ground, o s e
Freeman Mollie,* wife Roden, washerwoman
Freeman Thomas,* son Roden, res same, lab
Freeman Edward,* son Roden, res same, student
Freeman Minnie,* d Roden, res same, student
Freeman Norman,* hackman, e Martin, o s e
Freeman Nellie,* wife Norman, washerwoman
Freeman Bessie,* d Norman, res same, student
Freeman Jennie,* d Norman, res same, student
Freeman Bryant,* son Norman, res same, student
Freeman Mack,* lab, res 515 e Edenton
Freeman Laura,* wife Mack, washerwoman
Freeman George,* son Mack, res same, student
Frost Miss Julia, sister of Mrs Len H Royster, res same
Frost William A, boiler-maker, bds 108 n Saunders
Fryar Miss M V, attendant at Insane Asylum, res same
Fulcher W A, printer, res 521 s Bloodworth
Fulcher Mrs Katie, wife W A
Fulcher Miss Melissa, sister of W A, res same
Fuller Hon Thomas C, Judge U S Court of Land Claims, bds 130 Hillsboro'
Fuller William,* driver for Dr J R Rogers, res w Lane near R R
Fuller Harriet,* wife Wm, washerwoman
Fuller Mack,* hackman, res e Lane
Fuller Alice,* wife Mack, cook for Dr K P Battle Jr
Fuller Jennie,* house-servant, res 622 Elm
Fuller Lucinda,* washerwoman, res 324 Cannon
Fulgham Jas S, clk for W E Jones, bds Richardson House
Furlong William, boiler-maker, bds 108 n Saunders

GAITHINGS S H, inmate Soldiers' Home
Gales Mrs Seaton G, wid, res with Thos T Hay, 705 Hillsboro'
Gales Miss Altie, d Mrs Seaton G, res same
Gales Lane,* lab, res Nunn, o s s
Gales Jane,* wife Lane, washerwoman
Galvin Mrs Ann E, wid, res 519 n Person
Galvin Jno H, son Mrs Ann E, res same, eng S A L R R
Galvin Cicero, son Mrs Ann E, res same, fireman S A L R R
Gant Emit,* brick-mason, res Fayetteville below R R
Gardner Miss J, lives at F Shepard, cor Edenton and McDowell
Gardner W E, clk for J D Carroll, bds 513 s Bloodworth
Gardner C C, wks ice factory, res 218 s Harrington
Gardner Mrs Mattie, wife C C
Gardner Miss A, attendant at Insane Asylum, res same
Gargus James, lab, res 122 e Martin
Gargus Mrs Nannie, wife James
Gargus Janata, son James, res same, student
Gargus Miss Nellie, d James, res same
Garner Lucy,* washerwoman, res old Fair Ground, o s e
Garner Maggie,* d Lucy, res same, student
Garner Ida,* d Lucy, res same, student
Garrett Nancy,* farm hand, res 423 Smith
Gaston Ben,* servant at Thos N Bryant, res on lot
Gary Patsy,* seamstress, res 117 w Lenoir
Gary J O,* carp, res w Lenoir, Rex Hospital property
Gary Cornelia,* wife J O, house work
Gary Florence,* d J O, res same, seamstress
Gary Charlie,* son J O, res same
Gary Lula,* d J O, res same
Gary Hattie,* d J O, res same
Gatling John, cotton buyer, bds 311 w Martin
Gatling Bart M, lawyer, 3 Pullen bldg, res o s city
Gattis William, lives with E S Cheek, 114 n Dawson
Gattis W A, merchandise broker, res 316 s Dawson
Gattis Mrs Alice V, wife W A
Gattis Chas H, son W A, res same, clk for H S Leard
Gattis Louis P, son W A, res same, student
Gattis J Richard, carp, bds 313 w Lane
Gattis J T, flagman Southern R R, res 530 Hillsboro'
Gattis Mrs Bettie, wife J T
Gattis Charles, son J T, res same, clk for Betts Bros
Gattis H O, grocer Newbern ave, o s e, res same
Gay Solomon, inmate Soldiers' Home
Gear John,* gardener, res 404 Cannon
Gear Emeline,* wife John, washerwoman
Gelshenen J L, cot buyer for C E Johnson & Co, res 219 e Morgan
Gelshenen Mrs Maggie A, wife J L

Gelshenen Miss Mary A, d J L, res same
Germania House, 109½ Fayetteville, Mrs Katherine Deboy propr
Ghiselin Harding, nephew of B R Harding, r same, machinist app
Gibbs Miss Mary L, sister of Mrs F M Simmons, res same
Gibbs Hugh, beemer Caraleigh cot mill, bds 739 Fayetteville
Gibson Belle,* cook for Alice Patterson, res 805 Jenkins
Gilliam Lillie,* house-servant for Jacob Schwartz, res same
Gilliam Matthew,* student, res 214 w Lenoir
Gilliam Minerva,* chambermaid, res 25 w Worth
Gilliam Miss Lillie, attendant at Insane Asylum, res same
Gill David, lab, res Haywood
Gill Mrs Nancy, wife David
Gill Thomas, son David, res same, plumber
Gill Burley, son David, res same, lab
Gill Alonzo, son David, res same, lab
Gill Junius, son David, res same, student
GILL J H, founder and machinist, cor McDowell and Davie, res 325 s McDowell
Gill Miss Sallie, seamstress, res 546 Haywood
Gill Elmo, student, res 546 Haywood
Gill Ida,* washerwoman, res 401 s Dawson
Gill Solomon,* lab, res 102 w Cabarrus
Gill Eliza,* wife Solomon, cook for David Rosenthal
Gill Wright,* lab, res 207 w South
Gill Nat,* coachman, res 109 w Morgan
Gill Ellen,* wife Nat, washerwoman
Gill George, machinist S A L R R, bds Exchange Hotel
Gill Miss Nellie, dry goods, &c, 321 e Martin, res 208 e Morgan
Gill Katie,* servant at G W Morris, res same
Gill B T, gardener, res 208 e Morgan
Gill Miss Otie, d B T, res same
Gill Miss Nellie, d B T, res same
Gill Lewis, wks city market, res 208 e Morgan
Gill Spencer,* driver for J P Wyatt & Bros, res Adams' lane
Gill Fannie,* wife Spencer, washerwoman
Gill Anderson,* son Spencer, res same, student
Gill Ernest,* son Spencer, res same, student
Gill Henry,* lab, res 541 e Martin
Gill Martha,* wife Henry, res same, washerwoman
Gill Carrie,* d Henry, res same, student
Gill Arthur,* son Henry, res same, dining-room servant
Gill Eugene,* d Henry, res same, student
Gill Ernest, clk, rooms 327 e Hargett
Gill Katie,* house-servant, res 418 e Martin
Gill Sarah,* nurse, res 418 e Martin
Gill Henry,* blacksmith, res 321 s Bloodworth
Gilmore Austin,* painter, res 309 w South
Gilmore Adelaide,* wife Austin, house work

Gilmore John,* son Austin, res same, painter
Gilmore Minnie M,* d Austin, res same, house work
Gilmore Lizzie,* d Austin, res same, laundress
Gilyer John,* carp, bds 215 s Wilmington
Gilyer Eliza,* cook, wife John
Gladville Mrs Candace, wid, res 523 s Person
Glass George H, mgr Ral Telephone Exchange, res 527 Hillsboro'
Glass Mrs Geo H, res 527 Hillsboro'
Glass Riley, son Geo H, res same, student
Glen Miss Janet B, teacher in St Mary's School, res same
Glenn Frank M, printer, res 313 e Martin
Glenn Mrs Jennie, wife Frank M
Glenn Miss Mary, d Frank M, res same, student
Glenn Alonzo, painter, res n Blount, o s n
Glenn Mrs Annette, wife Alonzo
Glenn Ray, son Alonzo, res same, student
Glenn Miss Audry, d Alonzo, res same, student
Glenn Miss Lina, d Alonzo, res same, student
Glenn Mrs Bettie, mother of Alonzo, res same
Glenn Harlie, son Mrs Bettie, res same, clk
Glenn Annie,* nurse, res 802 Manly
Glenn Henry,* lab, res 802 Manly
Glennan Mrs Fannie, seamstress, res 119 w Morgan
Glennan John, son Mrs Fannie, res same
Glennan Fred, son Mrs Fannie, res same, wks Oak City Laundry
Glover B C, life ins agt, bds 321 e Lane
Gooch Alonzo, city hand, res 317 e Martin
Gooch Mrs Eliza, wid, res 327 w South
Gooch Chas H, son Mrs Eliza, res same, moulder
Gooch Miss Ida, d Mrs Eliza, res same, student
Gooch Miss Ella, d Mrs Eliza, res with M W Woodard
Gooch Mrs Nancy, res with L T Huddleston
Gooch Sallie,* cook, res 111 w Lenoir
Gooch Mary,* d Sallie, res same, house work
Gooch Ernest,* lab, res 111 w Lenoir
Gooch Fred,* son Sallie, res same, driver for Stevens & Son
Gooch W L, inmate Soldiers' Home
Goodwin Dr A W, physician and surgeon, office over Bobbitt's drug store, res 711 Hillsboro'
Goodwin Mrs Lovie C, wife Dr A W
Goodwin Loomis McA, son Dr A W, res same, student
Goodwin Miss Mildred H, d Dr A W, res same, student
Goodwin Mrs D, wid, mother Dr A W, res same
Goodwin Miss Ella, sister Dr A W, res same
Goodwin Mrs Martha E, wid, grocer, res 220 s East
Goodwin Miles, mgr for Royall & Borden, bds cor Newbern ave and Person
Goodwin Mrs Luta, wife Miles

Goodwin Geo T, inmate Soldiers' Home
Goodwin I M, inmate Soldiers' Home
Goodwin Frances,* laundress, res 320 w South
Goodwin Ned,* wood-sawyer, res 320 w South
Goodwin Wayland, grocer 534 Cannon, res same
Goodwin & Dupree, grocers, 534 Cannon
Goodwin Charles, motorman Ral Electric Co, bds 209 w Morgan
Goodwin Mrs Adeline, seamstress, res 416 w North
Godwin J B, blacksmith, res Fayetteville below R R
Godwin Mrs Cornelia E, wife J B
Godwin W H, son J B, res same
Godwin Frank, newspaper carrier, bds 203 n West
Good Lillie,* washerwoman, res 519 s Dawson
Goodloe Daniel R, newspaper correspondent, res with W G Randall, cor n Wilmington and Polk
Goeler Miss Lizzie, sister of Mrs A C Lehman, res same
Gorham Arthur L,* letter carrier, res 114 e Lenoir
Gorham Annie,* wife A L, seamstress
Gorham Edward,* son A L, res same, student
Gorham Beulah,* d A L, res same, student
Gorham Wesley,* son A L, res same, barber
Gorham Louise,* d A L, res same, student
Gorham Leah,* d A L, res same, student
Gorham Emma,* d A L, res same, student
Gorham Bessie,* d A L, res same, student
Gorham Addie,* d A L, res same, student
Gorman Mrs Mary E, dressmaker, res 226 e Cabarrus
Gorman Miss Effie, d Mrs Mary E, res same, wks Caraleigh cot mill
Gorman Miss Sadie O, d Mrs Mary E, res same, student
Gorman Miss May, d Mrs Mary E, res same
GORMAN MAXWELL J, proof-reader for Edwards & Broughton Printing and Publishing Co and correspondent of northern newspapers, res 408 n Person
Gorman James, painter, rooms 315 s McDowell
Goss Allen,* driver, res 303 s West
Goss Viney,* wife Allen, washerwoman
Goss Barbara,* d Allen, res same, student
Gower Wm A, butcher, res 515 s Harrington
Gower Mrs Ella L, wife W A, dressmaker
Grady E D, cot mill operator, res 538 w Peace
Grady Mrs Mary A, wife E D
Grady Miss Bettie F, d E D, res same
Grady Jno J, son E D, res same, wks Ral cot mill
Grady George, peddler, res 314 s East
Grady Mrs Alice, wife George, house work
Grady Tiller, lab, res 315 s Bloodworth
Grady Mrs Mary, wife Tiller
Grady Miss Willie, d Tiller, res same, student

Grady Chas, carp S A L shops, res 216 w Lane
Grady Mrs Mittie, wife Chas
Grady George, son Chas, res same, collector for G S Tucker & Co
Grandy Lottie,* washerwoman, res 556 Newbern ave
Grandy Mollie,* d Lottie, res same, cook
Grandy Cary,* son Lottie, res same, errand-boy
Grandy Nonie,* d Lottie, res same, servant
Grandy Hattie,* d Lottie, res same, cook for Chas Creighton
Grandy Willis, notary public, res 116 n Dawson
Graham Mack,* carp, res Martin, o s e
Graham Nancy,* wife Mack, washerwoman
Graham William,* son Mack, res same, driver
Graham Mary,* laundress, res 514 Smith
Graham Lillie,* d Mary, res same, student
Graham George,* lab, res 120 w South
Graham Sarah,* wife Geo, seamstress
Grant Lucy,* washerwoman, res 435 n Salisbury
Grant La Fayette, clk for L T Taylor, res same
Granville Cary,* dinner-carrier, res with Geo Montgomery
Graves Lena,* washerwoman, res 407 w Edenton
Graves Mollie,* d Lena, res same, washerwoman
Graves Josie,* d Lena, res same, washerwoman
Gray Eliza,* cook for J P Wyatt, res same
Gray Katie,* washerwoman, res Blount-st al
Gray Laura,* cook for Ed H Lee, res 224 e Cabarrus
Gray Mrs D H, wid, res cor Johnson and n Wilmington
GRAY ROBT T, lawyer, office 16 w Martin, res 530 n Blount
Gray Mrs Carrie, wife R T
Gray Robt L, son R T, res same, newspaper reporter
Gray Miss Lillie, d R T, res same, student
Gray Miss Carrie, d R T, res same, student
Gray Roxanna,* cook, res 302 w South
Gray Eva,* d Roxanna, res same, student
Greason H B, supt Ral cot mills, res cor Halifax and Franklin, o s n
Greason Mrs Catherine, wife H B
Greason Miss Annie, sister H B, res same
Greason Geo H, brother H B, res same, boss carder Ral cot mill
Gregory William,* gardener, res e Edenton
Gregory Leanna,* wife Wm, cook for Dr V E Turner
Green Monroe,* lab, res Townes' al
Green Allie,* cook for Miss Jennie Miller, res Townes' al
Green Tom,* lab, res 3 Stronach ave
Green Kate,* wife Tom, washerwoman
Green Miss Emma, res 308 w Jones
Green Miss Martha, res 308 w Jones
Green James, clk W B Mann, rooms 308 w Jones
Green Susan,* cook, res e Lane

Green Henry, conductor S A L R R, bds 10 e North
Green Austin,* blacksmith, res 508 s East
Green Fannie,* wife Austin, laundress
Green Thunia,* house work, res 326 s East
Green Mary,* nurse for Dr T E Skinner, res 522 e Martin
Green Sylvester,* nurse for E C Smith, res 522 e Martin
Green Archie,* hostler, res 547 e Davie
Green Emma,* wife Archie
Green Lucy,* gen house work, res 547 e Davie
Green Emma,* student, res 547 e Davie
Green Ellen,* washerwoman, res 620 Elm
Green A H, farmer, res 562 e Lenoir
Green Mrs Nannie W, wife A H
Green Wm W, son A H, res same, guano inspector
Green Oscar D, son A H, res same, farmer
Green Maurice M, son A H, res same
Green Miss Mary C, d A H, res same, student
Green Miss Nina W, d A H, res same, student
Green Miss Daisy, d A H, res same, student
Green A H Jr, son A H, res same, student
Green Emma,* washerwoman, res 517 s Dawson
Green Chas,* lab, res 405 s Dawson
Green Furney,* blacksmith, res Caswell lane
Green Austin,* blacksmith, s McDowell, res 508 s East
Green Mira,* house work, res Caswell lane
Green Walter,* lab, res Caswell lane
Green Abbie,* dining-room servant, res 711 s East
Green Frederick,* son Abbie, res same, student
Green George,* son Abbie, res same, student
Green Logan,* night watchman, res 616 s McDowell
Green Mattie,* wife Logan, house work
Green William,* lab, res 517 Cannon
Green Mary,* wife Wm, washerwoman
Green Gertrude,* d Wm, res same
Green Miss Victoria R, res 116 n East
Green Miss Sallie J, sister of Miss Victoria R, res same
Green Miss Lucy F, sister of Miss Victoria R, res same
Green John, brother of Miss Victoria R, res same
Green William,* drayman, res 12 w North
Green Minna,* wife Wm, washerwoman
Grey J S, broker, 120 Fayetteville, bds 108 Fayetteville
Grice Jesse, wks Ral cot mill, res 508 n West
Grice Mrs Zaley, wife Jesse
Grice Richard, son Jesse, res same, wks Ral cot mill
Grice Miss Maud, d Jesse, res same, wks Ral cot mill
Grice Claude, son Jesse, res same, wks Ral cot mill
Grice Wiley, son Jesse, res same, wks Ral cot mill
Grice Frank, son Jesse, res same, wks Ral cot mill

Griffis Penny,* cook for Dr T D Hogg, res on lot
Griffis Paschall, clk for R E Parham, res 307 e Martin
Griffis Mrs Mary, wife Paschall
Griffis Thomas, brother of Paschall, res same
Griffis Elizabeth,* boarding-house, 108 e Hargett
Griffith John,* lab, res 114 n West
Griffith Belle,* wife John, washerwoman
Grimes Mrs Elizabeth, wid, res cor Halifax and Lane
Grimes William H, son Mrs Elizabeth, res same, planter
Grimes Mrs Bettie, wife Wm H
Grimes Miss Nellie, d Mrs Elizabeth, res same
Grimes Jno G B, accountant, res 514 Fayetteville
Grimes Mrs Helen M, wife J G B
Groves Austin,* porter for Jno S Pescud, res Cotton lane, o s e
Groves Margaret,* wife Austin, washerwoman
Groves Annie,* d Austin, r same, student
Groves Belle,* d Austin, res same, student
Grissom Mrs L T, wid, res 404 w North
Gruendler Mrs E V, dressmaker, 314 s Blount
Gruendler Norman, son Mrs E V, res same, printer
Gruendler Leonard, son Mrs E V, res same
Gruendler Miss Myrtle, d Mrs E V, res same
Guess Philip,* lab, res 516 w South
Guess Lucy,* wife Philip, house work
Guess Willie,* son Philip, res same, student
Guess Joseph,* son Philip, res same, student
Gulley Jos P, trav salesman, res 425 s Wilmington
Gulley Mrs Repsie, wife Jos P
Gulley Miss Bernice, d Jos P, res same
Gulley Miss Garnett, d Jos P, res same
Gulley Miss Josephine, d Jos P, res same, student
Gulley Miss Repsie, d Jos P, res same, student
Gulley Jos P Jr, son Jos P, res same, student
Gulley Miss Melta, d Jos P, res same, student
Gulley Allen,* lab, res 15 Fowle
Gulley Kate,* wife Allen, washerwoman
Gulley Clarissa,* washerwoman, res 520 s Dawson
Gunter Laura B,* cook for B S Jerman, res on lot
Gunter Berry,* barber, bds 314 n Dawson
Gunter Eli,* gardener, res Idlewild
Gunter Rose,* wife Eli, washerwoman
Gunter Joe,* son Eli, res same, wks for W R Crawford
Gunter James,* son Eli, res same, student
Gunter Maggie,* nurse for Jas A Moseley, res same
Gunter George,* r r hand, res 126 Yearby's lane
Gunter Sylvia,* wife Geo, washerwoman
Gunter Gertrude,* d Geo, washerwoman
Gunter Thos,* son Geo, res same, student

Gunter Candace,* d Geo, res same, student
Gunter Nelson,* fireman S A L, res Yearby's lane
Gunter Ellen,* wife Nelson
Guy Sarah,* seamstress, res 609 e Cabarrus

HABEL Fred W, salesman for A D Royster & Bro, res 327 w Jones
Habel Mrs Hattie, wife F W
Habel Miss Mary, d F W, res same
Habel Mrs J G, wid mother of F W, res same
Habel Mrs W A, wid of Henry, res with F W Habel
Habel Wm H, son Mrs W A, res same, student
Hackney David,* lab, res 916 Manly
Hackney Jane,* wife David, washerwoman
Hackney Mary J,* d David, res same, cook
Hackney Dilly,* d David, res same, washerwoman
Hackney Charles,* son David, res same, lab
Hackney Cary,* son David, res same, student
Hackney William,* son David, res same, lab
Hackney Jane,* washerwoman, res 330 Cannon
Hackney R H,* letter-carrier, res 736 Fayetteville
Hackney Ella,* wife R H, teacher
Hailey Ed T, clk for N Deboy, res 228 s Swain
Hailey Mrs Sarah, wife Ed T
Hailey Robert, wks Peter Stumpf Beer Wks, res 224 s Swain
Hailey Miss Susan, chamber-maid at Central Hotel, res same
Hailey Moses, porter for Jacob Schwartz, res same
Haithcock Jesse, inmate Soldiers' Home
Hale Miss Mabel, teacher at Centennial Graded School, bds 103 s McDowell
Hales Thomas, grocer, Martin, res 747 Fayetteville
Hales Mrs Kate, wife Thomas
Hales Miss Julia, d Thomas, res same, student
Hales Miss Pattie, d Thomas, res same, student
Hales Hartwell, son Thomas, res same, student
Hales Williard, son Thomas, res same
Hall E T, clk at Berwanger Bros, res 412 Fayetteville
Hall Mrs M T, wife E T
Hall E T Jr, son E T, res same
Hall Wm H, salesman, res 412 Fayetteville
Hall Sam,* porter at Chas Bretsch's, rooms 405 s Dawson
Hall Dicey,* washerwoman, res 760 Fayetteville
Hall Thomas,* lab S A L R R, res o s e
Hall Virginia,* wife Thos, washerwoman
Hall Sherwood,* son Thos, res same, lab
Hall Effie,* d Thos, res same, washerwoman
Hall Caroline,* washerwoman, res 14 Matthews' lane

Hall Robert,* son Caroline, res same, wks city market
Hall Ben,* son Caroline, res same, wks for C D Arthur
Hall Della,* house-servant, res 24 McKee
Hall William,* lab, res 24 McKee
Hall Isaac,* lab, res 24 McKee
Hall Mollie,* sick-nurse, res 802 s Blount
Hall Virtruvins,* brick-mason, bds 215 Bledsoe ave
Hall Lewis,* carp, res 221 Bledsoe ave
Hall Sarah,* wife Lewis
Hall Eddie,* son Lewis, res same, student
Hall James,* son Lewis, res same, student
Hall Luke,* driver for Wyatt & Co, res 511 n Salisbury
Hall Mollie,* wife Luke, dressmaker
Hall Isaac,* carp, res 318 s Blount
Hall Bedie,* wife Isaac, washerwoman
Hall William,* son Isaac, res same, farm hand
Hall Laura,* d Isaac, res same, washerwoman
Hall John,* son Isaac, res same, laborer
Hall Eddie,* son Isaac, res same, servant
Hall Sarah A,* servant, res 8 s Harrington
Hall Eddie,* son Sarah A, res same, student
Hall Lottie,* washerwoman, res rear 219 s Person
Hall Patience,* house-servant, res 417 s East
Hall Thomas,* hackman, res 582 e Cabarrus
Hall Lena,* wife Thomas, cook
Hall Jerry,* son Thomas, res same, student
Hall Isaac,* brick-mason, res 210 w South
Hall Abbie,* wife Isaac, house work
Hall Carrie,* student, res 117 w Lenoir
Hall Robert,* lab, res 334 w South
Hall Zora,* wife Robt, washerwoman
Hall George,* son Robt, res same, hostler
Hall Walter,* son Robt, res same, lab
Hall John,* student, res 516 s McDowell
Hall Isaac,* house-servant, res 419 s McDowell
Hall Malinda,* wife Isaac, washerwoman
Hall Eggie,* d Isaac, washerwoman
Hamill & Hunnicutt, brick and stone contractors, s Salisbury
Hamill H J (Hamill & Hunnicutt), brick and stone contractor, res 559 e Martin
Hamill Mrs M C, wife H J
Hamilton William, city hand, res 111 e South
Hamilton Frances, wife Wm
Hamilton Oscar, son Wm, res same, wks Caraleigh mill
Hamilton Miss Sadie, d Wm, res same, student
Hamilton D S, boiler inspector, res 225 w Martin
Hamilton Mrs Ella J, wife D S
Hamilton Wesley, inmate Soldiers' Home

Hamilton Robert, drug clerk, bds 326 Newbern ave
Hamilton Wesley, lab, res Cannon
Hamlet James, weaver Caraleigh cot mills, bds 739 Fayetteville
Hamlet J T, trav salesmen, res 119 s Blount
Hamlet Mrs Annie P, wife J T
Hamlet Roland, son J T, res same, student
Hamlet Reginald, son J T, res same, student
Hamlet Roy, son J T, res same, student
Hamlet John, son J T, res same, student
Hamlin Jas E & Co,* saloon, 205 s Wilmington
Hamlin Jas E,* saloon, res 15 w North
Hamlin Annie,* wife Jas E, teacher
Hampton Mrs J S, wid, res 109 n Salisbury
Hampton John S, son Mrs J S, res same, printer
Hampton Clarence, son Mrs J S, res same, printer
Hampton Algenon, son Mrs J S, res same, clk for Jones & Powell
Hampton Miss Maggie, d Mrs J S, res same, student
Hampton Miss Lillie, d Mrs J S, res same, student
Hampton Miss Katie, d Mrs J S, res same, student
Hampton Sophia,* waiter for Jno S Pescud, res 402 s Blount
Hancock J R, inmate Soldiers' Home
Hanff Alexander, clk for J M Monie, res 235 n Saunders
Hanff Mrs Della, wife Alex
Hanff Samuel M, son Alex, res same, student
Hanff Mrs Mary, d Alex, res same, student
Hanks Geo L, supt Virginia Life Ins Co, office over Citizens National Bank, res e North
Hanks Mrs Nannie, wife Geo L
Hanks W H, machinist S A L, bds 427 Halifax
Hannah Jas W, driver ice wagon, res 122 w Cabarrus
Hannah Mrs Mary E, wife Jas W
Hanner Jesse,* bridge builder, bds 611 s Harrington
Hanner Pressley, hostler, res 526 e Davie
Hanner Mrs Edith, wife Pressley
Hansom Joseph,* lab, res 322 Cannon
Hanson James,* blacksmith, res s Swain
Hardie P C, turnkey city station-house, res 126½ Fayetteville
Hardie Mrs M A, wife P C
Hardie Miss Maggie, d P C, res same, student
Hardie Jas I, son P C, res same, student
Hardie Ellen,* servant at Peace Institute, res 620 Harp's lane, o s n
Hardie Lula,* washerwoman, res 618 Harp's lane, o s n
Hardie Booker,* whitewasher and plasterer, res 410 e Martin
Hardie Mary,* wife Booker, washerwoman
Hardie John,* lab, res rear Manly
Hardie Sarah,* wife John, washerwoman
Hardie Mary,* washerwoman, res 124 w Lenoir
Hardie Booker,* whitewasher, 110 e Hargett

Hardie Mrs Jemima, wid, seamstress, res 224 w Cabarrus
Hardie Harry, son Mrs Jemima, res same, clk for A V Emery
Hardie Miss Rena, d Mrs Jemima, res same, student
Hardie Miss Rosa, seamstress, res 222 w Cabarrus
Hardin J W Jr, bkkpr Nat Bank of Ral, res same
Harding Walter, eng S A L, res cor Bloodworth and Oakdale ave, o s n
Harding Mrs Laura, wife Walter
Harding Miss Ruby, d Walter, res same, student
Harding Israel, son Walter, res same, student
Harding B R, railroader, res 526 n Blount
Harding Mrs Kate, wife B R
Harding Miss Henrietta, d B R, res same
Harding Fred, son B R, res same, machinist
Hardy H B, trav agt for News and Observer, res 118 Halifax
Hardy Mrs Claudia K, wife H B
Hardy H B Jr, son H B, res same, student
Hardy Miss Mary M, d H B, res same, student
Hardy T F, son H B, res same, student
Hardy Mrs J E, wid, mother H B, res same
Hargrove Mann,* driver for Dr J W McGee Jr
Hargrove Lula,* cook, res 408 w Jones
Hargrove Mary,* cook for Albert Johnson, res on lot
Harilee Mrs Elizabeth, music teacher at Blind Institution, res same
Harp Edna,* cook for S F Mordecai, res 620 Elm
Harper Jacob J, carp, res 317 Polk
Harper Mrs Susan, wife Jacob J
Harper James H, carp, res 317 Polk
Harper Mrs Lizzie, wife Jas H
Harper Miss Willie, d Jas H, res same
Harrell E G, mgr N C Book Co, res 220 s Dawson
Harrell John, son E G, res same, clk in N C Book Co store
Harrington Henry, locomotive eng S A L R R, bds Exchange Hotel
Harris Bettie,* cook for R E Lumsden, res 225 e Lane
Harris Miss Lucy, seamstress, res 413 w South
Harris J W, attendant at Insane Asylum, res same
Harris Abram,* gardener, res Newbern ave, o s e
Harris James M, city weigher, res 426 s Wilmington
Harris Mrs Annie E, wife James M, boarding-house
Harris J Hubert, son James M, res same
Harris Miss Beulah M, d James M, res same
Harris John,* hostler, res 35 Hunter
Harris Mary,* wife John, cook
Harris Annie,* d John, res same, student
Harris W T, inmate Soldiers' Home
Harris Jesse, inmate Soldiers' Home

Harris J T, inmate Soldiers' Home
Harris Badger,* lab, res 743 Manly
Harris Mary,* nurse for V C Royster, res 326 w Edenton
Harris Fannie,* washerwoman, res 420 n Wilmington
Harris Harriet,* washerwoman, res 116 w Peace
Harris Lucinda,* washerwoman, res 116 w Peace
Harris William,* lab, res Yearby's lane
Harris Nannie,* wife Wm, washerwoman
Harris & Hill, saloon, 227 s Wilmington
Harris Lizzie,* cook for Madame E Besson, res same
Harris Sol, saloon, 207 s Wilmington, res o s w
Harris Miss Ella, seamstress, bds 211 Smithfield
Harris Emeline,* servant, 324 w Morgan
Harris Sherdman,* driver for C E Johnson, res 740 s Person
Harris Mary,* wife Sherdman, washerwoman
Harris Thomas,* son Sherdman, res same, student
Harris Silvia,* cook for C O Ball, room 740 s Person
Harris George,* bro Sherdman, res same student
Harris George,* brick-mason, res 114 w Cabarrus
Harris C R, clerk, res 308 Smithfield
Harris Mrs Fannie, wife C R
Harris Feribee,* washerwoman, res Bledsoe ave
Harris Julia,* washerwoman, res 224 Blount-st al
Harris Nat,* brakeman S A L R R, res 215 w North
Harris Rachel,* wife Nat, washerwoman
Harris Bessie,* cook for James Lyons, res same
Harris Jos, fish dealer, res Prairie bldg
Harris Mrs Bettie, wife Jos, wks in cot mill
Harris Miss Lillie, d Jos, res same
Harris Walter,* horseshoer and repairer, s Wilmington, near Central Hotel, res 218 s East
Harris Margaret,* wife Walter
Harris Bessie,* d Walter, res same, student
Harris Mary,* d Walter, res same, student
Harris Walter Jr,* son Walter, res same, student
Harris Nancy,* cook, room up-stairs 116 e Morgan
Harris Thos,* son Nancy, res same, lab
Harris D W C, dyer, res 310 s Bloodworth
Harris Mrs Henrietta, wife D W C
Harris Miss Blanche P, d D W C, res same, student
Harris Miss Ruby E, d D W C, res same, student
Harris Mrs Ella, wid, dressmaker, res 224 e Davie
Harris Miss Julia, d Mrs Ella, res same, student
Harris Thomas, son Mrs Ella, res same, student
Harris Irvin, son Mrs Ella, res same, student
Harris Bettie,* seamstress, res 409 s Blount
Harris David H,* son Bettie, res same, wks in restaurant
Harris J J, saloon and grocer, 210 s Wilmington, res 415 s Person

Harris Mrs Dora E, wife J J
Harris James C, son J J, res same, student
Harris Arthur G, son J J, res same
Harris Wm S, farmer, res 222 e Martin
Harris Mrs Mary A, wife Wm S, boarding-house
Harris John J W, eng Southern Rwy, res w Lane
Harris Mrs Berta, wife Jno J W
Harris Miss Sallie, d Jno J W, res same
Harris William, bkkpr at Whiting Bros, bds Jno J W Harris
Harris T C, engraver, res 14 n Saunders
Harris Mrs Anna, wife T C
Harris Stanford, son T C, res same, student
Harris Miss Martha, d T C, res same, student
Harris Miss Nannie, d T C, res same, student
Harris J C L, lawyer, office in Frap's bldg, res 213 e Hargett
Harris Mrs Florence U, wife J C L
Harris J C L Jr, son J C L, res same, wks Ral Elec Co
Harris Ceburn D, son J C L, res same, student
Harris Miss Margaret B, d J C L, res same, student
Harris Chas W, son J C L, res same, student
Harris Gordon, son J C L, res same, student
Harris Wm C, son J C L, res same, student
Harris Winder R, son J C L, res same, student
Harris W N, grocer, 606 e Davie, res same
Harris Mrs Arthelia, wife W N
Harris Miss Ida, d W N, res same, seamstress
Harris W E, son W N, res same, blacksmith
Harris Lizzie,* cook, res 523 e Davie
Harris Clarissa,* washerwoman, 521 e Davie
Harris Bettie,* cook, res 535 e Davie
Harris James,* son Bettie, res same, hackman
Harris Roberta,* d Bettie, res same, nurse
Harris Henrietta,* washerwoman, res 309 s Bloodworth
Harris Lillie,* d Henrietta, res same, cook
Harris Della,* d Henrietta, res same, cook
Harris Ferdinand,* son Henrietta, res same, porter for Levine & Brown
Harris Walter,* son Henrietta, res same, tobacco stemmer
Harris James,* son Henrietta, res same, student
Harris M F, chief clk to Wm Moncure, res 319 Polk
Harris Mrs Lillie N, wife M F
Harris Miss Eugenia M, d M F, res same, student
Harris Frederick, son M F, res same, student
Harris Scott, son M F, res same, student
Harris Lucy A,* house-servant, res 319 Cannon
Harris Miss Bessie, seamstress, res 114 w South
Harris Helen,* washerwoman, res rear 517 s Dawson
Harris E L, merchandise broker, office with Jones & Powell, bds J R Barkley

Harris Mrs Emma S, wife E L
Harris Miss Gladdys B, d E L, res same
Harris Clarissa,* washerwoman, res 127 n Harrington
Harrison Charles,* painter, res 402 w North
Harrison Helen * wife Charles
Harrison Mrs Lottie S, matron Blind Institution, res same
Harrison & Thornton,* painters, 16 s Salisbury
Harrison Mrs E M, proprietress Harrison House, 104 e Davie
Harrison Miss Lula E, d Mrs E M, res same
Harrison James A, son Mrs E M, res same
Harrison James W, mechanic, bds 408 n East
Harrison Annie,* washerwoman, res 425 s East
Harrison Maria,* nurse for Mrs Chas McKemmon, res on lot
Harrison Charles G, student, lives with Rev Dr I McK Pittenger
Harrison Jno L,* upholsterer, res 513 s Person
Harrison Elizabeth,* wife Jno L
Harrison Jno L Jr,* son Jno L, res same, upholsterer
Harrison Miss Geneva, lives with Mrs R W Smith
Harrison Robt,* trucker, res 409 Hillsboro'
Harrison Annie,* wife Robt, cook
Harrison Hattie B,* d Robt, res same, student
Harrison Wilber,* son Robt, res same, student
Harrison Mrs Rebecca, wid, res 538 e Jones
Harrison Miss Ethel, d Mrs Rebecca, res same, cash-girl at W H & R S Tucker & Co
Harrison Miss Lucy, d Mrs Rebecca, res same, cash-girl at W H & R S Tucker & Co
Harrison Robt, son Mrs Rebecca, r same, wks Law-Book Exchange
Hart John, inmate Soldiers' Home
Hart Chas B (Julius Lewis Hardware Co), hardware merchant, res 409 Oakwood ave
Hart C A, father of Chas B, res same
Hart Mrs A J, wife C A, res same
Hartsfield Wm A, watchmaker, res Oakdale ave, o s n
Hartsfield Mrs Rilla, wife Wm A
Hartsfield Nellie,* nurse at W P Whitaker, res same
Hartsfield Henry,* driver, res 813 Manly
Hartsfield Gracie,* wife Henry, house work
Hartsfield Edward,* barber, res 207 w South
Hartsfield Henry,* blacksmith, res 536 e Lenoir
Hartsfield Mary,* wife Henry, washerwoman
Hartsfield George,* son Henry, res same, janitor Gov guard armory
Hartsfield Etta,* d Henry, res same, house-servant
Hartsfield Thomas,* son Henry, res same, student
Hartsfield Lewis,* son Henry, res same, student
Harvey William, turpentine worker, res 528 e Lenoir
Harvey Mrs Silvia, wife Wm
Harvey Miss Winnie, d Wm, res same, bkpr

Harvey Jno H, son Wm, res same, student
Harward John,* porter, res 833 Fayetteville
Harward Mrs A M, wid, res 208 Newbern ave
Harward Miss Annie, d Mrs A M, res same
Harward Miss Addie, d Mrs A M, res same, stenographer and typewriter at Ætna Life Ins office
Harward James, son Mrs A M, res same, student
Hatcher John,* carp, res Martin, o s e
Hatcher Emma,* wife John, laundress
Hatcher Janet,* d John, res same, student
Hatchet Parthenia, house-servant, res 116 e Morgan
Hatch F A, machinist S A L shops, res 11 w Peace
Hatch Mrs F C, wife F A
Hatch Miss Mary, seamstress, res 109 s Blount
Hatch Miss Susan, seamstress, res 109 s Blount
Hatton W B, carp S A L, res 600 n Salisbury
Hatton Mrs V F, wife W B
Hauck Miss Myrtle, student, res with A G Atwood
Haughton Mrs M A, wid, res 111 s Bloodworth
Haughton Miss Pearl, d Mrs M A, res same, student
Hawkins Annie, housekeeper for Chas N Hunter, res same
Hawkins Lethia,* house-servant for Wm H Grimes, res on lot
Hawkins Colin M, pres N C Phosphate Co, office cor Fayetteville and e Davie, res 210 n Wilmington
Hawkins Mrs Janet, wife Colin M
Hawkins G W,* brick-maker, res 501 e Cabarrus
Hawkins Annie J,* wife G W, house work
Hawkins George,* son G W, res same, student
Hawkins Illinois,* d G W, res same, student
Hawkins Samella C,* d G W, res same, house work
Hawkins James,* brick-moulder, res 501 e Cabarrus
Hawkins Benzina,* house-servant, res 501 e Cabarrus
Hawkins James,* servant at F H Busbee's, res on lot
Hawkins Tamer,* cook, res 425 s McDowell
Hawkins Harry,* grocer, res 339 w South
Hawkins Eliza,* wife Harry, washerwoman
Hawkins Miss Jane A, aunt of Col A B Andrews, res same
Hawkins Dr A B, planter, res cor Blount and North
Hawkins Sallie,* asst matron in colored D D & B Inst, res same
Hawkins Creasy,* house-servant for A B Andrews, res on lot
Hawkins Fanny,* cook for A B Andrews, res on lot
Hawkins James,* driver for Insane Asylum, res 512 w South
Hawkins Danie,* wife James, washerwoman
Hawkins Louisa,* d James, res same, student
Hawkins Ella,* nurse, res 712 Fayetteville
Hawkins Lee,* lab, res 210 Cannon
Hawkins Frances J,* wife Lee, house work
Hawkins Siles,* driver for Dr W I Royster, res 210 Cannon

Hawkins Geo,* lab, res 210 Cannon
Hawkins Rebecca,* d Lee, res same, nurse
Hawkins Lee Jr,* son Lee, res same, student
Hawkins Syla,* dish-washer, res 124 w Davie
Hawkins Willie,* lab, res 124 w Davie
Hawkins Mamie D,* washerwoman, res 425 s McDowell
Hawkins Tamer,* student, res 425 s McDowell
Hawkins Minerva,* student, res 425 s McDowell
Hawkins Stephen Jr,* wks S A L R R, res Tarboro rd, o s e
Hawkins Helen,* wife Stephen, washerwoman
Hawkins Tom,* fireman S A L, bds 435 n Salisbury
Hawkins Pattie,* washerwoman, res 525 e Edenton
Hawkins John,* lab, res e Lenoir
Hawkins Maggie,* wife John, washerwoman
Hawkins Stephen,* hostler, res 557 e Edenton
Hawkins Grace,* wife Stephen, washerwoman
Hay Thos T, life ins agt, office in Fisher bldg, res 705 Hillsboro'
Hay Mrs Isabella G, wife Thos T
Hay Miss Mary S, d Thos T, res same, student
Hay Miss Belle, d Thos T, res same, student
HAY T T & BRO, fire ins agts, office in Citizens Nat Bk bldg
Hay O P, merchandise broker, 216½ Fayetteville
Hay Dr T T, retired physician, res Hillsboro' rd, o s w
Hay W D, ins agt, res Hillsboro road, o s w
Hay Miss M E, d Dr T T, res same
Hay Miss Rosalie, d Dr T T, res same
Hay Albert, ins agt, res Hillsboro' rd, o s w
Hay O P, merchandise broker, res Hillsboro' rd, o s w
Hayes Hader,* cook for Mrs A S Merrimon, res on lot
Hayes Austin C,* brick-mason, res 523 Smith
Hayes Bettie,* wife Austin C
Hayes Charlie,* son A C, res same, student
Hayes Thomas,* porter Branson House, res 4 Dodd
Hayes Winnie,* wife Thos, washerwoman
Hayes Lewis,* wks Mills Mfg Co, res 4 Dodd
Hayes Edward,* son Thomas, res same, student
Hayes James T,* son Thomas, res same, student
Hayes Rosianna,* mother Thomas, res same
Hayes W B, silversmith, wks for E Fasnach, bds 108 Fayetteville
Hayes Edward,* lab, res 20 Railroad
Hayes Jennie,* wife Ed, washerwoman
Hayes Maj E M, U S army officer, bds Yarboro' House
Hayes Mrs Emma, wife Maj E M
Hayes John,* lab, res 540 e Cabarrus
Hayes Charlotte,* wife John, washerwoman
Hayes John,* porter for Ed V Denton, res old Fair Ground, o s e
Hayes Hattie,* wife John, washerwoman
Hayes Mrs S G, bds 250 Peace

HAYES J J, gen agt Staunton Life Ins Co, office over James I Johnson's drug store, res 514 Hillsboro'
Hayes Mrs Alice, wife J J
Hayes J H,* grocer, Hargett, o s e, res same
Hayes Washington,* brick-mason, res Hargett, o s e
Hayes Nancy,* wife Washington, washerwoman
Hayes Mary,* d Washington, res same, student
Hayes Glasgow,* son Washington, res same, student
Hayes Violet,* d Washington, res same, student
Hayes Jacob,* son Washington, res same, student
Hayes Samuel,* carp, res e Hargett, o s e
Hayes Lavinia,* wife Samuel, washerwoman
Hayes William,* son Samuel, res same, student
Hayes Minnie,* d Samuel, res same, student
Hayes Maggie,* d Samuel, res same, student
Hayes Samuel Jr,* son Samuel, res same, student
Hayes Clarissa,* d Samuel, res same, cook for N B Broughton
Hayes Mrs Bettie, wid, res 209 Smithfield
Hayes Miss Cora, d Mrs Bettie, res same, seamstress
Hayes John H, son Mrs Bettie, res same
Hayes Miss Belle, d Mrs Bettie, res same, student
Hayes Miss Mary, d Mrs Bettie, res same, student
Hayes James, son Mrs Bettie, res same, student
Hayes Richard Jr,* musician, res 822 s Blount
Hayes Mollie,* wife Richard Jr, house work
Hayes Richard Sr,* carp, res 822 s Blount
Hayes Eliza,* wife Richard Sr
Hayes Geo,* son Richard Sr, res same, carp
Hayes Thomas,* son Richard Sr, res same, brick-mason
Hayes Alexander,* son Richard Sr, res same, lab
Hayes Joseph,* son Richard Sr, res same, lab
Haynes Mrs S A, wid, res 567 Newbern ave
Haynes A H, son Mrs S A, res same, policeman
Haynes Miss Sadie T, g d Mrs S A, res same
Haynes Mont R, cabinet-maker, shop 106 s Blount, r 218 s Blount
Haynes Mrs Sallie M, wife Mont R
Haynes Miss Susie May, d Mont R, res same, student
Haynes Miss Emma I, d Mont R, res same
Haynes Mrs Mary L, dressmaker, res 619 s Blount
Haynes Florizell, son Mrs Mary L, res same, tel opr
Haynes Miss Claudia, d Mrs Mary L, res same, student
Haynes Merrill, son Mrs Mary L, res same, student
Haynes Miss Florence, d Mrs Mary L, res same, student
Haynes Charles, son Mrs Mary L, res same
Haynes M L, clerical work, res 604 Elm
Haynes Mrs Isa, wife M L, dressmaker
Haynes Miss Dessie, d M L, res same
Haynes Miss Mamie, d M L, res same

Haynes Miss Ethel, d M L, res same, student
Haynes Carl, son M L, res same, student
Haywood Braswell,* waiter, room 229 Blount-st al
Haywood Dr Fab J, physician and surgeon, office and res 126 Halifax
Haywood Mrs Nannie G, wife Dr Fab J
Haywood Fab J Jr, son Dr Fab J, res same, student
Haywood W G, son Dr Fab J, res same, student
Haywood Mrs Martha, wid, mother Dr Fab J, res same
Haywood Adaline,* washerwoman, res e Hargett, o s e
Haywood William,* stone-mason, res Hargett, o s e
Haywood Annie,* d William, res same
Haywood Willis,* house-servant Thos H Briggs, res same
Haywood F P Sr, res with Mrs R C Badger
Haywood Frank P Jr, bkkpr Citizens National Bank, bds 103 s McDowell
Haywood Mary,* house-servant, res 829 Fayetteville
Haywood Miss Mary, res cor Johnson and n Wilmington
Haywood Miss Martha, sister to Miss Mary, res same
Haywood Miss Margaret C, sister to Miss Mary, res same
Haywood William,* carp, res 324 w Edenton
Haywood Jennie,* wife Wm, cook for Jesse Jones
Haywood Miss Martha, res with Wm M Boylan Sr
Haywood Miss Katherine, res with Wm M Boylan Sr
Haywood Miss Elsie, student, res with Wm M Boylan Sr
Haywood Miss Elizabeth G, res with E S Trapier
Haywood Miss Sallie B, res 110 Newbern ave
Haywood Miss Lucinda, sister of Mrs Sallie B, res same
Haywood Mrs R B, wid, res 127 e Edenton
Haywood Sherwood, son Mrs R B, res same, lawyer
Haywood Graham, son Mrs R B, r same, clk J Lewis Hardware Co
Haywood Marshall DeLancey, son Mrs R B, res same, secretary to Attorney-General
Haywood Miss Eleanor H, d Mrs R B, res same
Haywood Miss Miriam T, d Mrs R B, res same
Haywood Miss Maria T, res 127 e Edenton

T. T. HAY & BRO.,
FIRE INSURANCE AGENCY,

Largest American and English
Companies represented.

Office over Citizens National Bank, Fayetteville Street,
RALEIGH, N. C.

Haywood Dr Hubert, physician and surgeon, res 218 Newbern ave, office same
Haywood Mrs Emily, wife Dr Hubert
Haywood Edward, son Dr Hubert, res same, student
Haywood Miss Lucy, d Dr Hubert, res same, student
Haywood Miss Emmie, d Dr Hubert, res same, student
Haywood Mrs Lucy A, wid, res cor Newbern ave and Blount
HAYWOOD ERNEST, lawyer, office over Jas I Johnson's drug store, res cor Newbern ave and Blount
Haywood Edgar (A Williams & Co), merchant, res cor Newbern ave and Blount
Haywood Jno D, son Mrs Lucy A, res same, cotton buyer
Haywood Budley,* lab, res 321 s East
Haywood Annie,* wife Budley, cook
Haywood Henry,* lab, res 541 e Martin
Haywood Primus,* drayman, res 13 Hayti
Haywood Charlotte,* wife Primus, house work
Haywood Elnora,* d Primus, res same, house work
Haywood Ernest,* son Primus, res same, lab
Haywood Dock,* porter for T H Briggs & Sons, res 402 Cannon
Haywood Lizzie,* wife Dock, washerwoman
Haywood Mary,* music teacher, res 117 w Lenoir
Haywood Nancy,* washerwoman, res 13 w Worth
Haywood Lovina,* music teacher, res 13 w Worth
Haywood Rufus H,* orchestra leader, res 13 w Worth
Haywood Geo W,* musician, res 13 w Worth
Haywood Jno C,* musician, res 13 w Worth
Haywood Lewis,* janitor, res 128 w Lenoir
Haywood Eugenia,* wife Lewis, house work
Haywood Lewis Jr,* son Lewis, res same, porter at E V Denton
Haywood Effie,* d Lewis, res same, student
Haywood Eugene,* son Lewis, res same, student
Haywood Gertrude,* d Lewis, res same, student
Haywood Lovie,* washerwoman, res s Harrington
Haywood Chick,* lab, res rear 525 s Dawson
Haywood Mary,* servant, res o s e
Haywood W C,* shoemaker, res Smith
Haywood Ida,* wife W C, laundress
Haywood Anty A,* d W C, res same, student
Haywood Lucius,* son W C, res same, student
Haywood Mary,* washerwoman, res 117 n Swain
Haywood Phil,* son Mary, res same, porter N C Home Ins office
Haywood Delia,* d Mary, res same, washerwoman
Haywood Robert,* son Mary, res same, student
Haywood W C,* shoemaker, 407 Hillsboro'
HEARTT CHAS D, chief of police, office in City Hall, res 128 s Dawson
Heartt Mrs Isabella, wife Chas D

Heartt Miss Fannie E, d Chas D, res same
Heartt Thomas B, son C D, res same, clk for A B Andrews
Heartt Miss Nelia, d Chas D, res same
Heartt Dennis, son Chas D, res same, clk for Jas I Johnson
Heartt Miss Belle C, d Chas D, res same, student
Heartt Miss Elise B, d Chas D, res same, student
Heartt Miss Blanche, d Chas D, res same, student
Heck Mrs J M, wid, res cor n Blount and North
Heck Miss Fannie, d Mrs J M, res same
Heck Miss Susie, d Mrs J M, res same
Heck Miss Pearl, d Mrs J M, res same, student
Heck Charlie, son Mrs J M, res same, student
Heck Wm H, son Mrs J M, res same, student
Hedgepeth Delia,* clothes dyer, res 324 w Edenton
Hedgewood Miss Sarah, hkpr for W L Riddle, res same
Heflin R L, boarding-house, 309 w Martin
Heflin Mrs Flora, wife R L
Heflin Miss Kate, d R L, res same
Heflin Hugh, son R L, res same
Heflin Miss Hallie, d R L, res same
Hege Frank E, mgr of Poultry Division of Experiment Station, res Hillsboro' rd, o s w
Hege Mrs Minnie G, wife F E
Hege Miss Ethel L, d F E, res same
Heileg H J, eng S A L, res n Salisbury, o s n
Heileg Mrs Mary E, wife H J
Heilig K, general merchandise, 309 s Wilmington
Heller Julius, merchant, bds Germania House
Heller Bros, shoes, 134 Fayetteville
Heller Herman, clk Heller Bros, res same
Heller Sam H, clk Heller Bros, res same
Henderson Sam,* tobacco worker, res Smith
Henderson Sallie,* wife Sam, laundress
Henderson Elnora,* cook, res 205 w Lenoir
Henderson Clara,* house-servant, res 110 w Cabarrus
Henderson Frank,* student, res 110 w Cabarrus

FRANK HERMANN,

Artistic Tailor,

14 West Hargett Street,   Raleigh, N. C.

Hendon Miss Fannie, bleacher of hats, res 328 s McDowell
Henly Isabella,* cook for H S Leard, res same
Henly Theo,* city hand, res 820 s Wilmington
Henly Dilly,* wife Theo, chambermaid Park Hotel
Henly James,* lab, res 521 w South
Henly Octavia,* wife James, house work
Henly Lizzie,* d James, res same, student
Henry Nancy,* cook for Jas M Harris, res same
Henry Mrs A F, wid, res 507 s West
Henry L B, tel opr, res 507 s West
Henry Miss Ida F, d Mrs A F, res same
Hermann Frank, tailor, up-stairs, 122 Fayetteville, res same
Herndon Alonzo, wks Caraleigh mill, res Cannon
Herndon Mrs Annie, wife Alonzo
Herndon Henry,* hostler, res 118 w Cabarrus
Herndon Walter,* lab, res 28 Fowle
Herndon Ella,* seamstress, res 542 e Cabarrus
Herndon Florence,* d Ella, res same, student
Herring Miss Madge, student, bds 225 w Edenton
Hester Clara,* washerwoman, res 712 s Dawson
Hester Louisa,* servant, res 228 Blount-st al
Hervey Charles C, clk in office Edwards & Broughton, room over 134 Fayetteville
Hervey Mrs R E, boarding-house, 506 s Salisbury
Hervey Miss Rheta, d Mrs R E, res same, student
Hervey R T, son Mrs R E, res same, student
Hervey R P, bkkpr at W C Stronach & Sons, res 503 s West
Hervey Mrs Sallie G, wife R P
Hervey Henry J, son R P, res same, student
Hervey Miss Carolina C, d R P, res same, student
Hervey Miss Kate F, d R P, res same, student
Hicks Col Wm J, builder, contractor and architect, res 204 w Edenton
Hicks Miss Julia L, d Col Wm J, res same,
Hicks Miss Lizzie W, d Col Wm J, res same
Hicks Miss Bertha M, d Col Wm J, res same
Hicks Wm B, with N C Building & Supply Co. r 204 w Edenton
Hicks Mrs Josephine P, wife Wm B
Hicks Wm J Jr, son Wm B, res same
Hicks F P, son Wm B, res same
Hicks Miss Fannie, bkpr for J P Wyatt, 113 n Dawson
Hicks Wm H, huckster, res 215 Smithfield
Hicks Corinna, wife Wm H, seamstress
Hicks Walter, son Wm H, res same, candy-maker
HICKS & ROGERS, druggists, 101 Fayetteville
Hicks Jennie,* washerwoman, res 510 w Morgan
Hicks Eugenia,* d Jennie, res same, nurse for Rufus Horton
Hicks Joe,* son Jennie, res same, wks with Isham Fields

Hicks Major,* son Jennie, res same, wks Ral oil mill
Hicks Silvia,* laundress at Yarboro' House, res 123 e Cabarrus
Hicks Mrs C V, wid, res over 331 Hillsboro'
Hicks Miss Sallie, d Mrs C V, res same
Hicks Edgar A, son Mrs C V, res same
Hicks Robt M, son Mrs C V, res same, carp
Hicks Nettie,* nurse for Wm S Primrose, res on lot
Hicks Ransom,* whitewasher and plasterer, res rear 605 Hillsboro'
Hicks Ida,* wife Ransom, washerwoman
Hicks Miss Lillie S, g-d Geo V Strong, res same, teacher in Murphy Graded School
Hicks Henry T (Hicks & Rogers), druggist, bds 226 e Morgan
Hicks Mrs Ida, wife H T
Hicks J W, lab, res 535 e Martin
Hicks Lonnie, son J W, res same, lab
Hicks Miss Mary I, d J W, res same
Hicks Wyatt G, son J W, res same, lab
Hicks Junius A, son J W, res same, farm hand
Hicks Miss Hattie, d J W, res same, house-girl
Hicks Miss Callie, d J W, res same, student
Hicks Dan, eng S A L, res 418 n Person
Hicks Mrs Annie, wife Dan
Hicks Chas D, son Dan, res same, student
Hicks Willie F, son Dan, res same
Hicks Mrs Susan, wid, mother of Mrs Annie H Landis, res same
Hicks J E, wks for A J Ellis, res same
Hicks Ernest,* lab, res 30 Railroad
Hicks Mrs Catherine, mother H T Hicks, res 412 e Morgan
Hicks Mary,* student, res 533 Newbern ave
Hicks Henry,* driver, res Smith
Hicks Carrie,* wife Henry
Hicks Blanche,* d Henry, res same, student
Hicks Frank,* painter, res 309 w South
Hicks Otho,* lab, res w Lenoir
Hicks Toscus,* brakeman S A L, res w Lenoir
Hicks Mrs Gertrude, wid, artist and dressmaker, r 513 n Salisbury

GUARANTEED.

Dr. Nagle's Certain Cough Cure,	- 25c.
Hicks' Capudine, for Headache,	- 25c.
Fragrant Almonds, for the Skin,	- 25c.

Correct Prescription work.
Money refunded if you are not satisfied with the remedies.

HICKS & ROGERS,
Prescription Druggists, RALEIGH, N. C.

Hicks Miss Rosa, d Mrs Gertrude, res same, student
Hicks Miss Ida, d Mrs Gertrude, res same, student
Hicks Burton,* farmer, res 829 Fayetteville
Hicks Rebecca,* wife Burton, washerwoman
Hicks Luther,* son Burton, res same, student
Hicks Beulah,* d Burton, res same, student
Hicks Maud,* d Burton, res same, student
Hicks Agnes,* d Burton, res same, student
Hicks Berta,* cook for G M Lassater, res same
Highbarger Chas L, foreman broom dept Blind Institution, r same
High Wm H, father Mrs V C Royster, res same
High George,* lab, res 408 w Edenton
High Amanda,* wife Geo, washerwoman
High Lizzie,* d Geo, res same, servant at J M Fleming
High Jane,* d Geo, res same, servant at Exchange Hotel
High Mamie*, d Geo, res same, servant
High John,* son Geo, res same, servant at J W Hinsdale
High Mack,* brakeman S A L R R, res 420 n Wilmington
High Fannie,* wife Mack, washerwoman
High R C, mechanic, res Fayetteville below R R
High Miss Estelle, d R C, res same, student
High Stella,* house-servant, res 126 w South
High Joseph,* city hand, res 513 Haywood
High Rosetta,* wife Jos
High Swepson,* son Jos, res same, student
High Dony,* son Jos, res same, student
High Thomas,* son Jos, res same, student
High Jos Jr,* son Jos, res same, student
Hight Mumford D,* hostler for J W Brown, res on lot
Higgs Austin,* lab, res 722 s Dawson
Higgs Cena,* sick-nurse, res 722 s Dawson
Higgs Isabella,* d Austin, res same
Higgs Sherwood,* son Isabella, res same, student
Higgs James M,* lab, res 523 Newbern ave
Higgs Celia,* wife Jas M
Higgs Charles,* d James M, res same, student
Higgs Hugh,* d James M, res same, student
Higgs Marion,* d James M, res same, student
Higgs Ella,* cook for W T Tucker, res 14 n East
Higgs Miss Jennie, d Mrs Laura Watkins, res same, student
Higgs Miss Laura, d Mrs Laura Watkins, res same, student
Higgs James A, traveling salesman, res 417 n Blount
Higgs Mrs Pattie, wife Jas A
Higgs Miss Mattie, d Jas A, res same
Higgs Miss Jessie, d Jas A, res same, student
Higgs Miss Emmie, d Jas A, res same, student
Higgs James A Jr, son Jas A, res same, student
Higgs Allen, son Jas A, res same, clk for C A Sherwood & Co

Higgs Sherwood, merchant, res 417 n Blount
Higgs Mrs Lucy H, wife Sherwood
Hiler Ben,* huckster, res 530 e Martin
Hiler Lucy,* wife Ben, house work
Hiler Fannie,* d Ben, res same, student
Hiler Vinson,* son Ben, res same, student
Hill William,* lab S A L, res 413 n Salisbury
Hill Lula,* wife William
Hill A D, inmate Soldiers' Home
Hill George,* porter for Mrs E E Moffitt, res s East
Hill Mary,* wife George, house-servant at Mrs E E Moffitt
Hill Augustus,* watchman Park Hotel, res 707 s East
Hill Maggie,* wife Augustus
Hill James,* lab, res 431 Smith
Hill Thos,* lab, res 206 w Lenoir
Hill Hattie,* wife Thos, washerwoman
Hill Mrs R P, wid, res 314 Hillsboro'
Hill Jos D, farmer, res s Blount, o s s
Hill Mrs Isabelle, wife Jos D
Hill Miss Annie, d Jos D, res same
Hill Jno S, son Jos D, res same, lab
Hill Bud, son Jos D, res same, lab
Hill Thomas,* lab, res Nunn, o s s
Hill Belle,* wife Thos, sick-nurse
Hill Jennie,* d Thos, res same, student
Hill Lizzie, d Thos, res same, washerwoman
Hill James,* son Thos, res same, porter
Hill Joe & Son,* blacksmiths, 126 s Blount
Hill Mrs Ella, d Wm H Jones, res 705 s Blount
Hill I C (Hill & Harris), saloon keeper, res 314 e Martin
Hill Mrs Millie M, wife I C
Hill Theo H, poet, res St Mary's, o s w
Hill Mrs Mary G, wife Theo H
Hill Miss Rosa G, d Theo H, res same
Hill Miss Tempie B, d Theo H, res same, student
Hill Mrs C A, wid, res 225 Pace, o s n
Hill Miss Esther, d Mrs C A, res same, weaver Pilot cot mill
Hill Miss Della, d Mrs C A, res same, weaver Pilot cot mill
Hill Edgar, son Mrs C A, res same, weaver Pilot cot mill
Hill Claude, son Mrs C A, res same, weaver Pilot cot mill
Hill Miss Nettie, d Mrs C A, res same, student
Hill Clarence, son Mrs C A, res same, student
Hill Joshua B (J R Ferrell & Co), merchant, res 128 Newbern ave
Hill Mrs Maggie B, wife J B
Hill Miss Annie C, d J B, res same
Hill Miss Maggie V, d J B, res same
Hill Hubert, son J B, res same, student
Hill Ida,* washerwoman, res e Davie

Hill Henry,* driver, res 311 s Bloodworth
Hill Citie,* wife Henry, cook,
Hill Willie,* son Henry, res same, student
Hill Joseph,* blacksmith, res 23 Hayti
Hill Eliza,* wife Joseph, house work
Hill Chas R,* blacksmith, res 23 Hayti
Hill Annie,* wife Chas R, house work
Hill Thomas,* son Chas R, res same, blacksmith striker
Hill Charles,* porter Ral Savings Bank, res 519 s McDowell
Hill Corinna,* wife Chas, chambermaid at Peace Institute
Hill Thomas,* lab, res 513 s McDowell
Hill Ida,* wife Thomas
Hill Nettie,* house-servant for Mrs Fannie M Williams, res on lot
Hill Annie,* washerwoman, res rear 114 w Cabarrus
Hill Frances,* sister of Annie, res same, cook
Hill Minnie,* d Annie, res same, student
Hill Cora,* house-servant, res Martin, o s e
Hill John,* son Cora, res same, driver for Dr L A Scruggs
Hill Aaron,* farmer, res Rock Quarry rd
Hill Maria,* sister of Aaron, res same, washerwoman
Hill Maggie,* wife Aaron, house-servant for Dr P E Hines
Hill Hattie,* d Maria, res same, student
Hill Lula,* house-servant, res 115 w Lenoir
Hill Mary,* servant for W R Richardson, res same
Hill D H, Professor of English A & M College, res Hillsboro' rd, o s w
Hill Mrs P W, wife D H
Hill Miss Pauline, d D H, res same, student
Hill D H Jr, son D H, res same
Hill Mrs D H, wid, res Maiden Lane, o s w
Hill Miss Nannie, d Mrs D H, res same
Hilton Peyton,* teacher Shaw University, res 808 s Blount
Hilton Martha,* wife Peyton
Hilton Philip,* son Peyton, res same, student
Hines Isaac,* porter Mrs Lucy B Evans, res same
Hines Dr. Peter E, physician and surgeon, res 214 Newbern ave, office same
Hines Mrs Francis I, wife Dr Peter E
Hines Diana,* cook for Rev A M Simms, res 319 s Bloodworth
Hines James,* son Diana, res same, student
Hines Robert,* gardener, res Martin, o s e
Hines Emily,* wife Robt, laundress
Hines Pattie,* d Robt, res same, student
Hines Gracie,* washerwoman, res 527 Newbern ave
Hines Bettie,* d Gracie, res same, nurse Yarboro' House
Hines Nelson,* son Gracie, res same, driver
Hines Fannie,* d Gracie, res same, house-girl
Hines Alice,* d Gracie, res same, house-girl

Hines Thomas,* son Gracie, res same, coachman
Hines Laura,* d Gracie, res same, student
Hines Emma,* d Gracie, res same, student
Hinnant L S, lab, res 120 n Harrington
Hinnant Mrs Harriet, wife L S
Hinnant Jas A, driver for Standard Oil Co, res 120 n Harrington
Hinnant Mrs Serina, wife J A
Hinnant Charlie, son J A, res same, student
Hinnant Miss Minnie D, d J A, res same
Hinnant Miss Mildred, d J A, res same
HINSDALE Col J W, lawyer, office in Fisher bldg, res 330 Hillsboro'
Hinsdale Mrs Ellen, wife Col J W
Hinsdale Miss Margaret D, d Col J W, res same
Hinsdale Miss Elizabeth C, d Col J W, res same
Hinsdale Miss Ellen D, d Col J W, res same
Hinsdale Miss Annie D, d Col J W, res same
Hinsdale Sam J, son Col J W, res same, clk S A L R R
Hinsdale Jno W Jr, son Col J W, res same, clk for father
Hinson Miss Effie, hkpr William Starling, res same
Hiscock Ernest A, life ins agt, res 510 Halifax
Hiscock Mrs Catherine, wife Ernest A
Hiscock Miss Mary, d Ernest A, res same
Hinton Octavius,* lab, res old Fair Ground, o s e
Hinton Lucy,* wife Octavius, washerwoman
Hinton Frances,* d Octavius, res same, nurse
Hinton Laura,* d Octavius, res same, student
Hinton Edward,* son Octavius, res same, student
Hinton Caroline,* washerwoman, res Martin, o s e
Hinton Gaston,* marble-rubber, res 20 w Worth
Hinton Ferribe,* wife Gaston, washerwoman
Hinton Clarence,* son Gaston, res same, student
Hinton Sterling,* son Gaston, res same, student
Hinton Ben,* son Gaston, res same, student
Hinton Ella,* d Gaston, res same, student
Hinton Luvinia,* d Gaston, res same, student

JOHN W. HINSDALE,
Attorney at Law,
RALEIGH, N. C.,

Practises in any Court and any part of the State.

Railroad, Insurance, Corporation and Commercial Law.

REFERENCES: The Governor, the Supreme and the Superior Court Judges of North Carolina, and the Banks of Raleigh.

Hinton William,* wks Caraleigh mill, bds 722 Fayetteville
Hinton Albert,* lab, res 217 w Lenoir
Hinton Eliza,* wife Albert, washerwoman
Hinton Daniel,* son Albert, res same, lab
Hinton William,* driver for N C Car Co, res 10 n East
Hinton Mary,* wife Wm
Hinton Charles,* porter N C Car Co, res 10 n East
Hinton Louis,* porter Julius Lewis Hardware Co, res 827 s Wilmington
Hinton Maggie,* wife Louis, servant R H Battle, r 827 s Wilmington
Hinton Emma,* washerwoman, res w Peace
Hinton Jane,* washerwoman, res Cotton lane, o s e
Hinton Charles,* son Jane, res same, student
Hinton Hannah,* d Jane, res same, cook for Ivan M Proctor
Hinton Kate,* d Jane, res same, cook for Jno M Monie
Hinton Arthur,* whitewasher, res 508 e Edenton
Hinton Isabella,* wife Arthur, cook
Hinton John,* hackman, res rear e Davie, o s e
Hinton Jane,* wife John, washerwoman
Hinton Frank,* son John, res same, student
Hinton Bessie,* d John, res same, student
Hinton Annie,* d John, res same, student
Hinton Paul,* son John, res same, student
Hinton Reuben,* lab, res 752 e Davie
Hinton Sarah,* wife Reuben, cook
Hinton Lucy,* servant, res 529 s East
Hinton Laura,* invalid, res Hargett, o s e
Hinton Frank,* blacksmith, res 306 s Bloodworth
Hinton A G,* grocer, Yearby's lane
Hinton Abe,* lab S A L, res 423 n Salisbury
Hinton Sam,* farm hand, res 551 e Edenton
Hinton Bettie,* wife Sam, washerwoman
Hinton Mary,* cook for Geo H Glass, res same
Hinton Millie,* nurse at B G Cowper, res on lot
Hinton Susan,* house servant at J D Bushall, res same
Hinton Chaney,* servant at Mrs M L Little, res on lot
Hinton Maggie,* nurse for W R Tucker, res on lot
Hinton Mary,* nurse for R O Burton, res on lot
Hinton Allen,* lab, res 525 e Davie
Hinton Fannie,* wife Allen, washerwoman
Hinton Martha,* washerwoman, res 521 e Davie
Hinton Major,* lab, res 550 e Martin
Hinton Dicey,* wife Major, washerwoman
Hinton Roxie,* d Major, res same, student
Hinton Cornelia,* d Major, res same, cook
Hinton Frances,* washerwoman, res 513 e Davie
Hinton Rufus,* son Frances, res same, hostler

Hinton Robert,* driver, res 588 e Cabarrus
Hinton Lula,* d Robert, res same, house-servant
Hinton Daisy,* d Robert, res same, house-servant
Hinton Fannie,* d Robert, res same, student
Hinton Dempsey,* lab, res 710 e Davie
Hinton Happy,* wife Dempsey, washerwoman
Hinton Mills,* son Dempsey, res same, lab at p o
Hinton Anna,* d Dempsey, res same, student
Hinton Nellie,* d Dempsey, res same, student
Hinton Mattie,* nurse for Mrs Emma Swindell, res same
Hinton Daniel,* lab, res 323 s Bloodworth
Hinton Sallie,* wife Daniel, cook
Hinton John D,* son Daniel, res same, hackman
Hinton Frances,* d Daniel, res same, house-servant
Hinton William,* lab, res old Fair Ground, e Ral
Hinton Tamer,* wife Wm, washerwoman
Hinton A C, clk at Cross & Linehan, res 249 s Swain
Hinton Mrs Bessie, wife A C
Hinton Cain,* lab, res Hayti
Hinton Fannie,* wife Cain, washerwoman
Hinton Mack,* son Cain, res same, lab
Hinton Mary,* d Cain, res same, student
Hinton Nannie,* cook, res 526 s Dawson
Hinton Wiley, tailor, res 615 e Hargett
Hinton Miss Sarah, dressmaker, res 615 e Hargett
Hinton Charles,* hackman, res e Martin, o s e
Hinton Emily,* wife Charles, laundress
Hinton Richard,* son Charles, porter for W B Mann
Hinton Laura,* d Charles, res same, nurse for W B Mann
Hinton Emma,* d Charles, res same, servant
Hinton Moses,* lab, e Martin, o s e
Hinton Anna,* wife Moses, washerwoman
Hinton Frances,* d Moses, res same, house-servant
Hinton Lewis,* lab, res e Martin, o s e
Hinton Caroline,* cook J T Watts, rooms 229 Blount-st al
Hinton Robert,* lab, res 224 s Blount
Hinton Hattie,* wife Robert
Hinton Frank,* gardener, res Cotton lane, o s e
Hinton Patrick,* lab, res e Hargett, o s e
Hinton Mrs Indiana, dressmaker, res Hargett, o s e
Hinton Miss Florence, d Mrs Indiana, res same, dressmaker
Hinton Henry,* lab at Allen & Cram Machine Co, res o s e
Hinton Sarah,* cook, res Idlewild
Hinton Albert,* son Henry, res same, wks E R Pace
Hinton Charity,* washerwoman, res 112 n West
Hinton Sarah,* d Charity, res same, washerwoman
Hinton Caswell,* gardener, res 833 Fayetteville
Hinton Elizabeth,* wife Caswell

Hinton Addie,* d Caswell, res same, seamstress
Hinton Benj,* wood-cutter, res rear 130 e Hargett
Hinton Lucy,* wife Benj, washerwoman
Hinton Minerva,* res rear 124 e Hargett, washerwoman
Hinton Miss Emma, seamstress, res 523 s Wilmington
Hinton Agnes,* washerwoman, res w Lane near R R
Hinton Nannie,* cook for W R Newsom, res near railroad crossing at n West
Hinton L B,* harness-maker, 106 s Wilmington, res Oberlin, o s w
Hinton Hardy,* farm hand, res 617 Elm
Hinton Cenia,* wife Hardy, washerwoman
Hinton Olivia A,* d Hardy, res same, student
Hinton General,* son Hardy, res same, student
Hinton Perry,* son Hardy, res same, student
Hinton Ida,* d Hardy, res same, student
Hobby Green,* blacksmith, res 713 s Dawson
Hobby Julia,* wife Green, washerwoman
Hockaday Roberta,* cook, 531 Halifax
Hockady Lizzie,* servant at Insane Asylum, res 605 e Cabarrus
Hockady Bettie,* d Lizzie, res same, cook for Wm Brown
Hockady Della,* d Lizzie, res same, servant
Hockady Junius,* son Lizzie, res same, lab
Hockady Aaron,* fireman S A L R R, res Idlewild
Hockady Alice,* wife Aaron
Hockady Irene,* d Aaron, res same, cook
Hockady Edward,* son Aaron, res same, lab
Hockady William,* driver for Dr W H Bobbitt, res same
Hodge Lucy,* washerwoman, res 126 e Hargett
Hodge Rachel,* cook for S W Brewer, res on lot
Hodge W T, clk for James Freeman, res 548 e Hargett
Hodge Mrs Mittie F, wife W T
Hodge Miss Nettie, d W T, res same
Hodge Albert, son W T, res same, student
Hodge Ivan, son W T, res same, student
Hodge Kemp,* carp, res 22 Fowle
Hodge Sarah,* washerwoman, res 417 w South
Hodge Julia,* d Sarah, res same, washerwoman
Hodge Henry,* grocer, e Martin, o s e, res same
Hodge Lina,* cook, res 113 w Peace
Hodge Ruffin,* farm hand, res 596 e Lenoir
Hodge Lina,* wife Ruffin
Hodge Willie,* son Ruffin, res same, farm hand
Hodge Robert,* son Ruffin, res same, farm hand
Hodge Naddie,* son Ruffin, res same, farm hand
Hodge Eddie,* son Ruffin, res same, farm hand
Hodge Lina,* cook for Thos W Allen, res on lot
Hodges Miss Bessie, student, bds cor Newbern ave and Person
Hodges R W, clk Southern Express Co, res 217 w Martin

Hodges Mrs Florence, wife R W
Hogan Mrs Amanda, wid Robt Hogan, 420 w Lane
Hogan Capt J B, conductor S A L, res Hicks lane
Hogan Mrs Kate L, wife Capt J B
Hogan Miss Norman, d Capt J B, res same, student
Hogan Joseph, son Capt J B, res same, student
Hogan Eddie, son Capt J B, res same, student
Hogan James,* driver for B G Cowper, res on lot
Hoget Charles, clk, res 217 s Bloodworth
Hoget Mrs Stella, wife Charles
Hogg Dr Thos D, capitalist, res 210 n Wilmington
Hogg Miss Sallie, d Dr Thos D, res same
Hogg Gabriel,* porter Robt Simpson, druggist, res on lot
Hogue Mrs C A, wid, res with Mrs Ella Harris
Hogue Wm E, painter, res 322 s Person
Hogue Mrs Lucy H, wife Wm E
Hogue Geo E, son Wm E, res same, student
Hogue Miss Ellen M, d Wm E, res same, student
Hogue Chas N, son Wm E, res same, student
Hoke Gen R F, pres G C & N R R, res cor Edenton and Dawson
Hoke Mrs Lillie Van W, wife Gen R F
Hoke Miss Fannie, d Gen R F, res same
Holderfield Isaac, guard penitentiary, res 811 Jenkins
Holderfield Mrs Margaret, wife Isaac
Holderfield William, son Isaac, res same, painter
Holderfield Ruffin, son Isaac, res same, weaver Caraleigh mill
Holderfield Miss Laura, d Isaac, res same
Holderfield John, guard penitentiary, res 712 s West
Holderfield Mrs Agnes C, wife John
Holderfield Miss Nora E, d John, res same, student
Holderfield Hubert E, son John, res same, student
Holderfield Henry, guard penitentiary, res Cox ave, o s w
Holderfield Mrs Annie, wife Henry
Holderfield Malia, son Henry, res same, student
Holderfield Miss Bessie, d Henry, res same, student
Holden Mrs L V, wid, res 127 w Hargett
Holden Miss Lula T, d Mrs L V, res same
Holder John W,* lab, res 217 w North
Holder Penny,* wife John W, washerwoman
Holder Mary,* cook for W G Nottingham, res same
Holder Miss Lee, seamstress, res 314 e Davie
Holder Rufus, wks Pace stable, bds 203 n West
Holder Mrs Amanda, wife Rufus
Holder George, printer, res 719 s East
Holder Henry,* driver for Thomas & Maxwell, res 408 Smith
Holder Mary,* wife Henry, washerwoman
Holding J N, lawyer, res 528 s Salisbury
Holding Mrs Maggie M, wife J N

Holding Arthur N, son J N, res same
Holding & Vass, lawyers, 6 w Martin
HOLLADAY ALEX Q, pres Agricultural and Mechanical College, res Hillsboro' road, o s w
Holladay Mrs V R B, wife Alex Q
Holladay Chas B, son A Q, res same, student
Holland C D, clk for Royall & Borden, res 110 n Saunders
Holland Mrs Lillie G, wife C D
Holland Gideon,* foreman broom shop at Colored Deaf, Dumb and Blind Institution, res same
Holland Henry,* servant for Dr A W Goodwin, res on lot
Holland Hessie,* niece of Sam Stewart, res 806 s Blount
Hollinkrake John, spinner Ral cot mill, res Firwood ave, o s n
Hollinkrake Mrs Nannie, wife John
Hollinkrake Miss Emmie, d John, res same, student
Hollingsworth John R, ins agt, bds 125 e South
Hollingsworth Mrs Sammie, wife John R
Hollingsworth John R Jr, student
Hollister Mrs Martha, wid, res 324 w Morgan
Holloday Jane,* washerwoman, res 620 Harp's lane, o s n
Holloman Mrs W H, wid, res 309 Hillsboro'
Holloman Mrs E C, wid, sister of Mrs C H Anderson, res same
Holloman J D, section master, res 405 s Dawson
Holloman Mrs Mollie, wife J D
Holloman Jane,* washerwoman, res old Fair Ground, o s e
Holloman Clara,* d Jane, res same, washerwoman
Holloman Oscar,* son Jane, res same, lab
Holloman Richard,* son Clara, res same, student
Holloman Lavenia,* cook for W B Hutchings, res Womble lane
Holloman Tom,* lab, res Womble lane
Holloman William,* lab, res Womble lane
Holloway Creasy,* cook for S A Ashe, res on lot
Holloway W H, wagon-maker and repairer, 121 e Hargett, res 327 s Person
Holloway Mrs Eliza H, wife W H
Holloway S Webb, son W H, res same, wks with father

THE NORTH CAROLINA COLLEGE OF
AGRICULTURE AND MECHANIC ARTS

Begins its next Session September 3, 1896.

Expenses for one year, INCLUDING BOARD:

For County Students, - - $ 87 00
For all other Students, - - 117 00

For Catalogue, apply to   ALEXANDER Q. HOLLADAY, President,
Raleigh, N. C.

Holloway Cecil H, son W H, residence same, bus mgr Progressive Farmer
Holloway Miss Carrie M, d W H, res same, student
Holloway W A, carp, res 606 Hunter
Holloway Sarah J, wife W A
Holloway Miss Eliza J, d W A, spooler Caraleigh mill
Holloway W D, son W A, res same, carp
Holloway James B, son W A, res same
Holloway Miss Lidia L, d W A, res same
Holloway Henry G, son W A, res same
Holloway F I, bkkpr for N C Cot Oil Co, res 410 s Person
Holloway Mrs Lorene, wife F I
Holloway Martha,* washerwoman, res Bloodworth, o s u
Holloway Albert W, mechanic, res 708 n Person
Holloway Mrs Mary E, wife Albert W
Holloway Miss Ella, d Albert W, res same, teacher
Holloway Miss Irene, d Albert W, res same
Holloway Oscar, son Albert W, res same, wks Linnell Laundry
Holloway Miss Sudie, d Albert W, res same, student
Holloway Miss Lillie, d Albert W, res same, student
Holloway Ella,* washerwoman, res Adams lane
Holman W C, farmer and miller, res 209 e Morgan
Holman Mrs Annie, wife W C
Holman Miss Lizzie, d W C, res same
Holman Robert, son W C, res same
Holman Lewis, son W C, res same, student
Holman Miss Mamie, d W C, res same, student
Holman Miss Bertha, d W C, res same, student
Holman George, son W C, res same, student
Holman Sidney, son W C, res same, student
Holman Dempsey,* hackman, res 423 s Blount
Holman Martha,* wife Dempsey, cook for O J Carroll
Holman Martha,* d Dempsey, res same, cook Joe Weathers
Holman Mary,* d Dempsey, res same, house servant
Holman Lee,* son Dempsey, res same, student
Holman Squire,* waiter at B P Williamson, res 305 w South
Holman Ellen,* wife Squire, washerwoman
Holman Robert,* drayman, res 417 Cannon
Holman Jane,* laundress, res 417 Cannon
Holman Fannie,* d Robert, res same, ironer
Holman Sallie J,* d Robert, res same, ironer
Holman Nancy,* house work, res 417 Cannon
Holman Rosabelle,* washerwoman, res 305 w South
Holmes Squire,* farmer, res Idlewild
Holmes Mary,* wife Squire, cook
Holmes Henderson,* lab, res 515 Cannon
Holmes Rose,* wife Henderson, washerwoman
Holmes Odell,* d Henderson, res same, student

Holmes Amy,* washerwoman, res 23 Fowle
Holmes Betsy,* washerwoman, res rear 548 e Hargett
Holmes J P, wks for S A L R R, res 121 Polk
Holmes Mrs Mona, wife J P
Holmes W B, son J P, res same, printer
Holmes Mrs Ethel, wid, mother of J P, res same
Holmes Peter,* porter S A L R R, res 221 w North
Holmes Mary,* wife Peter, washerwoman
Holmes Willie,* son Peter, res same, student
Holmes O C, wks cot mill, res 227 n Dawson
Holmes Mrs Margaret, wife O C
Holt Sophia,* washerwoman, res 519 s Dawson
Holt L Banks, capitalist, res cor n Blount and Polk
Holt Mrs M C, wife L B
Holt Miss Carrie, d L B, res same, student
Holt Miss Cora, d L B, res same, student
Holt Miss Louise, d L B, res same, student
Holt Miss Mattie, d L B, res same, student
Holt Mrs Martha R, mother of Mrs Wm R Blake, res same
Holt D G, foreman cot oil mill, res 520 s West
Holt Mrs Helen S, wife D G
Holt Alonzo,* head-waiter Yarboro' House, res 716 Manly
Holt Johnnie A,* wife Alonzo, house work
Holt George W,* son Alonzo, res same, student
Holt Albert,* son Alonzo, res same, student
Holt William,* son Alonzo, res same, student
Holtzman R L, machinist at S A L R R
Hood Wm H Jr, clk, res 220 s Blount
Hood Mrs Florence M, wife Wm H Jr
Hood Miss Mildred M, d Wm H Jr, res same
Hood Ed H, painter, bds 231 e Lenoir
Hood Miss Rosa E, seamstress, bds 231 e Lenoir
Hood Miss Ida L, dressmaker, bds 231 e Lenoir
Hood Wm H Sr, clk for R E Parham, bds 214 e Martin
Hood M A,* servant, res with Rev A G Davis*
Hooks Ellen,* washerwoman, res 215 w Lenoir
Hooks Clara,* chair-bottomer, res 215 w Lenoir
Hooks Katie,* washerwoman, res 215 w Lenoir
Hoover Chas W,* saloon, 213 s Wilmington, res 117 e South
Hoover Louisa,* wife Chas W
Hoover Chas T,* son Chas W, res same, student
Hoover Mabel H,* d Chas W, res same, student
Hopkins William, wks Ral cot mill, res 524 n West
Hopkins Mrs Sarah, wife Wm, wks Ral cot mill
Hopkins Miss Marion, d William, res same, wks Ral cot mill
Hopkins Dr Allen, medicine dealer, res 122 e Martin
Hopkins Robert,* drayman, res rear Catholic church
Hopkins Annie,* wife Robert

Holmes Amy,* washerwoman, res 23 Fowle
Holmes Betsy,* washerwoman, res rear 548 e Hargett
Holmes J P, wks for S A L R R, res 121 Polk
Holmes Mrs Mona, wife J P
Holmes W B, son J P, res same, printer
Holmes Mrs Ethel, wid, mother of J P, res same
Holmes Peter,* porter S A L R R, res 221 w North
Holmes Mary,* wife Peter, washerwoman
Holmes Willie,* son Peter, res same, student
Holmes O C, wks cot mill, res 227 n Dawson
Holmes Mrs Margaret, wife O C
Holt Sophia,* washerwoman, res 519 s Dawson
Holt L Banks, capitalist, res cor n Blount and Polk
Holt Mrs M C, wife L B
Holt Miss Carrie, d L B, res same, student
Holt Miss Cora, d L B, res same, student
Holt Miss Louise, d L B, res same, student
Holt Miss Mattie, d L B, res same, student
Holt Mrs Martha R, mother of Mrs Wm R Blake, res same
Holt D G, foreman cot oil mill, res 520 s West
Holt Mrs Helen S, wife D G
Holt Alonzo,* head-waiter Yarboro' House, res 716 Manly
Holt Johnnie A,* wife Alonzo, house work
Holt George W,* son Alonzo, res same, student
Holt Albert,* son Alonzo, res same, student
Holt William,* son Alonzo, res same, student
Holtzman R L, machinist at S A L R R
Hood Wm H Jr, clk, res 220 s Blount
Hood Mrs Florence M, wife Wm H Jr
Hood Miss Mildred M, d Wm H Jr, res same
Hood Ed H, painter, bds 231 e Lenoir
Hood Miss Rosa E, seamstress, bds 231 e Lenoir
Hood Miss Ida L, dressmaker, bds 231 e Lenoir
Hood Wm H Sr, clk for R E Parham, bds 214 e Martin
Hood M A,* servant, res with Rev A G Davis*
Hooks Ellen,* washerwoman, res 215 w Lenoir
Hooks Clara,* chair-bottomer, res 215 w Lenoir
Hooks Katie,* washerwoman, res 215 w Lenoir
Hoover Chas W,* saloon, 213 s Wilmington, res 117 e South
Hoover Louisa,* wife Chas W
Hoover Chas T,* son Chas W, res same, student
Hoover Mabel H,* d Chas W, res same, student
Hopkins William, wks Ral cot mill, res 524 n West
Hopkins Mrs Sarah, wife Wm, wks Ral cot mill
Hopkins Miss Marion, d William, res same, wks Ral cot mill
Hopkins Dr Allen, medicine dealer, res 122 e Martin
Hopkins Robert,* drayman, res rear Catholic church
Hopkins Annie,* wife Robert

Holloway Cecil H, son W H, residence same, bus mgr Progressive Farmer
Holloway Miss Carrie M, d W H, res same, student
Holloway W A, carp, res 606 Hunter
Holloway Sarah J, wife W A
Holloway Miss Eliza J, d W A, spooler Caraleigh mill
Holloway W D, son W A, res same, carp
Holloway James B, son W A, res same
Holloway Miss Lidia L, d W A, res same
Holloway Henry G, son W A, res same
Holloway F I, bkkpr for N C Cot Oil Co, res 110 s Person
Holloway Mrs Lorene, wife F I
Holloway Martha,* washerwoman, res Bloodworth, o s u
Holloway Albert W, mechanic, res 708 n Person
Holloway Mrs Mary E, wife Albert W
Holloway Miss Ella, d Albert W, res same, teacher
Holloway Miss Irene, d Albert W, res same
Holloway Oscar, son Albert W, res same, wks Linnell Laundry
Holloway Miss Sudie, d Albert W, res same, student
Holloway Miss Lillie, d Albert W, res same, student
Holloway Ella,* washerwoman, res Adams lane
Holman W C, farmer and miller, res 209 e Morgan
Holman Mrs Annie, wife W C
Holman Miss Lizzie, d W C, res same
Holman Robert, son W C, res same
Holman Lewis, son W C, res same, student
Holman Miss Mamie, d W C, res same, student
Holman Miss Bertha, d W C, res same, student
Holman George, son W C, res same, student
Holman Sidney, son W C, res same, student
Holman Dempsey,* hackman, res 423 s Blount
Holman Martha,* wife Dempsey, cook for O J Carroll
Holman Martha,* d Dempsey, res same, cook Joe Weathers
Holman Mary,* d Dempsey, res same, house servant
Holman Lee,* son Dempsey, res same, student
Holman Squire,* waiter at B P Williamson, res 305 w South
Holman Ellen,* wife Squire, washerwoman
Holman Robert,* drayman, res 417 Cannon
Holman Jane,* laundress, res 417 Cannon
Holman Fannie,* d Robert, res same, ironer
Holman Sallie J,* d Robert, res same, ironer
Holman Nancy,* house work, res 417 Cannon
Holman Rosabelle,* washerwoman, res 305 w South
Holmes Squire,* farmer, res Idlewild
Holmes Mary,* wife Squire, cook
Holmes Henderson,* lab, res 515 Cannon
Holmes Rose,* wife Henderson, washerwoman
Holmes Odell,* d Henderson, res same, student

Hopkins Felix,* son Robert, res same, student
Hornbuckle R T, grocer, cor Person and Cabarrus, res 709 s Blount
Hornbuckle Mrs Stella, wife R T
Hornbuckle Miss Lillian, d R T, res same
Horne Jesse, inmate Soldiers' Home
Horner Miss Eleanor H, teacher, res 123 w Martin
Horton James, fireman S A L, bds 508 Halifax
Horton & Lee, grocers, cor Bloodworth and Lane
Horton E G (Horton & Lee), merchant, res 321 e Lane
Horton Mrs Carrie E, wife E G, boarding-house
Horton Jennie,* washerwoman, res Martin, o s e
Horton Annie,* cook for T B Crowder, res 44 Matthews ave
Horton Sam,* son Annie, res same, porter Crowder & Rand
Horton Mary,* d Annie, res same, washerwoman
Horton Lula,* d Mary, res same, student
Horton Audry,* d Mary, res same, student
Horton Addison,* lab, res 9 Gatling's lane
Horton Dicey,* wife Addison
Horton Lula,* washerwoman, res 58 Hunter
Horton John W, yard master S A L, res 223 n Salisbury
Horton Miss Emmie, d J W, res same
Horton Miss Annie, d J W, res same, student
Horton Miss Mamie, d J W, res same, student
Horton John W Jr, son J W, res same, machinist
Horton Rufus,* milker for B G Cowper, res on lot
Horton George, drayman, res Bledsoe ave
Horton Emma,* wife George, washerwoman
Horton Thomas,* son George, lab
Horton Henry, blacksmith S A L, res 239 n Dawson
Horton Furney,* driver Julius Lewis Hardware Co, res Nunn, o s n
Horton Susan,* wife Furney, washerwoman
Horton Miriam,* d Furney, res same, student
Horton Ivan,* son Furney, res same, student
Horton Mrs Sallie J, seamstress, res 719 s Blount
Horton Rufus H, eng S A L R R, bds 703 n Salisbury, o s n
Horton W T, eng S A L R R, res 703 n Salisbury, o s n
Horton Mrs Mary A, wife W T
Horton Miss Julia, artist, res s Wilmington
Horton Miss Ina, stenographer and typewriter, res s Wilmington
Horton Parthenia,* washerwoman, res rear Catholic church
Horton Marie,* d Parthenia, res same, laundress
Horton Henry,* son Bettie Mitchell, res same, student
Horton Wm A, carp, res 117 e Hargett
Horton Mrs Della, wife Wm A, seamstress
Horton Hubert, son Wm A, res same, student
Horton Miss Mabel, d Wm A, res same, student
Horton Rufus, clk J R Ferrall & Co, res 514 w Morgan
Horton Mrs Lula, wife Rufus

Horton Hubert, son Rufus, res same
Horton Miss Annie, d Rufus, res same
Horton Robert L, clk Cross & Lenehan, bds 327 s Person
Horton Mrs Clyde H, wife Robert L
Horton P S,* blacksmith, 321 s Blount, res 310 e Cabarrus
Horton Mamie,* wife P S
Horton Ella,* d P S, res same, student
Horton Augustus,* son P S, res same, student
Horton Wm H, carp, res 526 n East
Horton Mrs Maria L, wife W H
Horton Mrs Rebecca, wid, res with W E Hogue
Horton Walter A, eng S A L R R, res n Blount, o s n
Horton Mrs Etta T, wife Walter A
Horton Edward M, son Walter A, res same, student
Horton James D, son Walter A, res same, student
Horton Hironimus R, carp, res 507 n East
Horton Mrs Augusta, wife H R
Horton Miss Ella, d H R, res same, dressmaker
Horton Miss Sarah, d H R, res same, saleslady at Woollcott & Son
Horton Addison, son H R, res same, student
Horton Miss Flora, d H R, res same, student
Horton Reuben,* lab, res old Fair Ground, o s e
Horton Mary,* wife Reuben, res same, washerwoman
Horton Telfair, clk for Whiting Bros, res s Wilmington
House Mrs Caroline, seamstress, res 757 s Blount
House Miss Ellie, d Mrs Caroline, res same, wks Caraleigh mill
House Miss Myrtle, d Mrs Caroline, res same, wks Caraleigh mill
House Miss Lolla, d Mrs Caroline, res same, student
House John T, carp, res 547 e Hargett
House Mrs Annie F, wife John T
House Miss Lucy E, d John T, res same, dressmaker
House F T, son John T, res same, wagon-maker
House Miss Eugenia, d John T, res same
House John W, son John T, res same, office-boy Wynne, Ellington & Co
House Knelm, son John T, res same, grocery clk
House Woodford, son John T, res same, student
House Joseph, son John T, res same, student
House Miss Estelle, d John T, res same, student
House Ida, seamstress, res 521 s Dawson
HOUSE S V, painter, office s Salisbury, res 427 Halifax
House Mrs Margaret, wife S V
House Miss Annie M, d S V, res same
House S V Jr, son S V, res same, painter
House Mrs Drusilla, wife S V Jr
Houch Solomon, inmate Soldiers' Home
Howard Miss Lovie, tailoress, bds 117 e Hargett
Howard Scott, student, bds 117 e Hargett

Howard Walter, cigarmaker, bds 117 e Hargett
Howard Mary,* cook, res 717 s Dawson
Howard Mary,* washerwoman, res rear 517 s Dawson
Howell John, painter, res Avent Ferry rd, o s w
Howell Mrs Annie, wife John
Howell Mrs Bedie, wid, res Avent Ferry rd, o s w
Howell Miss Mattie M, d Mrs Bedie, res same
Howell Miss Ponnie L, d Mrs Bedie, res same
Howell Miss Golia B, d Mrs Bedie, res same
Howell Frank H, son Mrs Bedie, res same
Howell Miss Jessie C, d Mrs Bedie, res same
Howell A A, conductor Ral Elec r r, res Cox ave
Howell Mrs Nannie H, wife A A
Howell W A, supt Pullen Park, res at park
Howell Mrs Ida, wife W A
Howell Miss Myrtle M, d W A, res same
Howell Jesse,* fireman S A L, res 437 n Salisbury
Howell Rev Freeman R,* pastor Blount-Street Baptist church
Howell Mary E,* wife Rev F R
Howell Prof Logan D, supt Raleigh Graded Schools, bds 404 Hillsboro
Howell Jack,* shoemaker, e Hargett, res Martin, o s e
Howell Fannie,* wife Jack, washerwoman
Howell Martha,* washerwoman, res 599 e Cabarrus
Hubbard Diania,* cook T Margo, res 552 e Cabarrus
Huddleston L T, gardener at capitol, res 113 w Cabarrus
Huddleston Mrs Maggie, wife L T
Huddleston William, son L T, res same, moulder app
Huddleston Miss Hattie, d L T, res same, student
Hudgepeth Mrs I A, wid, res cor Swain and e Hargett
Hudgins W C, agt for Peter Stumpf beer, bds 117 e Davie
Hudgins A C, revenue service, bds 104 e Davie
Hudson Miss Martha, yeast dealer, res 743 s Blount
Hudson Mrs Susie A, wid, boarding-house, res 823 s Wilmington
Hudson Miss Mary H, sister Mrs Susie A, res same
Hudson W L, nephew Mrs Susie A, res same, hostler R E Parham

S. V. HOUSE, SR.,
CONTRACTOR FOR
All kinds of House Painting and Sign Work.

Plastered Walls Painted in Oil Colors or Plastoco. Tin Roofs Painted with best Iron Paint, warranted water-proof and not to scale off. All work done at short notice and in first-class style.

Shop and Office: S. Salisbury Street,   Raleigh, **N. C.**

Huggins H R, printer Barnes Bros, res 17 s East
Huggins Mrs Lina, wife H R
Huggins Wm M, son H R, res same, app printer
Huggins Miss Lessie M, d H R, res same, student
Huggins Allen,* lab, res 517 Newbern ave
Huggins Nancy,* wife Allen, house-servant
Hughes Emily,* nurse for Dr A W Knox, res on lot
Hughes Nannie,* cook for W T Stainback, res on lot
Hughes H I,* barber, Exchange Place, res 521 e Cabarrus
Hughes Sallie A,* wife H I, seamstress
Hughes Silla,* washerwoman, res Caswell lane
HUGHES W H, crockery, glassware, &c, 127 Fayetteville, res 221 w Martin
Hughes Mrs Lizzie H, wife W H
Hughes C M, son W H, res same, clk for father
Hughes Miss Ruth E, d W H, res same, student
Hughes Wm H Jr (Young & Hughes), plumber, res 221 w Martin
Hughes David,* lab, res 413 w South
Hughes Chaney,* wife David, washerwoman
Hughes Ellen,* washerwoman, res 112 e Morgan
Hughes Olive,* washerwoman, res 310 w South
Hughes Ella,* cook, res 310 w South
Hughes Lizzie,* cook, res 310 w South
Hughes Henrietta,* nurse, res 310 w South
Hughes Amanda,* cook, res 310 w South
Hughes John D,* lab, res 310 w South
Hughes James,* drayman, res e Lenoir, o s e
Hughes Gracie,* wife James
Hughes Edward,* son James, res same, student
Hughes Junius, son James, res same, student
Hughes Henry,* son James, res same, student
Hughes Mary,* d James, res same, student
Hulin A D, carp, res 315 s Harrington
Hulin Mrs Elizabeth E, wife A D
Hulin Miss Nellie R, d A D, res same
Hulin Miss Lucy C, d A D, res same
Hulin Miss Sallie E, d A D, res same, student
Hulin Thos D, son A D, res same, student
Hundley, Frank P, carp, room 10 Frap's bldg
Hunnicutt J D, attendant at Insane Asylum, res same.
Hunnicutt C B, eng S A L R R, bds 10 e North
Hunnicutt J H, brick-mason, res 530 s Bloodworth
Hunnicutt F H, brick-mason, res 557 e Martin
Hunnicutt Mrs Lula V, wife F H
Hunnicutt Fab J, son F H, res same, student
Hunnicutt Wm G, brick-mason, res Haywood
Hunnicutt Mrs Essie, wife W G
Hunnicutt Emmitt, son W G, res same, student

Hunnicutt Miss Mabel, d W G, res same, student
Hunnicutt George E, son W G, res same, student
Hunnicutt D O, carp, res 412 e Morgan
Hunnicutt Miss Metta, d D O, res same
Hunnicutt Miss Martha, res with Mrs Lacy Belvin
Hunnicutt Fab W (Hamill & Hunnicutt), contractor, res 230 s Swain
Hunnicutt Mrs Annie, wife F W
Hunnicutt Miss Lohren, d F W, res same
Hunt J W, carp, res 218 s Harrington
Hunt Mrs Dollie F, wife J W
Hunt J W Jr, son J W, res same, moulder
Hunt Miss Lottie I, d J W, res same, student
Hunt Miss Daisy M, d J W, res same, student
Hunt Harry G, son J W, res same, student
Hunt Sam,* wks oil mill, res rear Catholic church
Hunt Jane,* wife Sam
Hunt Wm J,* son Sam, res same, student
Hunt Gertrude,* d Sam, res same, student
Hunt Gracie,* nurse, bds 215 s Wilmington
Hunt, Mrs Lucetta, wid, res 402 w Morgan
Hunter Effie,* student, res 302 w South
Hunter Rosa,* cook, res on lot cor Hillsboro' and Salisbury
Hunter Mrs Mattie, wid, res 565 e Hargett
Hunter Miss Zula, d Mrs Mattie, res same, saleslady at A B Stronach
Hunter Joseph, son Mrs Mattie, res same, errand-boy Whiting Bros
Hunter Geo E (Latta & Hunter), grocer, res 124 Hillsboro'
Hunter Mrs C N, wife Geo E
Hunter Geo T, son Geo E, res same
Hunter Henry,* whitewasher, res 12 Kildee lane
Hunter Kittie,* wife Henry, washerwoman
Hunter Susan,* washerwoman, res 735 e Davie, o s e
Hunter Bennett,* son Susan, res same, lab
Hunter Robert,* harness maker, res 28 Hunter
Hunter Mary,* wife Robert, washerwoman
Hunter S J, carp, res 600 n Salisbury
Hunter Mary H,* student, res with Lee Rowland
Hunter Henry,* house-servant, res 561 e Edenton
Hunter J W, frt dept Southern R R, bds 305 Hillsboro'
Hunter Mrs Corinna, wife J W
Hunter Violet,* washerwoman, res Hargett, o s e
Hunter Chas N,* teacher at Garfield Graded School, res Cotton lane, o s e
Hunter Eliza,* wife Chas N, dressmaker
Hunter Emma,* d Chas N, res same, student
Hunter Eva,* d Chas N, res same, student

Hunter Lena, d Chas N, res same, student
Hunter Chas,* son Chas N, res same, student
Hunter Joseph,* shoemaker, 130 e Hargett, res 305 e Martin
Hunter Maria,* wife Joseph, seamstress
Hunter Kittie,* d Jos, res same, student
Hunter Ida,* d Jos, res same, student
Hunter B W, mgr McKimmon drug store, rooms over 133 Fayetteville
Hunter Mattie,* nurse for M G Jones, res same
Hunter Harriet,* washerwoman, res 121 e Cabarrus
Hunter William,* son Harriet, res same, tobacco worker
Hunter Wiley A,* waiter Park Hotel, room 409 s Blount
Hunter Wiley,* lab, res 316 e Cabarrus
Hunter Lucile,* wife Wiley, teacher
Hunter Lucy A,* washerwoman, res 421 s Swain
Hunter, Job,* shoemaker, res 305 s East
Hunter Maria,* wife Job, res same, seamstress
Hunter Kittie,* d Job, res same, seamstress
Hunter Ida,* d Job, res same, seamstress
Hunter Henry,* coachman, res 522 e Martin
Hunter Alice,* wife Henry, washerwoman
Hunter Allie,* d Henry, res same, student
Hunter Lee,* son Henry, res same, student
Hunter Eliza,* d Henry, res same, student
Hunter Susan,* cook, res Watson
HUNTER CARY J, gen agt Union Central Life Ins Co, office Commercial and Farmers Bank bldg, res 400 n Person
Hunter Mrs E A, wife C J
Hunter Mary E,* washerwoman, res 325 s Bloodworth
Hunter Hattie,* d Mary E, res same, servant
Hunter Lena,* d Mary E, res same, house-servant
Hunter Mattie A,* d Mary E, res same, house-servant
Hunter Charles,* city pump director, res 423 s McDowell
Hunter Sarah,* wife Charles, washerwoman
Hunter Lucy,* d Charles, res same, washerwoman
Hunter Robert,* son Lucy, res same, student

Our Old vs. other Co.'s New.

The **Union Central Life Insurance Co.** is the largest financial institution in next to the richest State in the U. S., and for many years has written the most liberal Policy contracts of any Company, giving the longest possible extension clause, largest possible paid-up value, and have kept the full legal value (as per the highest standard of valuation of any State) at the command of the insured in cash on his Policy, which he may still keep in force at the smallest possible cost.

PERFECT POLICY. FIRST EVER ISSUED LIKE IT.

CARY J. HUNTER, Sup't Va. and N. C., Raleigh, N. C.

Hunter Harriet,* d Lucy, res same, student
Hunter Osborn,* carp, res 208 w Cabarrus
Hunter Nancy,* wife Osborn, cook
Humphries Rev L A,* Methodist minister, res e Edenton
Humphries Fannie,* wife Rev L A
Hurst Katie,* cook for Mrs R E Hervey, res on lot
Hutchings Miss Narcissa, teacher, res 110 n Person
Hutchings Miss Julia, teacher, res 110 n Person
Hutchings C D, clk for C A Sherwood & Co, res 3 s Wilmington
Hutchings Mrs F A, wife C D
Hutchings Miss Julia, d C D, res same, student
HUTCHINGS WM B, city tax collector, office City Hall, res 412 Elm
Hutchings Mrs A R, wife Wm B
Hutchings Henry,* servant John S White, res on lot
Hutchings Maria,* washerwoman, res w Jones, near r r crossing
Hutchings Frances,* d Maria, res same, washerwoman
Hutchings George,* son Maria, res same, wks Jones & Powell
Hutchings Marshall,* son Maria, res same, laborer
Hutchings I D, car inspector S A L R R, res 313 w Lane
Hutchings Mrs Fannie F, wife I D
Hutchings Louis, son I D, res same
Hutchings James, son I D, res same

IDEN George E, tinner Julius Lewis Hardware Co, r 9 s East
Iden Mrs Eleanor, wife Geo E
Iden Miss Susie, d Geo E, res same, student
Irby B, prof of agriculture at A & M Col, res Maiden lane, o s w
Irby Mrs Jessie, wife B
Irby R E, clk Julius Lewis Hardware Co, res Maiden lane, o s w
Irby Mrs H F, mother of Prof B Irby, res same
Irby Miss Franc, niece of Prof B Irby, res same, student
Iredell Nancy,* cook, res 221 w Cabarrus
Iredell Fannie,* cook, res 221 w Cabarrus
Iredell Mollie,* laundress, res 221 w Cabarrus
Iredell Nannie,* chambermaid, res 221 w Cabarrus
Iredell Joseph,* porter N C Book Co, res 221 w Cabarrus
Ingraham Phoebe,* washerwoman, res 112 e Lenoir
Irvin Mary C,* seamstress, res 122 w Lenoir
Irvin Sophia,* cook, res 123 e Cabarrus
Ivey H M, store-keeper S A L, res 521 Halifax
Ivey Mrs Bettie, wife H M
Ivey Alley, fireman S A L, res 521 Halifax
Ivey Dora,* washerwoman, res w Lane, near R R
Ivey Hannah,* d Dora, res same, student
Ivey Henry,* clothes-cleaner, res 207 w Morgan

JACKSON Andrew J, carp Deaf, Dumb and Blind Institution, res 606 n Saunders
Jackson Mrs Lena, wife A J
Jackson Lawrence, son A J, res same, wks Ral cot mill
Jackson Miss Pattie M, d A J, res same, student
Jackson Claude, son A J, res same, student
Jackson Andrew J Jr, son A J, res same, student
Jackson Miss Ethelyn, d A J, res same, student
Jackson Herbert W, asst cashier Commercial and Farmers Bank, res 611 Fayetteville
Jackson Mrs Annie P, wife H W
Jackson Geo H, hostler, res 533 e Martin
Jackson Mrs Sarah, wife Geo H
Jackson Miss Laura B, d Geo H, res same
Jackson Andrew,* lab, res old Fair Ground, o s e
Jackson Chaney,* wife Andrew, washerwoman
Jackson Andrew Jr,* son Andrew, lab
Jackson Willie,* son Andrew, res same, lab
Jackson Semon,* son Andrew, res same, student
Jackson Mary,* washerwoman, res 6½ s Harrington
Jackson Minnie,* d Mary, res same, student
Jackson John L,* son Mary, res same, student
Jackson Adam,* fireman Mills Mfg Co, res 827 Jenkins
Jackson Ida,* wife Adam
Jackson Ada,* d Adam, res same, student
Jackson Claudius, student, lives with J J Hayes
Jackson Miss Hattie, student, lives with J J Hayes
Jackson Charlotte,* washerwoman, rear 609 Hillsboro'
Jackson Chas,* painter, res 401 s Dawson
Jackson Martha,* wife Chas, washerwoman
Jackson Mrs C S, wid, res 527 s Salisbury
Jackson Wm,* cook at Insane Asylum, res 523 Cannon
Jackson Annie,* wife Wm, washerwoman
Jackson H J,* shoemaker, res 804 Manly
Jackson Jane,* house-servant, res 312 Cannon
Jackson Bettie,* cook, res 312 Cannon
Jackson A M, lab, res Cox ave, o s w
Jackson Mrs Etta, wife A M
Jackson Oris, son A M, res same, student
Jader M, gen merchandise, 202 w Cabarrus, res same
Jader Joe, clk for M Jader, res same
Jader Miss Silvia, sister of M Jader, res same
Jeffreys Sonnie,* butler, res 113 n Swain
Jeffreys Rebecca,* wife Sonnie, washerwoman
Jeffreys Charles,* son Sonnie, res same, house-servant
Jeffreys Jane,* d Sonnie, res same, washerwoman
Jeffreys Ruth,* d Sonnie, res same, washerwoman

Jeffreys Minnie,* d Sonnie, res same, student
Jeffreys Fannie,* d Sonnie, res same, student
Jeffreys Livingston,* son Sonnie, res same, student
Jeffreys Laura,* cook, res Bledsoe ave
Jeffreys Sallie,* cook, res Bledsoe ave
Jeffreys Josephine,* d Laura, res same, washerwoman
Jeffreys Annie, d Laura, res same, washerwoman
Jeffreys Flora,* d Laura, res same, nurse
Jeffreys Maggie,* d Laura, res same, student
Jeffreys Fred,* son Laura, res same, student
Jeffreys Laura,* cook at Institution for the Blind, res 107 n Harrington
Jeffreys Lena,* d Laura, res same, student
Jeffreys Hattie,* d Laura, res same, student
Jeffreys Hubert,* son Laura, res same, student
Jeffreys Frank,* son Laura, res same, student
Jeffreys Medora,* student, res 425 Haywood
Jeffreys Mattie,* sister of Medora, res same, student
Jeffreys Clarence A,* brother of Medora, res same, student
Jeffreys Fred J,* brother of Medora, res same, student
Jeffreys P J,* grocer, 209 w South, res 207 w South
Jeffreys Burline,* wife P J, house work
Jeffreys William,* son P J, res same, lab
Jeffreys Claudie,* son P J, res same, lab
Jeffreys Rebecca,* cook, res 207 w South
Jeffreys Sylvester,* drayman, res 110 w Lenoir
Jeffreys Sarah S,* wife Sylvester, washerwoman
Jeffreys Otho T,* son Sylvester, res same, student
Jeffreys Laura,* washerwoman, res e Hargett, o s e
Jeffreys Alex,* son Laura, res same, lab
Jeffreys Ada,* nurse for Mrs H F Smith, res on lot
Jeffreys Matilda,* washerwoman, res 746 s Wilmington
Jeffreys George,* lab, res 529 e Cabarrus
Jeffreys Lavina,* wife George, washerwoman
Jeffreys Lucy,* cook for C D Holland, res same
Jeffreys Mary,* washerwoman, res Smithfield alley
Jeffreys Medora,* student, res 822 s Blount
Jeffreys Sallie,* washerwoman, res 207 e South
Jeffreys Classie,* washerwoman, res 207 e South
Jefferson Bettie,* washerwoman, res 314 w Lenoir
Jefferson Annie,* d Bettie, res same, student
Jenkins J W, associate editor News and Observer, bds 404 Fayetteville
Jenkins Oscar,* carp, res 215 s Harrington
Jenkins Louisa,* wife Oscar, washerwoman
Jenkins Nannie,* d Oscar, res same, washerwoman
Jenkins Amanda,* d Oscar, res same, nurse
Jenkins Sarah,* d Oscar, res same, student

Jenkins Fred,* d Oscar, res same, student
Jenkins Mamie,* d Oscar, res same, student
Jenkins Bessie,* d Oscar, res same, student
Jenkins Lucy,* wks Colored Deaf and Dumb Asylum, res 602 s Person
Jenkins John,* son Lucy, res same, student
Jenkins Henry,* son Lucy, res same, student
Jenkins Basil,* son Lucy, res same, wks cot yard
Jenkins Mrs Sallie, dressmaker, res 217 s East
Jenkins Henry,* lab, res 760 Fayetteville
Jenkins Sarah,* washerwoman, res 738 s Person
Jenkins Rosa,* farm hand, res 738 s Person
Jenkins Virginia,* d Sarah, res same, student
Jenkins Miss Salina, seamstress, res 307 w Morgan
Jenkins Miss Mary, hkpr for W H Fetner, res same
Jerman B S, cashier of Commercial and Farmers Bank, res 102 e North
Jerman Mrs Isabella M, wife B S
Jerman Wm B, son B S, res same
Jewett Chas W, sec and asst treas Shaw University, res same
Jewett Mrs Jennie, wife Chas W
Johns Nicholas, fish dealer, res 327 e Martin
Johns Mrs Mary, wife Nicholas
Johns Joseph,* lab, res 229 Blount-st al
Johns Susan,* wife Joseph, washerwoman
Johns Samuel,* porter for Wm McClure, res 229 Blount al
Johns Becky,* cook for E G Horton, res on lot
Johns Jos,* lab, res rear 521 s Dawson
Johnson Chas E, cot broker, 303 s Wilmington
Johnson Chas E (C E Johnson & Co), cot broker, office 303 s Wilmington, res 120 Hillsboro'
Johnson Mrs M E, wife Chas E
Johnson Miss Mary W, d Chas E, res same
Johnson Chas E Jr, son Chas E, res same
Johnson Miss Fannie H, d Chas E, res same
Johnson Mrs F L, mother Chas E, res same
Johnson D T, agt, grocer and commission merchant, 16 e Hargett, res 513 Hillsboro'
Johnson Mrs Anna, wife D T
Johnson Miss Gertrude, d D T, res same, teacher
Johnson Clarence, son D T, res same, clk N C Home Ins office
Johnson Harvey, son D T, res same, student
Johnson Miss Emma, d D T, res same, student
Johnson Miss Hattie, d D T, res same, student
Johnson Benj, son D T, res same, student
Johnson Thomas, son D T, res same, student
JOHNSON J R, mgr for N C of The Sun Life Assurance Co of Canada, office 238 Fayetteville, res cor Cabarrus and Salisbury

Johnson Mrs Jennie, wife J R
Johnson Harold C, son J R, res same
Johnson Eric F, son J R, res same
Johnson Miss Flossie M, d J R, res same
Johnson Wm P, son J R, res same
Johnson Andrew, cot mill opr, res n Boylan ave
Johnson Mrs Susan, wife Andrew
Johnson Miss Julia, d Andrew, res same, cot mill opr
Johnson Miss Sallie, d Andrew, res same, cot mill opr
Johnson Miss Henrietta, d Andrew, res same, cot mill opr
Johnson Andrew Jr, son Andrew, res same, cot mill opr
Johnson Jos J, merchant, e Hargett, o s e, res cor Newbern ave and Blount
Johnson Mrs P S, wife Jos J
Johnson Miss Ella B, d Jos J, res same
Johnson Chas C, supt Ral Elec Co, res cor Newbern ave and Blount
Johnson Mrs Maude E, wife Chas C
JOHNSON JAMES I, wholesale and retail druggist and mfr of anticephalalgine, cor Fayetteville and e Martin, res 226 Hillsboro
Johnson Mrs Rebecca, wife James I
Johnson Iredell, son James I, res same, student
Johnson Miss Elizabeth, d James I, res same
Johnson Lenox, son James I, res same
Johnson Rufus L (Nixon & Johnson), board and sale stable, res 421 s Wilmington
Johnson Mrs Jane E, wife Rufus L
Johnson James B, son R L, res same, student
Johnson Tapley O, son R L, res same, student
Johnson Thomas, lab, res 536 e Cabarrus
Johnson Mrs Stella, wife Thos
Johnson Miss Mattie, d Thos, res same, dressmaker
Johnson Miss Jennie, d Thos, res same, wks at Royster candy factory
Johnson William, carp, res in Prairie bldg
Johnson Joseph, son William, res same, carp
Johnson John, son William, res same, student
Johnson Martha,* restaurant, 221½ s Wilmington
Johnson Marion, turnkey at city station-house, res 219 Smithfield
Johnson Mrs Rebecca, wife Marion
Johnson Tessie McGee, d Marion, res same
Johnson Miss Margaret, seamstress, res 229 s Bloodworth
Johnson Mrs Susan, wid, seamstress, res 505 s Swain
Johnson Wiley,* train porter for Park Hotel, res same
Johnson Brasil,* lab, res 760 Fayetteville
Johnson Lizzie,* washerwoman, res 714 s McDowell
Johnson Miss Frances A, seamstress, res 327 s Bloodworth
Johnson Jane,* washerwoman, res 534 Halifax

Johnson Henrietta,* washerwoman, res 722 s Dawson
Johnson Alice,* washerwoman, res 212 Blount-st alley
Johnson Kissie,* washerwoman, res 503 Cannon
Johnson & Johnson, wood and coal dealers and com merchants, 109 Fayetteville
Johnson Miss Mattie, dressmaker, bds 231 e Lenoir
Johnson John, stone-mason, res Idlewild ave
Johnson Mrs Angeline, wife John
Johnson Miss Mary E, d John, res same, seamstress
Johnson George,* lab, res Pugh
Johnson John,* son Geo, res same, lab
Johnson Alex,* son Geo, res same, lab
Johnson Sallie,* d Geo, res same, student
Johnson Maggie,* d Geo, res same, student
Johnson Mary,* d Geo, res same, nurse
Johnson W A,* tobacco worker, res 760 Fayetteville
Johnson Annie,* wife W A, washerwoman
Johnson Enliee,* son W A, res same, tobacco worker
Johnson Burlina,* cook, res 514 w South
Johnson Geneva,* nurse, res 514 w South
Johnson Julia,* house-servant, res 514 w South
Johnson Rachel,* washerwoman, res 311 w South
Johnson Hannah,* d Rachel, res same, house-servant
Johnson Sarah,* d Rachel, res same, house-servant
Johnson Luvinia,* washerwoman, res 302 w South
Johnson Frank, lab, res 223 w Davie
Johnson Mrs Minnie, wife Frank
Johnson J S (Johnson & Johnson), coal and wood dealer, res 108 n McDowell
Johnson Mrs M B, wife J S
Johnson Felix,* coachman for Mrs V B Swepson, res same
Johnson Henrietta,* wife Felix, servant of Mrs V B Swepson
Johnson John, lab, res 15 Hayti
Johnson Mrs Gertrude, wife John
Johnson Mrs Cora, seamstress, res 212 s Harrington
Johnson James,* wks at Park Hotel, res 312 Cannon
Johnson Rosa,* wife James, house work
Johnson Ferribee,* house-servant, res 12 McKee
Johnson Rev Caesar,* Baptist minister, res 540 e Edenton
Johnson Lucy,* washerwoman, res 579 e Lenoir
Johnson Jennie,* d Lucy, res same, cook for A P Bryan
Johnson Luther,* son Lucy, res same, laborer
Johnson A R D (Johnson & Johnson), commission broker, wood and coal dealer, res 513 Hillsboro'
Johnson James O, clk for J J Johnson, res e Hargett, o s e
Johnson Mrs Lula, wife James O
Johnson James,* lab, res old Fair Ground, o s e
Johnson Rosa,* wife James, washerwoman

Johnson Laura,* washerwoman, r 221 w North
Johnson Miss Ervy, operator Telephone Exchange, bds 527 Hillsboro'
JOHNSON THOS B, photographer, gallery over 115 Fayetteville, res 223 e Davie
Johnson Mrs Jane, wife Thos B
Johnson Miss Jennie, teacher in Peace Institute, res same
Johnson Miss Janie, wks Royster candy factory, bds 216 w Lane
Johnson Ed, house painter, res 416 w North
Johnson Mrs Elizabeth, wid, mother Ed, res same
Johnson Miss Alice, d Mrs Elizabeth, res same
Johnson John, son Mrs Elizabeth, res same, painter
Johnson David, merchant, bds 317 w Morgan
Johnson Mrs Ida, wife David
Johnson O H, grocer, 331 Hillsboro', bds 527 Hillsboro'
Johnson Patsy,* laundress, res s Saunders
Johnson Handy,* son Patsy, res same, laborer
Johnson Mary,* d Patsy, res same, washerwoman
Johnson Ransom,* porter at Stronach & Sons, res 121 w Lenoir
Johnson Susan,* wife Ransom, house work
Johnson Frank,* carp, res 521 s Wilmington
Johnson Martha A,* wife Frank, sick-nurse
Johnson Hattie,* d Frank, res same, school teacher
Johnson Lizzie,* d Frank, res same
Johnson Sallie,* sick-nurse, res same, 519 s Wilmington
Johnson Jacob,* landscape gardener, res 510 s East
Johnson Mary,* wife Jacob, laundress
Johnson Richard,* son Jacob, res same, porter for L J Walker
Johnson Courtland,* son Jacob, res same, student
Johnson Josephine, nurse for Mrs C A Riddle, res same
Johnson W S, wks ice factory, bds 218 s Harrington
Johnson Henry C, machinist, res 408 n Bloodworth
Johnson Mrs Joanna, wife H C
Johnson E A,* lawyer, res 519 s West
Johnson Lena A,* wife E A, teacher
Johnson Columbus,* father of E A, res same

T. B. JOHNSON,

High=Art Photographer,

113½ Fayetteville St., Raleigh, N. C.

All styles of Photographs made and work guaranteed. A trial will convince the most sceptical. Lowest prices consistent to good workmanship.

Johnson Frederick,* brother of E A, res same, student
Johnson John, stone-cutter, res 529 s Harrington
Johnson Mrs Rachel, wife John
Johnson Sarah,* cook for John Johnson, res same
Johnson W B, tailor, res 409 s Person
Johnson Miss Manie, d W B, res same, student
Johnson Sam, wks Farina roller mills, bds 109 s Blount
Johnson Albert, mechanic, res 329 Hillsboro'
Johnson Mrs Elizabeth, wife Albert
Jolly Mrs Bettie, seamstress, res Fayetteville, below R R
Jolly Miss Lila A, d Mrs Bettie
Jolly William, quiller at Caraleigh mill, res Fayetteville, below R R
Jolly Mrs Hattie, wife Wm, weaver at Caraleigh mill
JOLLY B R, jeweler and silversmith, 128 Fayetteville, res 116 s McDowell
Jolly Frank M, son B R, res same, wks with father
Jolly Miss Lucy E, d B R, res same
Jolly Mrs Nancy, wid, res 116 s McDowell
Jolly Miss Bettie, d Mrs Nancy, res same, dressmaker
Jones A A, butcher, res Cox ave, o s w
Jones Mrs Martha, wife A A
Jones Alonzo, son A A, res same, painter
Jones Wm O, son A A, res same
Jones Charles, son A A, res same, student
Jones Mrs M C, wid, res with J M Barbee
Jones Samuel, butcher, cor s Harrington and Hillsboro', res same
Jones R H, spinner Ral cot mill, res 130 Firwood ave, o s n
Jones Mrs L V, wife R H
Jones Miss Bessie, d R H, res same, spinner Ral cot mill
Jones Miss Laura, d R H, res same, student
Jones Lonnie, wks Raleigh cot mill, bds 211 e South
Jones Miss Ella, seamstress, res 175 Hunter
Jones Miss Lurie, seamstress, bds 122 e Martin
Jones Alfred, oil merchant, res 411 Elm
Jones Mrs Lizzie C, wife Alfred
Jones Miss Nannie R, d Alfred, res same, student
Jones Miss Fannie C, d Alfred, res same, student
Jones Miss Mildred McKee, d Alfred, res same, student
Jones Miss Margaret R, d Alfred, res same, student
Jones Mrs Winnie, wid, res 519 s Bloodworth
Jones Wiley A, son Mrs Winnie, res same, printer
Jones Alonzo, clk J J Harris, res 226 s Bloodworth
Jones Mrs Lucy, wife Alonzo, seamstress
Jones Robert, lab, res 226 e Bloodworth
Jones Miss Adna, sister Mrs Ed V Denton, res same
Jones Mrs Annie, wid, seamstress, res 121 s West
Jones John, beemer Caraleigh cot mill, bds 739 Fayetteville

Jones G M, city policeman, res 405 n West
Jones Mrs Lula, wife G M
Jones Miss Margaret, d G M, res same, student
Jones Miss Annie, d G M, res same, student
Jones Miss Jessie, d G M, res same, student
Jones L H, guard at penitentiary, res 213 Tucker
Jones Mrs Susan, wife L H
Jones Chas H, son L H, res same, printer
Jones Lewis A, son L H, res same, wks Ral cot mill
Jones C C, restaurant, over 210 s Wilmington
Jones Wm H, grocer, 705 s Blount, res same
Jones Mrs Elizabeth, wife Wm H
Jones Patrick, son Wm H, res same, wks Ral cot mill
Jones Miss Cornelia, d Wm H, res same, saleslady
Jones Mrs Jessie, wid, res 518 w North
Jones Albert, son Mrs Jessie, res same, machinist
Jones Herald, son Mrs Jessie, res same, student
Jones Charlie, son Mrs Jessie, res same, student
Jones Wm J, blacksmith S A L shops, res 205 n Salisbury
Jones Mrs Maggie, wife Wm J
Jones Miss Lillie, d Wm J, res same, student
Jones Armistead, lawyer, office Commercial and Farmers Bank bldg, res Hillsboro' near Dawson
Jones Mrs Nannie B, wife Armistead
Jones Miss Nannie B, d Armistead, res same
Jones Miss Mary A, d Armistead, res same
Jones Wm B, son Armistead, res same, student
Jones Robert H, ins agt, res 305 Hillsboro'
Jones Mrs Sue B, wife R H
Jones J Wiley, revenue officer, bds 314 Hillsboro'
Jones Cullen, mechanic, bds 11 s Wilmington
Jones Matt G, eng Ral Elec Co, res 122 Dawson
Jones Mrs Julia, wife Matt G
Jones W H, salesman, bds 407 Fayetteville
Jones Mrs Etta, wid, seamstress, 110 s McDowell
Jones L, motorman Ral Elec Co, bds 209 w Morgan
Jones T A, section hand, bds 314 n McDowell
Jones Melissa,* washerwoman, res Womble lane
Jones Elijah,* son Melissa, res same, porter G S Tucker & Co
Jones Archie,* son Melissa, res same, student
Jones Eliza,* d Melissa, res same, nurse
Jones Essie,* d Melissa, res same, student
Jones James,* fireman S A L R R, res 223 w North
Jones Mollie,* wife James, washerwoman
Jones Emma D,* d James, res same, student
Jones S W,* carp, res 31 Hayti
Jones Annie M,* wife S W, house work
Jones Wayman,* son S W, res same, brick-mason app

Jones Furman,* son S W, res same, driver for Dr J W McGee
Jones Wade H,* son S W, res same, house-servant
Jones Ballard,* son S W, res same, student
Jones Ernest,* son S W, res same, student
Jones Wiley,* lab, res Manly-st alley
Jones Maggie,* d Wiley, res same, cook
Jones Harriet,* d Wiley, res same, nurse
Jones Penny,* washerwoman, res 405 Cannon
Jones Victoria,* d Penny, res same, student
Jones Edgar,* son Penny, res same, student
Jones Octavia,* cook, res 819 Manly
Jones John,* lab, res 819 Manly
Jones Harriet,* house-servant, res 813 Manly
Jones E G,* baker, 603 s McDowell, res same
Jones Martha,* wife E G
Jones Alice,* cook, res 109 w Lenoir
Jones George,* son Alice, res same, student
Jones Isabella,* cook for H Crossan, res same
Jones Hubert,* son Isabella, res same, student
Jones Sylvia,* cook, res Pugh
Jones Arthur,* lab, res Oakwood ave
Jones Lula,* wife Arthur
Jones Richard,* lab, res 224 e Cabarrus
Jones Alice,* wife Richard, washerwoman
Jones Chas E,* son Richard, res same, student
Jones Walter,* son Richard, res same, student
Jones Mary,* washerwoman, res Manly
Jones Isham,* lab, res Manly
Jones Willis,* lab, res Forsythe alley
Jones Rufus,* carver Yarboro' House, res 750 s Person
Jones Ailsey,* wife Rufus
Jones Robert,* porter Farmers and Commercial Bank, res 750 s Person
Jones Fannie,* d Rufus, res same, cook Ed Adams
Jones Judson,* son Rufus, res same, laborer
Jones Maggie,* d Rufus, res same, student
Jones Buck,* son Rufus, res same, porter Dr J A Sexton
Jones Wayland,* son Rufus, res same, student
Jones James,* son Rufus, res same, student
Jones Sidney,* farmer, res 835 Fayetteville
Jones Sarah,* wife Sidney, washerwoman
Jones Mary,* nurse, res 835 Fayetteville
Jones Maggie,* d Sidney, res same, student
Jones Sidney,* lab, res 739 s Blount
Jones Louisa,* wife Sidney, cook for W L Sunderford
Jones Lewis,* son Sidney, res same, porter for M A Bledsoe Jr
Jones Gertrude,* d Sidney, res same, student
Jones Everlina,* cook for Mrs H Mahler, res 739 s Blount

Birthplace of ANDREW JOHNSON, 17th President of the United States, Raleigh, N. C.

Jones Caroline,* cook, res Bledsoe ave
Jones Minor,* carp, res Bledsoe ave
Jones Carrie,* d Caroline, res same, student
Jones Ernest,* works Southern R R, bds 35 Hunter
Jones Sallie,* house-servant, res 35 Hunter
Jones Rev Milliard,* Baptist minister, res 745 s Blount
Jones Dora,* wife Rev Milliard
Jones Sam,* laborer, res with John O'Kelly
Jones Malsey,* servant, res 106 Smithfield
Jones Wm,* servant for F E Hege, res same
Jones Lucy A,* washerwoman, res w Lane near R R
Jones Norfleet,* house-servant for Mrs Elizabeth McSnow, res on lot
Jones Andrew,* lab, res 529 s Wilmington
Jones Sarah,* wife Andrew, cook Elvin Fleming
Jones Lewis,* coachman, res 529 s Wilmington
Jones Valley,* cook, res near r r crossing at n West
Jones Mary,* cook, res near r r crossing at n West
JONES W N, lawyer, office 16 w Martin, res 522 Fayetteville
Jones Mrs Sallie B, wife W N
Jones Miss Annie B, d W N, res same, student
Jones Mrs L J, wid, res with son W N Jones
Jones D W, shoemaker, res 219 s West
Jones Miss Mary J, dressmaker, res 219 s West
Jones Miss Jennie, dressmaker, res 219 s West
Jones Justin S, tel opr, bds 404 Fayetteville
Jones Mrs Mattie, wife Justin S
Jones William,* whitewasher, res Rock Quarry rd
Jones Laura,* wife Wm, washerwoman
Jones Ben M,* son Wm, res same
Jones James T,* son Wm, res same
Jones Madison,* fireman S A L R R, res 314 n Dawson
Jones Adalaide,* wife Madison, washerwoman
Jones Hilliard,* son Madison, res same, lab
Jones Wm,* whitewasher, res Rock Quarry rd
Jones Laura,* wife Wm, washerwoman
Jones Ben M*
Jones Cornelia,* washerwoman, res 517 s McDowell
Jones Gertie,* d Cornelia, res same, student
Jones Jane,* washerwoman, res 408 Smith
Jones Millie,* d Jane, res same, house-servant
Jones Carrie,* d Jane, res same, student
Jones W F,* shoemaker, res 709 Manly
Jones Fannie E,* wife W F, house work
Jones Willis,* porter for Pool & Moring, res 531 e Edenton
Jones Florence,* wife Willis, washerwoman
Jones Frank,* lab, res 515 e Edenton
Jones Lizzie,* wife Frank, washerwoman

Jones Miss Emma, weaver Caraleigh mill, bds at Mrs Bettie Jolly
Jones Lewis,* shoemaker, res 712 s McDowell
Jones R K, wks Caraleigh mill, res 418 w South
Jones Mrs C A, wife R K, house work
Jones Oscar, son R K, res same, wks Caraleigh mill
Jones Miss Dora, d R K, res same, student
Jones Daniel,* lab, res 529 e Edenton
Jones Matilda,* wife Daniel, cook
Jones Rev W A,* Baptist minister, res 308 w South
Jones Adelaide,* wife Rev W A, house work
Jones George,* lab, rooms 405 s Dawson
Jones Jane, laundress, res 503 Smith
Jones James,* lab, res 739 s Blount
Jones Harriet,* washerwoman and scourer, res 108 Newbern ave
Jones S M & Bros, shoemakers, 140 s Wilmington
Jones Narcissa,* laundress, res 503 Cannon
Jones Fannie,* d Narcissa, res same, student
Jones Frank,* lab, res 405 w South
Jones Julia,* wife Frank, cook
Jones Lula,* washerwoman, res 401 s Dawson
Jones Emily,* wid, washerwoman, res 410 w Edenton
Jones Ella,* washerwoman, res 317 s Bloodworth
Jones Alonzo,* son Ella, res same, lab
Jones Sam,* son Ella, res same, lab
Jones Harry,* lab, res 225 s Bloodworth
Jones Harry Jr,* son Harry, res same, student
Jones Matilda,* cook for W G Martin, res on lot
Jones Minerva,* cook for W R Tucker, res 512 e Edenton
Jones Nellie E,* house-servant, res 718 s Dawson
Jones Annie,* cook, res 556 e Edenton
Jones Mary,* house-servant, res 12 w Worth
Jones Louisa,* cook for Mrs Jas McKimmon, res on lot
Jones Miss Maggie, dressmaker, res 427 s Wilmington
Jones Pattie S,* student, res with Wm Pool
Jones Mary,* sister of Pattie S, res same, student
Jones Rev Milliard,* Baptist minister, res 526 s Dawson
Jones Dora,* wife Rev Milliard, house work
Jones William,* hackman, res 728 Manly
Jones Becky,* wife Wm, house work
Jones Willie,* son Wm, res same, student
Jones Daniel, lab, res 312 w Lenoir
Jones Rosa, wife Daniel, washerwoman
Jones Washington, lab, res 720 s Dawson
Jones Jane,* wife Washington, house-servant
Jones Albert,* brick-mason, res 720 s Dawson
Jones Blanche,* wife Albert, house work
Jones Sallie,* d Albert, res same, student
Jones John, upholster, res 542 e Martin

Jones Annie, wife John
Jones Arthur, son John, res same, student
Jones Seth, sexton city cemetery, res 403 e Morgan
Jones Mrs Delia, wife Seth
Jones Wesley, son Seth, res same, clk Ed Scarboro
Jones Miss Pattie, d Seth, res same
Jones Miss Florence, d Seth, res same, student
Jones Sherman,* wks phosphate mill, res Caswell lane
Jones Mary,* wife Sherman, cook Mrs Nixon
Jones W A, printer, res 519 s Bloodworth
Jones Narcissa,* cook W T Ultey, res same
Jones Chaney,* washerwoman, res Hargett, o s e
Jones Miss Annie T, teacher in kindergarten dept Deaf and Dumb Asylum
Jones Daniel,* lab, res 2 Johnson ave
Jones Matilda,* wife Daniel, washerwoman
Jones Catherine,* milker for W C Upchurch, res 324 e Edenton
Jones Manuel,* lab, res 24 McKee
Jones Sarah,* wife Manuel, washerwoman
Jones Archie,* wks in city market, res 429 s Person
Jones Sherman,* shoemaker, res 508 Newbern ave
Jones Emma,* wife Sherman
Jones Robert,* butler Major W W Vass, res 533 Newbern ave
Jones Mittie,* wife Robt, washerwoman
Jones J W, clk, bds 326 Newbern ave
Jones Susan,* cook, res 303½ w South
Jones Helen,* washerwoman, res rear e Cabarrus
Jones Jas M,* shoemaker, 545 Newbern ave, res 543 Newbern ave
Jones Henrietta, cook Peter Watkins, res same
Jones Mrs Cornelia, wid, seamstress, res 109 Grimes alley
Jones Frank,* wks N C Car Co, res 523 Newbern ave
JONES & POWELL, com merchants, wood and coal dealers, 107 Fayetteville
Jones Jesse A (Jones & Powell), com merchant, wood, coal and ice dealer, res 509 Hillsboro'
Jones Mrs Mollie, wife Jesse A
Jones Miss Annie, d Jesse A, res same, student
Jones Willie, son Jesse A, res same, student
Jones Corydon, son Jesse A, res same, student
Jones Garland, sec and treas Ral oil mills, res 531 Hillsboro'
Jones Mrs Florence H, wife Garland
Jones Irwin T, son Garland, res same, bkkpr Citizens Nat Bank
Jones Chas D, son Garland, res same, collector Nat Bank of Ral
Jones Miss Florence H, d Garland, res same
Jones Miss Fannie A, d Garland, res same, student
Jones Garland Jr, son Garland, res same, student
Jones Lawrence T, son Garland, res same, student
Jones W E, dry goods, notions, millinery, &c, 206 Fayetteville, res 540 n Blount

Jones Mrs Helen, wife W E
Jones Miss Hattie H, d W E, res same, student
Jones Miss Mary L, d W E, res same
Jones John, clk Chas Anderson, bds Exchange Hotel
Jones T R, beer and soda bottler, res 422 s Dawson
Jones Mrs Minnie E, wife T R
Jones Miss Bessie M, d T R, res same, student
Jones Miss Mabel A, d T R, res same, student
Jones Harry E, son T R, res same, student
Jones Miss Maud E, d T R, res same, student
Jones T A, shoe mfr, res 215 w Jones
Jones Mrs E C, wife T A
Jones Thomas A, flagman S A L R R, res 215 w Jones
Jones Miss Emma V, d T A, res same, student
Jones Andrew J, bkkpr, res 628 w Jones
Jones Mrs Mollie, wife A J
Jones Miss Pearl, d A J, res same, student
Jones Jesse, son A J, res same, student
Jones Miss Emma, d A J, res same, student
Jones Robert, son A J, res same, student
Jones Carter, son A J, res same, student
Jones R P, millwright, res 525 s Harrington
Jones Mrs Annie L, wife R P
Jones Fernando, son R P, res same, student
Jones Floyd, son R P, res same, student
Jones Miss Pearl E, d R P, res same, student
Jones Haywood, wks Ral cot mill, res 211 e South
Jones Mrs Texanna, wife Haywood
Jones Mrs Mason, wid, res with Haywood
Jones Miss Judie, d Mrs Mason, res same, wks cot mill
Jones John H, stationary eng for N C Car Co, bds 703 n Salisbury, o s n
Jones Turner,* lab, res old Fair Ground, o s e
Jones Fannie,* wife Turner, laundress
Jones Esther,* washerwoman, res old Fair Ground, o s e
Jones Ellen,* d Esther, res same, nurse
Jones J W, clk, bds 326 Newbern ave
Jones A L,* lab, res old Fair Ground, o s e
Jones Susie,* wife A L
Jones Dr A O, res 118 n Person
Jones Mrs Lizzie, wife Dr A O
Jones Sam,* driver for Stronach & Sons, res 541 e Martin
Jones Delia,* wife Sam
Jones Annie,* d Sam, res same, house work
Jones Lizzie,* d Sam, res same, house work
Jones Hattie,* d Sam, res same, student
Jones Lewis,* shoemaker, 317 w Cabarrus
Jones Lem, basket maker, res 527 Cannon

Jones Mrs Emily, wife Lem
Jones Emma,* nurse at C W Newcomb's, res on lot
Jones Henrietta,* washerwoman, res old Fair Ground, o s e
Jones Ann,* farm hand, res old Fair ground, o s e
Jones Hester,* washerwoman, res 328 w Edenton
Jones Daniel,* drayman, res 104 w Edenton
Jones Eliza,* washerwoman, res old Fair Ground, o s e
Jones Nannie,* cook, res 116 e Morgan
Jones Harriet,* washerwoman, res 114 n Harrington
Jones W J,* shoemaker, 16 n McDowell, res 709 Manly
Jones Miss Emma, lives with Mrs E S Cheek, 114 n Dawson
Jones Frances, washerwoman, res 32 Hunter
Jones Rev Alex,* Baptist minister, res 32 Hunter
Jones Rev Isaac,* Baptist minister, res 32 Hunter
Jones Logan,* wks Yarboro' House, res 9 Stronach ave
Jones Frank,* porter J Y McRae, res 9 Stronach ave
Jones George,* porter at Potter & Scott, res 563 e Cabarrus
Jones Janie,* wife Geo, washerwoman
Jones Hettie,* cook for Chas Creighton, res same
Jones William H, stone-cutter, res 105 s Bloodworth
Jones Mrs Mary, wife William H
Jordan John C, blacksmith, shop cor s Blount and Morgan, bds 109 s Blount
Jordan Mrs Salina, wife John C
Jordan A E, bkkpr for Thomas & Maxwell, res 314 e Morgan
Jordan Mrs Emma, wife A E
Jordan Armond, son A E, res same, student
Jordan Mrs C H, wid, res 565 e Hargett
Jordan James F, moulder, res 565 Hargett
Jordan Mrs Annie M, wife James F
Jordan Jacob,* lab, res 226 s East
Jordan Laura E,* wife Jacob
Jordan Lula M,* d Jacob, res same, teacher
Jordan Junius,* son Jacob, res same, janitor
Jordan Martha,* d Jacob, res same, student
Jordan Lovie G,* d Jacob, res same, student
Jordan Jacob Jr,* son Jacob, res same, student
Jordan Stephen,* lab, res e Hargett
Jordan Kate,* wife Stephen, washerwoman
Jordan Della,* washerwoman, res e Hargett, o s e
Jordan Walter,* son Della, res same, lab
Jordan Willie,* son Della, res same, lab
Jordan John,* lab, res e Hargett, o s e
Jordan Bettie,* washerwoman, res 553 e Edenton
Jordan Charles,* farm hand, res 553 e Edenton
Jordan Albert,* son Bettie, res same, lab
Jordan Noah,* lab, res 514 w Morgan
Jordan Pattie,* wife Noah, washerwoman

Jordan Lee,* son Noah, res same, lab
Jordan Harriet,* d Noah, res same, nurse
Jordan Miss G, student, lives with H B Hardy, 118 Halifax
Jordan William, shoemaker, res Johnson
Jordan Mrs Elizabeth, wife William
Jordan Rosa,* cook for Jos G Brown, res 328 w Edenton
Jordan Nettie,* cook for T B Yancey, res on lot
Jordan Miss Clara, sister of Mrs Elizabeth Betts, res same
Jordan Riley,* lab, res 622 Elm
Jordan Martha,* wife Riley, house work
Jordan Mary,* washerwoman, res 426 s Swain
Jordan Mrs J B, wid, res 122 w Jones
Jordan Miss Stella E, d Mrs J B, res same
Jordan W D, grocer, 106 w North, res same
Jordan Mrs Etta, wife W D
Joseph Wm H,* shoemaker, res 14 s Harrington
Joyner Martha,* washerwoman, res 6 Matthews' lane
Joyner Meddicus,* son Martha, res same, brick-mason
Joyner Eucus,* son Martha, res same, lab
Joyner Emma,* cook for Rev Curtis, res 6 Matthews' lane
Joyner Miss Annie, wks Caraleigh mill, bds 417 s Dawson
Joyner Marie,* housekeeper for Geo Renshaw, res same
Joyner Robert W, inmate Soldiers' Home
Joyner Alice,* cook, res 22 w Worth
Justice Walter, weaver Caraleigh mill, bds 744 Fayetteville
Justice J W, inmate Soldiers' Home
Justice Elizabeth,* cook for W A Lamb, res on lot

KAPLAN Isaac, peddler, res 414 s Blount
Kaplan Mrs Annie, wife Isaac
Karrar Miss Emma, stamping and embroidering, 115 Fayetteville, bds w Edenton near Edenton-st church
Kayler Chas H, supt Caraleigh phosphate mill, res 408 e Hargett
Kayler Mrs Elizabeth C
Kayler Chas C, son Chas H, res same
Keely Chas, wks S A L R R, bds 209 w Morgan
Kehoe R H, machinist, res Firwood ave
Keith Mrs Frances, wid, res 130 Firwood ave, o s n
Keith Miss Roberta, d Mrs Frances, res same, spinner Ral cot mill
Keith John S, plasterer, res n Bloodworth
Keith Mrs Emma L, mother J S, res same
Kelly Miss Ada C, attendant at Insane Asylum, res same
Kelly Stephen, wks Caraleigh mill, res 409 Cannon
Kelly Mrs Loan, wife Stephen, wks Caraleigh mill
Kelly Charlotte,* house work, res 406 Cannon
Kelly Chas,* son Charlotte, res same
Kelly John, driver for A V Emery, res over store

Kelly Mrs Susan, wife John
Kelly Junius,* huckster, res 725 s East
Kelly Annie,* wife Junius
Kelly Wesley, cot mill operator, res Prairie bldg
Kelly Winslow, cot mill operator, res Prairie bldg
Kelly Mrs Hawkins, wife Winslow
Kelly Miss Viola, d Winslow, res same
Kelly Paul, son Winslow, res same
Kenan Thos S, clk Supreme Court of N C, office Supreme Court bldg, res 201 n Wilmington
Kenan Mrs S D, wife Thos S
Kenan Miss M L, d Thos, res same
KENDRICK W B, gen agt University Pub Co, N Y, res 435 Halifax
Kendrick Mrs M N, wife W B
Kendrick Gerald O'K, son W B, res same, student
Kendrick Hugh O'K, son W B, res same, student
Kennedy & Jackson,* shoemakers, 802 Manly
Kenneth Bros (J E & W R), grocers, cor Jones and Salisbury
Kenneth W R (Kenneth Bros), grocer, res cor Jones and Salisbury
Kenneth J E (Kenneth Bros), grocer, res cor Jones and Salisbury
KENNY JOHN B, broker, real estate and ins agt, 2 Pullen bldg, res 526 n Wilmington
Kenny Mrs M S, wife J B
Kenster L A, plumber and gas-fitter, res 508 s West
Kenster Mrs Ada, wife L A
Kenster Miss Sadie, d L A, res same, student
Kenster Miss Lula, d L A, res same, student
Kenster Miss Lovie, d L A, res same
Kenster Mrs L S, wid, res 317 w Jones
Kenster A T, son Mrs L S, res same, plumber
Kenster Miss Bettie, d Mrs L S, res same
Kienzle Charles, candy maker, bds 606 Hunter
Killian Elvis,* cupalo tender, res 31 Hayti
Killian Geneva,* wife Elvis, house work
Kimbrough Miss M S, res 435 Halifax
King Rufus, wks Pilot mill, res Avent Ferry road, e s w
King Mrs Lillie, wife Rufus
King Walter, son Rufus, res same
King Miss Mary, d Rufus, res same, wks Pilot cot mill
King Miss Nannie, d Rufus, res same
King Willie, son Rufus, res same, student
King Harry, son Rufus, res same, student
King Rev James,* Episcopal minister, res 15 s Harrington
King Polly A,* wife Rev James
King John, printer, res 713 s Blount
King Miss Sallie, sister John, res same
King Mrs Clara, seamstress, res 11 w Peace

King Miss Martha, seamstress, res 11 w Peace
King & Hales, grocers, 116 e Martin
King Wesley W, grocer, 324 n Saunders, res 326 n Saunders
King Mrs Ann, wife Wesley W
King Ed H, son Wesley W, res same, salesman
King Mrs Mary A, sister Wesley W, res same
King Andrew J, traveling salesman, res 402 e Hargett
King Mrs Ida E, wife A J
King Miss Estelle E, d A J, res same, student
King Miss Maggie A, d A J, res same, student
King Wm S, son A J, res same, moulder
King John C, blacksmith, res 215 s West
King Mrs Mary T, wife J C
King Miss Lovie, d J C
King Miss Myrtle, d J C, res same, student
King Rufus W, son J C, res same, merchant
King Mrs Lizzie C, wid, res 213 w Martin
King Miss Minnie T, d Mrs L C, res same, student
King Mrs Anna, wid, res 416 s Salisbury
King Rev C H,* Methodist minister, res 116 w South
King Ella M,* wife Rev C H
King O G, druggist, cor Wilmington and Hargett, res 613 e Hargett
King Mrs A E, wife O G
King Miss Mary A, sister of Mrs Jos Creighton, res same
King Robert O, traveling salesman, res s Blount
King Mrs Sarah J, wife R O
King Edgar, clk Jesse G Ball, res 314 s Bloodworth
King Mrs Lucy, wife Edgar
King Delmar, son Edgar, res same, wks Ral cot mill
King Miss Maggie, d Edgar, res same, student
King Miss Bertha, d Edgar, res same, student
King Emily,* washerwoman, room 214 e Cabarrus
King C C, carp S A L R R, res 2 Franklin, o s n
King John, son C C, res same
King Richard, watchman cot yard, res 227 n Dawson
King Mrs N M, wife Richard
King Miss Nannie, d Richard, res same, student
King David, son Richard, res same, student
King Joseph, wks N C penitentiary, res 121 s West
King Miss Nora, sister Jos, res same
King Mrs L M, wid, boarding-house, res 404 Hillsboro'
King Miss Nannie, d Mrs L M, res same, saleslady N C Book Co
King Miss Ellen, d Mrs L M, res same
King Miss Laura, d Mrs L M, res same
King Missouri,* cook, res 124 w Lenoir
King Mary,* d Missouri, res same, student
King Jessie, d Missouri, res same, student

King Devereux,* d Missouri, res same, student
King Margaret,* d Missouri, res same, student
King David H, collector frt dept S A L R R, room over Robert Simpson's drug store
King Wm F, painter, res Firwood ave
King Mrs Emma J, wife W F
King Miss Janet L, d W F, res same
King D M, trav eng S A L, res 224 n McDowell
King Mrs Nelia, wife D M
King Chas R, mechanic, res 550 e Jones
King Mrs Sallie, wife Chas R
King Robt, loom-fixer Caraleigh mill, bds with P M Davis
King Mrs Sallie, wife Robert
King Mrs C H, wid, res 223 w Jones
King Wm E, son Mrs C H, res same, clk for W E Carter
King Herbert A, son Mrs C H, res same
KING W H & CO, druggists, cor Fayetteville and e Hargett
King W H (W H King & Co), druggist, room over store
King Eveline,* cook for C B Park, rooms 510 n Bloodworth
King & Pool, grocers, e Hargett, o s e
King Miss Sallie, dressmaker, res 323 Pace
King Phil,* porter for Roger Nott, res 553 e Martin
King Charles, merchant, res 614 e Davie
King Mrs Annie, wife Charles
King William, son Chas, res at Blind Institution
King Miss Minnie, d Chas, res same
King Miss Ida, d Chas, res same
King Miss Mattie, d Chas, res same
King Oscar, son Chas, res same, student
King Cody, son Chas, res same, student
King Miss Lenora, d Chas, res same, student
King Theodore, son Chas, res same, student
King Mrs Charlotte, wid, res 218 e Lenoir
King Robert, son Mrs Charlotte, res same, wks Caraleigh mill
King Paschall K, son Mrs Charlotte, res same, wks Caraleigh mill
King Leonidas K, son Mrs Charlotte, res same, wks Caraleigh mill

W. H. KING & CO.,

Druggists,

Corner Fayetteville and Hargett Sts.

King Miss Octavia, d Mrs Charlotte, res same
King Miss Dora, d Mrs Charlotte, res same, student
King James C, plumber, res 210 s Bloodworth
King Mrs Laura R, wife Jas C
King James E, son Jas C, res same, ins agt
King Ernest L, son Jas C, res same, baggage master S A L
King Roy, farmer, res 222 e Lenoir
King Miss Juanetta, d Roy, res same
Kirby Dr Geo L, supt N C Insane Asylum, res same
Kirby Miss L M, attendant at Insane Asylum, res same
Kirby Miss E G, stenographer Insane Asylum, res same
Kirkland W D, lab S A L shops, res 228 w North
Kirkland Mrs F E, wife W D
Kirkland A M, son W D, res same, wks in boiler shop S A L
Kirkland Miss E S, d W D, res same, student
Kirkland W D Jr, student, res 228 w North
Kirkland Miss M J, d W D, res same, student
Kirkland J S, attendant at Insane Asylum, res same
Kirkland Augusta,* cook Ed Vaughan, res same
Kirkpatrick Miss A B, attendant at Insane Asylum, res same
Kittrell Henry,* upholsterer, res 130 w Lenoir
Kittrell Lizzie,* wife Henry, house work
Kleighbacker B W, steward Central Hotel, res same
Kleighbacker Mrs Katie, wife B W
Kleighbacker Norman, son B W, res same
Klueppelberg Chas, pattern mkr S A L R R, res 220 n Harrington
Klueppelberg Mrs Mary, wife Chas
Klueppelberg Miss Bertha, d Chas, res same
Klueppelberg Henry, son Chas, res same, machinist apprentice
Klueppelberg Miss Lottie, d Chas, res same, student
Klueppelberg Howell, son Chas, res same, student
Klouse D B, painter, res 229 w Cabarrus
Klouse Mrs Olie, wife D B
Klouse Miss Iola, d D B, res same, student
Knight Mark,* lab, res 714 s Dawson
Knight Mary,* wife Mark, washerwoman
Knight Hugh, flagman S A L, bds W C Eatman
Knight Mattie,* seamstress, res Adams lane
Knight Miss Emma, lives with Mrs Rosa K Smith
Knox Dr A W, physician and surgeon, office over James McKimmon's drugstore, res 516 n Blount
Knox Mrs Eliza, wife Dr A W
Knox Miss Eliza, d Dr A W, res same
Knuckles Geo,* porter for E Fasnach, res rear 11 e Lane
Koehler H R, watchmaker at H Mahler's sons, bds cor McDowell and Hargett
Koonce Mrs B A, wid, res 204 e Lenoir
Koonce Chas F, son Mrs B A, res same, printer

Koonce Miss Addie O, d Mrs B A, res same, seamstress
Koonce John S, son Mrs B A, res same, clk at Thomas & Maxwell
Koonce Richard, night watchman, res 314 Hillsboro'
Koonce Mrs Sarah F, wife Richard
Koonce Chas G, son Richard, res same, printer
Koonce Miss Lillie E, d Richard, res same, student
Kreth Fernando, cigarmaker, res 212 Smithfield
Kreth Mrs Fostine, wife Fernando
Kreth Alex, cleaner and scourer, res 122 s McDowell
Kreth Mrs E, wife Alex
Kreth Mrs Joseph, wid, res 116 w Edenton
Kreth Miss Fruletta, d Mrs Joseph, res same, artist
Kuhnie George, cot buyer, bds cor Newbern ave and Person
Kyle Jane E, washerwoman, res Womble lane

LACY Benj R, Commissioner of Labor Statistics and cashier of the Mechanics Dime Savings Bank, res 539 n Blount
Lacy Mrs M B, wife B R
Lacy Miss Mary, d B R, res same, student
Lacy Miss Irene, d B R, res same, student
Lacy B R Jr, son B R, res same, student
Lacy Miss Frances, d B R, res same, student
Lacy Robert,* teacher, res rear 104 Hillsboro'
Lacy Jane,* wife Robert
Lamb Wm A, carp, res 323 Peace
Lamb Mrs Sallie, wid, res 328 e Martin
Lambeth Chas W, bkkpr, res 308 e Jones
Lambeth Miss Cora, d Chas W, res same
Lambeth Miss Lillie, d Chas W, res same, student
Lambeth Sam F, son Chas W, res same, collector for Royall & Borden
Lambeth W M, son Chas W, res same, clk in U S p o
Lambeth Ernest W, son Chas W, res same, clk for J B Kenny
Lambeth Charles S, bkkpr, res 121 n Bloodworth
Lambeth Mrs Jennie, wife Chas S
Lambert John,* train hand Southern R R, res 325 w Edenton
Lambert Cora,* wife John
Lampkin F M, clk for Whiting Bros, res 313 e Lane
Lampkin Mrs Carrie, wife F M
Lampkin Miss Marion, d F M, res same, student
Lancaster Mrs M M, wid, res 217 n Harrington
Lancaster Miss Bettie G, d Mrs M M, res same
Lancaster Miss Lula, d Mrs M M, res same
Lancaster F S, son Mrs M M, res same, painter
Lancaster L W, son Mrs M M, res same, clk T H Briggs & Sons
Lancaster Mrs Jennie, wife L W
Lancaster Wm H, liveryman, res 548 e Jones

Lancaster Mrs Alice, wife Wm H
Lancaster Miss Claudia, d W H, res same, student
Lancaster Robert, son W H, res same, student
Lancaster Earle, son W H, res same, student
Lancaster Robert E, painter, res n Boylan ave
Lancaster Mrs Lucy, wife Robert E
Lancaster G W, inmate Soldiers' Home
Landis C E, inmate Soldiers' Home
Landis Mrs Annie H, wid, boarding-house, Park Place n Blount
Landis Thomas, son Mrs Annie H, res same
Landis Gertrude, d Mrs Annie H, res same
Lane York,* lab, res 22 Railroad
Lane Lou,* wife York, cook
Lane Harriet,* servant Rev Dr I McK Pittenger, res same
Lane David,* lab, res 729 Manly
Lane Julia J,* wife David, house work
Lane Cora,* cook, res 553 e Edenton
Lane Catherine,* washerwoman, res 737 e Davie
Lane Benj,* son Catherine, res same, lab
Lane Pattie,* d Catherine, res same, house work
Lane Hattie,* d Catherine, res same, student
Lane Allen,* city hand, res 412 Smith
Lane Fletchie,* wife Allen
Lane Edward G,* lab, res 612 e Cabarrus
Lane David P * (Leary & Lane), lawyer, res e Davie
Lane Adriana,* wife D P
Lane Wm H,* son D P, res same, student
Lane Adeline,* cook, res basement 554 e Hargett
Lane Susie,* nurse for Dan Hicks, res on lot
Lane Mary,* house-servant, res e Davie
Lane Kate,* invalid, res Martin, o s e
Lane Sarah,* d Kate, res same, washerwoman
Lang Chester, cigarmaker, res 228 e South
Lang Mrs Ludia, wife Chester
Lang Mrs Winnie, wid, res 228 e South
Langston Capt P T, conductor S A L R R, bds 115 Johnson
Langston Mrs Nellie C, wife Capt P T
Langston David, merchant, bds at Rev Dr J B Bobbitt
Lanier Ed,* lab, res Cannon
Lanier Harriet,* wife Ed, washerwoman
Lanier Miss Fannie, seamstress, res 208 e Lenoir
Lanier Thos, painter, bds 554 e Davie
Lanier J H, carp, bds 559 Newbern ave
Lanier Mrs Fannie, wife J H
Lanier Walter, son J H, res same
Larsen E, yard hand S A L R R, res 529 n Salisbury
Larsen Mrs A, wife E
Larsen A, son E, res same, student

Larsen Wm, son E, res same, student
Larsen Fred, son E, res same, student
Larsen Sophia, d E, res same, student
Larsen Lillie, d E, res same, student
Lashley Y P, carp, res 424 s West
Lashley Mrs Sarah H, wife Y P
Lashley Miss Mina, d Y P, res same, student
Lassater G M, conductor S A L R R, res 408 w Morgan
Lassater Mrs Annie, wife G M
Lassater Miss Lena, d G M, res same, student
Lassiter Eugene, wks city fire dept, 122 e Davie
Lassiter Mrs Maggie, wife Eugene
Lassiter Teemer,* lab, res 812 Manly
Lassiter Frances,* wife Teemer, washerwoman
Lassiter Isaac,* lab, res Green Level
Lassiter Martha,* wife Isaac, washerwoman
Lassiter Dock,* wood worker, res 4 Stronach ave
Lassiter Eliza,* wife Dock, washerwoman
Lassiter Hattie,* cook, res e South
Latta C G (Latta & Wright), cot broker, res 216 n Person
Latta Mrs Mary, wife C G
Latta Miss Mary, d C G, res same
Latta Miss Lena, d C G, res same, student
Latta Miss Maud, d C G, res same, student
Latta Albert, son C G, res same, student
Latta Chas G Jr, son C G, res same
Latta & Wright, cot brokers, 317 s Wilmington
Lawrence James E, eng S A L R R, res 711 n Salisbury, o s n
Lawrence Mrs Mary E, wife James E
Lawrence Miss Lelia A, d James E, res same, teacher
Lawrence Miss Lillie P, d James E, res same
Lawrence Miss Kate, d James E, res same, teacher in Central Graded School
Lawrence Miss Birdie, d James E, res same, student
Lawrence Dora,* washerwoman, res 426 e Hargett
Lawrence Miss Virgie, bkpr for Mrs Jno A Simpson, res same
Laws Frank,* driver for T H Briggs & Sons, res s East
Laws Bettie,* wife Frank, washerwoman
Laws Nannie,* d Frank, res same, student
Laws Burt,* son Frank, res same, student
Laws Alfonzo,* student, res 413 w Martin
Laws Nancy,* washerwoman, res 225 e South
Lawton Miss Ella, res 549 e Martin
Leach Cora,* washerwoman, res 215 Bledsoe ave
Leach Maria,* cotton chopper, res Adams lane
Leach William,* lab S A L R R, res 539 Newbern ave
Leach Emma,* wife William, washerwoman
Leach M T, cotton buyer, bds 128 n Blount

Leach G E, cotton broker, bds Yarboro' House
Leach Silvia A,* washerwoman, res w Davie
Leach Dempsey,* son Silvia A, res same, student
Leach Ola,* d Silvia A, res same, student
Leach R B, life ins agt, res 121 s McDowell
Leach Miss C S, sister R B, res same
Leach Miss N, sister R B, res same
Leak Rev R H W,* pastor A M E church, res 316 e Davie
Leak Mary M,* wife Rev R H W
Leak Gertrude E,* d Rev R H W, res same, student
Leak Maggie W,* d Rev R H W, res same, student
Leak Robert C,* son Rev R H W, res same, student
Leak Julia H,* d Rev R H W, res same, student
Leak R H W Jr,* son Rev R H W, res same, student
Leak James G,* son Rev R H W, res same, student
Leak Frank,* brakeman S A L, res 437 n Salisbury
Leard H S, soliciting agent for S A L R R, office Yarboro' House bldg, res 123 n McDowell
Leard Mrs Nellie, wife H S
Leard Allen D, son H S, res same
Leard, Miss Margaret, d H S, res same
Leard Mrs Maggie, mother H S, res same
Leary & Lane,* lawyers, office cor e Davie and s Wilmington
Ledbetter William, deputy warden N C penitentiary, res same
Lee Battle,* lab, res 12 Hayti
Lee Ellen,* wife Battle, washerwoman
Lee Bud,* son Battle, res same, errand-boy
Lee Nathan,* son Battle, res same, errand-boy
Lee Dock,* crossing watchman S A L R R, res 325 w Edenton
Lee Della,* washerwoman, res 715 s West
Lee Lucy, d Della, res same, house work
Lee John,* son Della, res same, errand-boy
Lee C R, clk S A L R R, res 105½ Fayetteville
Lee Mrs Nannie T, wife C R, boarding-house
Lee Miss Mary M, d C R, res same, student
Lee Edwin R, son C R, res same, student
Lee Miss Nannie D, d C R, res same
Lee Mike,* lab, res 529 s Wilmington
Lee Betsy,* wife Mike, cook for C C Crow
Lee Hackney,* lab, res 108 n West
Lee Estella,* wife Hackney, washerwoman
Lee Claude C, carp, wks N C Car Co, res 526 n Salisbury
Lee Mrs Eleanor, wife C C
Lee Paul, son C C, res same, student
Lee Elijah,* fireman S A L R R, res Fleming's lane
Lee Rosa,* wife Elijah, washerwoman
Lee Dock,* fireman S A L R R, res Fleming's lane
Lee Lonnie,* son Elijah, res same, student

Lee Blanche, seamstress, res Hood's alley
Lee John,* city hand, res 205 Cannon
Lee Ella,* d John, res same, cook
Lee Narcissa,* d John, res same, student
Lee Van,* son John, res same, student
Lee Stewart,* son John, res same student
Lee Ed H, cot buyer, office 307 s Wilmington, res 220 Hillsboro'
Lee Mrs Annie, wife Ed H
Lee Mrs Mary, mother Ed H, res same
Lee Miss Lizzie, d Mrs Mary, res same
Lee Coy, wks Caraleigh mill, res 218 e Lenoir
Lee Mrs Delia, wife Coy
Lee John,* driver for T R Jones, res 714 s Dawson
Lee Geo,* lab, res 714 s Dawson
Lee Henry, inmate Soldiers' Home
Lee Mary,* cook for Mrs E B Haywood, res e Edenton
Lee Miley,* washerwoman, res 428 Smith
Lee Tempie,* cook, res old Fair Ground, o s e
Lee Augustus,* farm hand, res old Fair Ground, o s e
Lee Paul, farmer, res 304 e Jones
Lee Mrs Ellen, wife Paul
Lee Miss Margaret, d Paul, res same, student
Lee E H (Horton & Lee), merchant, bds 321 e Lane
Lee Robert E, printer, res 321 e Cabarrus
Lee Mrs Annie M, wife Robert E
Lee Robert E Jr, son Robert E, res same
Lee John,* hostler, res 715 s West
Leggett Minerva,* cook for Geo D Meares, res on lot
Leggett Miss A L, attendant at Insane Asylum, res same
Lehman A C, clk Southern R R frt office, res 10 n Saunders
Lehman Mrs L D, wife A C
Lehman Miss Emily, d A C, res same, student
Lehman Robert, son A C, res same, student
Lehman Miss Eva, d A C, res same, student
Leonard Aaron,* city hand, res 715 s East
Leonard Tempie,* wife Aaron, cook
Leonard Medical School, 750 s Wilmington, under management of Shaw University
Levine & Brown, clothing and shoes, 208-216-220 s Wilmington
Levine Dave (Levine & Brown), merchant, bds 12 e Davie
Levy Robert H, painter, res 755 s Blount
Levy Mrs Bettie, wife R H
Levy Miss Etta, d R H, res same
Levy Willie H, son R H, res same, student
Levy Lewis L, son R H, res same student
Levy Miss Lucy, d Robt, lives with Mrs C R Harris
Levy Emmett E, son Mrs Fannie Harris, res same, trav salesman
Lewellyn Mrs Ida, wid, wks book bindery, res 527 s Person

Lewellyn Edward, son Mrs Ida, res same, printer's app
Lewellyn Eugene, son Mrs Ida, res same, student
Lewis Maj A M, lawyer, res 529 n Wilmington
Lewis Mrs Sarah M, wife A M
Lewis Mrs R G, wid, lives with Maj A M Lewis
Lewis Robert G, son Mrs R G, res same
LEWIS JULIUS HARDWARE CO, 224 Fayetteville, wholesale and retail dealers in hardware, &c
Lewis Julius, capitalist, res cor Hillsboro' and Saunders
Lewis Mrs Abagail B, wife Julius
Lewis Mrs Sarah W, wid, res 520 n Person
Lewis Miss Ethel C, d Mrs Sarah W, res same, student
Lewis James J, printer, res 113 w Morgan
Lewis Mrs Amanda V, wife James, dressmaker
Lewis Alfred, carp, res 113 w Morgan
Lewis Arilla,* washerwoman, res 562 e Cabarrus
Lewis Wilson,* son Arilla, res same, student
Lewis Hilliard,* son Arilla, res same, student
Lewis Anderson,* farm hand, res old Fair Ground, o s e
Lewis Rosa A.* wife Anderson, washerwoman
Lewis Susie,* d Anderson, res same, farm hand
Lewis Mary,* d Anderson, res same, farm hand
Lewis Ruffin,* son Anderson, res same, farm hand
Lewis Stamps,* son Anderson, res same, student
Lewis Penny,* d Anderson, res same, student
Lewis Fannie,* washerwoman, res 319 Cannon
Lewis Florence,* house-servant, res 319 Cannon
Lewis John,* lab, res 319 Cannon
Lewis Hattie,* cook for C P Wharton, res Cotton lane, o s e
Lewis Mattie,* cook, res Cotton lane, o s e
Lewis David,* student, res Cotton lane, o s e
Lewis James H,* shoemaker, res 14 s Harrington
Lewis Mrs Rosa, wid, res 524 n West
Lewis Sarah,* student, res w Peace
Lewis Thomas,* student, res w Peace
Lewis & Battle, eye, ear and throat specialists, office 217 n Wilmington
Lewis Dr R H, eye, ear and throat specialist, r 227 n Wilmington
Lewis Mrs M E, mother Dr R H, res same
Lewis Jane,* cook, res 310 w Lenoir
Lewis James,* lab, res 310 w Lenoir
Lewis Addison,* lab, res Smith
Lewis Hattie,* cook for C P Wharton, res on lot
Lewis Charles W, brick-mason, bds 326 n Saunders
Lewis Dora,* servant at James Maglum, res rear 10 e North
Lewter A S, railroader, res 110 w Martin
Lewter Mrs Carrie H, wife A S
Lewter Miss Lillian, d A S, res same

Southern Railway,

The Greatest Southern System,

Penetrating

the States of Georgia, Alabama, Mississippi, Virginia, North Carolina, South Carolina, Kentucky and Tennessee.

Operating

the famous WASHINGTON AND SOUTHWESTERN LIMITED, composed of Pullman Drawing-Room Sleeping Cars, elegant Day Coaches and Southern Railway Dining Cars, between New York, Philadelphia, Baltimore, Washington and Atlanta, Birmingham, Memphis, Montgomery, New Orleans, Asheville and Hot Springs (N. C.) Savannah, Jacksonville and Tampa.

W. H. GREEN,   J. M CULP,   W. A. TURK,

General Offices: Washington, D. C.

Litchford Jas O, teller of Raleigh Savings Bank, bds 404 Fayetteville
Little Mrs C M, dressmaker, res 127 n Dawson
Little Miss Addie B, d Mrs C M, res same, seamstress
Little Robert S, son Mrs C M, res same, tinner apprentice
Little Miss Fannie, d Mrs C M, res same
Little Miss Lucy, d Mrs C M, res same, student
Little Mrs M L, wid, res 11 n Blount
Little Henry M, son Mrs M L, res same, clk Southern R R frt office
Little Albert H, son Mrs M L, res same, machinist app
Little Wm P, son Mrs M L, res same, mgr Everhart's ice factory
Little Burke H, son Mrs M L, res same, student
Little Thos, pressman, bds 305 s Person
Littlepage J W, board and sale stable, cor e Martin and s Blount
Littlejohn Henrietta,* cook, res 407 s Dawson
Littlejohn Doctor,* lab, res 407 s Dawson
Littlejohn Jno,* driver for Oak City Laundry, res old Fair Ground, o s e
Littlejohn Emma,* wife John, washerwoman
Littlejohn Mary E,* d John, res same, student
Littlejohn Bessie,* d John, res same, student
Littlejohn Susan* washerwoman, res old Fair Ground, o s e
Lippard Marcus, inmate Soldiers' Home
Livingston Lydia, seamstress, res 585 e Cabarrus
Lockhart Amanda,* washerwoman, res 415 s Blount
Lockhart John A,* son Amanda, res same, student
Locklear Henry,* lab, res w South
Locklear Lottie,* wife Henry, washerwoman
Locklear James,* son Henry, res same, lab
Locklear Ella,* d Henry, res same, house-servant
Locklear Mary,* d Henry, res same, house-servant
Locklear Sarah,* d Henry, res same, house-servant
Locklear Frank,* son Henry, res same, lab
Locklear Caswell,* barber, res 420 s Salisbury
Locklear Jennie,* washerwoman, res 525 e Lenoir
Locklear Benton,* son Jennie, res same, blacksmith
Locklear Hosten,* son Jennie, res same, blacksmith striker
Locklear Charles,* baker, res 503 Cannon
Locklear Ella,* wife Charles, washerwoman
Locklear Frank,* lab, res 308 w Cabarrus
Lockre William Sr, stone-mason, res cor Jones and Dawson
Lockre Mrs Bettie, wife William
Lockre William Jr, boiler-maker S A L R R, res cor Jones and Dawson
Lockre Charles, son William Sr, res same, student
Lockre Alexander, son William Sr, res same, student
Lodge W A, druggist, res 16 s Salisbury
Lodge Mrs C F, wife W A, dressmaker

Logan William,* tobacco worker, res Cotton lane, o s e
Logan Emma,* tobacco worker, res Cotton lane, o s e
Logan Daisy,* tobacco worker, res Cotton lane, o s e
Logan Annie,* cook for Mrs Lucy Ferrell, res Cotton lane, o s e
Loman J W, yardmaster Southern R R, res 416 s Dawson
Loman Mrs Lizzie L, wife J W
Long Mrs M M, mother Mrs Mary E Heileg, res n Salisbury, o s u
Long Abe, huckster, res 725 s East
Long William,* shoemaker, res 420 Smith
Long Mary,* wife William, washerwoman
Long Ella,* cook, res 205 w Lenoir
Lougee Mrs L O, wid, res 324 s Person
Lougee E M, clerk for Hicks & Rogers, res 324 s Person
Lougee Omer, student, res 324 s Person
Lougee Louis, student, res 324 s Person
Love Hannah,* washerwoman, res 719 s West
Love Pattie M,* d Hannah, res same, teacher
Love Mary A,* d Hannah, res same, teacher
Love George P,* son Hannah, res same, lab
Love Hattie B,* d Hannah, res same, student
Love Marion,* son Hannah, res same, student
Love Ada L,* d Hannah, res same, student
Love Hannah,* d Hannah, res same, student
Love Thomas L, tobacco buyer, res 413 Newbern ave
Love Mrs N S, wid, res 413 Newbern ave
Love Fred W, son Mrs N S, res same, student
Love Miss Annie, d Mrs N S, res same, student
Love's Cupid, smoking-tobacco factory, 118 e Hargett, Jesse G Ball propr
Love E H, hide and fur dealer, 118 e Hargett, res 515 Oakwood ave
Love Mrs Martha H, wife E H
Love Alonzo R, son E H, res same, ministerial student
Love Miss Florence N, d E H, res same
Love Miss Emma C, d E H, res same
Love Miss Alice L, d E H, res same
Love John,* son Cora Cotten, res same, student
Love Thomas,* son Cora Cotten, res same, student
Love Eddie,* son Cora Cotten, res same, student
Lovejoy Hettie,* farm hand, res old Fair Ground, o s e
Lowery J A, mechanic, res Oakdale ave, o s n
Lowery Mrs E A, wife J A
Lowery Clarence, son J A, res same
Lowery Henry C, merchant, res 230 e Martin
Lowery Mrs Mollie, wife Henry C
Lowe Mrs M V, wid, res 530 Cannon
Lowe Denie, son Mrs M V, res same, student
Lowe Merriel, son Mrs M V, res same, student
Lloyd Wm L, loco engineer, res 520 s Harrington

Lloyd Mrs Nannie E, wife Wm L
Lloyd Wm W, son Wm L, res same
Loyd Joseph, wks Pilot cot mill, res Oakdale ave, o s n
Loyd Mrs Flora, wife Joseph
Loyd A J, weaver Pilot cot mill, res Pace, o s n
Loyd Mrs Fannie, wife A J
Loyd Roden,* gardener, res Hargett, o s e
Ludden & Bates, Southern Music House (Ral branch), 332 Fayetteville, Miller & Uzzle mgrs
Lumsden J C S, hardware merchant, 226 Fayetteville, res 413 Hillsboro'
Lumsden Mrs M J, wife J C S
Lumsden Frank H, tinner and coppersmith, res 326 w Jones
Lumsden Mrs Martha L, wife Frank H
Lumsden Thomas, son F H, res same, flagman S A L
Lumsden Miss Mary Lucile, d F H, res same
Lumsden Chas F, tinner and iron worker, shop 108 s Wilmington, res 216 n Harrington
Lumsden Mrs Mattie, wife Chas F
Lumsden John, son Chas F, res same, taxidermist
Lumsden Miss Lida E, d Chas F, res same
Lumsden Chas, son Chas F, res same, student
Lumsden R E, mailing clk at Union Depot, res 312 w Martin
Lumsden Mrs Minnie F, wife Robt E
Lumsden Robt E, son R E, res same, student
Lumsden Miss Minnie R, d R E, res same, student
Lumsden Clarence H, son R E, res same, student
Lumsden Lonnie H, tinner, res 215 n Salisbury
Lumsden Mrs Lucy, wife L H
Lumley Mrs T J, wid, res 546 e Jones
Lumley Miss Ida, d Mrs T J, res same, dressmaker
Lumley Samuel, son Mrs T J, res same, candy-maker
Lumley Mrs Olie, res with Mrs T J
Lumley Geo W, pressman at E M Uzzell, res 416 e Edenton
Lumley Mrs Rosa B, wife Geo W, dressmaker
Lumley Sam W, candy-maker, res 418 s Person
Lumley Mrs Carrie O, wife Sam W
Lunsford Mary,* cook for B F Park, res on lot
Lunsford Frances,* servant, res 234 w Lenoir
Lyons James, machinist S A L, res 415 n Wilmington
Lyons Mrs Mary A, wife James
Lyons Herman, son James, res same, fireman S A L R R
Lyons Lawrence D, son James, res same, app boiler making
Lyons Miss Christine, d James, res same, student
Lyons Fred J, son James, res same, student
Lyons Emmett H, son James, res same, student
Lyons Edward P, son James, res same, student
Lyon Miss Caroline, dressmaker, res 319 e Morgan

Lyon Miss Janie, sister of Miss Caroline, res same, dressmaker
Lyon W H, dry goods, notions, &c, 16 Martin, res 103 s Bloodworth
Lyon Mrs Mary E, wife W H
Lyon Winfield H, son W H, res same, student
Lyon Mary E, d W H, res same, student
Lyon Racket Store, dry goods, notions, &c, 16 e Martin, W H Lyon proprietor
Lyon Thomas,* carp N C Car Co, res 215 w North
Lyon Mack,* laborer, res 516 Newbern ave
Lyon Mary,* wife Mack, store-keeper
Lyon John,* son Mack, res same, student

MABRY Mrs W T, wid, res 219 e Hargett
Mabry Miss Susie E, d Mrs W T, res same, saleslady
Mabry Wm A, son Mrs W T, res same, drug clk
Mabry Miss Etta L, d Mrs W T, res same
Mabry Frank K, son Mrs W T, res same, ice dealer
Mabry Geo W, son Mrs W T, res same, student
Mack Albert A, musical director in St Mary's School, res same
Macklin Sylvia,* servant, res o s e
MAC RAE JOHN Y, druggist, cor s Wilmington and e Martin and cor e Martin and Fayetteville, res 327 e Hargett
Macy Mrs A E, wid, res 313 w Morgan
MACY WM R, son Mrs A E, res same, painter, office s Salisbury
Maglum James, master mechanic S A L R R shops, r 214 Halifax
Maglum Mrs Annie, wife James
Maglum Dan, son James, res same, machinist
Maglum Cornelius, son James, res same, student
Maglum Miss Rose, d James, res same, student
Maglum Bernard, son James, res same, student
Mahler F Louis, bkkpr at National Bank of Raleigh, r 533 n Blount
Mahler Mrs Henrietta R, wife F L
Mahler Miss Margaret L, d F L, res same
Mahler Fred W, son F L, res same, student

W. R. MACY,

S. Salisbury St., *Artistic Sign Writer,*

Near Cor. Hargett Street.

Mail Orders promptly attended to.   Your patronage solicited.

Mahler's Sons H, jewelers, opticians and silversmiths, 228 Fayetteville
Mahler L A (H Mahler's Sons), jeweler and chief of fire department, rooms 228 Fayetteville
Mahler Mrs H, wid, res 430 Fayetteville
Mahler Fred (H Mahler's Sons), jeweler and optician, r 430 Fayetteville
Mahony J R, inmate Soldiers' Home
Mallaby Miss Margie, dressmaker, res 615 e Hargett
Mallett Silas P,* farmer, res Tarboro' rd, o s e
Mallett Charlotte,* wife Silas
Mallett Charlie,* son S P, res same
Mallett Wm,* son S P, res same
Malone John H,* brick-mason and plasterer, res 12 Stronach ave
Malone Mattie,* wife John H, washerwoman
Malone Maggie,* farm hand, res old Fair Ground, o s e
Mangham Miss, res with J C Drewry
Mangum D C, saloon, 303 s Blount, res Holloman rd
Mangum Mrs Sallie, wife D C
Mangum Miss Nelia, d D C, res same
Mangum Miss Rosa, d D C, res same
Mangum Miss Gertrude, d D C, res same
Mangum Albert, livery stable, res 313 s Blount
Mangum Mrs Sarah, wife Albert, dressmaker
Mangum John, son Albert, res same, wks Caraleigh mill
Mangum Miss Dessie, d Albert, res same, student
Mangum Jno W, lineman for Fire Dept, res 305 e Martin
Mangum Mrs Lola, wife Jno W,
Mangum Engelhard, son Jno W, res same
Mangum William H, farmer, res 529 s Bloodworth
Mangum Mrs Sallie, wife Wm H
Mangum Miss Kate, d Wm H, res same
Mangum Tim, son Wm H, res same, driver
Mangum Burleigh, son Wm H, res same, driver
Mangum Jno C, hostler, res 122 w Cabarrus
Mangum Mrs Gertrude, wife Jno C
Mangum Wm E, son Jno C, res same, driver
Mangum Palmetto, son Jno C, res same, student
Mangum Mack,* driver for Stronach & Sons, res 508 e Edenton
Mangum Mary,* washerwoman, res Idlewild
Manly Phoebe,* washerwoman, res 301 s East
Manly Wm E,* son Phoebe, res same, wks for F A Watson
Manly James,* son Phoebe, res same, lab
Manly Mary,* d Phoebe, res same, washerwoman
Manly Bessie,* d Phoebe, res same, washerwoman
Manly Sidney,* city hand, res 409 Hillsboro'
Manly Maria,* wife Sidney, washerwoman
Manly Geo P,* son Sidney, res same, student

Manly Rosa B,* d Sidney, res same, student
Manly Dolly,* house-servant, res 705 s Dawson
Mann W B, grocer, 5 e Hargett, res 553 e Hargett
Mann Mrs Phoebe, wife W B
Manor W E, ins agt, bds Park Hotel
Manor Mrs W E, wife W E
Manor Miss Marjorie, d W E, res same, student
Manor Miss Shirlie, d W E, res same, student
Marable Miss Daisy, teacher in Peace Institute, res same
Marcom James C, justice of the peace, office Central Hotel bldg, res 211 n Harrington
Marcom Miss Agnes, sister James C, res same
Marcom J W, printer, res 416 e Hargett
Marcom Mrs Sallie L, wife J W
Marcom Charles B, son J W, res same, moulder
Marcom Milton L, son J W, res same, boiler-maker
Marcom Bud, motorman Ral Electric Co, bds 209 w Morgan
Marcom Mrs Lucy, wife Bud
Marcom A F, carp, res 555 e Davie
Marcom Mrs Fannie, wife A F
Marcom Miss Myrtle, d A F, res same, student
Marks Edward T, marble-cutter, shop w Martin, res 517 s Person
Marks James R, lab, res 517 s Person
Marks Mrs Henrietta W, wid, res 517 s Person
Marks William, wks for S A L R R, res 227 n Dawson
Marks Mrs Ella, wife William
Marks Eddie, son William, res same, student
Marrow Henry,* restaurant cook, res 757 e Davie, o s e
Marrow Saluda,* wife Henry, washerwoman
Marrow James,* son Henry, res same, lab
Marrow Lolla,* d Henry, res same, student
Marsh G W, huckster city market, res 225 w Edenton
Marsh Mary V, d G W, res same, teacher Central Graded School
Marsh Miss Hattie A, d G W, res same, saleslady W H & R S Tucker
Marsh Miss Annie W, d G W, res same
Marsh George, son G W, res same, mgr Johnson & Johnson wood yard
MARSHALL REV DR M M, rector Christ Episcopal church, res 6 Newbern ave
Marshall Mrs Margaret S, wife Rev M M
Marshall Miss Margaret S, d Rev M M, res same, student
Marshall Miss Theodora, d Rev M M, res same, student
Marshall J K (Page & Marshall), laundryman, bds 6 Newbern ave
Marshall Corinna,* washerwoman, res e Davie, o s e
Marshall Lydia,* d Corinna, res same, washerwoman
Marshall Vircie,* d Corinna, res same, nurse
Marshall Lucy,* d Corinna, res same, student

Marshall J H, janitor at City Hall, res 221 s Bloodworth
Marshall Mrs Jessie, wife J H
Marshall Miss Maud, d J H, res same
Marshburn Otis M, drug clk, res 404 n Bloodworth
Marshburn Mrs Nora, wife Otis M
Martin E M, proprietor City livery stable, res w Jones
Martin Miss Lizzie, d E M, res same, student
Martin Walter, son E M, res same, student
Martin Wm G, life ins agt, res 111 n Bloodworth
Martin Mrs Minnie, wife Wm G
Martin W H, clk for Charitable and Penal Institutions, office Treasurer's office, res Idlewild
Martin Mrs M M, wife W H
Martin James H, son W H, res same, student
Martin Chester A, son W H, res same, student
Martin Howard D, son W H, res same, student
Martin Alonzo, son W H, res same, student
Martin Matthew,* driver for So Ex Co, res 515 s Blount
Martin Louise,* wife Matthew
Martin Ernest M, locomotive eng S A L R R, bds 215 w Jones
Martin Mrs Mamie, wife Ernest M
Martin Annie,* washerwoman, res old Fair Ground, o s e
Martin T E, conductor S A L R R, bds 10 e North
Martin Mrs Kate, housekeeper, res 314 e Davie
Martin Dr T D, retired physician, res Hillsboro' rd
Martin Mrs H P, wife Dr T D
Massenburg Susan,* cook for Mrs Samuel Ruffin, res same
Massey W F, prof of horticulture, arboriculture and botany in A & M Col, res Hillsboro' rd, o s w
Massey Mrs Arrilla J, wife W F
Massey Miss Nellie, d W F, res same
Massey Miss Annie H, d W F, res same
Massey Miss Mabel P, d W F, res same, student
Massey Miss Winifred R, d W F, res same, student
Massey Miss Elizabeth W, d W F, res same, student
Massey Arthur B, son W F, res same
Massey Henry,* wks for Water Co, res 19 w Worth
Massey Biddy,* wife Henry, washerwoman
Massey Wm,* wks Rex Hospital, res 19 w Worth
Massey Lula,* d Henry, res same, house work
Massey Corrina,* d Henry, res same, nurse
Massey Seymour,* son Henry, res same, errand-boy
Massey C F, eng Ral cot mill, bds cor n Halifax and Franklin, o s n
Massey Andy,* lab, res 720 Manly
Massey Bella,* wife Andy, cook
MASSEY A P, lawyer, office in Citizens Nat Bank bldg, bds Park Hotel
Massey Jos, farmer, res Rock Quarry rd

Massey Mrs Sue H, wife Jos
Massey Norwood L, son Jos, res same, farm hand
Massey Allen G, son Jos, res same, farm hand
Massey Miss Mona M, d Jos, res same
Massey James T,* barber app, res 729 Manly
Massey Lucy A,* wife James T, washerwoman
Massey Kittie,* cook for J C Drewry, res on lot
Mason Mrs S B, wid, res 121 n Wilmington
Mason Miss Lorena, d Mrs S B, res same, student
Mason Samuel, son Mrs S B, res same, student
Mason Hattie,* washerwoman, res 563 e Cabarrus
Matthews Lou,* washerwoman, res 710 s West
Matthews George,* son Lou, res same, lab
Matthews Alex,* son Lou, res same, lab
Matthews James,* son Lou, res same, lab
Matthews Zeb,* son Lou, res same, lab
Matthews Alfred W, driver, res 222 s Harrington
Matthews Mrs Delia, wife A W
Matthews Miss Chessie E, d A W, res same, student
Matthews Leroy, son A W, res same
Matthews Allison, wks at Caraleigh mill, bds 222 s Harrington
Matthews W J,* brick-mason, res w South
Matthews W H,* brick contractor, res 211 w South
Matthews Sarah R,* wife W H
Matthews Robert,* son W H, res same, brick-mason
Matthews Frank, grocer, cor s Blount and Lenoir, res 228 e Lenoir
Matthews Mrs Corrina E, wife Frank
Matthews Arabella,* washerwoman for Soldiers' Home, res Hargett, o s e
Matthews Miss Georgia, tailoress at Physioc & Co's, bds 407 Fayetteville
Matthews Jonas M, blacksmith S A L, res 210 n McDowell
Matthews Mrs M E, wife Jonas M
Matthews Powie, son Jonas M, machinist S A L, r 210 n McDowell
Maxie W A, train hand S A L, bds 120 Johnson
Maxwell Herbert, conductor S A L R R, bds 105½ Fayetteville

A. P. MASSEY,
ATTORNEY AND COUNSELLOR
——AND——
NOTARY PUBLIC.

Special attention to Claims and Collections and furnishing Financial Reports and Statements. Depositions taken for use in any of the States.

Office of Col. Jno. W. Hinsdale, Citizens National Bank Building.

Maxwell Mortimer, saloon keeper, bds 105½ Fayetteville
Mayfield Wesley,* lab, res Smith
Mayfield Annie,* wife Wesley
Mayfield Fred,* son Wesley, res same, student
Mayfield Arthur,* son Wesley, res same, lab
Mayfield Mamie,* d Wesley, res same student
Mayho Sallie,* washerwoman, res rear 420 s Salisbury
Mayho Anna,* cook for R T Bishop, res same
May Annie,* house-servant for Mrs C H Smith, res on lot
May George,* milker for B G Cowper, res on lot
May James,* wks C H Beine, res o s e
May Martha,* wife James, washerwoman
Mays Miss Jennie, seamstress, res 541 e Cabarrus
Maynard W T, section foreman S A L, res 314 n McDowell
Maynard Mrs M A, wife W T
Maynard Miss Cassie, d W T, res same
Maynard Luther, son W T, res same
Maynard Mrs Eliza, wid, res Bledsoe ave
Maynard Allen, son Mrs Eliza, res same, city hand
Maynard Miss Sallie, d Mrs Eliza, res same
Maynard Miss Delia, d Mrs Eliza, res same
Maynard Miss Emma, d Mrs Eliza, res same
Maynard Willie, son Mrs Eliza, res same, student
Maynard Miss Anna, lives with R B Leach
Maynard Ernest P (Peele & Maynard), lawyer, res 120 n Person
Maynard Mrs Albertine, wife E P
Maynard Green, grocer, res 107 w South
Maynard Miss Emma, d Green, res same
McAden Mrs B T, wid, res 535 n Blount
McAden Rufus Y, son Mrs B T, res same, student
McAden James T, son Mrs B T, res same, student
McBee Mrs Anna, teacher in St Mary's school, res same
McCain Miss Maggie, student, lives with M J Adams
McCain Miss Virgie, student, lives with M J Adams
McCauley Wm, ins agt, bds Branson House
McCauley Roger E,* tailor, 16 s Salisbury, res Newbern ave, o s e
McCauley Martha A,* wife Roger E
McCauley Lewyn E,* son Roger E, res same, student
McCauley Ethel G,* d Roger E, res same, student
McCauley Rachel H,* d Roger E, res same, student
McCauley Maggie,* laundress, res Rock Quarry rd
McClenehan Robert N,* lab, res 315 e Lenoir
McClennahan Lizzie,* cook, res 124 Davie
McClennahan Peggie,* cook, res 124 w Davie
McCloud Thornton,* blacksmith striker, res rear 10 e North
McClure Wm, saloon, 232 Fayetteville, bds 104 e Davie
McCracken Eliza,* seamstress, res 715 s McDowell
McCray John,* barber, res 118 w Cabarrus

McCullers Jim,* tobacco worker, res 120 e Cabarrus
McCullers Lena,* wife Jim, res same, washerwoman
McCullers Miss Willie, res with R L Heflin
McCullers Susan,* washerwoman, res rear 217 w South
McCullers Annie,* d Susan, res same, student
McCullers Sallie, cook, res 828 s Wilmington
McCullers Della, seamstress, res 828 s Wilmington
McCulloch E F, clk in rev dept, res 540 e Hargett
McCulloch Mrs Viola H, wife E F
McCulloch Edgar, son E F, res same, student
McDade W A, farmer, res 402 w Morgan
McDade Mrs Rosa, wife W A
McDade Miss Blanche, d W A, res same
McDade Arthur, son W A, res same
McDade Ormond, son W A, res same
McDade Inez, d W A, res same
McDaniel Rosa,* teacher of music in colored D D & B Institute, res same
McDONALD CHARLES C, mgr and sec of Ral branch of the Southern Building and Loan Association of Knoxville, Tenn, office 107 Fayetteville, res 437 Halifax
McDonald Mrs Lula T, wife C C
McDonald Miss Lula S, d C C, res same, student
McDonald John S, son C C, res same, student
McDonald Eugene G, son C C, res same, student
McDonald Charles C Jr, son C C, res same, student
McDowell W F, blacksmith, res 412 n East
McDowell Mrs Hattie, wife W F
McDowell Miss Maud, d W F, res same
McDowell J, traveling salesman, bds Park Place
McFadden Miss Fannie, student, res with John A Collier
McFarland Reuben,* wks on telephone line, r rear 527 Hillsboro'
McFarland Senia,* wife Reuben
McGeachy Dr R S, second asst physician N C Insane Asylum, res same
McGee Dr J W Sr, physician and surgeon, office and res cor Edenton and Dawson
McGee Mrs S E, wife Dr J W
McGee Miss Emma, d Dr J W, res same
McGee Miss Ella, d Dr J W, res same
McGee Dr J W Jr, physician and surgeon, office 127 res 129 w Martin
McGee Miss Florrie B, wife Dr J W Jr
McGee Miss Susie N, d Dr J W Jr, res same
McGee James W, son James W, res same
McGee Wm T, collector for Ral Gas Co, res 227 Hillsboro'
McGee Mrs Louise, wife W T
McGee Miss L C, d W T, res same, student

McGhee Geo B, tobacco broker, bds 103 e Edenton
McGhee Mrs Eliza S, wife Geo B
McGhee Miss Annie L, d Geo B, res same
McGhee Miss Mary P, d Geo B, res same
McGowan P W, printer, rooms 328 s McDowell
McGuider Miss Esther, cashier for A B Stronach, rooms at Mrs M A Hardie, 126½ Fayetteville
McIntosh J W, grocer, 122 e Martin, bds s Person
McIntyre Lewis,* painter, res 724 Manly
McIntyre Lena,* wife Lewis, cook
McIntyre Susan,* cook, res 724 Manly
McIntyre William,* lab, res 724 Manly
McIntyre Nancy,* nurse C J Hunter, res Townes al
McIntyre Bessie,* d Nancy, res same, student
McIntyre Willie,* son Nancy, res same, student
McIntyre Laura,* d Nancy, res same
McKee Dr James, physician and surgeon, res 128 n Blount
McKee Mrs Mildred, wife Dr James
McKee Wm H, son Dr James, res same, clk Southern frt office
McKee John S, son Dr James, res same, student
McKee James B, son Dr James, res same, student
McKee Edwin B, son Dr James, res same, student
McKee Lewis M, son Dr James, res same, student
McKee Philip, son Dr James, res same, student
McKee Miss Priscilla, aunt of Mrs Eliza Battle, res same
McKimmon Charles, mgr of A B Stronach's dry goods store, res Park Place, n Blount
McKimmon Mrs Jennie, wife Chas
McKimmon Mrs James, wid, res 512 n Blount
McKimmon James, son Mrs James, res same, student
McKimmon Miss Mary, d Mrs James, res same, student
McKimmon Miss Lelia M, d Mrs James, res same, student
McKimmon Miss Kate, teacher in St Mary's School, res same
McKimmon Jas & Co, druggists, 133 Fayetteville
McKinzie J E,* lab, res 117 n Swain
McKinzie Hattie,* wife J E, washerwoman
McKoy Lewis,* drayman, res s Saunders
McKoy Ida,* wife Lewis, washerwoman
McKoy Lewis,* son Lewis, res same, farm hand
McKoy Larry,* lab, res Whitaker ave
McKoy Bettie,* wife Larry, washerwoman
McKoy Willie,* son Larry, res same, student
McKoy Jesse,* son Larry, res same, student
McKoy Penny,* d Larry, res same, student
McKoy Neill,* shoemaker, res Whitaker ave
McKoy Florida,* wife Neill, house work
McKoy Mabel,* d Neill, res same, student
McKoy Leana,* d Neill, res same, student

McKoy Jerry,* lab, res 818 Manly
McKoy Fannie,* wife Jerry, washerwoman
McKoy Caetta,* d Jerry, res same
McKoy Clarence,* son Jerry, res same
McKoy Wm,* shoemaker and Christian minister, res Smith
McKoy Dicey,* wife Wm
McKoy Wm Jr,* son Wm, res same, porter at Hornbuckle
McKoy Lucy,* washerwoman, res 511 e Davie
McKnight Nellie,* washerwoman, res Blount-st al
McLean Stella,* cook for Jesse E Adams, res same
McLeod Clara,* house-servant, res 207 w South
McLean Ellen,* farm hand, res 207 s East
McLean Bessie,* d Ellen, res same, student
McLean James D, painter S A L, res 602 n Salisbury
McLean Mrs Emma, wife Jas D
McLean Lucy,* cook for Nick Deboy, res 812 s Wilmington
McLean Sam,* lab, res 917 Manly
McLean Lucy,* washerwoman, res Green Level
McLean Florence,* washerwoman, res 124 s Davie
McLeod Annie,* cook, res 716 Fayetteville
McLeod Priscilla,* cook at Peace Institute, res 421 s Swain
McLeod Willie,* son Priscilla, res same, lab
McLester Miss Maggie, matron at Rex Hospital, res same
McMackin W C, road supervisor, res 122 s Harrington
McMackin Mrs A E, wife W C
McMackin Miss Nannie, d W C, res same
McNair Hugh,* porter for A B Andrews, res 525 e Lenoir
McNair Ary,* wife Hugh
McNair Maggie,* cook for Dr P E Hines, room 106 e Cabarrus
McNair Mary J,* house-girl, res 120 w Peace
McNair Susan,* cook for J C Neimyer, res same
McNeill James,* lab, res rear 501 Hillsboro'
McNeill Jane,* wife James, washerwoman
McNeill Thomas,* son James, res same, porter for D T Johnson
McNeill Charles,* son James, res same, lab
McNeill James Jr,* son James, res same, lab
McNeill Annie,* d James, res same, nurse
McNeill Henrietta,* washerwoman, res Cotton lane, o s e
McNeill Clarence,* farm hand, res Cotton lane, o s e
McNeill Parker,* wks brick-yard, res Cotton lane, o s e
McNeill Lucy,* nurse, res Cotton lane, o s e
McNeill Alice,* cook D S Avera, res Cotton lane, o s e
McNeill Alex,* wks wagon factory, res 58 Hunter
McPheeters A M, stock and bond broker, res 114 s Dawson
McPheeters Mrs Fannie L, wife A M
McPheeters A M Jr, sec and supt Ral Water Co, res 114 s Dawson
McPheeters Miss Fannie L, d A M, res same
McPheeters Sam B, son A M, res same, student

McPheeters Wm L, son A M, res same, student
McPheeters Miss Sudie D, d A M, res same, student
McPheeters Miss Marguerite L, d A M, res same, student
McRae & Day, lawyers, office 217 Fayetteville
McRae James C (McRae & Day), lawyer, bds 120 Halifax
McRary J N, business mgr Press-Visitor, res 309 w Davie
McRary Vernon, son J N, res same, bkkpr for Press-Visitor
McRary Willie, son J N, res same, student
McRary Miss Annie, d J N, res same, student
McRary John, son J N, res same, student
McSwain Kinny,* porter MacRae drug store, res rear 228 e Cabarrus
McSwain Maggie,* wife Kinny
McSwain Lawrence,* son Kinny, res same, wks for Jno W Brown
McSwain Martin,* son Kinny, res same, wks city market
McSwain Andrew,* son Kinny, res same, nurse
McSwain Dickinson,* son Kinny, res same, milker
McSwain Nannie,* d Kinny, res same, cook
McSwain Agnes,* d Kinny, res same, student
McSwain Berta,* d Kinny, res same, student
McSwain J H,* dairyman, res 615 s McDowell
McSwain Ora A,* wife J H, house work
McSwain Rody,* blacksmith, res 125 e Cabarrus
McSwain Lula,* washerwoman, res 30 Fowle
McSwain Phœbe,* cook, res 121 n Harrington
McVea Miss Emilie W, teacher in St Mary's School, res same
Mechanics Dime Savings Bank, 117 Fayetteville, Chas E Johnson pres, B R Lacy cashier
Meacham Miss Bessie, nurse at Rex Hospital, res same
Meacham Ann V,* cook for Major W W, res on lot
Meadows Mrs Willie, wid, dressmaker, res 506 e Hargett
Meadows Rufus A, son Mrs Willie, res same, student
Meadows Miss Willie, d Mrs Willie, res same, seamstress
Meadows W J C,* waiter Yarboro' House, room 320 e Davie
Meares Geo D, music teacher and mgr Academy of Music, res 627 w Jones
Meares Mrs Minnie, wife Geo D
Measles Hannah,* washerwoman, res 224 s Bloodworth
Mebane Miss Mattie, res with L Banks, Holt
Mebane Thos,* lab, res 738 s Person
Mebane Helen,* wife Thos, washerwoman
Mebane Jerry,* fireman S A L, res Yearby's lane
Mebane Alice,* wife Jerry, washerwoman
Medlin Wm A, sexton at Tabernacle church, res 301 s Bloodworth
Medlin Mrs S J, wife Wm A
Medlin D H, son Wm A, res same, printer
Medlin J C, son Wm A, res same, printer
Medlin Thos A, son Wm A, res same, student
Medlin Miss Martha, seamstress, res 301 s Bloodworth

Medlin L F, grocer, 328 e Martin, res same
Medlin W S, clk for L F Medlin, res same
Medlin Wm T, son W S, res same, student
Medlin John H, bookbinder, res 114 w Martin
Medlin Mrs Carrie, wife John H
Medlin Miss Minnie M, d John H, res same, student
Medlin John P, bookbinder, res 318 s Person
Medlin Mrs Lula B, wife John P
Medlin Thomas, city overseer, res 530 e Davie
Medlin Mrs Lizzie, wife Thos
Medlin George, city hand, res 609 e Cabarrus
Medlin David H, soliciting agt, res cor Bloodworth and Martin
Medlin Lizzie, seamstress, res 521 s Dawson
Medlin Mrs Eunice, janitress S A L reading-room, 109 Grimes' al
Merritt J Mal, conductor S A L R R, bds 10 e North
Merritt Kemp W, bkkpr for Crowder & Rand, res 20 s Swain
Merritt Mrs Roxie M, wife Kemp W
Merritt Sarah,* nurse for Wm H Grimes, res on lot
Merritt Hector,* lab, res Rock Quarry rd
Merritt Alice,* wife Hector, washerwoman
Merritt Robert,* son Hector, res same, lab
Merritt Jerry,* son Hector, res same, lab
Merritt Bettie,* d Hector, res same, nurse
Merritt Addie,* d Hector, res same, nurse
Merritt Elsie,* laundress at Rex Hospital, res 307 w Lenoir
Merritt George,* lab, res 307 w Lenoir
Merritt Bunny,* son Elsie, res same, student
Merritt Wm H,* lab, res 311 w Lenoir
Merritt Maggie,* cook, res Bloodworth, o s n
Merritt Frances,* cook, res 219 s East
Merritt Jane,* washerwoman, res 519 e Davie
Merritt F L, associate editor News and Observer, bds Park Hotel
Merritt Sarah,* nurse, res 32 Railroad
Merritt James,* hostler, res 720 Fayetteville
Merritt Bettie,* servant for Wm H Grimes, res on lot
Merrimon Mrs A S, wid, res 526 n Wilmington
Merrimon Miss Maud L, d Mrs A S, res same
MESERVE CHAS F, Pres Shaw University, res cor South and Wilmington
Meserve Mrs Abbie, wife Chas F
Meserve Miss Alice, d Chas F, res same
Messick Miss Clara, wks dress dept W H & R S Tucker & Co, bds Park Hotel
Mial Jos,* lab, res e Hargett, o s e
Mial Harriet,* wife Jos
Mial Norman,* son Jos, res same, wks at city market
Mial Madison,* son Jos, res same, wks B N Mitchell
Mial Oscar,* son Jos, res same, student

Mial Scott,* lab, res Idlewild
Mial Cathanda,* wife Scott, washerwoman
Mial Louise,* cook for Mrs W T Mabry, res 321 s Bloodworth
Mials Lem,* eng Jones & Powell, res 2 Stronach ave
Middleton Robert, blacksmith, bds 324 w Lane
Millery Robert,* gardener, res Cotton lane, o s e
Millery Charity,* wife Robert, washerwoman
Miller W H, bookbinder, res 511 s Bloodworth
Miller Mrs Emma, wife W H
Miller Miss Beulah, d W H, res same, cash-girl at W H & R S Tucker & Co
Miller H F, son W H, res same, student
Miller Miss Mary L, d W H, res same, student
Miller Miss Sallie, d W H, res same, student
Miller Henry, traveling salesman, bds cor Newbern ave and Person
Miller Mrs Lorraine, wife Henry
Miller Miss Jennie, boarding-house, cor Newbern ave and Person
Miller Miss Louie, d Henry, res same, student
Miller Sam A, mailing clk News and Observer, bds 628 Hillsboro'
Miller Robert,* lab, res Martin, o s e
Miller Ellen,* wife Robert, washerwoman
Miller Lula,* d Robert, res same, washerwoman
Miller Tempie,* cook, res 225 s Bloodworth
Miller Lou,* cook for Dr J M Ayer, res 125 n West
Miller Jesse,* brick-mason, bds 108 e Hargett
Miller Amanda,* restaurant, res 408 s Blount
Miller Mary,* d Amanda, res same, cook restaurant
Miller Mrs L C, res n Person
Miller Miss Mary C, d Mrs L C, res same
Miller Henry W, private sec to Col A B Andrews, res n Person
Miller Nancy,* cook for I C Blair, res same
Millican Jennie,* nurse for H D Blake, res same
Millican Judy,* washerwoman, res 429 s Person
Millican Jennie,* d Judy, res same, nurse
Millican Robert,* barber, rooms rear 124 e Hargett
Millinden Miss Bertha, res with B S Liles
MILLS MFG COMPANY, wagons, building material, &c, Fayetteville st R R crossing
Mills John A, wagon mfg, &c, res 413 w Hargett
Mills Mrs J I, wife John A
Mills Maple, son John A, res same, student
Mills Hartrick, son John A, res same, student
Mills Miss Myrtle, d John A, res same
Mills Mrs Bettie, wid, d Mrs Lucy B Evans, res same
Mills Miss Mary, d Mrs Bettie, res same
Mills L, assistant yard master S A L R R, bds 104 n McDowell
Mills Ben, mechanic S A L R R, bds 104 n McDowell
Mills J B,* huckster, 718 s Saunders, res same

Mills Sarah, wife J B, house work
Mills J D, weaver Pilot cot mill, bds 225 Pace, o s n
Mills Mrs Jennie, wife J D, weaver Pilot cot mill
Mills Fenner, peddler, res 412 s Swain
Mills Mrs Dora, wife Fenner
Mills Nula,* house-servant for Mrs Annie M Parker, res on lot
Miner Miss Minnie, niece Mrs L T Grissom, res same
Miner John,* porter J J Thomas, res 230 e South
Miner Millie,* wife John, washerwoman
Miner Wm A,* mechanic, res 202 w Lenoir
Minger Mrs Celia, wid, res 227 n Dawson
Minger Miss Lillie, d Mrs Celia, res same, student
Minger Miss Pearl, d Mrs Celia, res same
Minter Cain,* whitewasher, res 213 s Harrington
Minter Julia,* wife Cain, washerwoman
Minter George,* son Cain, res same, student
Minter Simon,* son Cain, res same, student
Mitchell Hilliard L, carp, 304 n Dawson
Mitchell Mrs Ella, wife Hilliard L
Mitchell Miss Irene, d Hilliard L, res same, student
Mitchell John E, carp, res 321 w Jones
Mitchell Mrs Hannah, wife John E
Mitchell Benj H, harness and saddle dealer, res 202 w Lane, shop 331 s Wilmington
Mitchell Mrs Mary S, wife B H
Mitchell Fred E, son B H, res same, student
Mitchell Miss E, d B H, res same, student
Mitchell Wm,* brick-mason, res 315 e Davie
Mitchell Altona F,* wife Wm
Mitchell James O,* son Wm, res same, brick-mason
Mitchell Elenora C,* d Wm, res same, student
Mitchell Annie B,* d Wm, res same, student
Mitchell Maywood,* d Wm, res same, student
Mitchell Hilliard, dairyman, bds 224 w Lane
Mitchell Susan,* hkpr for Cas Pollard, res on lot
Mitchell A C, revenue dept, bds cor McDowell and Hargett
Mitchell Bettie,* washerwoman, res 212 e Cabarrus
Mitchell Isabella,* washerwoman, res 223 e Cabarrus
Mitchell Mrs Lethia, mother of Mrs W N Harris, res same
Mitchell Abe, machinist, res 604 e Davie
Mitchell Mrs Belle, wife Abe
Mitchell Miss Carrie, d Abe, res same
Mitchell John W, city hand, res 610 e Davie
Mitchell Mrs Martha, wife John W
Mitchell John W Jr, son J W, res same
Mitchell J H, blacksmith, res 538 e Martin
Mitchell Mrs Caroline, wife J H
Mitchell Walter J, son J H, res same, machinist

Mitchell William,* lab, res old Fair Grounds, o s e
Mitchell Cornelia,* wife William, washerwoman
Mitchell Charles, machinist, res 553 e Martin
Mitchell Mrs J Gertrude, wife Charles
Mitchell Miss Hazel E, d Charles, res same, student
Mitchell Lucy J,* matron in colored D D & B Inst, res same
Mitchell George W, printer, res 410 e Edenton
Mitchell Mrs Esther, wife George W
Mitchell Mrs Mary, mother George W, res same, dressmaker
Mitchell Miss Mamie, d Mrs Mary, res same, dressmaker
Mitchell Miss Daisy, d Mrs Mary, res same, student
Mitchell Rufus, son Mrs Mary, res same, student
Mitchell Clarence, son Mrs Mary, res same, student
Mitchell Grant,* lab, res 423 e Lenoir
Mitchell Anna,* wife Grant, washerwoman
Mitchell Arrington,* lab, res Manly
Mitchell Dilsey,* wife Arrington, washerwoman
Mitchell J D,* fireman Southern R R, res 816 Manly
Mitchell Georgia,* wife J D, house work
Mitchell Mattie E,* d J D, res same, student
Mitchell Allen T,* grocer, cor Worth and Manly, res 331 Cannon
Mitchell Sarah A,* wife A T
Mitchell Walter,* lab, res 823 Manly
Mitchell Chas,* son Walter, res same, student
Mitchell Emmanuel,* son Walter, res same, student
Mitchell Maggie,* d Walter, res same, student
Mitchell Walter Jr,* son Walter, res same, student
Mitchell Walter,* lab, res 212 w South
Mitchell William,* lab, res 212 w South
Mitchell James,* carp, res 212 w South
Mitchell Amanda,* wife James, house work
Mitchell Miss Anna B, student, res with D S Hamilton
Mitchell Miss Josephine V, student, res with D S Hamilton
Mitchell Thomas, res 407 n West
Mitchell Mrs Fannie, wife Thos
Mitchell Wm S,* business mgr for the Gazette, res 214 Cannon
Mitchell Ida M,* wife W S, teacher
Mitchell Sallie N,* d W S, res same, student
Mitchell Wm A,* son W S, res same, student
Mitchell P B,* son W S, res same
Mitchell Fannie,* washerwoman, res 332 w South
Mitchell Chaney,* washerwoman, res 332 w South
Mitchell William,* wks for Jno C Drewry, res e Jones, Idlewild
Mitchell Emma,* wife Wm, washerwoman
Mitchener Lucy,* cook for W H Worth, res 318 w South
Mitchener Fannie,* d Lucy, res same, nurse
Mitchener Virinda,* d Lucy, res same, nurse at T B Crowder's
Mitchener Willie,* son Lucy, res same, lab

Mitchener Walter,* son Lucy, res same, musician
Mitchener Thomas,* lab, res 611 s McDowell
Mitchener Patsy,* wife Thos, washerwoman
Mitchener Eliza,* d Thos, res same, cook
Mitchener Green,* son Thos, res same, porter at J Hal Bobbitt's
Mitchener Minnie,* d Thos, res same, student
Moffitt Jos, wks S A L R R, res 213 w North
Moffitt Mrs Lou, wife Jos
Moffitt John, son Jos, res same, student
Moffitt James, son Jos, res same, student
Moffitt Miss Maggie, d Jos, res same, student
Moffitt Joe, son Mrs Lou, res same, student
Moffitt Elijah, lawyer, bds cor McDowell and Hargett
Moffitt E L, editor Christian Sun, bds cor McDowell and Hargett
Moffitt Mrs E E, wid, res 611 Fayetteville
Moncure Wm, division supt S A L R R, res 525 n Blount
Moncure Mrs Belle, wife Wm
Moncure Miss Belle, d Wm, res same, student
Moncure Miss Vivian, d Wm, res same, student
Moncure Wm Jr, son Wm, res same, student
Monk Mary,* house-servant for Thos S Kenan, res on lot
Monk Louis,* cook for Thos S Kenan, res on lot
Monie J M, dry goods, notions, &c, 217 s Wilmington, res corner Bloodworth and Jones
Monie Mrs Fannie M, wife J M
Monie Miss Mary A, d J M, res same
Monie J M Jr, son J M, res same, student
MONTAGUE B F, lawyer and pres Board of Trustees of N C Institution for the Blind, office in Commercial and Farmers Bank bldg, res 313 Newbern ave
Montague Mrs Bettie L, wife B F
Montague Miss Mary L, d B F, res same, student
Montague Miss Annie L, d B F, res same, student
MONTGOMERY WALTER A, associate justice of Supreme Court of N C, res 529 n Person
Montgomery Mrs Lizzie, wife Walter A
Montgomery Walter A Jr, son Walter A, res same, student
Montgomery Miss Elizabeth, d Walter A, res same, student
Montgomery Mrs S H, wid, res 330 w Hargett
Montgomery Miss Pattie, d Mrs S H, res same
Montgomery Frank,* stone-worker, res Whitaker ave
Montgomery Martha,* wife Frank, washerwoman
Montgomery Wm B,* son Frank, res same
Montgomery Patsy,* house-servant, res Whitaker ave
Montgomery George,* hostler at R E Parham, res e Martin, o s e
Montgomery Janet,* wife George, washerwoman
Montgomery J P,* lab, res old Fair Ground, o s e
Montgomery Minerva R,* wife J P, laundress

Montgomery Mattie,* washerwoman, res rear 404 Fayetteville
Monroe Miss Janie,* attendant at Insane Asylum, res same
Mood D J, printer, res Oakwood ave
Mood Mrs Maggie, wife D J
Mooneyham A H, clk at W H & R S Tucker & Co, res 408 n East
Mooneyham Mrs Ellen, wife A H
Mooneyham Miss Lizzie, d A H, res same, student
Mooneyham Herbert, son A H, res same, student
Moore David, clk for John C Scarboro, res 328 e Morgan
Moore Mrs Bettie, wife David
Moore Miss May, d David, res same
Moore Vick, son David, res same, clk for Johnson & Johnson
Moore Miss Dixie, d David, res same, student
Moore David Jr, son David, res same, clk for D T Johnson
Moore Mrs Drusilla, wid, dressmaker, res 129 e Hargett
Moore Fred, son Mrs Drusilla, res same, student
Moore Junius N, son Mrs Drusilla, res same, student
Moore John M, son Mrs Drusilla, res same, student
Moore George G, son Mrs Drusilla, res same, student
Moore A L, conductor S A L R R, res 218 w Jones
Moore Mrs C H, wife A L
Moore Miss Eliza, d A L, res same, teacher
Moore Thos E, grocer 114 w Peace, res same
Moore Mrs Lucy A, wife Thos E
Moore William, shoemaker, res Haywood
Moore Mrs Mary F, wife Wm
Moore John R, son Wm, res same, painter
Moore Frank G, son Wm, res same, student
Moore Harriet,* servant, res 220 Blount-st alley
Moore Mary,* d Harriet, res same, washerwoman
Moore & Johnson, tobacco prize-room, cor s Blount and Cabarrus
Moore John C, salesman, res Elm
Moore Mrs Emma, wife John C
Moore Miss Lois, d John C, res same, student
Moore V B, tobacco buyer, res 311 w Martin
Moore Mrs Bessie C, wife V B
Moore Miss Lucy C, d V B, res same
Moore Miss Albertine, d V B, res same
Moore Nathan,* lab, res 411 w South
Moore Martha,* wife Nathan, house work
Moore John,* son Nathan, res same, lab
Moore Gertrude,* d Nathan, res same, student
Moore James,* son Nathan, res same, student
Moore Neill H, shoemaker, res 309 e Martin
Moore Mrs Fronie E, wife Neill H
Moore W, shoemaker, shop basement Jones & Powell
Moore Lizzie, house work, bds 317 s East
Moore Indiana,* cook for R H Battle, res 618 Elm

Moore Blanche, seamstress, res 535 e Lenoir
Moore Ben M, real estate, res 310 s Dawson
Moore Catherine,* cook, res 710 s McDowell
Moore Miss A T, attendant at Insane Asylum, res same
Mordecai Samuel F (Battle & Mordecai), lawyer, r 303 n Boundary
Mordecai Mrs Bettie, wife S F
Mordecai Miss Bessie, d S F, res same
Mordecai Geo W, son S F, res same, student
Mordecai Henry L, son S F, res same, student
Mordecai Edward W, son S F, res same, student
Mordecai Alfred, son S F, res same, student
Mordecai Miss Ellen, d S F, res same, student
Mordecai Mrs Martha, wid, res n Person, o s n
Mordecai Miss Pattie, res n Person, o s n
Mordecai Lucy,* washerwoman, res e Davie, o s e
Mordecai Rosa,* d Lucy, res same, nurse
Mordecai Peggie,* cook for Mrs Kate Perry, r 306 s Bloodworth
Mordecai Lizzie,* cook for W S Boone, res on lot
Morgan Mrs Bettie, wife Robert, res 747 Fayetteville
Morgan Miss Ella, d Mrs Bettie, res same, weaver Caraleigh mill
Morgan Miss Eva, d Mrs Bettie, res same, weaver Caraleigh mill
Morgan Miss Marcey, d Mrs Bettie, res same, student
Morgan Ernest, son Mrs Bettie, res same, student
Morgan Miss P, teacher in Peace Institute, res same
Morgan J O, clk W B Mann, bds 111 s Bloodworth
Morgan Goings,* umbrella mender, res e Raleigh
Morgan Alpheus,* farm hand, res e Hargett, o s e
Morgan Love,* wife Alpheus, cook for E P Maynard
Morgan Elizabeth,* d Alpheus, res same, servant
Morgan Mary,* washerwoman, res rear 407 s Dawson
Morgan Ellen,* washerwoman, res 510 e Edenton
Morgan Matilda,* cook for W L Nowell, res same
Morgan Robert,* painter, res 513 Newbern ave
Morgan Louise,* wife Robt, washerwoman
Morgan Len,* driver for C W Young, res e Jones, Idlewild
Morgan Lina,* wife Len, washerwoman
Moring F O (Pool & Moring), merchant and sec of Caraleigh cot mill, res 127 n Blount
Moring Mrs P A, wife F O
Moring Miss Maggie, d F O, res same, student
Moring Miss Daisy, d F O, res same, student
Moring Miss Helen, d F O, res same, student
Moring Alfred, father of F O, res same
Moring M J J,* barber Prairie bldg, res same
Moring Martin J,* barber, res 6 s Harrington
Moring Alice,* wife Martin J
Morris John T, upholsterer and furniture repairer, cor e Morgan and s Wilmington, res same

Morris Mrs Rosa, wife Jno T
Morris Mark C, section hand S A L R R, res 406 w Lane
Morris Mrs Della, wife Mark C
Morris Miss Lillian, d Mark C, res same, student
Morris Miss Lula, d Mark C, res same, student
Morris A, clothing and shoes, 223 s Wilmington, res 408 s Person
Morris Mrs Fannie, wife A
Morris Jacob, son A, res same, student
Morris Louis, son A, res same, student
Morris Sandy,* lab, res 25 McKee
Morris Adelaide,* wife Sandy, washerwoman
Morris Rena,* house-servant, res 25 McKee
Morris Jos, moulder, res 745 Fayetteville
Morris Mrs Hattie, wife Jos
Morris Gideon W, cabinet maker, res 212 e Lenoir
Morris Mrs Hattie E, wife G W, seamstress
Morris Mrs M L, wid, mother of Wm A Faison, res same
Morris Miss Luvenia E, bkpr for Mrs W O Scott, res same
Morris Florence, seamstress, res 515 s McDowell
Morris Sidney M, blacksmith, bds 538 w Peace
Morris Miss Minnie, res 523 s Wilmington
Morris Mrs Solicitor, seamstress, res 109 Grimes' al
Morson Hugh, prin (Morson & Denson) Ral Male Academy, res 317 e Jones
Morson Mrs Sallie, wife Hugh
Morson Miss Harriet, d Hugh, res same
Morson Hugh A, son Hugh, res same, student
Morson Wm F, son Hugh, res same, student
Morson John, son Hugh, res same, student
Morson Miss Sallie L, sister Hugh, res same
Morton Mittie,* cook, res 212 w Cabarrus
Moseley N S, prop Moseley dining-hall, 130 Fayetteville, res same
Moseley Frank W, son N S, res same, clk for father
Moseley Jos B, son N S, res same, bkkpr Ral Electric Co
Moseley Nathan, son N S, res same
Moseley Miss Louise, d N S, res same
Moseley Jas A, traveling salesman, res 114 s Salisbury
Moseley Mrs A C, wife Jas A
Moseley Geo G, clk W H & R S Tucker & Co, bds 105½ Fayetteville
Moseley Dolly,* servant for Dr A O Jones, res same
Moseley Thos B (J M Broughton & Co), ins and real estate agt, bds 528 e Jones
Moseley Wesley,* clk, res 301 Cannon
Moseley Nancy,* wife Wesley, house work
Moseley Nannie,* student, res 301 Cannon
Moser Mike A, carp, bds 513 Polk
Moses Amy,* wks for Chas I Proctor, res 110 n Harrington

Moss Emeline,* washerwoman, res Adams lane
Moss Thomas,* son Emeline, res same, tobacco worker
Moss William,* son Emeline, res same, tobacco worker
Moss Maggie,* d Emeline, res same, tobacco worker
Moss Frankie,* d Emeline, res same, nurse
Moss Eldridge, city hand, res 524 e Lenoir
Moss Cassanda, wife Eldridge
Moss Miss Lillie F, d Eldridge, res same, student
Moss Miss Bedie A, d Eldridge, res same
Mott Miss Mary A, seamstress, res 217 s East
Moye J M,* lab, res 409 w South
Moye Mollie,* wife J M, house work
Moye Exie,* d J M, res same, student
Moye Hattie,* d J M, res same, student
Moye Louise,* d J M, res same, student
Muckle William,* train hand S A L R R, res w Lane, near crossing at n West
Muckle Virginia,* wife Wm, washerwoman
Muckle John,* train hand S A L R R, res Fleming's lane
Muckle Martha,* wife John, washerwoman
Mullenix M S, shoemaker, res 311 e Martin
Mullin Mrs Clara, wid, res 11 McKee
Mullin Ernest, wks Caraleigh mill, res 11 McKee
Mullin Miss Lula, student, res 11 McKee
Mullin Offy, wks Caraleigh mill, res 816 Fayetteville
Mullin Mrs Nora, wife Offy, wks Caraleigh mill
Mullin Junins H, policeman, res rear s East
Mullin Miss Mollie M, sister Junins H, res same
Muir Sandy, ins agt, bds 404 Fayetteville
Munson J B, Southern R R Division frt and passenger agt, office rear Citizens National Bank
Murdock Robert,* lab, res 712 s McDowell
Murphy Mrs Emma, boarding-house, 508 w Morgan
Murphy Miss Lizzie, d Mrs Emma, res same, teacher
Murphy John, son Mrs Emma, res same, wks for Jones & Powell
Murphy Willie J, son Mrs Emma, res same, student
Murphy Alonzo, son Mrs Emma, res same, student
Murphy Archie,* lab, res 516 e Davie
Murphy Moses,* porter, res 516 e Davie
Murray Mrs Della D, wid, res w Davie
Murray Miss Bessie L, d Mrs D D, res same, student
Murray Mrs E S, wid, res 313 w Hargett
Murray T H, ticket agt S A L, res 313 w Hargett
Murray Miss Nellie, d Mrs E S, res same
Murray Jesse O, carp, res 507 Newbern ave
Murray Mrs Martha A, wife Jesse O
Murray Henry, son Jesse O, res same, driver
Murray Jesse E, son Jesse O, res same, driver

Murray Robert B, son Jesse O, res same, clk Miss Julia Woodward
Murray Miss Lucy E, d Jesse O, res same, student
Murray Guy, son Jesse O, res same, student
Murray Ida,* cook for Mrs C H King, res 113 n Harrington
Murray Otis,* driver for Woollcott & Son, bds 223 w North
Murray Mrs D D, seamstress, res w Davie
Murrell Miss J C, bds 250 Peace
Myatt W A (Myatt & Hunter), merchant, res 121 n Blount
Myatt Mrs C S, wife W A
Myatt Miss Nellie, d W A, res same
Myatt Miss Lula, d W A, res same, student
Myatt Wm, son W A, res same, student
Myatt Garland, son W A, res same, student
Myatt Edwin, son W A, res same, student
Myatt Ernest, son W A, res same, student
Myatt & Hunter, wholesale grocers and commission merchants, 17 e Martin and 18 Exchange Place
Myatt Annie,* d Eliza Reid, res same, student
Myatt Mrs Ann, wid, lives with Edward Teasley
Myatt Mrs Emma, wid, boarding-house, 109 s Blount
Myatt Alice,* house-servant, res 718 s Dawson
Myatt Ferrebe,* washerwoman, res 323 w South
Myers Luther A, ins agt, bds 305 Hillsboro'
Myers Geo,* wks State Library, res 435 n Salisbury
Myers Sallie,* wife Geo

NASH Louise,* house-servant of Dr Thos D Hogg, res on lot
Neal L C, grocer, cor West and r r crossing, res 301 n West
Neal Mrs K M, wife L C
Neal Miss Mollie, d L C, res same, wks Ral cot mill
Neal Miss Lelia, d L C, res same, wks Ral cot mill
Neal Miss Caddie, d L C, res same, wks Ral cot mill
Neal Frances,* housekeeper for Reuben Cole, res same
Neathery Edward, bookbinder, bds 112 Halifax
Neathery Mrs J B, wid, res 220 s Dawson
Neimyer J C, eng S A L, res 118 Firwood ave, o s n
Neimyer Mrs Sallie, wife J C
Neimyer J E, son J C, res same, drug clk for Wynne & Birdsong
Neimyer Miss Annie, d J C, res same, student
Nellis Miss Mamie, seamstress, res 226 e Cabarrus
Nelson Charles,* lab, res Martin, o s e
Nelson Louise,* wife Chas
Nelson Jackie,* mother of Chas, res same, sick-nurse
Nelson Catherine,* washerwoman, res 602 s Person
Newcomb Chas W, bkkpr for Pool & Moring, res 513 Halifax
Newcomb Mrs Annie B, wife C W
Newcomb Miss Alice B, d C W, res same

Newcomb Miss Lula, saleslady at Fred A Watson's, r with brother, C W Newcomb
Newell Miss Annie, dressmaker, res 547 e Martin
Newell Scott,* lab, res 413 n West
Newell Pattie,* wife Scott, washerwoman
Newell Sallie,* d Scott, res same, cook for C B Barbee
Newell Lewis,* son Scott, res same, lab
Newell Brittian,* son Scott, res same, wks for Wm J Saunders
Newell Charlotte,* house-servant for F H Briggs, res on lot
Newkirk Miss M L, attendant at Insane Asylum, res same
Newman Wm W, clk J R Ferrall & Co, res 515 w Morgan
Newman Miss Mamie, d W W, res same, student
Newman Miss Lelia, d W W, res same
Newman Mrs Annie, wid, hkpr Harrison House, res same
Newman Miss Mabel, d Mrs Annie, res same, student
Newsom J D, clk for C H Beine & Co, res 302 w Jones
Newsom Mrs Sarah A, wife J D
Newsom Miss Laura D, d J D, res same, teacher
Newsom Chas F, son J D, res same, printer
Newsom W R, clk W E Jones, res 525 Halifax st
Newsom Mrs Maggie, wife W R
Newsom Julia,* washerwoman, res 414 s Swain
Newton Geo, wks for city, res 402 rear Smithfield
Newton Mrs Lillie, wife Geo
Newton Miss Cora, d Geo, res same, wks Caraleigh mill
Newton Willie, son Geo, res same, student
Newton Geo Jr, son Geo, res same, student
Newton Miss Sallie, d Geo, res same, student
Newton John, invalid, res 310 s Salisbury
Newton Mrs Mary, wife John, seamstress
Nesbitt R H, with Franklin Pub Co, N Y, res 435 Halifax
Nevels William,* lab, res 804 s Wilmington
Nevels Florence,* wife William, washerwoman
Nichols John, justice of peace and sec N C Agricultural Society, office w Martin opp U S p o, rooms 126½ Fayetteville
Nichols Mrs Virginia C, wife John
Nichols J J,* grocer, 423 n West, res same
Nichols Eliza,* wife J J, cook for Dr W I Royster
Nichols Kate B,* d J J, res same, student
Nichols Wm J,* waiter Park Hotel, room 409 s Blount
Nichols Marthena,* res Fayetteville below R R
Nichols Louisa,* invalid, res Fayetteville below R R
Nichols Tena M,* d Louisa, res same, teacher
Nichols Stanford, printer, res 408 n Bloodworth
Nichols Mrs Caroline, wife Stanford
Nichols Laurie, son Stanford, res same, brick-mason
Nichols Miss Gertie, d Stanford, res same
Nichols James,* farm hand, res e Hargett, o s e

Nichols Sarah,* wife James, washerwoman
Nichols Viney,* d James, res same, waiter at Mrs Mary Banks
Nichols Mary,* d James, res same, nurse for Len Johnson
Nichols James,* driver for Bart Gatling, res Hargett, o s e
Nicholson Victoria,* washerwoman, res 574 e Cabarrus
Nicholson Belle,* d Victoria, res same, cook
Nicholson Mary,* d Victoria, res same, cook
Nicholson Wm, son Victoria, res same, milker
Nicholson Moses,* son Victoria, res same, lab
Nicholson John, son Victoria, res same, lab
Nicholson Patsy,* d Victoria, res same, student
Nicholson Thomas,* son Victoria, res same, student
Nicholson Joe,* train hand S A L, res 122 w Peace
Nicholson Sallie,* wife Joe, washerwoman
Nivins Willis,* lab S A L, res 122 w Peace
Nivins Hannah,* wife Willis
Nivins Arthur,* son Willis, res same, student
Nivins Ben,* son Willis, res same, student
Nixon Dr T F, physician, res 531 n Saunders
Nixon Mrs F A, wife Dr T F
Nixon Miss F E, d Dr T F, res same, dressmaker
Nixon R Y, son Dr T F, res same, tel opr
Nixon Miss Maud, d Dr T F, res same, stenographer and typewriter
Nixon Chas R, son Dr T F, res same, student
Nixon N N, son Dr T F, res same, student
Nixon & Johnson, sale, boarding and camp stable, s Wilmington bet Davie and Cabarrus
Nixon W A (Nixon & Johnson), horse dealer, res 412 Fayetteville
Nixon Mrs E A, wid, res 412 Fayetteville
Nixon Miss Mollie, sister of W A, res same
Nixon Miss Laura, sister of W A, res same
Noble Ferry,* barber W G Otey, res 5 n Swain
Noble Mary,* wife Ferry
Noble Floyd,* son Ferry, res same, student
Noble Eugene,* son Ferry, res same, student

THE N. C. HOME INSURANCE CO.,
RALEIGH, - N. C.
ORGANIZED 1868.
Affords Indemnity for Loss by Fire.

Home Office: Raleigh, N. C.   Agencies throughout the State.

W. S. PRIMROSE, PRESIDENT.   CHAS. ROOT, SECRETARY AND TREASURER.
E. CHAMBERS SMITH, VICE-PRESIDENT.   P. COWPER, ADJUSTER.
R. B. DeVAULT, SPECIAL AGENT.

Noble Hazel,* son Ferry, res same, student
Noland Patrick, inmate Soldiers' Home
NORMAN Rev Dr W C, pastor Edenton-st Methodist church, res 228 w Edenton
Norman Mrs Sallie C, wife Rev Dr W C
Norman Rev Moses W D, teacher in Shaw University, res same
Norman Jos R, carp, res 536 e Jones
Norman Mrs Rebecca, wife Jos R
Norris Sam B, mgr for W E Jones, dry goods, &c, res 103 n McDowell
Norris Mrs Minnie F, wife Sam B
Norris Wm H, son Sam B, res same, student
Norris Delmer M, son Sam B, res same
Norris M T & Bro, wholesale grocers and commission merchants, 239 s Wilmington
Norris M T (M T Norris & Bro), merchant, res 421 n Blount
Norris Mrs C A, wife M T
Norris Miss Mary E, d M T, res same, student
Norris Miss Ethel M, d M T, res same, student
Norris Miss Willa, d M T, res same, student
Norris Miss Ruby, d M T, res same, student
Norris W C (M T Norris & Bro), bds 421 n Blount
Norris C F, wks oil mill, res 514 s Harrington
Norris Mrs Caroline, wife C F
Norris C B, son C F, res same, quiller Caraleigh mill
Norris Miss Eadie L, d C F, res same, weaver Caraleigh mill
Norris James R, son C F, res same, cloth inspector
Norris Miss Nella C, d C F, res same, weaver Caraleigh mill
Norris Miss Irene H, d C F, res same, student
Norris Lonnie R, son C F, res same, student
NORTH CAROLINA HOME INS CO, 220 Fayetteville
NORTH CAROLINA BLDG & SUPPLY CO, n West, builders and contractors
North Carolina Phosphate Co, office 331 Fayetteville, C M Hawkins pres, B S Jerman sec & treas
NORTH CAROLINA CAR CO, Franklin, builders and cont'rs

W. I. HICKS, Pres.   C. H. BECKWITH, Vice-Pres.   W. I. ELLINGTON, Treas. and Sup't.

NORTH CAROLINA
Building and Supply Company,
CONTRACTORS AND BUILDERS.

NORTH CAROLINA BOOK CO, 129 Fayetteville, E G Harrell mgr
North-Side Drug Store (Wynne J S & Birdsong E G proprietors), 445 Halifax
Northam E R, clk A B Stronach, bds 329 Hillsboro'
Norwood Geo T, bookbinder, res 415 Elm
Norwood Mrs Annie R
Norwood's Cigar Factory, 214 s Wilmington, J M Norwood propr
Norwood J M, cigar mfg, res 309 s Person
Norwood Mrs Lula C, wife J M
Norwood Mrs D C, mother of J M, res same
Norwood William, cigar maker, room 214 s Wilmington
Norwood Burton,* lab, res 512 e Edenton
Norwood Mary,* wife Burton, washerwoman
Norwood Nora,* d Burton, res same, cook for T K Bruner
Norwood Grizzie,* washerwoman, res 506 Haywood
Norwood Ben,* lab, res 304 s Harrington
Norwood Janie,* wife Ben, washerwoman
Norwood Lizzie,* d Ben, res same, nurse
Norwood Minnie,* d Ben, res same, student
Norwood Ella,* d Ben, res same, student
Norwood Mary,* washerwoman, res Forsythe al
Norwood Lucy,* d Mary, res same, washerwoman
Nott Roger, rooms 331 Fayetteville
Nottingham J T, keeper of market, res 220 n Salisbury
Nottingham Mrs E C, wife J T
Nottingham Miss Alma L, d J T, res same
Nottingham Miss Gracie B, d J T, res same
Nottingham Geo S, son J T, res same, drug clk J Y MacRae
Nottingham Miss Emily, d J T, res same, student
Nottingham Wm G, wks S A L R R, res 218 n Harrington
Nottingham Mrs Mollie, wife Wm G
Nottingham Wm T, son Wm G, res same
Nowell Alvin, boarding-house, 209 w Morgan
Nowell W L, eng S A L, res 112 Firwood ave, o s n
Nowell Mrs E G, wife W L

The North Carolina Car Company,
Raleigh, N. C.,

Manufacturers of Railroad Machinery and Mill Castings, Log Cars, &c.,

——ARE PREPARED TO——

Repair Locomotives, Stationary Engines, and do general Machine Work.

Nowell Ralph G, son W L, res same, wks S A L
Nowell E B, son W L, wks Ral cot mill
Nowell Miss Nannie, d W L, res same
Nowell R M, clk for Woollcott & Son, bds 321 e Lane
Nowell Patrick,* fireman Ral Electric Co, res 225 e Lane
Nowell Lucy,* washerwoman, res old Fair Ground, o s e
Nowell Alice,* cook, res w Lenoir, Rex Hospital property
Nowell Chas,* son Alice, res same, student
Nunn Roscoe, asst meteorologist U S Weather Bureau, res 118 w Edenton
Nunn Mrs Hattie D, wife Roscoe
Nunn Daniel,* lab, res rear 508 s West
Nunn Caroline,* wife Daniel, house work
Nunn Ruffin,* son Daniel, res same, farm hand
Nunn Wm,* lab, res 516 e Davie
Nunn Laura,* wife Wm, house work
Nunn Rev Henry,* Methodist minister, res Nunn
Nunn Harriet,* wife Rev Henry, nurse
Nunn Lula,* d Rev Henry, res same

OAK CITY STEAM LAUNDRY, 216 Fayetteville, Page & Marshall proprietors
Oakley Annie,* washerwoman, res 212 w South
Oakley Marshall,* lab, res 212 w South
Oatney Wm,* crossing watchman S A L R R, res near cor West and Lane
Oatney Annie,* wife Wm, washerwoman
O'Bryant Lizzie,* nurse for Dr Hubert Haywood, res on lot
O'Connell Douglas, blacksmith, res 212 s East
O'Connell Mrs Ida M, wife Douglas
Ogburn Isabella,* washerwoman, res Smithfield alley
Ogburn Louisa,* washerwoman, res Smithfield alley
Ogburn Ned,* hackman, res Smithfield alley
O'Kelly Delphia,* house work, res Avent Ferry rd, o s w
O'Kelly Fannie,* d Delphia, res same
O'Kelly Nannie,* d Delphia, res same
O'Kelly John,* hackman, res Avent Ferry rd, o s w
O'Kelly Anna,* wife John
O'Kelly John,* student, res 421 s Blount
O'Kelly Roger,* student, res 421 s Blount
O'Kelly Wm,* student, res 421 s Blount
O'Kelly Charles,* student, res 421 s Blount
O'Kelly Isaac,* livery stable, e Martin
O'Kelly John,* hackman, res o s w
O'Kelly Roger,* hackman, res o s e
Olds Fred A, newspaper correspondent, res Park Hotel
Olds Mrs K A, wife Fred A

Olds Fred C, son Fred A, clk C E Johnson & Co, res Park Hotel
Oldham M L, clk for H H Crocker, res 205 e Hargett
Oldham Mrs Maggie, wife M L
Oldham Miss Bessie, d M L, res same, student
Olive Mrs Jennie, dressmaker, res 309 s Blount
Olive Henry, son Mrs Jennie, res same, restaurant
Olive Anderson, inmate Soldiers' Home
Olive W C, tel opr, bds 317 w Jones
Olive Mrs Lovie, wife W C
Olmstead Alton E, carp, res 216 e Lenoir
Olmstead Mrs Sarah F, wife A E, dressmaker
Olmstead Robt T, son A E, res same, tinner
Olmstead Miss Dora R, d A E, res same student
Olmstead Jno W, son A E, res same, student
Olmstead Harvey B, son A E, res same, student
Olmstead Thos C, machinist, res 602 e Davie
Olmstead Miss Eula M, d Thos C, res same
Olmstead Miss Ida B, d Thos C, res same
O'Neill William, bkkpr, res Smith
O'Neill Mrs Bettie, wife Wm
O'Neill Miss Ordrey, d Wm, res same, student
O'Neill J R, clk revenue office, res 215 w Cabarrus
O'Neill Miss Annie M, d John R
O'Neill David,* lab, res rear 515 s Harrington
O'Neill Eliza,* wife David, cook
O'Neill Alice,* cook for W H Holloway, res Martin, o s e
O'Neill Maggie,* d Alice, res same, teacher of music
O'Neill Cameron,* lab, res rear 548 e Hargett
O'Neill Frances,* wife Cameron, washerwoman
O'Neill Armada,* d Cameron, res same, nurse
O'Neill Floyd,* son Cameron, res same, student
O'Neill Roxanna,* cook, res 720 Fayetteville
O'Neill Pleasant,* cook, res old Fair Ground, o s e
O'Neill Mrs M E, seamstress, res 415 s Person
O'Quinn Jesse, florist at H Steinmetz, bds 109 s Blount
Ormand Miss Elnora, niece of W W Newman, res same

W. G. OTEY,

Shaving and Hair-Dressing Saloon,

315 Fayetteville Street, RALEIGH, N. C.

Polite and Prompt Service.   **Hot and Cold Baths.**

Osborn Nancy,* washerwoman, res s Harrington
OTEY W G,* barber, shop Yarboro' House bldg, res 125 w Cabarrus
Otey Henry,* barber, res 511 s McDowell
Otey Josephine,* wife Henry
Otey Cloe,* house-servant, res 418 s McDowell
Outlaw Mary A,* seamstress, res 715 s McDowell
Outlaw Eliza,* d Mary A, res same, student
Outlaw Mary A,* house-servant, bds 611 s Harrington
Outlaw Julia,* cook, res 516 s East
Outlaw David,* son Julia, res same
Overby W H, grocer, 201 Smithfield, res same
Overby Mrs Eliza, wife W H
Overby Alex,* fireman S A L, res 2001 Yearby's lane
Overby Lucy,* wife Alex, washerwoman
Overby Elgie,* greaser S A L, res Yearby's lane
Overby Annie,* wife Elgie
Overby Jane,* cook at Park Place, res same
Overby Lewis,* train hand S A L R R, res 543 n Wilmington
Overby Matilda,* wife Lewis, washerwoman
Overton W H, sec Young Men's Christian Association, bds Newbern ave and Person
Owen E C, printer, res 517 s Person
Owen Mrs Mattie D, wife E C
Owen Miss Hazel E, d E C, res same, student
Owen Miss Susie V, d E C, res same, student
Owens Miss Lucy, d Mrs F A Hutchings, res same, student
Owens Mary,* nurse for Robert L Burkhead

PACE Elias R, grocer, 702 n Person, res 704 n Person, o s n
Pace Mrs W H, wid, res cor Blount and Polk
Pace Miss Mattie, d Mrs W H, res same, student
Pace Willie, son Mrs W H, res same, student
Pace J M, sales stable, buggy and wagon dealer, 111 e Martin
Pace Elias Jr, guard at penitentiary, res 724 Pace
Pace R A, grocer, 713 n Person, res 711 n Person
Pace Mrs Annie, wife R A
Pace Miss Ellen, d R A, res same, student
Pace E R, machinist S A L R R, res Franklin, o s n
Pace Mrs Lula, wife E R
Pace Mrs Isabella, mother E R, res same
Pace Sallie,* washerwoman, res Adams lane
Pace Bunny,* porter for J E Duke, res 724 e Davie
Pace Ada,* washerwoman, res 22 Fowle
Pace Nat,* lab, res old Fair Ground, o s e
PAGE & MARSHALL, proprietors Oak City Laundry, 246 Fayetteville

Page Robert L, laundryman, bds 404 Fayetteville
Page Mrs S E, wid, res 620 w Jones
Page Miss Louise, d Mrs S E, res same
Page Miss Mary A, d Mrs S E, res same, teacher
Page Miss Lucy, d Mrs S E, res same, student
Page Dock,* gardener, res 533 s Harrington
Page Maria,* wife Dock, washerwoman
Page Alva,* cook for S G Ryan, res on lot
Page Henry H,* carp, res 405 Haywood
Page Mary J,* wife Henry H, house work
Page Malpheas,* hackman, res n Bloodworth, o s n
Page Candace,* wife Malpheas, cook for Elias Pace
Page Hattie,* restaurant, 221 s Wilmington, res same
PAGE M W, sheriff Wake co, res Morrisville, N C
Pair Gracie,* washerwoman, res 112 e Cabarrus
Pair Lizzie,* washerwoman, res 406 Smith
Palmer Amanda,* washerwoman, res 505 s Blount
Palmer Wm H,* son Amanda, res same, porter for Miss M Reese
Palmer Luvenia,* d Amanda, res same, house-servant for F O Moring
Palmer James,* son Amanda, res same, lab
Palmer Lillie,* d Amanda, res same, student
Palmer Frank,* fireman S A L R R, res 205 w North
Palmer Hannah,* wife Frank
Palmer Hattie D,* d Frank, res same
Palmer W H,* hotel waiter, res 517 s Dawson
Pardon Mary,* cook for Jas H Ennis, res same
Parham Hugh, salesman, bds Newbern ave and Person
Parham James T, carp, res 102 n Saunders
Parham Mrs Valia, wife Jas T
Parham Miss Pattie C, d Jas T, res same
Parham Miss Lydia B, d Jas T, res same
Parham Jas L, son Jas T, res same, printer
Parham Miss Evie S, d Jas T, res same
Parham Robert E, saloon, board, sale and livery stable, 17 Exchange Place, 325 and 329 s Wilmington, res 214 e Martin
Parham Mrs Rosa, wife R E
Parham Miss Sallie, d R E, res same, student
Parham Miss Bessie, d R E, res same, student
Parham Miss Katie, d R E, res same, student
Parham Willie, son R E, res same, student
Parham Robert E Jr, son R E, res same, student
Parham James, son R E, res same
Parham A W, piano and organ agt, res 223 s West
Parham Mrs Mary A, wife A W
Parham Irwin, son A W, res same, student
Parham Allen,* lab, res 104 w Cabarrus
Parham Catherine,* wife Allen, washerwoman

Parham Henrietta,* cook, res 104 w Cabarrus
Parham Eliza,* mother of Allen, res same
Parham Anise,* cook for R O Burton, res on lot
Parham Etta,* chamber-maid at Park Place, res same
Parham Hugh, salesman, bds cor Newbern ave and Person
Park Charles B, instructor in mechanics at A & M College, res 314 Polk
Park Mrs Effie L, wife C B
Park Peyton H, son C B, res same
Park Miss Frances, d C B, res same
Park Benj F (N C Bldg and Supply Co), yard and shop mgr, res 207 n West
Park Mrs Fannie C, wife Benj F
Park John Alsey, son Benj F, res same
Parker & Terrell, merchandise brokers, 312 s Wilmington
Parker M A (M A Parker & Co), cot buyer, res 304 Oakwood ave
Parker Mrs Martha J, wife M A
Parker Eugene L, son M A, res same, student
Parker Linus M, son M A, res same, student
Parker Clyde E, son M A, res same, student
Parker Miss Ethel G, d M A, res same, student
Parker Miss Nelia C, matron Blind Institution, res same
Parker Mrs Maggie, wid, res 114 w Martin
Parker Milliard, son Mrs Maggie
Parker Thos, wks Ral cot mill, res 446 Halifax
Parker Mrs Lear, wife Thos
Parker Claude S, clk at W E Jones, res cor McDowell and Martin
Parker Mrs Sallie L, wife C S
Parker C L, son C S, res same, student
Parker Miss Mary O, d C S, res same, student
Parker Miss Violet M, d C S, res same, student
Parker Miss Lula E, d C S, res same, student
Parker J W, grocer, 329 w Martin, res same
Parker Mrs Mollie, wife J W
Parker Harvey, son J W, res same, wks Caraleigh mill
Parker Brantley, son J W, res same, weaver Caraleigh mill
Parker Miss Arcey, d J W, res same, student
Parker W H, inmate Soldiers' Home
Parker W B, inmate Soldiers' Home
Parker W Howell, inmate Soldiers' Home
Parker Mrs C N, wid, boarding-house, 117 Fayetteville (up-stairs)
Parker Miss Minnie B, d Mrs C N, res same, student
Parker Miss Lillie, d Mrs C N, res same, student
Parker Scott, son Mrs C N, res same, student
Parker Miss Ann, res with W A Linehan
Parker Mrs Annie M, wid, res 117 e Edenton
Parker Bartholomew Moore, son Mrs Annie M, res same, student

Parker F W, drug clk for Jas I Johnson, rooms over store 301 Fayetteville
Parker Anthony,* drayman, res 26 Railroad
Parker Cornelia,* wife Anthony, house work
Parker Lillie,* cook, res 588 e Cabarrus
Parker Hardy,* lab, res 564 Newbern ave
Parker Emily,* wife Hardy
Parker Reuben,* farm hand, res 834 s Wilmington
Parker Eliza,* wife Reuben, washerwoman
Parker Ann,* washerwoman, res Manly
Parker Abram,* lab, res old Fair Ground, o s e
Parkinson J L, stenographer and typewriter, bds Harrison House
Parish Mrs Margaret L, wid, res 547 e Jones
Parish Sam M, son Mrs M L, res same, teacher of music
Parish Iowa S, painter, res 547 e Jones
Parish Mrs Minnie T, wife Iowa S
Parish Walter W, painter, res 542 e Jones
Parish Mrs Allie, wife W W
Parish Willie, son W W, res same, student
Parish Edward, son W W, res same, student
Parish Lonnie, son W W, res same, student
Parish Thomas, son W W, res same, student
Parish John, painter, res 316 w Edenton
Parish Mrs Sarah, wife John
Parish Miss Mollie, d John, res same
Parish Ephraim,* grocer, res 224 Newbern ave
Parish Ira,* cook, res rear 224 Newbern ave
Parish Edith,* washerwoman, res 421 s Salisbury
Parish Eva,* d Edith, res same, student
Parish Lula,* d Edith, res same, nurse
Parrish Baxter, mechanic S A L, res 109 Johnson
Parrish Mrs Sophia, wife Baxter
Parrott G E, salesman, bds 554 e Hargett
Parsons Wm R, gen merchandise, Prairie bldg, res same
Parsons Mrs Mattie M, wife Wm R
Parsons Miss Annie, d W R, res same, student
Parsons Leroy, son Wm R, res same, student
Partin Mrs E F, wid, res cor w Jones and St Mary's
Partin Miss Julia B, d Mrs E F, res same, saleslady at Miss M Reese's
Partin Thos A, clk at A B Stronach's, r cor w Jones and St Mary's
Partin Mrs Annie G, wife Thos A
Partin Donald B, son Mrs E F, res same, machinist
Partin Leander H, clk, res Oakwood ave
Partin Mrs Gertrude E, wife L H
Partin G W, asst sec Y M C A, res cor Oakwood ave and East
Partin Mrs Luenza, wife G W

Partin Miss Lena W, d G W, res same, stenographer at Agricultural Dept
Partin Noah,* lab, res Tarboro' rd, o s e
Partin Isabella,* cook for C G Latta, res on lot
Patterson S L, Commissioner of Agriculture, bds Yarboro' House
Patterson Mrs Martha, wid, teacher in Centennial Graded School, bds 549 n Person
Patterson Henry S, son Mrs Martha, res same, student
Patterson Samuel, carp, res 803 Jenkins
Patterson Mrs Alice, wife Samuel
Patterson Miss Fannie, d Samuel, res same, student
Patterson Willie, son Samuel, res same, student
Patterson Miss Emma, d Samuel, res same, student
Patterson James, son Samuel, res same, student
Patterson Henry C,* huckster, res 17 w Worth
Patterson Lucy A,* wife H C, house work
Patterson Esau,* fireman at ice factory, res 208 w South
Patterson Henrietta,* wife Esau, washerwoman
Patterson Willimetta,* d Esau, res same, student
Patterson James T,* train hand, res 116 w Peace
Patterson Indiana,* wife James T, washerwoman
Patterson Annie,* d James T, res same, washerwoman
Patterson Amanda,* restaurant, res 311 w Cabarrus
Patterson Sam,* lab, res 311 w Cabarrus
Patterson John,* lab, res 307 Cannon
Patterson Sarah,* wife John, house work
Patterson Annie,* washerwoman, res 743 Manly
Patterson W H,* merchant, res 744 s Wilmington
Patterson Alice A,* wife W H
Patterson James R,* son W H, res same, student
Patterson Willie H,* son W H, res same, student
Patterson Martin L,* son W H, res same, student
Paschall Frank P,* butler for R H Battle, res 746 s Wilmington
Paschall Cora,* wife F P, washerwoman
Paschall Frank,* son F P, res same, student
Paschall Hattie,* d F P, res same, student
Passmore Chas B, clk C A Sherwood & Co, bds 108 w Edenton
Patrick Isaac,* lab, res 820 Smithfield al
Patrick Charlotte,* wife Isaac, washerwoman
Patrick Eunice,* d Isaac, res same, washerwoman
Patrick Nathaniel,* son Isaac, res same, laborer
Pauli Hubert, student, res 119 w Martin
Payne Jas H,* shoemaker, res 407 Hillsboro'
Peace Annie,* cook for Mrs C Durham, res same
Pearce T C, quiller at Caraleigh mill, res 711 s West
Pearce Mrs Lula, wife T C
Pearce Jeff, moulder, res 214 w Cabarrus
Pearce Mrs Emma, wife Jeff

Pearce Miss Lillie, d Jeff, res same, student
Pearce J B, clk W H & R S Tucker & Co, res 119 Hillsboro'
Pearce Mrs O M, wife J B
Pearce Miss I O, attendant at Insane Asylum, res same
Pearce Nancy,* nurse for T M Argo, res on lot
Pearce Sarah,* cook for J C Moore, res on lot
PEARSON CHARLES, architect, office in Pullen bldg, bds 520 n Person
Pearson D O, saloon clk, bds 407 Fayetteville
Peatross J M, painter, res Oberlin, o s w
Peddy T N, wks cot oil mill, res 317 s Harrington
Peddy Mrs Lucetta, wife T N
Peddy Miss Effie, d T N, res same, saleslady at Woollcott & Son
Peddy Lester, son T N, res same, drug clk
Peddy Miss Annie, d T N, res same, student
Peddy John A, mechanic, res 205 e Hargett
Peddy Miss Hattie, saleslady Lyon Racket Store, res 205 e Hargett
Peddy D M, printer, res 205 e Hargett
Peebles W F, inmate Soldiers' Home
Peebles Lawrence W,* drayman, res 320 s Blount
Peebles Lucy L,* wife L W, washerwoman
Peel P A, carp, res 409 n Salisbury
Peel Mrs T X, wife P A
Peele & Maynard, lawyers, office over 239 s Wilmington
Peele W J (Peele & Maynard), lawyer, bds 329 Hillsboro'
Pegram L B, traveling salesman, res 622 w Jones
Pegram Mrs Ella, wife L B
Pegram Louis, son L B, res same, student
Pegram Frank,* porter at A V Emery, res rear 405 s Dawson
Pegram John,* lab, res 225 e Lane
Pegues Prof A W,* supervisor of the colored D D & B Inst, res same
Pegues Ella C,* wife Prof A W, teacher in oral department of the colored D D & B Inst
Pegues Adaline,* mother of Prof A W, res same
Pell Mrs Annie P, wid, seamstress, res 326 w Jones
Pell Harden, son Mrs Annie P, res same, student
Pemberton John, nephew R T Gray, res same, student
Pence Thomas, butcher, res 222 e Morgan
Pence Mrs Annie E, wife Thomas
Pence Thomas J, son Thomas, res same, city editor Press-Visitor
Pennington Wm, collector for Thomas & Maxwell, r 209 Tucker
Pennington Mrs Belle, wife Wm
Pennington S P, blacksmith, res 209 w Davie
Pennington Mrs Octelia, wife S P
Pennington Manney, clk for W A Upchurch, res 209 w Davie
Penny W S, clk for D T Johnson, res same
Penny Orvid, clk M T Norris & Bro, bds 222 e Martin

Penny Ransom S, clk for J M Monie, bds 105 Freeman
Penny Sarah J,* cook, res 422 s Swain
Penny Lucinda,* cook, res 422 s Swain
Penny Mary M,* cook, res 422 s Swain
Penny Georgiana,* cook, res 422 s Swain
Penny Lavina,* nurse, res 422 s Swain
Penny David,* lab, res 211 Cannon
Penny Joseph,* city hand, res 211 Cannon
Penny Charles,* lab, res 211 Cannon
Penny Alex,* porter for Dewar & Wilder, res 211 Cannon
Penny Robt,* lab, res 531 e Edenton
Penny Ann,* wife Robt, washerwoman
Penny Simon,* lab, res 422 s Swain
Penny Louise,* wife Simon
Penny Ada,* washer and ironer, res 529 s Wilmington
Penny William, lab, rooms 109 w Lenoir
Penny Winnie,* cook, rooms 738 s Person
Penny Bettie,* cook, res 423 n Salisbury
Perdue Mrs Sophia, wid, res Pace, o s n
Perdue Samuel, son Mrs Sophia, res same, invalid
Perdue Miss Bettie, housekeeper for W W Newman, res same
Perkins Emily,* washerwoman, res Blount-st al
Perkins T A, machinist S A L R R
Perkinson Mrs E J, wid, res 111 s Bloodworth
Perkinson Miss Evie, d Mrs E J, res same, saleslady for W E Jones
Perkinson B J, son Mrs E J, res same, app machinist
Perkinson Wm,* porter M T Norris & Bro, res 821 Smithfield al
Perkinson Mary,* wife Wm
Perkinson Louisa,* d Wm, res same, student
Perkinson Sarah,* g-d Wm, res same, student
Perkinson Docie,* washerwoman, res 425 Smith
Perkinson Cora,* d Docie, res same, laundress
Perkinson Isaac,* son Docie, res same, lab
Perry Mrs Mary D, wid, res Hillsboro' rd, o s w
Perry Henry J, son Mrs Mary D, clk for A J Ellis
Perry Miss Mattie R, d Mrs Mary D, res same, cashier at C A Sherwood & Co
Perry Henry, supt Raleigh Ice & Refrigerating Co, res cor Hargett and West
Perry Delia N, wife Henry
Perry Miss Zelma, d Henry, res same
Perry W B, butcher, res 119 Polk
Perry Mrs S A, wife W B
Perry M C, street hand, res 227 n Dawson
Perry Mrs Winnie, wife M C
Perry Columbus H, carp, res 223 s Person
Perry Mrs Kate, wife C H
Perry Con, son C H, res same, plasterer

Perry Hubert, son C H, res same, student
Perry Mrs B L, wid, res with J A Duncan
Perry John, son Mrs B L, res same, student
Perry Miss Etta, d Mrs B L, res same, student
Perry Thomas,* driver for D T Johnson, res near Soldiers' Home, o s e
Perry Lucinda,* wife Thos, washerwoman
Perry Thomas,* student, res same
Perry Millie,* d Thomas, res same, student
Perry Maggie D,* d Thomas, res same, student
Perry Emma,* d Thomas, res same, student
Perry Judy,* cook, res 28 Hayti
Perry Norfleet,* lab, res 28 Hayti
Perry Hixie,* house-servant, res 28 Hayti
Perry Chas H,* butcher, res 402 e Davie
Perry Nannie,* wife Chas H
Perry Charles,* son C H, res same, student
Perry Mabel,* d C H, res same, student
Perry Ezekiel,* son C H, res same, student
Perry Gertrude,* d C H, res same, student
Perry Christina,* d C H, res same, student
Perry Goldie,* d C H, res same
Perry Narcissa,* dressmaker, res 409 s Bloodworth
Perry Sarah,* seamstress, res 409 s Bloodworth
Perry Alexander,* son Narcissa, res same
Perry Leander,* son Narcissa, res same
Perry Rev Geo W,* Baptist minister, res 812 s Blount
Perry Chloe,* wife Rev Geo W, house work
Perry Burt,* lab, res 527 e Lenoir
Perry Della,* wife Burt, cook
Perry Henry,* musician, res Watson
Perry Lula,* wife Henry, house work
Perry Sophronia,* house-servant, res 417 s Swain
Perry Luke,* son Sophronia, res same, farm hand
Perry Joe,* driver for Dr A W Knox, res rear 309 Hillsboro'
Perry Ella,* wife Joe, cook for Mrs W H Holloman
Perry Rachel,* nurse for R T Gray, res 120 e Cabarrus
Perry Hannah,* d Rachel, res same, servant
Perry Alex,* son Rachel, res same, wks city market
Perry Robert,* son Rachel, res same, lab
Perry Mooney,* son Rachel, res same, lab
Perry Julia,* cook, res 210 w Lenoir
Perry Charles,* driver, res old Fair Ground, o s e
Perry Cora,* wife Charles, washerwoman
Perry Maria,* cook, res 714 Fayetteville
Perry Charles,* son Maria, res same, butler
Perry Ella,* d Maria, res same, cook
Perry Mary,* d Maria, res same, cook

Perry Mary W,* house-girl Jas Baker, res s McDowell
Perry Winnie,* washerwoman, res 121 w Davie
Perry Ephraim, farmer, res 120 Johnson
Perry Mrs L W, wife Ephraim, boarding house
Perry Luvenia,* cook for D H Crawford, res same
Perry Richard,* servant, res 403 Smithfield
Perry Lee H, huckster, res 567 Newbern ave
Perry Mrs Olia C, wife Lee H
Perry Miss Julia, d Lee H, res same
Perry Thomas,* bell-boy Park Hotel, rooms 522 e Martin
Perry Rev Joseph,* Baptist minister, res 517 e Davie
Perry Annie,* wife Joseph, house work
Perry Elijah,* blacksmith, res Bledsoe ave
Perry Eliza,* nurse, res 324 w Edenton
Perry Burton C, lab, res e Lenoir
Perry Mrs Ann, wid, res 126 w Lane
Perry Theo, weaver Caraleigh cot mill, bds 739 Fayetteville
Person Henry,* waiter at Park Hotel, res Watson
Person Dora,* wife Henry, house work
Person Silva,* cook, res e Davie, o s e
Pescud John S, druggist, 118 Fayetteville, res 546 n Person
Pescud Mrs Isabella W, wife John S
Pescud Miss Jane H, d John S, res same
Pescud Miss Mary W, d John S, res same, student
Pescud Miss Beile W, d John S, res same, student
Pescud Miss Annie L, d John S, res same, student
Pescud John S Jr, son John S, res same, student
Pescud Ed F, mgr N C Book Co, res 107 n Saunders
Pescud Thomas, grocer, 214 Fayetteville, res 107 n Saunders
Pescud Miss Mary T, sister of E F Pescud, res same
Pescud J T, clk for A B Stronach, res 107 n Saunders
PESCUD THOMAS, wholesale and retail grocer, 214 Fayetteville, res n Saunders
Peterson A J, machinist S A L, res 421 n Salisbury
Peterson Mrs Addie, wife A J
Peterson Louis, son A J, res same, student

THOMAS PESCUD,
The Family Grocer,
214 Fayetteville Street, - - RALEIGH, N. C.

Everything in the Grocery Line that a Family needs.

Peterson Miss Susie, d A J, res same, student
Pettiford Elizabeth,* servant, res Rock Quarry rd
Pettiford Eliza,* d Elizabeth, res same, house-servant
Pettigrew William,* painter, res 125 e Cabarrus
Petty Rev Jerry,* Christian minister, res 18 Hayti
Petty Annie,* wife Rev Jerry, washerwoman
Petty Julia,* d Rev Jerry, res same, washerwoman
Petty Priscilla,* d Rev Jerry, res same, student
Petty John,* son Rev Jerry, res same, student
Petty Robt,* lab, res Cannon
Petty Mattie,* wife Robt, washerwoman
Phifer David,* brick-mason, res 525 e Lenoir
Phifer Lonise,* wife David
Phillips & Co, grocers, 329 s Wilmington
Phillips L B (Phillips & Co), merchant, res 310 s Person
Phillips W A, clk for Phillips & Co, res 310 s Person
Phillips F B, son L B, clk for Frank Stronach, res same
Phillips Jarvis, son L B, res same, wks Linnell laundry
Phillips Miss Carrie, d L B, res same, milliner
Phillips Miss Roberta, d L B, res same, student
Phillips Miss Rosa, d L B, res same, student
Phillips Miss Veva, d L B, res same, student
Phillips J W, clk for Robt E Parham, res cor Martin and Swain
Phillips Mrs Jimmie, wife J W
Phillips Fletcher, clk for M T Norris & Bro, res 502 s Salisbury
Phillips Mrs Eula H, wife Fletcher
Phillips Mrs Salina, housekeeper for Wm C Upchurch, res same
Phillips Frank,* cook at Soldiers' Home, res Kildee lane
Phillips Maggie B,* wife Frank, washerwoman
Phillips Mary E,* d Frank, res same, chamber-maid Dr V E Turner
Phillips Maggie F,* d Frank, res same, chamber-maid F H Cameron
Phillips Janet E,* d Frank, res same, washerwoman
Phillips Delia A,* d Frank, res same, student
Phillips Annie B,* d Frank, res same, student
Phillips Frank R,* son Frank, res same, porter for Dr V E Turner
Phillips Ned,* nurse hospital Soldiers' Home, res 17 s Swain
Phillips Chloe,* wife Ned
Phillips Mary,* teacher parochial school of Episcopal church, res 17 s Swain
Phoebus Miss A E W, res with Prof W F Massey
PHYSIOC J E, merchant tailor, 131½ Fayetteville
Physioc Mrs Laura V, wife J E
Physioc Louis V, son J E, res same, clk at Experimental station
Physioc Fenix T, son J E, res same, student
Physioc Miss Jessie P, d J E, res same
Pickett Miss Nannie, res with W A Howell

Pierce Mrs D F, wid, res 306 n Person
Pierce Miss Ada, d Mrs D F, res same, student
Pierce Ernest, son Mrs D F, res same, student
Pierce Miss Kate, d Mrs D F, res same, student
Pierce Miss Polly M, wks Edwards & Broughton bookbindery, rooms 422 s Wilmington
Pierce Mrs Matilda, wid, bkpr for T C Olmstead
Pierce Thomas, son Mrs Matilda, res same
Pierce Miss Minnie, d Mrs Matilda, res same
Pierce Brittain,* huckster, res 546 e Cabarrus
Pierce Louise A,* wife Brittain, house work
Pierce Mariam,* d Brittain, res same, student
Pierce Alice,* cook for R H Brooks, res Hargett, o s e
Pierce Mrs Mary, wid, res with J S Keith
Pierce Sarah,* washerwoman, res Hargett, o s e
Pike John W, keeper of arsenal, res 311 w Davie
Pike Mrs Etta, wife John W
Pike B N, son John W, res same, wks for Jones & Powell
Pike J R, son John W, res same, wks for Jones & Powell
Pike Peter,* gardener, res 215 s Harrington
Pike Barney, wks for Gas Co, res 315 s McDowell
Pike Mrs Charlotte L D, wife Barney
Piper John, tailor, bds 117 Fayetteville
PITTINGER Rev Dr I McK, rector Good Shepherd church, res 129 Hillsboro'
Pittinger Mrs L W G, wife Rev Dr I McK
Pittinger Miss Louise, d Rev Dr I McK, res same, student
Pittinger Paul, son Rev Dr I McK, res same, student
Pittman J C, printer, res 543 e Hargett
Pittman Mrs Mary C, wife J C
Pittman Miss Mary D, d J C, trained nurse Rex Hospital
Pittman Miss Gracie W, d J C, res same
Pittman Wm J, son J C, res same, clk for John C Drewry
Pittman Joseph, son J C, res same, student
Pitts Sharp,* wks Oak City Laundry, res 825 Manly
Pitts Nannie,* wife Sharp, washerwoman

J. E. PHYSIOC,

Merchant Tailor,

LEADER OF FASHION.

High-Class Tailoring at reasonable prices.

Will Save you 10 to 15 Dollars on a Suit.

FAYETTEVILLE STREET, RALEIGH, N. C.

Pitts Pattie,* d Sharp, res same, student
Pitts Lovie,* d Sharp, res same, student
Pitts Tempie,* cook for Geo C Upchurch, res 554 e Edenton
Pitts Mary,* d Tempie, res same, washerwoman
Pitts Lula,* d Tempie, res same, washerwoman
Pitts Arlina,* d Tempie, res same, house-servant
Pitts Henry,* wks Oak City Laundry, res Bledsoe ave
Pitts Blanche,* wife Henry
Pleasant B S, wks Pullen Park, res 119 Johnson
Pleasant Mrs Annie, wife B S
Pleasant B B, son B S, res same, wks Ral cot mill
Pleasant Miss Hattie, d B S, res same, wks Ral cot mill
Pleasant Wm A, son B S, res same, student
Pleasant Miss Maud, d B S, res same, student
Pleasant Thad H, eng S A L R R, res 217 n Dawson
Pleasant Mrs Penny, wife Thad H
Pleasant Miss Adelaide, d Thad H, res same
Pleasant Miss Evalina, d Thad H, res same
Plummer William,* porter for J R Ferrall & Co, res 612 s McDowell
Plummer William,* lab, res 120 w South
Plummer Silvia,* wife Wm, house work
Plummer Harriet,* washerwoman, res w Lane, near R R
Plummer Frank,* farm hand, res 423 e Lenoir
Plummer Mary,* washerwoman, res 423 e Lenoir
Plummer Kemp,* lab, res 114 e Morgan
Plummer Peter,* carp, res 114 e Morgan
Plummer Fannie,* wife Peter, washerwoman
Plummer Ben,* lab, res 517 e Lenoir
Plummer Laura,* wife Ben, washerwoman
Plummer Rachel,* d Ben, res same, servant
Plummer Mabel, d Ben, res same, servant
Poe H, cashier Southern Express Co, res 107 s McDowell
Poe Mrs Bessie, wife H
Poe John,* train hand S A L, res 116 w Peace
Poe Ida,* wife John, washerwoman
Pogue Jos E, tobacco mfr, factory 315 s Wilmington, res 18 e Cabarrus
Pogue Mrs Henrietta, wife Jos E
Pogue Jos E Jr, son Jos E, res same, student
Pointer Lizzie,* washerwoman, res 514 s Dawson
Pointer Merriman,* driver for Chas Bretsch, res 514 s Dawson
Pointer Lucinda, seamstress, res 514 s Dawson
Polk Dan K,* porter for Col A B Andrews, res 716 s McDowell
Polk Matilda,* wife Dan K, house work
Polk Mary,* d Dan K, res same, student
Polk Ethel,* d Dan K, res same, student
Polk Bessie,* d Dan K, res same, student

Polk Mrs L L, wid, res 565 n Person
Polk Miss Carrie, d Mrs L L, res same, art student
Polk Nellie,* seamstress, res 418 e Martin
Polk Hannah,* d Nellie, res same, cook
Poindexter Peter,* chief cook Park Hotel, res same
Pollard Caswell, farmer, res Smithfield
Pool & Moring, wholesale grocers and commission merchants, 237 s Wilmington
Pool S C (Pool & Moring), merchant, res 323 Hillsboro'
Pool Mrs Jennie, wife S C
Pool Miss Janet, d S C, res same, student
Pool Harry, son S C, res same student
Pool Pool Miss Martha L, d S C, res same
Pool Miss Christine, d S C, res same
Pool R C, driver for City Fire Dept, res 119 w Morgan
Pool Mrs Eva, wife R C
Pool Bud, driver for City Fire Dept, res 119 w Morgan
Pool Miss Bessie, d R C, res same, student
Pool Miss Mildred, d R C, res same, student
Pool Robert, son R C, res same, student
Pool Epenetus N, grocer, e Davie, res 506 e Hargett
Pool Mrs Lillie, wife E N
Pool Miss Clyde, d E N, res same, student
Pool Miss Eva, sister of E N, res same
Pool Burborn, wks at penitentiary, res 121 w Morgan
Pool Mrs Ellen, wife Burborn
Pool Miss Ellen, d Burborn, res same, wks Ral cot mills
Pool John, son Burborn, res same, lab
Pool Selly, son Burborn, res same
Pool Miss E A, prin Murphy Graded School, bds 116 n Dawson
Pool J H, clk, res 313 s Harrington
Pool Mrs Ada F, wife J H
Pool Alonzo, res 313 s Harrington
Pool Lonnie, son Alonzo, res same, gateman at Union depot
Pool M B (King & Pool), merchant, rooms at store
Pool J M, inmate Soldiers' Home
Pool Eliza,* washerwoman, res e Davie, o s e
Pool Caesar,* son Eliza, res same, driver for N W West
Pool Australia,* son Eliza, res same, hotel waiter
Pool Ransom, shoemaker, res 430 s East
Pool Mrs Elizabeth, wife Ransom
Pool Wm,* lab, res 553 e Edenton
Pool Bertan A,* washerwoman, res 553 e Edenton
Pool Willie,* son Wm, res same, student
Pool Mary,* d Wm, res same, student
Pool Susan,* washerwoman, res rear 217 w South
Pool Harry,* son Susan, res same, student
Pool Wm,* gardener, res Townes alley

Pool Caroline,* wife Wm, washerwoman
Pool Patsy,* washerwoman, res Martin, o s e
Pool Jack,* carp, res Martin, o s e
Pool Anna,* wife Jack, groceries
Pool Violet,* cook, res 580 e Cabarrus
Pool Bettie,* d Violet, res same, student
Pool Rena,* washerwoman, res old Fair Ground, o s e
Pool Fannie,* cook James Freeman, res same
Pool Mrs J F, wid, res 119 Hillsboro'
Pope J A (Barbee & Pope), candy mfg, res n Saunders
Pope Mrs Alice, wife J A
Pope Arthur, son J A, res same, student
Pope Miss Blanche, d J A, res same, student
Pope Miss Bessie, d J A, res same, student
Pope Mrs Martha, wid, dressmaker, res 513 n Salisbury
Pope Levy,* porter for W H King & Co, res rear 404 Hillsboro'
Pope Hannah,* wife Levy
Pope Burton,* son Levy, res same, student
Pope Bertha,* d Levy, res same, student
Pope William,* carp, res 312 Cannon
Pope Holland,* wife Wm, washerwoman
Pope Herbert,* son Wm, res same, student
Pope Anthony,* lab, res 407 w South
Pope Lizzie,* wife Anthony, cook
Pope Jane,* d Anthony, res same, cook
Pope Benj,* lab, res 119 n Harrington
Pope Leanna,* cook, res 512 e Davie
Pope Richard,* lab, res Avent Ferry rd, o s w
Pope Kate,* wife Richard, house work
Porter Edward, spinner Ral cot mill, res 510 n West
Porter Mrs Effie, wife Edward
Porter Miss Maggie, d Edward, res same, wks Ral cot mill
Porter John H, bkkpr, res Oberlin
Postal Telegraph and Cable Co, 11 e Martin, W J Crews mgr
Poster Patsy,* washerwoman, res 121 n Harrington
Poster Charles,* lab, res 127 n Harrington
Poster Fannie,* wife Chas, washerwoman
Poster Mary,* d Chas, res same, cook for Dr F J Haywood
Poster Millie,* d Chas, res same, cook for Geo D Meares
Poster Ella,* d Chas, res same, washerwoman
Poster Jennie,* d Chas, res same, servant
Poster Susie,* d Chas, res same, servant
Poster Annie,* washerwoman, res s s Harrington
Potter & Scott, saloon and livery stable, 114 e Martin
Potter J E (Potter & Scott), saloon keeper, res 600 s Salisbury
Potter Mrs Annie, wife J E
Porter Mrs Sarah, wid mother J E, res same
Potter Zach, carp, bds 402 w Morgan

Potter James,* lab, res 212 w South
Potter Sarah,* wife James, washerwoman
Potter E C, agt Norfolk and Southern R R, bds Dr R B Ellis
Potter Mrs Lula B, wife E C
Potts Miss Charity, house work, res Avent Ferry rd, o s w
Potts R L, agt Southern frt depot
Powell A M (Jones & Powell), merchant, res 502 Hillsboro'
Powell Mrs Jennie, wife A M
Powell Thomas, son A M, res same, wks Crystal Ice Factory
Powell Miss Lena, d A M, res same
Powell Miss Bessie, d A M, res same, student
Powell Miss Jennie, d A M, res same, student
Powell Miss Ethel, d A M, res same, student
Powell James, son A M, res same, student
Powell George,* blacksmith for T A Bowen, res n Swain
Powell Annie E,* wife Geo, washerwoman
Powell William,* son Geo, res same, lab
Powell Mary,* d Geo, res same, house-servant for C M Busbee
Powell Dennis,* son Geo, res same, student
Powell Robert,* son Geo, res same, student
Powell Geo Jr,* son Geo, res same, student
Powell Clara,* house-servant, res 712 s Saunders
Powell Simon,* lab, res 231 Freeman, o s s
Powell Helen,* wife Simon, washerwoman
Powell James,* son Simon, res same, lab
Powell Elnora,* d Simon, res same, student
Powell Turner,* son Simon, res same, student
Powell Spencer,* driver for Southern Express Co, res 320 w North
Powell Annie,* wife Spencer
Powell Lula,* d Spencer, res same, student
Powell Arthur,* son Spencer, res same, servant for Mrs L B Evans
Powell Sherman,* son Spencer, res same, student
Powell Junius,* son Spencer, res same, student
Powell Spencer Jr,* student, res 320 w North
Powell Charles,* lab, res 534 e Davie
Powell Elvira,* wife Chas, washerwoman
Powell Diana,* d Chas, res same, washerwoman
Powell Sam,* son Chas, res same, lab
Powell Frella, res n Salisbury
Powell Telfair, flagman S A L, res n Salisbury
Powell Hattie,* house-servant, res Martin, o s e
Powell Roanna,* washerwoman, 802 s Blount
Powell Mary,* d Roanna, res same, student
Powell Mattie,* d Roanna, res same, student
Powell Arthur,* carp, res 518 w Lane
Powell Thos,* porter at Cross & Linehan's, res 108 Newbern ave
Powell Ann,* cook for L B Pegram, res on lot
Prather Annie,* washerwoman, res Caswell lane

Prather Edgar,* son Annie, res same, porter at L H Adams'
Prather Frank,* son Annie, res same, porter at Moses Bledsoe's
Prather Joseph,* son Annie, res same, student
Prather David,* son Annie, res same, student
Prather Jennie,* d Annie, res same, student
Pratt David,* lab, res 310 w South
Pratt Emma,* washerwoman, res rear 405 s Dawson
Pratt Bettie,* d Emma, res same, washerwoman
Pratt Lillie,* d Emma, res same, washerwoman
Pratt Robert,* house-servant for Chas E Johnson, room 106 e Cabarrus
Prayer Tony,* lab, res 540 e Edenton
Prayer Penny,* wife Tony, washerwoman
Prayer Julia,* sister of Tony, res same, student
Prendergast Rev Father J M, pastor Church of the Sacred Heart, res 204 Hillsboro'
Price Thomas,* driver for Park Hotel, res 118 e Cabarrus
Price Silvia,* wife Thos, washerwoman
Price Henry,* son Thos, res same, student
Price Janie,* d Thos, res same student
Price W E,* butcher, res 715 Manly
Price Ella,* wife W E, house work
Price Alonzo,* teacher, res 108 n West
Price Elia,* wife Alonzo
Price Osborn,* city hand, res 617 e Lenoir
Price Sallie,* wife Osborn, washerwoman
Price Henry,* lab, res 545 e Edenton
Price Isabella,* wife Henry, washerwoman
Price Thos J, machinist, res 306 n Person
Price Sion D, machinist, res 306 n Person
Price Willis,* waiter at restaurant, res Martin, o s e
Price Martha,* wife Willis, servant
Price Lou,* cook, res e Davie, o s e
Price Harmon,* son Lou, res same, lab
Price Sue,* washerwoman, res rear 517 s Dawson
Price Anna,* washerwoman, res Adams lane
Priddy Edgar, clk for W E Jones, bds 540 n Blount
Prince Sandy, city hand, res Fayetteville
Prince Mrs Sarah, wife Sandy
Prince Miss Pearl, d Sandy, res same
Prince Miss Myrtle, d Sandy, res same
PRIMROSE WM S, pres N C Home Ins Co, res 621 w Jones
Primrose Mrs Ella P, wife Wm S
Primrose Henry, son Wm S, res same, student
Primrose Miss Jessie, d Wm S, res same, student
Primrose Miss Helen, d Wm S, res same, student
Primrose R Owen, son Wm S, res same, student
Primrose Hugh W, son Wm S, res same, student

Primrose Will S, son Wm S, res same
Primrose Miss Eliza, d Mrs F A Olds, res same
Pritchard J H & Co,* grocers, 212 e Cabarrus
Pritchard John,* lab, res Nunn, o s s
Pritchard Martha,* washerwoman, res Nunn, o s s
Privett Mason,* cook, res 521 e Lenoir
Privett Edward,* lab, res 521 e Lenoir
Privett Emma,* d Mason, res same, nurse
Privett Mart,* son Mason, res same, hostler
Privett Cherry,* washerwoman, res 228 w South
Privett Joseph,* son Cherry, res same, lab
Proctor Ivan M, planter, res Newbern ave, o s e
Proctor Mrs Lucy B, wife Ivan M
Proctor Robert M, son Ivan M, res same, student
Proctor Miss Jennie M, d Ivan M, res same, student
Proctor Chas I,* grocer, res 110 n Harrington
Proctor Lillie A,* wife Chas I
Pugh David, inmate Soldiers' Home
Pullen Jno T, cashier Ral Savings Bank, rooms over Y M C A
Pullen Miss Sallie, housekeeper for Sam Bogasse, res same
Pullen Sion, carp, res Avent Ferry rd, o s w
Pullen Mrs Sophronia, wife Sion
Pullen Miss Iona, d Sion, res same
Pullen Miss Sadie, d Sion, student
Pulley Rufus H, carp, res Haywood
Pulley Mrs Fannie, wife Rufus H
Pulley Melton, son Rufus H, res same, wks Caraleigh mill
Pulley Mrs Charlotte, seamstress, res 409 Haywood
Pulley Miss Carsie, d Mrs Charlotte, res same
Pulley Caroline,* washerwoman, res rear 205 e Hargett
Pulley J C, carp, res e Davie, o s e
Pulley Mrs Annie, wife J C, dressmaker
Purnell Thos R, lawyer, office in Mahlen bldg, res 422 n Person
Purnell Mrs Adelia, wife T R
Purnell Miss Lula V, d T R, res same
Purnell Miss Elizabeth, d T R, res same
Purnell Miss Annie B, d T R, res same, student
Purnell Miss Adelia, d T R, res same, student
Purnell Thos R Jr, son T R, res same, student
Purnell James McKee, son T R, res same
Puryear James, tobacconist, res with J W Cheek
Puryear Miss Addie, d James, res same
Puryear J R, inmate Soldiers' Home
Putney Wesley, printer, res 205 Smithfield
Putney Mrs Bettie, wife Wesley
Putney Miss Ella, d Wesley, res same
Putney Willie, son Wesley, res same, student
Putney Edward, son Wesley, res same, student

Putney Miss Emma, d Wesley, res same, student
Putney Richard, janitor Centennial Graded School, res rear of the school
Putney Miss Sabry, d Richard, res same, wks Caraleigh mill
Putney Miss Sallie, d Richard, res same, wks Caraleigh mill
Putney Miss Virginia, d Richard, wks Caraleigh mill
Putney Mrs Martha, wid, res 612 e Davie
Putney Miss Gertrude, d Mrs Martha, res same, seamstress
Putney Miss Laura, d Mrs Martha, res same, seamstress

RABY James, clk for J M Monie
Raines John, wood worker, bds 416 s Person
Raines Mrs Rebecca, wife John
Raleigh Gas Company, office cor McDowell and Cabarrus, B P Williamson pres, W T McGee sec and treas
Raleigh Crystal Ice Factory, 120 s West, Jones & Powell proprietors
RALEIGH STATIONERY COMPANY, mfg stationers, stationery, blank books, office and school supplies, 309 Fayetteville, W G Separk mgr
Raleigh Telephone Exchange, 110½ Fayetteville, Geo H Glass mgr
RALEIGH SAVINGS BANK, cor Fayetteville and Hargett
Raleigh Cotton Mills, near S A L shops, C G Latta pres, C E Johnson vice-pres, J S Wynne sec and treas, H B Greason supt, manufactures cot yarns
Raleigh Male Academy, cor Jones and Bloodworth, Morson & Denson principals
Raleigh Paper Company, mills at Falls Neuse, office 6 w Martin, J N Holding sec, treas and mgr
Ramie John,* fireman S A L R R, res Fleming's lane
Ramie Celia,* wife John, washerwoman
Ramie George,* son John, res same, grocer
Ramie Joseph,* son John, res same, student
Ramsey Miss Mary, sister of Mrs C A Separk, res same

W. C. STRONACH, Pres.   G. ROSENTHAL, Vice-Pres.
JNO. T PULLEN, Cashier.   J. O. LITCHFORD, Teller.

Raleigh Savings Bank.

CAPITAL, $15,000.   SURPLUS, $11,000.

Interest Allowed on Savings Deposits.

RALEIGH, N. C.

Ramsey J L, editor Progressive Farmer, rooms over Robt Simpson's drug store
Ramsey Mrs Martha J, wid, res 119 w Martin
Ramsey Miss Etta S, d Mrs Martha J, res same
Ramsey Annie,* washerwoman, res 107 n Harrington
Rand N M (Crowder & Rand), merchant, res 610 Fayetteville
Rand Mrs Salina E, wife N M
Rand Philip B, son N M, res same
Rand Julian A, son N M, res same
Rand Wm H, steward Institution for the Blind, res at Institution
Rand Mrs S F, wife Wm H
Rand Isabella,* washerwoman, res 117 e Cabarrus
Rand Maggie,* sister Isabella, res same, washerwoman
Rand William,* drayman, res 304 s East
Rand Maria,* wife Wm, res same, washerwoman
Rand Anna,* d Wm, res same, cook
Rand Lena,* d Wm, res same, student
Rand Briny,* washerwoman, res 412 e Martin
Rand Robert, clk Julius Lewis Hardware Co, bds 508 Fayetteville
Rand Clara,* house work, res 570 e Cabarrus
Rand Esther,* washerwoman, res 708 s McDowell
Rand Susie,* d Esther, res same, nurse
Randall W G, portrait painter, res cor n Wilmington and Polk
Randall Mrs Annie J, wife W G
Randall L Y, machinist, bds 314 Hillsboro'
RANEY R B, gen agt for N C of the Penn Mutual Life Ins Co, office Yarboro' House bldg, bds Yarboro' House
Ransom Robert L,* farm hand, res 615 s McDowell
Ransom Ida L,* student, res 214 Cannon
Ransom Ellen,* seamstress, res 102 w Cabarrus
Rattler Marzella,* washerwoman, 533 Cannon
RAY J W & CO, furniture dealers and repairers, 117 e Martin
Ray Austin,* lab, res near r r crossing, n West
Ray Laura,* wife Austin, washerwoman
Ray & Wallace, restaurant, up-stairs 309 s Wilmington
Ray William,* drayman, res 426 s Person
Ray Hattie,* wife Wm, dining-room servant
Ray Victoria,* d Wm, res same, student
Ray Sarah,* mother Wm, res same
Ray Louise,* seamstress, res 223 e Cabarrus
Ray Mrs A F, wid, boarding-house, 11 s Wilmington
Ray Miss Maud, d Mrs A F, res same, saleslady at A B Stronach
Ray Miss Hattie, d Mrs A F, res same, milliner
Ray John W (J W Ray & Co), furniture dealer, res 524 n East
Ray Mrs Ida, wife J W
Ray Mary,* washerwoman, res 516 e Davie
Ray Ralph,* son Mary, res same, dining-room servant R F Hoke
Ray Paul,* son Mary, res same, porter for N Deboy

Ray Myrtle,* d Mary, res same, student
Ray Emma,* d Mary, res same, student
Ray Mrs Sallie, grocer, cor e Davie and Haywood, res same
Ray Martha,* cook, res 211 w Davie
Ray Rosa,* d Martha, res same, student
Ray Estelle,* d Martha, res same, student
Ray M T, patent medicine, res 744 Fayetteville
Ray Mrs Nora J, wife M T
Ray Miss Minnie B, d M T, res same, student
Ray Hubert S, son M T, res same, student
Raynor Stephen,* carp, res 417 n West
Raynor Louise,* wife Stephen
Raynor Mary,* d Stephen, res same, servant
Raynor Lillie,* d Stephen, res same, servant
Raynor Annie,* d Stephen, res same, servant
Raynor Rufus,* son Stephen, res same, student
Raynor Norman,* son Stephen, res same, student
Raynor Jennie,* servant, res 318 s Bloodworth
Raynor Samuel,* gardener, res 108 s Harrington
Raynor Louise V,* wife Sam
Razor China,* servant, res 506 Haywood
Reading-Room Seaboard Air-Line R R, Grimes' al, Mrs Eunice Medlin janitress
Reaves Walter T, teacher at colored Institution for the Blind, res at white institution
Reavis W J, grocer, Hillsboro' rd, res same
Reavis Mrs M A, wife W J
Reavis Miss Mildred M, d W J, res same
Reavis Miss Lelia, d W J, res same
Reavis Catherine,* house-servant, res 411 Haywood
Reavis Dora,* d Catherine, res same, house work
Reavis Lula,* d Catherine, res same, cook
Reavis Carrie,* d Catherine, res same, house work
Reavis George,* son Catherine, res same, student
Redford John H, conductor S A L R R, res 410 w Morgan
Redford Mrs Mary F, wife John H
Redford Miss Lydia L, d John H, res same, student
Redford Miss V B, seamstress, res 502 s Salisbury
Redford Miss Minnie L, teacher in Centennial Graded School, res 502 s Salisbury
Redford Miss Mattie N, student, res 502 s Salisbury
Reed Annie,* washerwoman, res 715 s East
Reed Virginia,* cook, res 715 s East
Reid David,* barber app, res 118 w Cabarrus
Reid Eliza,* cook, res 234 e South
Reid Emmitt,* son Eliza, res same, lab
Reid Charlotte,* missionary, res 228 Blount-st al
Reid Hilliard,* lab, res 228 Blount-st al

Reese Miss M, millinery and fancy goods, 209 Fayetteville
Reese Mrs Elizabeth, wid, res 209 Fayetteville
Reese Miss Josephine D, saleslady for Miss M Reese, res 209 Fayetteville
Reese Miss Sallie N, milliner for Miss M Reese, r 209 Fayetteville
Reese Miss Janie, saleslady for Miss M Reese, res 209 Fayetteville
Reese Miss Mattie, d Mrs Elizabeth, res same
Reeves Mrs Elizabeth, wid, seamstress, res 821 s Blount
Reeves Miss Etta, d Mrs Elizabeth, res same, dressmaker
Reeves Tempie,* mother Caroline Whitaker, res same
Reeves W H,* lab, res 517 Haywood
Reeves Mrs Hannah, wid, grocer, 323 e Martin, res same
Reeves Lizzie,* cook H J Heileg, res same
Rensch Mlle Emma, teacher of French and German in St Mary's School, res same
Renfrow Berry, grocer, cor Cabarrus and s McDowell
Renfrow Mrs Christian, wife Berry
Renfrow Lula B, d Berry, res same
Renfrow Miss Mary I, d Berry, res same, student
Renfrow Miss Fannie E, d Berry, res same, student
Renn Dr Geo A, office Park Avenue Pharmacy, bds cor McDowell and Hargett
Renshaw George,* blacksmith, res 507 e Davie
Renshaw Lydia,* wife George, washerwoman
Renshaw James,* brakeman S A L, res 507 e Davie
Renshaw Captain,* son George, res same, blacksmith app
Renshaw John,* lab, res w Lenoir
Renshaw George,* blacksmith, res 114 n Harrington
Rhea Miss Mary A, attendant at Insane Asylum, res same
Rhodes Thomas,* student, res 522 e Martin
Rhodes George,* brother of Thomas, res same, student
Rhodes Jack,* asst furnace tender N C Car Co's foundry, res o s e
Rhodes Ella,* wife Jack, washerwoman
Rhodes Wm H, son Jack, res same, student
Rhodes Benj,* sexton Christ church, res 422 n West
Rhodes J H,* pressman Edwards & Broughton, res cor Cannon and Dawson
Rhodes Mary A,* wife J H, house work
Rhodes Sarah J,* d J H, res same, washerwoman
Rhodes Reuben,* lab, res 118 w South
Rhodes Florence,* wife Reuben
Rhodes Wesley,* lab, res 301 Cannon
Rhodes Mattie,* wife Wesley, house work
Rhodes Charity,* washerwoman, res 125 n West
Richardson W R, tel opr, res Avent Ferry rd, o s w
Richardson Mrs A C, wife W R
Richardson Miss Mattie S, d W R, res same
Richardson Wm H, son W R, res same

Richardson Mrs Ellen, mother W R, res same
Richardson W R Jr, son W R, res same
Richardson Jane,* washerwoman, res 31 McKee
Richardson Julia,* washerwoman, res w Peace
Richardson Henry,* crossing flagman S A L R R, res 420 n Wilmington
Richardson Carrie,* wife Henry, servant
Richardson Sandy,* wks frt depot S A L, res 217 w North
Richardson T N, cot weigher, res cor McDowell and Hargett
Richardson Mrs W A, wife T N, boarding-house
Richardson Miss Catherine L, d T N, res same
Richardson James, son T N, res same, student
Richardson Miss Ada, d T N, res same, student
Richardson London,* driver, res s West
Richardson Anna,* wife London, house work
Richardson S M, propr Richardson House, 120 e Hargett
Richardson Mrs Ada E, wife S M
Richardson Miss Myrtle A, d S M, res same, student
Richardson Willie M, son S M, res same, student
Richardson Miss Fannie K, d S M, res same, student
Richardson James,* restaurant, 207½ s Wilmington, res same
Richardson Leah,* wife James
Richardson Eugene, clk for Myatt & Hunter, bds 222 e Martin
Richardson Mary,* cook for Mrs F A Hutchings, res on lot
Richardson Thad, clk for J A Spence, bds 109 s Blount
Richardson Mrs Hattie, wid, res with O M Marshburn
Richardson Annie,* washerwoman, res s Swain
Richardson Miss Emma, seamstress, res 230 s East
Richardson Wm,* lab, res 213 s East
Richardson Cora,* wife Wm, washerwoman
Richardson Elizabeth,* cook, res 213 s East
Richardson Nancy A,* d Elizabeth, res same, cook
Richardson Florence,* d Elizabeth, res same, servant
Richburg J W, wks for Southern R R, res Johnson
Richburg Mrs Amelia, wife J W, dressmaker
Richburg Miss Laura, d J W, res same, dressmaker
Ricks Hugh, bds cor McDowell and Hargett
Ricks David,* barber, res 523 e Lenoir
Ricks Mary,* wife David, washerwoman
Ricks Louisa,* d David, res same, student
Ricks Silphia,* washerwoman, res 611 e Davie
Ricks Lillie,* d Silphia, res same, cook
Ricks Charles,* wks Jones & Powell's wood and coal yard, res 434 s Blount
Ricks Corinna,* wife Charles, washerwoman
Ricks Harry,* son Charles, res same, wks C P Wharton
Ricks Daisy,* d Charles, res same, student
Ricks Emmett,* son Charles, res same, student

Ricks Matilda,* d Charles, res same, student
Ricks Charles,* dining-room servant, res 408 Cannon
Ricks Henrietta,* wife Charles, house work
Ricks Rufus S.,* driver for Thos Pescud, res 419 s Swain
Ricks Mamie E.,* wife R S, house work
Ricks Frank,* brick-mason, res 114 n Harrington
Ricks Annie,* house-girl for Mrs Anna Rosenthal, r Bledsoe ave
Riddick W C, Professor of Mathematics and Civil Engineering A & M College, res Hillsboro' rd, o s w
Riddick Mrs Lillian D, wife W C
Riddick Violet,* washerwoman, res Hayti
Riddick Bessie,* d Violet, res same, nurse
Riddick N J, clk U S Circuit and District Court, office U S bldg, res 15 w Cabarrus
Riddick Charles,* lab, res 115 e Cabarrus
Riddick Lucy,* wife Charles, washerwoman
Riddick Weldon,* farmer, res 751 e Davie, o s e
Riddick Charity,* wife Weldon, washerwoman
Riddick Ernest,* son Weldon, res same, student
Riddick Gethro,* son Weldon, res same, student
Riddick Violet,* washerwoman, res 804 s Wilmington
Riddle C A, foreman house bldg N C Car Co, res 210 n Harrington
Riddle Mrs Annie M, wife C A
Riddle Geo B, son C A, res same, student
Riddle R H, son C A, res same, student
Riddle W L, son C A, res same, student
Riddle Lawrence E, son C A, res same, student
Riddle Capt J L, conductor S A L R R, res 301 n Harrington
Riddle Mrs R M, wife J L
Riddle Mrs C H, wid, mother J L, res same
Riddle W L, carp, res 404 w North
Riddle Ernest, son W L, res same
Riddle John S, carp, res 215 n West
Riddle Mrs Annie, wife John S
Riddle Arthur, son John S, res same, student
Riddle Hubert, son John S, res same, student
Riddle Miss Mabel, d John S, res same, student
Riddle Herman, son John S, res same, student
Riddle Mrs Martha T, wid, res 115 n McDowell
Riddle Sam M, son Mrs Martha T, res same, clk for Robert Simpson
Riddle Miss Lula, d Mrs Martha T, res same, teacher Centennial Graded School
Ridley John,* lab, res Cotton lane, o s e
Ridley Lina,* wife John, washerwoman
Ridley Ernest,* son John, res same, student
Ridley Ordney,* d John, res same, student

Riggan Jos D, toy and confectionery store, 132 Fayetteville, r 217 e Hargett
Riggan Mrs Amelia, wife Jos D
Riggan James M, ins agt, res 719 s Blount
Riggan Miss Mamie A, wife Jas M
Riggan Roy D, son Jas M, res same, student
Riggan Miss Fannie M, d Jas M, res same, student
Riggan Jas M Jr, son Jas M, res same
Riggan Mrs Roberta, wid, res cor Hargett and West
Riggan Jack, son Mrs Roberta, res same, machinist
Riggan Miss Anna, d Mrs Roberta, res same, student
Riggan Wade H, moulder, res 412 e Hargett
Riggan Mrs Juliet A, wife Wade H
Riggan Miss Miriam, d W H, res same
Riggan Miss Esther R, d W H, res same
Riggsbee L G, carp, res Cox ave, o s w
Riggsbee Mrs Mary E, wife L G
Riggsbee W M, carp, res Cox ave, o s w
Riggsbee Mrs Katie V, wife W M
Riggsbee Mrs Charlotte, lives with W W Fowler
Rivers R C, printer, res cor Oakwood ave and Bloodworth
Rivers Mrs Hattie N, wife R C
Rivers Miss Octavia, d R C, res same, student
Roak Julia,* washerwoman, res 514 s Dawson
Roak Mack,* lab, res 514 s Dawson
Robards W W, teller Citizens Nat Bank, bds 407 n Blount
Roan James, mgr Crystal ice factory, res 122 s West
Roan Mrs Mary V, wife James
Roan John, son James, res same, student
Roan Miss Mary, d James, res same, student
Roan Miss Isadore, d James, res same, student
Roan Michael, son James, res same, student
Roan Lucy,* washerwoman, res 545 e Edenton
Roan Susan,* d Lucy, res same, student
Roan Sophia,* mother Lucy, res same
Roan Henry,* lab, res 545 e Edenton
Roan Henry,* lab, res 108 e Hargett
Roan Octavia,* wife Henry
Robbins W W, machinist S A L R R, res 119 w Edenton
Robbins Mrs Sallie G, wife W W
Robbins Miss Pearl, d W W, res same, student
Robbins Miss Janet B, d W W, res same, student
Robbins Miss Harriet, d W W, res same, student
Robbins Miss Marie, d W W, res same, student
Robbins Miss Eliza, d W W, res same, student
Robbins Mrs G C, d James Maglum, res same
Robbins Miss Mamie E, sister Mrs W H Holloman, res same, 309 Hillsboro'

Robbins Will H, mgr for Mrs W H Holloman, res 309 Hillsboro'
Robbins Mrs Susie, wife Will H
Robbins J H, farmer, res 314 Newbern ave
Robbins Mrs Minnie E, wife J H
Robbins Miss Sadie, d J H, res same
Robbins Starkie, inmate Soldiers' Home
Roberts Edward B, clk in revenue office, res 519 Oakwood ave
Roberts Mrs Martha S, wife E B
Roberts Miss Bessie, d E B, res same, student
Roberts Miss Ebie, d E B, res same, student
Roberts Miss Ivey, d E B, res same, student
Roberts Miss Emma S, d E B, res same
Roberts Frances,* washerwoman, res 817 s Wilmington
Roberts Rev N F,* teacher Shaw Institute, res Oberlin
ROBERTS HARRY H, justice of the peace and notary public, office Frap's bldg, res 422 s Wilmington
Roberts Mrs Mary F, wife Harry H, dressmaker
Robests Miss Mary E, d H H, res same, student
Roberts Harry R, son H H, res same, student
Roberts Eugene H, son H H, res same, student
Roberts Miss Blanche L, d H H, res same
Roberts Mrs Mary D, wid, res 218 s Swain
Roberts Mrs Lucy, seamstress, res 324 w Morgan
Robertson Riley,* brakeman S A L R R, res 543 n Wilmington
Robertson Ellen,* wife Riley, washerwoman
Robertson Henry,* gardener, res 618 Elm
Robertson Celia,* wife Henry, cook for W E Jones
Robertson Ella,* d Henry, res same, servant
Robertson W F, machinist, bds 112 Halifax
Robertson Wm, machinist, bds 112 Halifax
Robertson J A J, janitor U S building, res 323 s Person
Robertson Mrs V J, wife J A J
Robertson Miss S E, d J A J, res same, teacher
Robertson Luther, son J A J, res same, wks at E M Uzzell
Robertson Robert A, son J A J, res same, cash-boy at A B Stronach

---

H. H. ROBERTS,
Justice of the Peace and Notary Public,
No. 3 Frap's Building. RALEIGH. N. C.

PROMPT ATTENTION TO ALL BUSINESS.

Copying, Book-keeping, Letter-Writing, Stating of Accounts.

Particular attention given to Stating Accounts of Administrators and Guardians; taking Inventories for Assignees and Making Returns; Searching Old Records; Writing Memorials and Reporting Public Meetings.

OFFICE HOURS: FROM 7 A. M. TO 9 P. M.

Robertson Paul J, son J A J, res same, student
Robinson John, eng S A L, res 214 n McDowell
Robinson Mrs Kate, wife John
Robinson Miss Mabel, d John, res same, student
Robinson Miss Bessie, d John, res same, student
Robinson B J,* grocer, 314 w Cabarrus, res same
Robinson Laura D,* wife B J
Robinson George,* brakeman Southern R R, res 221 w Lenoir
Robinson Creasy,* wife George, washerwoman
Robinson Curry,* son George, res same, lab
Robinson Cora,* d George, res same, ironer
Robinson Arthur, son George, res same, student
Robinson Janie,* house-servant, res 221 w Lenoir
Robinson Frank,* lab, res 917 Manly
Robinson Arry,* washerwoman, res old Fair Ground, o s e
Robinson Joe,* lab, res old Fair Ground, o s e
Robinson Nannie, wife Joe, washerwoman
Robinson Mary, d Joe, res same, student
Robinson Richard,* son Joe, res same, student
Robinson Ora,* d Joe, res same, nurse
Robinson Rebecca,* hkpr for Rev James King, 15 s Harrington
Robinson Susie,* house-servant at Executive Mansion, res same
Robinson Lucy,* washerwoman, res Adams lane
Robinson Delia,* cook for James R Watson, res same
Rochelle L S, restaurant and lodging-house, 235 s Wilmington
Rochelle Virginia,* house work, res 12 w Worth
Rochelle Green,* drayman, res Idlewild
Rochelle Sallie,* wife Green, washerwoman
Rochelle Emma,* d Green, res same, student
Rochelle Mary,* washerwoman, res Blount st al
Rogers M F, carp, res Prairie bldg
Rogers Mrs Cornelia, wife M F
Rogers Frank L, son M F, res same, lab
Rogers Wm M, son M F, res same, lab
Rogers I H, asst steward N C penitentiary, res 603 Hillsboro'
Rogers Mrs D E, wife I H
Rogers W A, merchant, bds 603 Hillsboro'
Rogers Flora,* dining-room servant Harrison House, res 415 s Blount
Rogers Isaac W, deputy U S marshal, res 228 e Martin
Rogers Mrs Lenorah, wife Isaac W
Rogers Miss Ruthendale, d I W, res same
Rogers Miss Lula, d I W, res same, student
Rogers Paul H, son I W, res same, clk
Rogers Miss Daisy, d I W, res same, student
Rogers Miss Pattie L, d I W, res same, student
Rogers Miss Jessie L, d I W, res same
Rogers J Rowan, farmer, res 117 Boylan ave

Rogers Mrs Annie S, wife J Rowan
Rogers Miss M A, d J R, res same, student
Rogers J R Jr, son J R, res same, student
Rogers Miss Narcissa, d J R, res same, student
Rogers Sion, son J R, res same, student
Rogers B W, clk in office Wm Moncure, supt S A L R R, bds 113 w Edenton
Rogers W M, traveling agt for News and Observer, res 534 Halifax
Rogers Mrs Lydia, wife W M
Rogers Miss Emmie, d W M, res same, student
Rogers Miss Bessie, d W M, res same, student
Rogers Bettie,* washerwoman, res e Raleigh
Rogers Junius,* son Bettie, res same, student
Rogers Goldie,* d Bettie, res same, student
Rogers Wm H, grocer and commission merchant, 12 Exchange Place, res 404 Oakwood ave
Rogers Mrs Kate, wife W H
Rogers Gaston, son W H, res same, student
Rogers Miss Catherine W, d W H, res same, student
Rogers Mehalia,* servant at Mrs R S Tucker, res on lot
Rogers Mrs Mary, wid, mother of Mrs Cornelia Taylor, res same
Rogers B C (Hicks & Rogers), druggist, bds cor Newbern ave and Person
Rogers Mrs Ludie, wife B C
Rogers Lillie,* washerwoman, res Bloodworth, o s n
Rogers Miss Sallie, d of Mrs W N Harris, res same, seamstress
Rogers Andrew J,* teacher, res 425 Haywood
Rogers Hattie,* wife A J, house work
Rogers Mrs Lena, wid, res 416 s Salisbury
Rogers E G, wheelwright, res Cannon
Rogers Mrs F T, wife E G, dressmaker
Rogers William, farm hand, res 527 Cannon
Rogers Mrs Charity, wife Wm
Rogers Maggie, d Wm, res same, student
Rogers Charlotte,* washerwoman, res e Hargett, o s e
Rogers Mannie,* washerwoman, res e Hargett, o s e
Rogers Winston, stenographer and typewriter S A L R R, bds 112 w Edenton
Rogers Luke,* farmer, res 413 n Salisbury
Rogers Candace,* wife Luke
Rogers Lizzie,* d Luke, res same, cook
Rogers Lewis,* farm hand, res Stronach ave
Rogers Patsy,* wife Lewis, cook for Ed Crow
Rogers Lucy,* d Lewis, res same, washerwoman
Rogers Thomas,* son Lewis, res same, waiter
Rogers Lewis Jr,* son Lewis, res same, waiter at Exchange Hotel
Rogers Fannie,* washerwoman, res 409 w South
Rogers Geo,* lab, res e Davie, o s e

Rogers Emma,* wife Geo, washerwoman
Rogers Geo Jr,* son Geo, res same, student
Rogers Jacob,* lab, res e Hargett, o s e
Rogers Louise,* wife Jacob, house work
Rogers Owen,* son Jacob, res same, farm hand
Rogers Squire,* son Jacob, res same, wks for Mrs J C Winder
Rogers Garfield,* son Jacob, res same, farm hand
Rogers Mary A,* d Jacob, res same, farm hand
Rogers Hilliard,* son Jacob, res same, farm hand
Rogers Martha J,* d Jacob, res same, student
Rogers Nettie J,* d Jacob, res same, student
Rogers Nick,* farm hand, res old Fair Ground, o s e
Rogers Hubert, son Mrs Annie Pulley, res same, student
Rogers Calvin,* lab, res old Fair Ground, o s e
Rogers Caroline,* wife Calvin, washerwoman
Rogers Margaret,* washerwoman, res old Fair Ground, o s e
Rogers Rosa,* nurse for A B Stronach, res on lot
Rogers Zelphia J, seamstress, res 523 s Wilmington
Rogers Hugh P, son Mrs Z J, res same, wks H Steinmetz
Rogers Alonzo, stationary eng, res 21 Hayti
Rogers Mrs Julia, wife Alonzo, house work
Rogers Sidney,* porter for J D Carroll, res 728 e Davie, o s e
Rogers Sophronia,* wife Sidney, seamstress
Rogers Mrs Louisa, seamstress, res 229 s Bloodworth
Rogers Alvis, painter, res 701 s Bloodworth
Rogers Mrs Piatty, wife Alvis
Rogers Eugene, son Alvis, r same, pressman Edwards & Broughton
Rogers Miss Gertrude, d Alvis, res same, wks Caraleigh mill
Rogers Miss Maud, d Alvis, res same, wks Caraleigh mill
Rogers Miss Beulah, d Alvis, res same, student
Rogers Jos T, carp, res s Bloodworth
Rogers Mrs Susan, wife Jos T
Rogers Norman, son Jos T, res same, wks Caraleigh mill
Rogers Miss Lillie, d Jos T, res same
Rogers Brodie,* carp, res 536 e Edenton
Rogers Cynthia,* wife Brodie
Rogers Geo T,* son Brodie, res same, barber
Rogers Eris,* son Brodie, res same, carp
Rogers Eula M,* d Brodie, res same
Rogers Meta D,* d Brodie, res same, teacher in Garfield Graded School*
Rogers L G, bkkpr for Cary Lumber Co, res 214 s Harrington
Rogers Mrs Ida D, wife L G
Rogers Dr J R, physician and surgeon, office and res Park Hotel
Rogers Mrs M A, wid, res 113 s Blount
Rogers R W, ins agt, 226 Fayetteville, res o s n
Roles Ruffin, furniture factory, cor w Jones and r r crossing, res cor w Jones and Saunders

Roles Mrs Emily, wife Ruflin
Roles Z L, furniture maker, res 227 n Saunders
Roles Mrs Mary F, wife Z L
Roles Lionel H, son Z L, res same
Roles Wm R, son Z L, res same
Rollins Delia,* cook, res 513 w South
Rollins Cora,* house work, res 514 s Dawson
Rollins Ella,* washerwoman, res 514 s Dawson
Root Chas, sec and treas N C Home Ins Co, res 749 Hillsboro'
Root Mrs Annie, wife Chas
Root Miss Sadie S, d Chas, res same, student
Root Aldert S, son Chas, res same, student
Root Miss Annie G, d Chas, res same, student
Root Chas B, res with son Chas Root
Roper Ewell, clk for W E Jones, bds 540 n Blount
Rosenau Fred, foreman cloth-room Caraleigh cot mill, bds 745 Fayetteville
Rosengarten J, clothing, shoes, &c, 218 s Wilmington, bds Germania House
Rosengarten A, salesman, bds Germania House
Rosenthal G, sec and treas Juanita cot mill, 122 Fayetteville, res 420 Fayetteville
Rosenthal Mrs Bertha, wife G
Rosenthal Miss Bertha, d G, res same
Rosenthal Miss Susie, d G, res same, student
Rosenthal David, res cor Fayetteville and Cabarrus
Rosenthal Mrs Frances, wife David
Rosenthal Lawrence, son David, res same
Rosenthal Miss Gertie, res with David Rosenthal, student
Rosenthal Jerome, res with David Rosenthal, student
Rosenthal M, grocer, cor Fayetteville and Hargett, res 529 Fayetteville
Rosenthal Mrs Hannah, wife M
Rosenthal Isador, dry goods and millinery, 211 Fayetteville, res 115 n McDowell
Rosenthal Mrs Sarah, wife Isador
Ross John T, clk U S post-office, res Sewell ave, Idlewild
Ross Mrs Jennie L, wife John T
Ross Miss Jennie B, d John T, res same, student
Ross C F, pastry cook Park Hotel, res same
Rowland Thornton, deputy sheriff, bds 109 s Blount
Rowland Delia,* cook for R E Parham, res Rock Quarry rd
Rowland Lee,* porter at Commercial and Farmers Bank, res 561 e Edenton
Rowland Sallie,* wife Lee
ROYALL & BORDEN, furniture dealers, 218 s Wilmington, also entrance through A B Stronach, Miles Goodwin mgr
Royall Flora,* cook, res 322 e Martin

Royster Dr W I, physician and surgeon, office and res 323 w Morgan
Royster Mrs Mary W, wife Dr W I
Royster Dr Hubert A, physician and surgeon, office and res 323 w Morgan
Royster James F, son Dr W I, res same
Royster Frank W, son Dr W I, res same, clk at Caraleigh mills
Royster Bunchy,* cook, res 524 Yearby's lane
Royster Lucy,* student, res with Wright Brasel
Royster Clarence,* student, res with Wright Brasel
Royster V C, candy mfr and merchant, 207 Fayetteville, res 306 Hillsboro'
Royster Mrs Hallie, wife V C
Royster Wilber, son V C, res same, student
Royster Percy, son V C, res same, student
Royster Vitruvius, U S Commissioner and deputy clk U S Circuit Court, office U S bldg, res 209 e Hargett
Royster Mrs Margaret, wife Vitruvius
Royster A D & Bro, candy mfrs, store and factory 207 Fayetteville
Royster Hettie,* cook, res 227 e Cabarrus
Royster W B, printer, res 210 Newbern ave
Royster Mrs J E, wife W B
Royster Miss Edith, d W B, res same, teacher in Graded School
Royster Frank, son W B, res same, conductor Ral Electric Co
Royster Miss Julia, d W B, res same
Royster Len H (N C Bldg and Supply Co), architect, contractor and builder, res 108 n Saunders
Royster Mrs Bettie A, wife Len H
Royster Thomas,* gardener, res 18 Fowle
Royster John,* student, res Manly
Royster D L, carp, res 209 e Hargett
Royster Mrs Sarah J, wife D L
Royster Miss Nellie, d D L, res same
Royster Miss Gertrude, d D L, res same, teacher
Ruffin Mrs Samuel, wid, res 315 Oakwood ave
Ruffin L A,* lab, res 716 Fayetteville
Ruffin Maria,* wife L A, house work
Ruffin Sarah,* d L A, res same, student
RUSS WM M, mayor city of Raleigh, res 124 n Wilmington
Russ Mrs Henrietta, wife Wm M
Russell Wm, lab, res 309 n West
Russell Frances,* house servant, res 407 w Martin
Russell Rena,* washerwoman, res Martin, o s e
Russell Emily,* laundress for A B Andrews, res on lot
Russell Ella,* nurse for John N Smith, res same
Ruth Mack F (Caudle & Ruth), grocer, res 501 Hillsboro'
Ruth Mrs Hattie, wife Mack F
Ruth Thos, son Mack F, res same, student

Ruth Sam L, carp, res 302 St Mary's, o s w
Ruth Mrs M K, wife Sam L
Ruth Miss Lena, d Sam L, res same, dressmaker
Ruth Tulice, son Sam L, res same, clk Ruth & Caudle
Ruth Marvin, son Sam L, res same, carp
Ruth Miss Minnie, d Sam L, res same, seamstress
Ruth H G, carp, res 530 Hillsboro'
Ruth Mrs Mary, wife H G
Ruth Geo H, carp, res 517 Hicks' lane
Ruth Mrs Mollie, wife Geo H
Ruth Miss Florence, d G H, res same, wks Ral cot mill
Ruth Samuel, son G H, res same, wks Ral cot mill
Ruth James O, carp N C Car Co, res 108 Johnson
Ruth Mrs Ida, wife James O
Ruth Willie, son James O, res same, clk Wyatt & Co
Ruth Miss Bettie, d James O, res same
Ruth Andrew, son James O, res same, student
Ruth Miss Jane, res 615 e Hargett
Ryan S G, lawyer, office in Pullen bldg, res 421 n Bloodworth
Ryan Mrs M G, wife S G
Ryan John, stone-mason, res 18 s Swain
Ryan Mrs Margaret, wife John
Ryan Patrick, son John, res same, stone-cutter
Ryan Miss Annie, d John, res same

SADLER Walter, moulder, res 132 w Cabarrus
Sadler Mrs Rosa L, wife Walter
Sadler Marion, tailor app, res 116 w Morgan
Saintsing Alex, carp, res 552 e Davie
Saintsing Mary, wife Alex
Saintsing Arthur, son Alex, res same, student
Saintsing John, son Alex, res same, student
Saintsing Clyde, son Alex, res same, student
Saintsing Miss Maud, d Alex, res same, student
Saintsing Atlas L, moulder Allen & Cram Co, res 559 Newbern ave
Saintsing Mrs Malissa, wife Atlas L
Saintsing Willie, son Atlas L
Saintsing Thomas, res 559 Newbern ave
Saintsing W H, mechanic S A L, res 118 Johnson
Saintsing Mrs L A, wife W H
Saintsing Miss India, d W H
Saintsing Waymouth, son W H, wks Ral cot mill
Saintsing Miss Gaitha, d W H, res same, student
Sale Thos P, sanitary officer, bds 105½ Fayetteville
Salmer John, farm hand, res 116 w Morgan
Salmon Mrs Cutlie, wid, res 18 McKee
Salmon Thomas, son Mrs Cutlie, wks Caraleigh mill

Salmon Miss Cornelia, d Mrs Cutlie, res same, spinner
Salmon Miss Vassar, d Mrs Cutlie, res same
Salter Moses,* farmer, res Cotton lane, o s e
Salter Emily,* wife Moses, washerwoman
Salter Jacob,* son Moses, res same, lab
Salter Rev D S,* Baptist minister, res Cotton lane, o s e
Salter Martha,* wife Rev D S
Salter Gertrude,* d Rev D S, res same, student
Salter Charlotte,* d Rev D S, res same, student
Salter William,* son Rev D S, res same, student
Salter Ernest,* son Rev D S, res same, student
Salter Thomas,* son Rev D S, res same, student
Salter Ed,* lab, res Idlewild
Salter John,* gardener, res Idlewild
Salter Venus,* wife John, cook Normal School
Salter Emily,* d John, res same, washerwoman
Salter Annie,* d John, res same, washerwoman
Salter Maggie,* d John, res same, student
Salter Katie,* d John, res same, student
Salter Della,* d John, res same, student
Salter Isaac,* son John, res same, student
Salter Mile,* lab, res e Hargett, o s e
Salter Mile,* wife Mile, washerwoman
Sanderford, Wm L, grocer, cor s Blount and Smithfield, res 813 s Blount
Sanderford Mrs Annie, wife Wm L
Sanderford J W, grocer, e Hargett, o s e, res same
Sanderford Mrs Olivia L, wife J W
Sanders Jas A, trav salesman, res 328 w Jones
Sanders Mrs Henrietta, wife Jas A
Sanders Miss Louise, d Jas A, res same, student
Sanders Samuel, son Jas A, res same
Sanders Charlie, son Jas A, res same
Sanders B W,* carp, res 222 Smithfield
Sanders Sarah J,* wife B W
Sanders Mary O,* d B W, res same, student
Sanders Sarah J,* d B W, res same, student
Sanders Amelia,* d B W, res same, student
Sanders James E,* son B W, res same, student
Sanders Benj W,* son B W, res same, student
Sanders Emily,* cook for R J Conrad, res 229 e Cabarrus
Sanders Clossie,* cook for B W Upchurch, res 229 e Cabarrus
Sanders Troy,* farm hand, res 229 e Cabarrus
Sanders Rosa,* cook for W D Upchurch, res 229 e Cabarrus
Sanders Miss Cornelia, res with Geo Coffee
Sanders Miss, hkpr for Geo Medlin
Sanders Nancy,* cook for Mrs Emma Swindell, res same
Sanders Chaddie,* washerwoman, res rear 217 w South

Sanders Mary,* wks colored Deaf and Dumb Asylum, res 232 e South
Sanders Millie,* washerwoman, res 807 Jenkins
Sanders Charles,* painter, res 807 Jenkins
Sanders Nora,* cook for Col W J Hicks, res on lot
Sanders Robert,* wks Southern R R, bds 35 Hunter
Sanford Thos,* carp, res 520 Smith
Sanford Rebecca,* wife Thos, laundress
Sanford Wm,* son Thos, res same, wks on Outlook paper
Sanford Lovie,* d Thos, res same, laundress
Sanford James,* son Thos, res same, painter
Sanford Charles,* son Thos, res same, driver for W D Upchurch
Sanford Maggie,* d Thos, res same, student
Sanford Ætna,* d Thos, res same, student
Sandy Marion, city hand, res Prairie bldg
Sandy Mrs Sarah, wife Marion, seamstress
Sapp R L, electrician Ral Elec Co, res 122 n Dawson
Sapp Mrs Lula M, wife R L
Sapp Miss Ida B, d R L, res same, student
Sapp W E, son R L, res same, student
Sater A T, carp, res 230 Smithfield
Sater Mrs Mary E, wife A T
Sater Miss Mary B, d A T, res same, seamstress
Sater Henry W, son A T, res same, carp
Sater Miss Bettie, d A T, res same, student
Sater Miss Neva, d A T, res same, student
Sater Thomas, son A T, res same, student
Satterfield Lina,* washerwoman, res 715 s West
Satterfield Callie,* washerwoman, res 116 w South
Sauls Mrs Sallie, wid, res with W H Miller
Sauls Lina, house-girl for Chas E Stokes, res same
Saunders Col Wm J, ins agt, res 426 n Saunders
Saunders Mrs J M, wife Col Wm J
Saunders Miss Jennie C, d Col Wm J, res same
Saunders Fred, clk Sec of State office, bds Central Hotel
Saunders Miss Anne, in charge of infirmary at St Mary's School, res same
Savage Mrs Emma, wid, res Smithfield
Savage Geo, son Mrs Emma, res same, brick-mason
Savage Mrs Callia, wife Geo
Savage Alfred, machinist, bds 11 s Wilmington
Sawyer M D, stationary eng, res Hillsboro' rd, o s w
Sawyer Mrs Henrietta, wife M D
Sawyer Wm H, son M D, res same, student
Sawyer Jos E, son M D, res same, student
Sawyer W M,* butcher, res 330 s East
Sawyer Sarah,* wife Wm
Sawyer Mary,* d Wm, res same

Sawyer Lizzie,* servant, res Smith
Scales Miss Sadie, res with Mrs Geo Waters
Scales Jesse,* hostler for J Schwartz, res same
Scarboro John C, clk for J J Harris, res 6 s East
Scarboro Mrs Alice, wife Jno C
Scarboro Paul, son Jno C, res same
Scarboro George,* lab, res 562 E Cabarrus
Scarborough Jno C, Supt Public Instruction, office Supreme Court bldg, res 519 e Jones
Scarborough Mrs Julia V, wife Jno C
Scarborough Hartwell V, son J C, res same, student
Scarborough Miss Annie R, d J C, res same, student
Scarborough Miss Julia C, d J C, res same, student
Scarborough Miss Annie M, niece of J C, res same, student
Scarborough E F, grocer, 124 e Martin, res 212 e Davie
Scarborough A J, carp, res 212 e Davie
Scarborough Mrs M J, wife A J
Scarlette T J, watchman Union depot, res 315 s Dawson
Scarlette Mrs Martha E, wife T J, dressmaker
Scarlette G C, son T J, res same, tel opr
Schilling Eugene, painter, res 101 Johnson
Schilling Mrs Meekins, wife Eugene, dressmaker
Schenk Miss Mary, teacher literary dept at the Institution for the Blind, res at the Institution
Schiveley Miss Nellie, music teacher, bds Park Place
Schiveley Miss Lottie, music student, bds Park Place
Schwartz J, butcher, res cor Hargett and Harrington
Schwartz Mrs Lena, wife J
Schwartz Wm, son J, res same
Schwartz Miss Henrietta, d J, res same
Schwartz Isaac, son J, res same
Schwartz Samuel, butcher, res with son J Schwartz
Schwartz Jacob, clothing merchant, res 109 s Wilmington
Schwartz Mrs Minnie, wife Jacob
Schwartz Miss Fannie, d Jacob, res same, student
Scott Matilda,* washerwoman, res Martin, o s e
Scott Lucy,* cook, res Martin, o s e
Scott Frank,* son Matilda, res same, driver for Fab Brown
Scott Edward,* son Matilda, res same, lab
Scott Thomas,* son Matilda, res same, student
Scott Bettie,* washerwoman, res 819 Fayetteville
Scott Lizzie,* cook J M Barbee, res 819 Fayetteville
Scott Maria,* cook P C Enniss, res 819 Fayetteville
Scott Henrietta,* d Bettie, res same, student
Scott Cornelius,* son Bettie, res same, student
Scott James,* son Bettie, res same, student
Scott Charlie,* son Bettie, res same, student
Scott John M,* butcher, res 724 e Davie

Scott Cherry,* wife J M, washerwoman
Scott Wm,* pedler, res old Fair Ground, o s e
Scott Tabie,* wife Wm, laundress
Scott John,* son Wm, res same, student
Scott Pink,* d Wm, res same, student
Scott Walter O (Scott & Potter), saloon-keeper, 114 e Martin, res Smithfield
Scott Mrs Delia F, wife W O
Scott Miss Jennie, d W O, res same, student
Scott Laura,* cook, res 322 Cannon
Scruggs Dr L A,* physician, office and res 24 e Worth
Scruggs Clara B,* wife Dr L A
Scruggs Goldie,* d Dr L A, res same
SEABOARD AIR-LINE FREIGHT OFFICE, 305 Halifax, C S Allen agt
Seagraves Miss Sallie, dressmaker, res 514 s Bloodworth
Sears A L, traveling salesman, res Idlewild
Sears Mrs Martha, wife A L
Sears Eliza,* cook, res 116 w Peace
Seawell R B, farmer, res cor e Hargett and Swain
Seawell J L, son R B, res same, deputy clk Supreme Court
Seawell Miss Miriam, d R B, res same
Seawell R B Jr, son R B, res same, civil eng
Seawell Miss Pattie, res with Mrs Nellie Carver
Selby Mrs Mary, mother of Mrs Hattie N Rivers, res same
Self Calvin W, collector Thomas & Maxwell, res 326 s Blount
Self Mrs Bettie, wife C W
Self Miss Nannie, d C W, res same, wks Royster's candy factory
Self Griflis, son C W, res same
Self Lewis, son C W, res same
Self Lissie, d C W, res same
Separk Mrs Mary W, wid, res 307 w Jones
SEPARK WHARTON G, mgr Raleigh Stationery Co, res 307 w Jones
Separk Miss Mollie W, d Mrs Mary W, res same
Separk Miss Alma McKee, d Mrs Mary W, res same
Separk Joseph, son Mrs Mary W, res same, ministerial student
Separk Miss Maud, g-d Mrs Mary W, res same
SEPARK CHARLES A, compiler of Raleigh City Directory, bds 307 w Jones
Separk Mrs Bartie Ramsey, wife Charles A
Sexton Dr J A, physician and surgeon, office 507 Fayetteville, res same
Shadrack Thomas, harness maker, bds 416 s Person
Shaffer A W, civil eng, res cor Fayetteville and Lenoir
Shaffer Mrs Alice A, wife A W
Shaffer Miss Beulah S, d A W, res same
Shaffer Elmer M, son A W, res same, student

Shaffer Miss Honora, d A W, res same, student
Shaffer Miss Ethel A, d A W, res same, student
Shaffer George, machinist, bds 112 Halifax
SHAW UNIVERSITY, cor Wilmington and South, Prof Chas Meserve pres
Shaw Chas K, clk for W H & R S Tucker & Co, bds cor Newbern ave and Person
Shaw Henry,* lab, res 418 s Swain
Shaw Penny,* wife Henry, washerwoman
Shaw Caroline,* d Henry, res same, washerwoman
Shaw Henrietta,* d Henry, res same, cook for T J Bashford
Shaw Cornelia,* d Henry, res same, cook
Shaw Nelson,* son Henry, res same, lab
Shaw Madison,* son Henry, res same, errand-boy
Shaw W J, ticket gate-keeper Union depot, res 327 w Jones
Shaw Mrs Minnie, wife W J
Shaw Miss Mamie, d W J, res same, student
Shaw Hubert, son W J, res same
Shearin Henry,* porter Edward Fasnach, res 807 Jenkins
Sheets J A, ins agt, bds 514 Hillsboro'
Shelton Miss Rosa L, chief lady attendant Insane Asylum, res same
Shepard F, foreman S A L shops, res cor Edenton and McDowell
Shepard Mrs C, wife F
Shepard Miss M, sister F, res same
Shepherd W O, foreman machine shop and foundry N C Car Co, res 531 n Salisbury
Shepherd Mrs F L, wife W O
Shepherd W H, son W O, res same, boiler-maker S A L
Shepherd Miss E L, d W O, res same
Shepherd Bertram, son W O, res same, app machinist
Shepherd Jas E (Shepherd & Busbee), lawyer, bds Yarboro' House
Shepherd & Busbee, lawyers, office Pullen bldg
Shepherd Lizzie,* cook for Wm Simpson, res on lot
Sheppard Rev M B,* minister, res 732 e Davie, o s e
Sheppard Alice J,* wife Rev M B
Sherwood C A (C A Sherwood & Co), merchant, res 127 w Hargett
Sherwood Mrs Mary E, wife C A
Sherwood Wm H, son C A, res same, student
Sherwood Miss Mary H, d C A, res same, student
Sherwood Miss Lulie V, d C A, res same, student
Sherwood Mrs Frank, teacher in Murphy School, res 214 e Morgan
Sherwood C A & Co, dry goods, notions, &c, 205 Fayetteville
Sherrill Logan,* driver, res s West
Sherrill Josephine,* wife Logan, house work
Shipp Mrs Maggie, wid, res 226 n Person
Shipp Miss Mary, d Mrs Maggie, res same
Shipp Miss Kate C, teacher in St Mary's School, res same
Shipp Maria,* cook, res 414 Haywood

Shipp Samuel,* son Maria, res same, house-servant
Shobe Miss Leah, res with Rev I A Canfield
Shore R E, chief clk Park Hotel, res same
Short Beverly,* carp, res old Fair Ground, o s e
Short Mollie,* wife Beverly, washerwoman
Short George,* son Beverly, res same, student
Short John H,* carp, res 602 e Cabarrus
Short Jennie,* wife John H, laundress
Short Herodicas,* son John H, res same
Shroyer Mrs Alice A, wid, res 212 s East
Siligson Isaac, merchant, res 114 s Blount
Siligson Mrs Annie, wife Isaac, boarding-house
Silas Ann E,* cook, res 217 w South
Silas Bettie,* nurse, res 217 w South
Silas Dennis,* son Ann E, res same, student
Sills Matilda,* washerwoman, res Bledsoe ave
Sills John,* porter Madame Besson, res Bledsoe ave
Sills Lessie,* d Matilda, res same, music teacher
Sills Geneva,* d Matilda, res same, washerwoman
Sills Dora,* washerwoman, res 103 Smithfield
Sills Lilla,* d Dora, res same, student
Sills Alonzo,* son Dora, res same, student
Sills Jane,* washer and scourer, res 915 Manly
Sills Lethia,* d Jane, res same, house-servant
Sills Addie,* d Jane, res same, cook
Sills Harriet,* d Jane, res same, washerwoman
Sills James T,* son Jane, res same, student
Simonds John, lab, res 308 s Salisbury
Simonds Mrs Betsy, wife John
Simmons F M, internal revenue collector, res 528 Fayetteville
Simmons Mrs Belle, wife F M
Simmons Miss Mamie R, d F M, res same
Simmons Miss Eliza H, d F M, res same, student
Simmons Miss Ella M, d F M, res same, student
Simmons Miss Isabella G, d F M, res same, student
Simmons Allen,* lab, res 326 w South
Simmons Margaret,* wife Allen, washerwoman
Simmons Caroline,* washerwoman, res 207 w Davie
SIMMS Rev Dr A M, pastor Baptist Tabernacle church, res cor Newbern ave and Bloodworth
Simms Mrs Mary, wife Rev Dr A M
Simms Miss Evelyn, d Dr A M, res same, student
Simms Robert M, son Dr A M, res same, student
Simms Miss Mattie, d Dr A M, res same, student
Simms Moses,* wks Ral Gas Co, res 400 Cannon
Simms Mary,* wife Moses, washerwoman
Simms Ida,* d Moses, res same, student
Simms George,* lab, res e Martin, o s e

Simms Phillis,* wife George, washerwoman
Simms Bryant,* son George, res same, lab
Simms Eddie,* son George, res same, lab
Simms Georgiana,* d George, res same, nurse
Simms Hattie B,* d George, res same, nurse
Sims Mary,* washerwoman, res 613 e Lenoir
Sims Jessie,* d Mary, res same, nurse
Sims Mabel,* d Mary, res same, student
Sims Willie,* son Mary, res same, student
Sims Roney,* lab, res 426 s Blount
Sims Laura,* wife Roney, washerwoman
Sims William,* grocer, Newbern ave, o s e, res same
Sims Winnie,* wife Wm, washerwoman
Sims Bessie,* d Wm, res same, student
Sims Roberta,* washerwoman, res Hargett, o s e
Sims Wm H,* son Roberta, wks city market
Simons Mrs F E, wid, res with W E Fann
Simpson John A, music teacher Blind Institution, res 211 w Jones
Simpson Mrs Narcissa, wife Jno A, music teacher Blind Institution
Simpson Robt L, son Jno A, res same, student
Simpson Frank B, son Jno A, res same, student
Simpson Walter A, son Jno A, res same, student
SIMPSON WILLIAM, druggist, Pullen bldg, Fayetteville, res Park Place n Blount
Simpson Miss Annie, d Wm, res same
Simpson Thomas, son Wm, res same
Simpson Robert, druggist, cor Hillsboro' and Salisbury, res 115 n McDowell
Simpson Mrs Ella W, wife Robert
Simpson John F, son Robert, res same
Skinner Rev Dr Thos E, Baptist minister, res 403 e Edenton
Skinner Mrs Annie S, wife Rev T E
Skinner Chas W, son Rev T E, res same
Skinner J L, clk for C E Johnson & Co, res 504 n Person
Skinner Mrs Octavia, wife J L
Skinner Ida,* washerwoman, res 415 w South
Skinner Ella,* d Ida, res same, student
Skinner B S, supt N C A & M College farm, r Hillsboro' rd, o s w
Skinner Mrs L P, wife B S
Skinner Miss Nellie P, d B S, res same
Skinner Miss Nannie B, d B S, res same
Skinner J Leigh, son B S, res same, collector for Citizens National Bank
Skinner Miss Kate L, d B S, res same, student
Skinner Miss Lillie P, d B S, res same, student
Skinner Miss Rosa F, d B S, res same, student
Slade S M R,* farm hand, res 112 Smithfield
Slade Lenora,* wife S M R, house work

Slade Cary,* d S M R, res same, student
Slade Serlnda,* d S M R, res same, student
Slade Annie B,* d S M R, res same, student
Slade Walter,* son S M R, res same, student
Slater Miss Florence W, teacher in St Mary's School, res same
Slater Silas,* lab, res 552 e Martin
Slater Julia,* wife Silas, washerwoman
Sledge Matilda,* cook, res rear Park Place
Sledge Henry,* son Matilda, res same, fireman at N C Car Co
Sledge Claude,* son Matilda, res same, wks for C N Dixon
Sledge Nathan,* lab, res Cotton lane, o s e
Sledge Clarisa,* wife Nathan, seamstress
Sledge William,* lab, res old Fair Ground, o s e
Sledge Malinda,* wife Wm, servant
Sledge William,* fireman S A L, res s Yearby's lane
Sledge Belle,* wife William
Sledge David,* porter for J D Carroll, res 509 e Davie
Sledge Fannie,* wife David, washerwoman
Small Nellie,* cook, res 325 s Bloodworth
Small Charles,* porter for L J Walker, res 510 s East
Small Nancy,* washerwoman, res 116 w Peace

SMEDES BENNETT, D D, prin of St Mary's School, Hillsboro', res same
Smedes Mrs Henrietta, wife Dr Bennett
Smedes Miss Mary S, d Rev Bennett, res same
Smedes Miss Helen L, d Rev Bennett, res same
Smethurst W A, supt cotton-oil mill, res 510 s Salisbury
Smethurst Mrs M F, wife W A
Smethurst W S, son W A, res same, student
Smethurst Frank A, son W A, res same
Smith Jno O, eng S A L R R, res n Saunders
Smith Mrs A J, wife Jno O
Smith Stanley G, son Jno O, res same, student
SMITH HAM F, city clk, office in City Hall, res 513 n Bloodworth
Smith Mrs Nannie W, wife Ham F
Smith Miss Emily M, d Ham F, res same, student
Smith Mrs Orrin, wid, res 408 n Person
Smith M M, son Mrs Orrin, res same, prop Law-Book Exchange
Smith Ben F, son Mrs Orrin, res same, wks Ral Gas Co
Smith Miss Carrie E, d Mrs Orrin, res same, wks Telephone Ex
Smith Miss Corrina L, d Mrs Orrin, res same, wks Law-Book Ex
Smith Miss Nellie M, d Mrs Orrin, res same, student
Smith William, adjuster S A L R R, res 127 Halifax
Smith Mrs J M, wife William
Smith Wm Conway, son William, res same, app S A L
Smith Miss Roberta, d William, res same
Smith J H, life ins agt, res 313 Oakwood ave

Smith Mrs Alma, wife J H
Smith Wm E, son J H, res same, student
Smith Emma,* sick-nurse, res 528 e Davie
Smith William,* son Emma, res same, lab
Smith Sallie,* d Emma, res same, cook
Smith Sylvester,* son Emma, res same, wks at Dairy
Smith Charles,* son Emma, res same, farm hand
Smith Rader,* son Emma, res same, farm hand
Smith Tiny,* d Emma, res same, musician
Smith Virginia,* d Emma, res same, student
Smith Gaston,* son Emma, res same, student
Smith Mary,* cook for A H Green, res 418 s Swain
Smith Miss Bedie, dressmaker, res 410 w Jones
Smith Miss Lizzie, sister to Miss Bedie, res same
Smith Thos B, watchman, res 410 w Jones
Smith Mrs Florence C, grocer, e Davie, res same
Smith Foster, d Mrs Florence, res same
Smith Harry, son Mrs Florence, res same
Smith W H, asst train dispatcher S A L R R, bds Rev Alvin Betts
Smith George, shoemaker, cor s Wilmington and e Cabarrus, res East
Smith Martha,* washerwoman, res Fowle
Smith Howard,* son Martha, res same, lab
Smith Connie,* son Martha, res same, lab
Smith W R, mechanic, bds 404 Fayetteville
Smith John U, saloon, Exchange Place, res 107 w Jones
Smith Mrs Rosa K, wife John U
Smith Alex,* wks for Dr T D Hogg, res e Lane
Smith Pattie,* wife Alex, washerwoman
Smith Joseph,* lab, res 523 Smith
Smith W D, fish dealer, res 752 Fayetteville
Smith Mrs Hattie, wife W D, dressmaker
Smith Miss Mary, d W D, res same, student
Smith W D Jr, son W D, res same, student
Smith D B, son W D, res same
Smith Katie,* house-servant, res 720 Fayetteville
Smith Richard, wks News and Observer, res 743 s Blount
Smith Wm D, paper carrier, res 743 s Blount
Smith Walter, printer, bds 11 s Wilmington
Smith Robert,* wks for C H Beine, res 516 e Davie
Smith Sabina,* wife Robert, house work
Smith Alonzo,* driver for Dr A O, res on lot
Smith Miss Jennie, seamstress, cor e Davie and Swain
Smith Miss Sunnie, seamstress, cor e Davie and Swain
Smith James H, farmer, res 301 s Bloodworth
Smith Mrs Lydia A, wife James H
Smith Mary,* cook, res 321 s Bloodworth

Smith Dempsey,* lab, res Rock Quarry rd
Smith Mary E,* wife Dempsey, washerwoman
Smith Matilda,* d Dempsey, res same, student
Smith John,* farmer, res e Hargett, o s e
Smith Fannie,* wife John, washerwoman
Smith Lucy,* washerwoman, res 425 n West
Smith Edward, clk for Samuel Jones, res cor Harrington and Hillsboro'
Smith Silla,* cook, res 560 e Cabarrus
Smith Lucy,* cook, res 13 McKee
Smith Olivia,* cook, res 13 McKee
Smith Levy, shoemaker, 406 s Wilmington, res same
Smith John M, son Levy, res same, night watchman Nixon & Johnson
Smith Miss Culie, d Levy, res same, wks Caraleigh mill
Smith Stephen, son Levy, res same, wks Caraleigh mill
Smith Henry,* lab, res 513 Smith
Smith Ellen,* wife Henry, laundress
Smith Laura,* d Henry, res same, student
Smith Martha,* d Henry, res same, laundress
Smith Richard,* son Henry, res same, tobacco worker
Smith Charles,* son Henry, res same, lab
Smith Julia,* d Henry, res same, student
Smith Mrs R W, wid, proprietress Exchange Hotel, Hillsboro'
Smith Miss Fannie W, d Mrs R W, stenographer and typewriter for Edwards & Broughton, res Exchange Hotel
Smith Sarah,* washerwoman, res 710 Manly
Smith Daisy,* d Sarah, res same, washerwoman
Smith Leonard W, printer at Edwards & Broughton's, res 308 n Dawson
Smith Mrs Sarah, wife L W
Smith Leonard, son L W, res same, student
Smith Etta,* adopted d Dr L A Scruggs, res same
Smith David,* lab, res 517 Cannon
Smith Mary,* wife David, washerwoman
Smith Lee,* lab, rooms 320 w Lenoir
Smith Eldridge, ins agt, res 415 e Hargett
Smith Mrs Laura, wife Eldridge
    Jones Willie, son Mrs Laura Smith, res same
    Jones Miss Maud, d Mrs Laura Smith, res same, student
Smith Louise,* washerwoman, res 512 Newbern ave
Smith Dora,* d Louise, res same, washerwoman
Smith Thais,* son Louise, res same, student
Smith James,* son Louise, wks W G Otey
Smith Edward D,* grocer, cor Cabarrus and Blount, res 536 e Lenoir
Smith Minnie,* wife E D
Smith E DeWitt, salesman W H & R S Tucker, r Newbern ave, o s e

Smith Mrs Manie, wife E D
Smith Perrin,* lab, res w Lenoir
Smith Louise,* wife Perrin, washerwoman
Smith Calvin,* driver for M T Norris, res 615 e Lenoir
Smith Catherine,* wife Calvin, washerwoman
Smith Sarah,* d Calvin, res same, nurse
Smith Alonzo,* son Calvin, res same, house-servant
Smith Mary,* washerwoman, res 136 w Cabarrus
Smith Henry,* son Mary, res same, student
Smith John,* son Mary, res same, student
Smith Major,* barber, res 316 s Bloodworth
Smith Julia,* wife Major
Smith Mrs C H, wid, boarding-house, 118 n Wilmington
Smith Miss Lula, d Mrs C H, res same
Smith Thomas,* whitewasher, res Upperman lane
Smith Cornelia,* wife Thomas, washerwoman
Smith Minnie,* d Thos, res same, student
Smith Sam T, saloon, 11 Exchange Place, res 408 Hillsboro'
Smith Mrs Nora, wife Sam T
Smith Miss Katie, d Sam T, res same, student
Smith Simeon, pressman Edwards & Broughton, res 823 Fayetteville
Smith Mrs Amanda, wife Simeon
Smith Wm H, son Simeon, blacksmith, res same
Smith Mrs Emma, wife Wm H
Smith Chas E, lab, res 823 Fayetteville
Smith Mrs Virginia E, wife Chas E
Smith Creasy,* nurse at H D White, res on lot
Smith W O, printer, res 323 s McDowell
Smith Mrs Ellen B, wife W O
Smith Wm B, son W O, res same
Smith Miss Mary E, d W O, res same
Smith John,* painter, res 514 w South
Smith Viney,* d John, res same, house work
Smith Alfonzo,* son John, res same, painter
Smith John,* painter, res 323 s Bloodworth
Smith Alex,* servant at Dr T D Hogg, res 119 w Cabarrus
Smith Pattie,* wife Alex, washerwoman
Smith Eliza,* cook, res 122 w Peace
Smith Cora,* d Eliza, res same, servant
Smith Annie,* cook for J N Holding, res on lot
Smith Z P (Capital Printing Co), printing and binding, res 404 Hillsboro'
Smith Mrs Minnie, wife Z P
Smith Bettie,* washerwoman, res 125 n West
Smith William,* servant of Mrs R C Badger, res same
Smith Adeline,* servant, res 428 s Person
Smith Joseph, son Adeline, res same, wks for J W Beasley

S.A.L. THE SEABOARD AIR LINE

IS THE ONLY LINE OPERATING
DOUBLE DAILY EXPRESS TRAINS
DRAWING THROUGH
PULLMAN PALACE SLEEPING CARS.

RALEIGH
---TO---
HENDERSON, DURHAM, SOUTHERN PINES, CHESTER, CLINTON and GREENWOOD, S. C., ELBERTON, ATHENS and ATLANTA, GA.

THE SOUTH AND SOUTH-WEST.
THE NORTH AND NORTH-EAST.

THE ATLANTA SPECIAL.	THE S. A. L. EXPRESS.
Pullman Vestibuled Limited Train.	SOLID TRAIN.
DRAWING-ROOM, BUFFET SLEEPING-CARS AND DAY COACHES SOLID TO	SLEEPING CARS AND DAY COACHES,
WASHINGTON, D. C.,	To ATLANTA, GA.,
AND ATLANTA, GA.	PORTSMOUTH, VA.

VESTIBULED LIMITED TRAINS, FASTEST TIME AND THE MOST LUXURIOUS CARS WITHOUT EXTRA FARE.

INTERSTATE EXPRESS FREIGHT.
QUICKEST TIME TO THE
NORTH and EAST and to GEORGIA, FLORIDA and the SOUTH.

Ticket Offices: Union Depot and 317 Fayetteville St.

H. S. LEARD, Soliciting Pass'r Ag't, Raleigh, N C

E. St. JOHN,	H. W. B. GLOVER,	T. J ANDERSON,
Vice-President.	Gen. Freight Agent.	Gen. Passenger Agent

SUN LIFE ASSURANCE COMPANY
OF CANADA.

INCORPORATED 1865.

Life Assurance in force Dec. 31, 1895,	$34,754,840 00
Net Assets, besides uncalled capital,	5,365,770 53
Income for the year,	1,528,056 09
Surplus to policy-holders,	535,911 23

OUR NEW PLAN.

The Sun Life, of Canada, now offers the best thing you can get in Assurance, and we shall be glad to call and explain.

The *Unconditional, Automatically-Non-Forfeiting, Self-Premium-Paying Policy* now issued by this Company.

Send for particulars at once.

J. R. JOHNSTON, Manager,
238 Fayetteville Street.   -   -   Raleigh, N. C.

CHAS. F. BULLOCK,

SIGNS.

Best Reference.

Hargett Street,

RALEIGH, N. C.

Smith Phœbe,* washerwoman, res rear 210 e Cabarrus
Smith Mamie,* d Phœbe, res same, student
Smith Charlie,* son Phœbe, res same, student
Smith Pattie,* washerwoman, res 507 s Blount
Smith Sophia,* cook for J E Pogue, res 507 s Blount
Smith Miss Emie, teacher in Peace Institute, res same
Smith Sallie,* servant for W H Weatherspoon, res on lot
Smith Penina,* cook for F L Mahler, res 16 n East
Smith C N, attendant at Insane Asylum, res same
Smith Annie,* house-servant, res 2 Johnson ave
Smith Pompey,* lab, res s West
Smith Harriet,* house-servant, res s West
Smith Dr R A, res 112 e Davie
Smith Mrs Rebecca, wife Dr R A
Smith William, son Dr R A, res same
Smith Miss Mary, d Dr R A, res same, saleslady for W H & R S Tucker
Smith Miss Sallie E, d Dr R A, res same, saleslady for W H & R S Tucker
Smith Miss Mildred, d Dr R A, res same, teacher
Smith Maggie,* washerwoman, res 412 e Martin
Smith Catherine,* d Maggie, res same, student
Smith William,* son Maggie, res same, student
Smith Sarah,* d Maggie, res same, student
Smith Pleasant,* washerwoman, res 210 w Cabarrus
Smith Minerva,* d Pleasant, res same, student
Smith Edward,* son Pleasant, res same, student
Smith George,* fireman S A L R R, res 323 w North
Smith Annie,* wife Geo, washerwoman
Smith Sam,* son Geo, res same, student
Smith George,* shoemaker, res 613 s East
Smith Sarah,* wife George, washerwoman
Smith Sarah,* d Geo, res same, servant at Peace Institute
Smith Sonnie,* lab, res 611 s East
Smith Emma,* wife Sonnie, servant Colored Institution
Smith Maud,* d Sonnie, res same, student
Smith Minnie,* d Sonnie, res same, student
Smith Jennie,* d Sonnie, res same, student
Smith Peter W,* eng at Colored D D & Blind Institution, res 713 s East
Smith Jane,* wife Peter W
Smith Albert,* son P W, res same, student
Smith Ida,* d P W, res same, student
Smith Mary,* d P W, res same, student
Smith Jerry,* lab, res 518 s Dawson
Smith Mrs Amelia, wid, dressmaker, res 754 e Davie, o s e
Smith Henry W, son Mrs Amelia, res same, wks Caraleigh mill
Smith Miss Lula I, d Mrs Amelia, res same

Smith Miss Annie F, d Mrs Amelia, res same, student
Smith W W, gen fire ins agt, office 217 Fayetteville, res 3 e North
Smith Mrs Eula S, wife W W
Smith W N H, son W W, res same, student
Smith Louis M, son W W, res same, student
Smith Gordon, son W W, res same, student
Smith Ed Chambers, lawyer, office Pullen bldg, res 434 Halifax
Smith Mrs Annie B, wife Ed Chambers
Smith Mrs W N H, wid, mother Ed Chambers, res same
Smith Mrs Selina, wid, res 305 s Person
Smith S M, son Mrs Selina, res same, collector for J M Broughton & Co
Smith Miss Eva, d Mrs Selina, res same, retoucher at Johnson's gallery
Smith Miss Lillie, d Mrs Selina, res same, student
Smith Miss Evie, niece Mrs Maggie W Adams, res same
Smith Annie P,* cripple, res 804 s Wilmington
Smith Lena,* cook for W E Foster, res same
Smith Hamden S,* teacher, res 429 s Person
Smith Alice,* house-servant, res 305 w South
Smith Henry,* grocer, 317 w Cabarrus
Smith Ann,* washerwoman, res Hood's al
Snead Miss Gracie, student, res with Len H Royster
Sneed Haywood,* hackman, res 616 Harp's lane, o s n
Sneed Emma,* wife Haywood, washerwoman
Snellings Hattie,* washerwoman, res Blount-st al
Snelling W N, wholesale and retail grocer and commission merchant, 309 s Wilmington, res 226 e Morgan
Snelling Mrs L S, wife W N
Snipes Miss Etta, bkkpr for Mrs J N Denton, res 117 s Bloodworth
Snipes Nash,* lab, res 207 w Lenoir
Snipes Amanda,* wife Nash, washerwoman
Snipes Henry,* hackman, res 23 w Worth
Snipes Hannah,* wife Henry, washerwoman
Snipes Dorcas,* cook, res 114 w Cabarrus
Snipes Jane,* washerwoman, res 25 w Worth
Snow Mrs Elizabeth McC, wid Geo H, res 30 Boylan ave
Snow Wm B, son Mrs Elizabeth McC, res same, lawyer
Snow Geo H, son Mrs Elizabeth McC, res same, ins agt
Snow Miss Adelaide B, d Mrs Elizabeth McC, res same, student
Snow Wm,* barber, res rear 416 s Person
Snow Lou,* wife Wm
Snow Hattie,* d Wm, res same, servant
Snow Bettie,* d Wm, res same
Snow John,* r r brakeman, res 405 s Dawson
Snow Florence,* washerwoman, res 222 w Lenoir
Snugs Charles, carp, res 127 w Jones
Snugs Mrs Lizzie, wife Chas

Snugs Miss Fannie, d Chas, res same
Solomon Sydney, driver City Fire Dept, res 116 w Morgan
Solomon Mrs Caroline, wife Sydney, seamstress
Solomon William, son Sydney, res same, city hand
Solomon George, son Sydney, res same, lab
Solomon Miss Lillie, d Sydney, res same
Solomon Mrs Lizzie, wid, res 116 w Morgan
Solomon Miss Annie, d Mrs Lizzie, res same
Solomon Henry, wks for city, res 215 s Blount
Solomon Mrs Annie, wife Henry
Sorrell Mrs L W, wid, res 230 w Cabarrus
Sorrell F M, accountant, res 230 w Cabarrus
Sorrell D B, clk at C H Beine & Co, res 230 w Cabarrus
Sorrell T E, clk at A Morris, res 230 w Cabarrus
Sorrell Henry,* driver City Fire Dept, res 108 w Davie
Sorrell Laura,* wife Henry, washerwoman
Southerland T R, traveling salesman, bds Park Place
Southerland Mrs Bessie, wife T R

SOUTHERN RAILWAY DIVISION FREIGHT OFFICE,
7 e Martin, J B Munson agt
Southern Express Company, A P Bryan agt, 108 Fayetteville
Southern Law-Book Exchange, M M Smith prop, Y M C A bldg
Sowers C F, laundryman, bds 508 Fayetteville
Sowers Mrs M B, wife C F
Spears Eugene F, clk for E H Love, res 312 s Bloodworth
Spears Mrs Annie O, wife Eugene F
Spears Miss Arrie M, d E F, res same, student
Spears Lee D, carp, res 557 Newbern ave
Spears Mrs A R, wife Lee D
Spears Miss Burley, d Lee D, res same, dressmaker
Spears Miss Metta, d Lee D, res same, student
Spears Robert, son Lee D, res same, student
Spears Miss Bettie, d Lee D, res same, student
Spears Miss Nannie, d Lee D, res same, student
Spears Miss Helen, d Lee D, res same, student
Spell John,* lab, res 522 s Dawson
Spell Lethia,* wife John, washerwoman
Spence N A, merchant, res 423 s Wilmington
Spence Neill A, bicycle repairer, res 423 s Wilmington
SPENCE PLUMBING CO, 105 w Martin, Spence & Kenster
  proprietors
Spence G M, plumber, res 528 e Hargett
Spence Mrs Maggie B, d G M
Spence Miss Linda B, d G M, res same
Spence Mrs A N, gen merchandise, 126 e Martin, res 311 s Dawson
Spence J A, mgr for Mrs A N Spence, res 311 s Dawson
Spence Garland L, son J A, res same
Spencer E N, clk for W E Jones, bds 105½ Fayetteville

Spencer Lizzie,* house-servant, res 405 w South
Spencer Theo,* brick-mason, res 409 Cannon
Spencer Lillie,* wife Theo, house work
Spencer Maria,* house work, res 409 Cannon
Spencer Haywood,* brick-mason, res 409 Cannon
Spencer Sarah,* house-servant, res 330 Cannon
Spencer Mollie,* washerwoman, res 551 e Martin
Spencer Thos,* son Mollie, res same, student
Spencer Vance,* brakeman S A L R R, res 209 w North
Spencer Mary,* wife Vance, washerwoman
Spencer Lizzie,* washerwoman, res 534 e Davie
Spikes W B, carp, res 122 s Blount
Spikes Mrs S J, wife W B
Spikes Charles R, candy-maker, res cor e South and Blount
Spikes Mrs Elizabeth, wife Charles R
Spikes Florence,* servant, res 525 s Blount
Spikes Sarah,* cook, res 26 Fowle
Spikes Frank,* driver for Allen & Cram, res 15 Fowle
Spikes Tamer,* wife Frank, washerwoman
Spikes Janet,* d Frank, res same, house-servant
Spikes George H,* son Frank, res same, student
Spikes Frank Jr,* son Frank, res same, student
SPILLMAN Rev B W, Baptist Sunday-School Missionary, res 312 Newbern ave
Sprinkle John, inmate Soldiers' Home
Spruill C P, bkkpr for Thos H Biggs, bds 120 e Hargett
Staley Cicero H, carp, bds 313 w Lane
Stamps Mrs E R, wid, res 321 Oakwood ave
Stamps Miss Miriam, d Mrs E R, res same, student
Stamps Miss Elise, d Mrs E R, res same, student
Stamps Edward R, son Mrs E R, res same, student
Stancil E S, inmate Soldiers' Home
Stainback W T, clk for W H & R S Tucker & Co, r 504 n Blount
Stainback Mrs Annie J, wife W T
Stainback Miss Claire, d W T, res same, student
Stainback Thos, son W T, res same, student
Stainback Frank, son W T, res same, student
Stanford Ned,* carp, res rear 515 s Harrington
Stanford Mittie,* wife Ned
Stanford Ed,* son Ned, res same, errand-boy
Stanley Warren,* lab, res 324 e Edenton
Stanley Hester,* wife Warren, washerwoman
Stanley Mollie,* d Warren, res same, cook for C M Walters
Stanley Alice,* d Warren, res same, cook for W W Parish
Stanley Jeff,* driver for Myatt & Hunter, res 14 n East
Stanley Mary A,* wife Jeff, sec of Order of Grand Fountain
Stanley Maria,* washerwoman, res 114 n Harrington
Stanley Mamie G,* student, res 14 n East

Stark John,* lab, res 402 s Blount
Stark Annie,* wife John, restaurant cook
Stark Rebecca,* d John, res same, wks at Laundry
Stark Emma,* d John, res same, wks in restaurant
Stark William,* son John, res same, hackman
Stark John,* wks for N W West, res 402 s Blount
Starling William, soap agt, res 416 e Morgan
Starling Mrs Ellen, wife Wm
Starling Arthur, son Wm, res same, student
Starling Miss Ida, d Wm, res same, student
Starling Miss Ruth, d Wm, res same, student
Stanton Henry, carp, bds 211 w Morgan
Steel Henry, printer Edwards & Broughton, bds 411 e Morgan
Steine Charles, shoemaker, res 503 Newbern ave
Steine Miss Dixie, d Chas, res same, dressmaker
Steine Miss Nellie, d Chas, res same, dressmaker
Steine Miss Bertha, d Chas, res same, student
STEINMETZ FLORAL HALL NURSERY, n end Halifax, Henry Steinmetz propr
Steinmetz Henry, florist, res Halifax, o n
Steinmetz Mrs Emma L, wife Henry
Steinmetz Miss Emily, d Henry, res same, student
Steinmetz Miss Matilda, d Henry, res same, student
Steptoe Solomon,* drayman, res 13 McKee
Steptoe Luvenia,* wife Solomon, laundress
Street W D, inmate Soldiers' Home
Stephenson W R, cotton weigher, office cotton platform, res Swift creek
Stevens W C, baggage master S A L, bds W S Utley
Stevens Martha, house work, res 742 s Person
Stevens Mrs H M, wid, bds 204 Halifax
Stevens Festus, inmate Soldiers' Home
Stevens Melton, grocer Academy Music bldg, bds 407 Fayetteville
STEVENS & SON, grocers, cor s Salisbury and Martin
Stevens Effie,* nurse G W Brinkley, res same

Roses, Carnations

and other choice Cut Flowers. Floral Designs, Bouquets, Palms, Ferns and other Decorative Pot Plants.

PANSY PLANTS, Verbenas, Geraniums and all kinds of out-door Bedding Plants, Tuberose Bulbs, Magnolias, Evergreens, etc. Best varieties of transplanted Tomato Plants, Cabbage and Egg Plants.

H. STEINMETZ, Florist.

'Phone 113.   North Halifax Street, near Peace Institute.

Stevenson Thos S, plumber, steam and gas fitter, 15 w Hargett, res 316 e Jones
Stevenson Mrs E L, wife Thos S
Stevenson Wm A, son Thos S, res same, student
Stevenson Rev E G, Missionary Baptist minister, res 528 n Person
Stevenson Mrs Rena F, wife Rev E G
Stevenson Edward, son Rev E G, res same
Stevenson Major, son Rev E G, res same, wks Ral cot mill
Stevenson Lonnie, son Rev E G, res same, wks Ral cot mill
Stevenson Ernest, son Rev E G, res same
Stevenson Miss Julia, hkpr for Mrs Nancy Edwards, res same
Stewart P M, grocer, 816 Fayetteville, res same
Stewart Mrs Laura, wife P M
Stewart John, son P M, res same, weaver Caraleigh mill
Stewart Leonard,* city hand, res 14 Pugh
Stewart Mary,* wife Leonard, washerwoman
Stewart Cornelia,* d Leonard, res same, cook
Stewart Victoria,* d Leonard, res same, nurse
Stewart Irene,* d Leonard, res same, student
Stewart Georgiana,* d Leonard, res same, student
Stewart Jesse,* stone-cutter, res 214 w Lenoir
Stewart Miss Susan, rooms 116 s West
Stewart J M, wks Ral cot mill, res 526 n West
Stewart Mrs Lena, wife J M
Stewart Emma,* washerwoman, res Caswell lane
Stewart Neill C, wks cot compress, res o s e
Stewart Mary,* cook for H B Hardy, res same
Stewart Sam,* carp, res 806 s Blount
Stewart Lizzie,* wife Sam, nurse
Stewart Royal,* son Sam, res same, porter for Dr N G Carroll
Stewart Roxana,* d Sam, res same, student
Stewart Sam,* carp, res Smith
Stewart Lucinda,* wife Sam
Stewart Chaney,* pedler, res rear 405 s Dawson
Stewart Dan B,* lab, res 209 w North

THOS. S. STEVENSON,
PLUMBER, STEAM AND GAS-FITTER,
AND DEALER IN
PUMPS, HYDRAULIC RAMS,
RANGES, GAS FIXTURES,
LEAD, IRON AND EARTHEN PIPES.

HARGETT ST., 3 doors W. Raleigh Nat. Bank, RALEIGH, N. C.
JOBBING PROMPTLY ATTENDED TO.

Stewart C C,* wks cot yard, res 209 w North
Stewart Henrietta,* wife C C, washerwoman
Stewart Victoria, washerwoman, res Dodd
Stewart Sallie,* washerwoman, res s Harrington
Stith Mrs D B, wid, res 124 w Morgan
Stith Miss Maggie, d Mrs D B, res same, saleslady for Alfred Williams & Co
St Luke's Home of the King's Daughters, 226 e Davie, in charge of the King's Daughters, Miss Maggie Brockwell housekeeper
Stokes A P, carp, res 825 Fayetteville
Stokes Mrs Dora, wife A P
Stokes Chas E, car inspector S A L R R, r near north end Dawson
Stokes Mrs Peggie A, wife Chas E
Stone Mrs G A, wid, res n Blount, o s n
Stone Cecil G, son Mrs G A, res same, trav salesman
Stone Miss Esther E, d Mrs G A, res same
Stone Miss Lillian E, d Mrs G A, res same
Stone Virgil P, son Mrs G A, res same, bicycle repairer
Stone Carl V B, son Mrs G A, res same, student
Stone Miss Pearl G, d Mrs G A, res same, student
Stone Emmett P, conductor S A L R R, res 522 n Person
Stone Mrs Ida J, wife E P
Stone Iredell J, son E P, res same, student
Stone Miss Anna B L, d E P, res same, student
Stone Mrs Mary J, wid, res 115 Johnson
Stone Thos S, son Mrs Mary J, res same, locomotive eng S A L
Stone Moses A, son Mrs Mary J, res same, clk A B Stronach
Stone Miss Daisy, d Mrs Mary J, res same
Stone Vicey,* washerwoman, res 222 e Cabarrus
Stone Jennie,* waiter in restaurant, res 224 s Wilmington
Stone William,* lab, res Newbern ave, o s e
Stone Jensy,* wife William, washerwoman
Stone Annie,* cook for W W Robbins, res 116 n West
Stone Edward,* brakeman S A L R R, bds 320 w North
Stonebanks C H, merchant, res 217 Linden ave
Stonebanks Mrs Ida, wife C H
Stott Nathan T, carp, res 519 s Bloodworth
Stott Mrs Ann, wife N T
Stott Miss Hawkins, d N T, res same, dressmaker
Stott Miss Ida M, d N T, res same, hkpr
Stott Miss Effie A, d N T, res same, wks Caraleigh mill
Stott Miss Maggie L, d N T, res same, wks Caraleigh mill
Stout Jerry,* lab frt depot S A L R R, res 437 Johnson
Stout Corrina,* wife Jerry, washerwoman
Stout Flora,* d Jerry, res same, student
Stout Lina,* d Jerry, res same, student
Stout Emma,* d Jerry, res same, student
Stout Robert,* porter for O H Johnson, res 437 Johnson

Stout Lydia,* d Jerry, res same, nurse for G W Brinkley
Straughan F M, wks State capitol, res 129 e Hargett
Straughan Mrs Elizabeth, wife F M
Straughan Miss Zula, d F M, res same
Straughan Jos, son F M, res same
Straughan T B, eng, res Brooklyn, o s w
Straughan Wiley A, moulder, res Brooklyn, o s w
Straughan Miss Lula C, seamstress, res 223 n Harrington
Straughan T E, printer, res Brooklyn, o s e
Straughan John, wks State capitol, res 118 s Blount
Straughan Victoria, wife John
Strickland Henry, spinner Ral cot mill, res 17 w Peace
Strickland Mrs Fannie, wife Henry
Strickland Wm, son Henry, res same, spinner
Strickland Charlie, son Henry, res same, wks Ral cot mill
Strickland Taylor, son Henry, res same, wks Ral cot mill
Strickland Eddie, son Henry, res same, student
Strickland Fannie, d Henry, res same, student
Strickland Hynes S,* grocer, 815 Fayetteville, res 12 McKee
Strickland Martha,* wife H S, house work
Strickland Mamie,* cook for Phil Andrews, res 519 Haywood
Strickland Matilda,* laundress, res 519 Haywood
Strickland Darcus,* cook, res 519 Haywood
Strickland Fannie,* nurse, res 519 Haywood
Strickland Andrew,* bootblack, res 519 Haywood
Strickland Mrs Hexie T, dressmaker, res 303 w Cabarrus
Strickland Grover C, son Mrs H T, res same, student
Strickland August L, son Mrs H T, res same
Strickland Geo L, student, res with Barney Pike
Strickland N B, carp, res 315 s McDowell
Strickland Mrs Samantha C, wife N B
Strickland G A, undertaker, 128 s Wilmington, res 321 w Jones
Strickland Mrs Lula, wife G A
Strickland Lemuel, inmate Soldiers' Home
Strickland Miss Annie, house girl Mrs E F Wyatt, res same
Strickland Dennis,* porter at Raleigh Stationery Co, r 219 s East
Strickland Mary,* cook, res 219 s East
Strickland Nellie,* d Lucy Toney, res same
Strickland William,* lab, res 533 e Cabarrus
Strickland Hattie,* wife Wm, washerwoman
Strickland Henry,* son Wm, res same, lab
Stronach A B, dry goods, notions, &c, 215 Fayetteville, res 411 n Bloodworth
Stronach Mrs M A, wife A B
Stronach Miss Kate McK, d A B, res same
Stronach Miss Ethel J, d A B, res same, student
Stronach Van Dalen, son A B, res same, clk for A B Stronach
Stronach Miss Janet, d A B, res same, student

Stronach Donaldson, son A B, res same, student
Stronach Miss Ellen, d A B, res same, student
Stronach Wm M, son A B, res same, student
Stronach Miss Mary L, d A B, res same
Stronach's Horse, Harness and Carriage Emporium, 319, 321 and 323 s Wilmington, Frank Stronach propr
Stronach Frank, propr Stronach's Emporium, r 412 n Bloodworth
Stronach Mrs Mary C, wife Frank
Stronach James N, son Frank, res same
Stronach Wm C (Stronach & Sons), merchant and Chairman of County Commissioners, res Bloodworth and n Boundary
Stronach Alexander, son W C, r same, lawyer, office in Fisher bldg
Stronach Jno B, son W C, res same, merchant
Stronach Frank M, son W C, res same, merchant
Stronach Miss Annie B, d W C, res same, art student
Stronach Miss Alice K, d W C, res same, art student
Stronach Wm C Jr, son W C, res same, flagman S A L
Stronach & Sons, wholesale and retail grocers, 213 Fayetteville
Strong Robt G, lawyer, office over Julius Lewis Hardware Co, res 410 n East
Strong Mrs Daisy, wife Robt G
Strong George V, lawyer, office over Julius Lewis Hardware Co, res 504 n Blount
Strong Miss Carrie C, d Geo V, r same, teacher in Murphy School
Strong Mrs Geo V Jr, wid, res 504 n Blount
Strother W H, lab, res 404 s Dawson
Strother Mrs Mary A, wife W H
Strother Thos B, son W H, res same
Strother Miss Mary H, d W H, res same
Strother E S, yard master Southern R R, res 404 s Dawson
Strother Mrs C A, wife E S
Stroud Lizzie,* cook, res 520 s Dawson
Stroud Henrietta,* washerwoman, res 121 w Lenoir
Stunkel Mrs Isabella, wid, res 603 n Saunders
Stunkel Miss Bertha, d Mrs Isabella, res same
Stunkel Miss Maria, d Mrs Isabella, res same, stenographer and typewriter
Stunkel Miss Emma, d Mrs Isabella, res same, saleslady at Royster's candy store
Stunkel Richard, son Mrs Isabella, res same
Stutts John B, weaver Caraleigh cot mill, bds with Jno A Deans
Sugg Miss Emma, house-girl for J A Lowery, res same
Suggs Miss Lizzie, seamstress, res Smithfield
Summerlin Jesse J, tobacconist, res 323 s Person
Summerlin Mrs Ellen, wife J J
Summerlin Miss Vivian L, d J J, res same, student
Summerville Melissa,* washerwoman, res 228 w Lenoir
Summerville John,* son Melissa, res same student

Sumner Mrs Annie, housekeeper, 313 s Dawson
Sutton J M, printer, res cor Salisbury and North
Sutton Miss Lillie, sister of J M, res same
Sutton W A, cigar-maker, res 119 Johnson
Sutton Mrs Amanda, wife W A
Sutton Fred, son W A, res same, cabinet-maker
Sutton Arthur, son W A, res same, wks Ral cot mill
Sutton Miss Mildred, d W A, res same, student
Sutton Miss Nannie, d W A, res same, student
Sutton Miss Mary L, d W A, res same, student
Sutton Alfred,* driver for Dr James McKee, res Brookside Park
Sutton Maggie,* wife Alfred, washerwoman
Sutton Julia,* d Alfred, res same
Sutton Maggie,* d Alfred, res same
Sutton J D, inmate Soldiers' Home
Swain D Shelly, letter-carrier, res 322 Oakwood ave
Swain Mrs D S, res 322 Oakwood ave
Swain Mrs Josie, wid, res 322 Oakwood ave
Sweeny Patrick, gardener, res 406 Cannon
Sweeny Mrs Bettie, wife Patrick
Swepson Mrs V B, wid, res 104 Hillsboro'
Swindell J L, wks at A & M College, res Hillsboro' rd
Swindell Mrs Annie L, wife J L
Swindell J L Jr, son J L, res same, student
Swindell Wm R, son J L, res same, student
Swindell Miss Fannie H, d J L, res same, student
Swindell Miss Parnie, d J L, res same, student
Swindell Mrs Emma, wid, res 305 Newbern ave
Swindell Charles, salesman, res 305 Newbern ave
Syme Mrs Anna S, wid, res cor Person and North
Syme Andrew, son Mrs Anna S, res same, clk S A L frt office
Syme Geo F, son Mrs Anna S, res same, student
Syme William A, son Mrs Anna S, res same, student
Syme John C, invalid, res with Mrs M E Anderson
Syme Mrs Mildred C, res with Mrs M E Anderson
Syme Maria,* cook for Dr H B Battle, res on lot

TANT Frank B, clk for J J Thomas & Co, res 412 e Hargett
Tant Miss Alice G, sister F B, res same, bookbinder
Tant Miss Hattie V, sister Frank B, res same
Tarpley W G, eng, res 304 n Person
Tarpley Mrs Lizzie, wife W G
Tate Robert,* janitor Shaw University, res 403 Smithfield
Tate Annie,* wife Robert
Tate Acey,* cook for N G Whitfield, res Hargett, o s e
Tate Annie,* washerwoman, res 118 w Cabarrus
Tate Jesse,* fish dealer, res 118 w Cabarrus

Tate James,* cook at Park Hotel, res 118 w Cabarrus
Tate Miss Bettie, house work, res 130 w Cabarrus
Tate Mrs Eliza, wid, res 214 w Cabarrus
Tate Walter, son Mrs Eliza, res same, wks Caraleigh mill
Tate Della,* washerwoman, res 118 w Davie
Tate Ceburn,* gardener, res 118 w Davie
TAYLOR W A, merchant tailor, 10 w Martin, res 116 Polk
Taylor Rose,* servant for M Bowes, res on lot
Taylor Charles,* carp, res 118 n Dawson
Taylor Lina,* wife Chas, washerwoman
Taylor Mary,* d Chas, res same, washerwoman
Taylor Cora,* d Chas, res same, washerwoman
Taylor Susan,* laundress, res 612 e Cabarrus
Taylor Carrie M,* d Susan, res same, servant
Taylor Jennie H,* d Susan, res same student
Taylor Susie A,* d Susan, res same, student
Taylor Reuben,* lab, res 710 s Saunders
Taylor Priscilla,* wife Reuben, house work
Taylor Daisy,* d Reuben, res same, student
Taylor Miss Emma, res with T B Womack
Taylor Ed L, mechanic, res n Salisbury
Taylor Mrs Dannie, wife Ed L
Taylor Miss Edna L, d Ed L, res same
Taylor Mrs R W, wid, res 558 Newbern ave
Taylor Miss Lula, d Mrs R W, res same, saleslady for W H & R S Tucker & Co
Taylor Angus, merchant tailor, res 116 Polk
Taylor Mrs Cornelia, wife Angus
Taylor W A, merchant tailor, res 116 Polk
TAYLOR WM T, tailor and grocer, Haywood, res e Hargett
Taylor Mrs Lanie, wife Wm T
Taylor Charles, son Wm T, res same, tailor app
Taylor Miss Mary, sister of Wm T, res same
Taylor John R, father of Wm T, res same, tailor
Taylor L D, merchant, 219 s Wilmington, res 313 s East
Taylor Mrs Rebecca J, wife L D
Taylor Miss Minnie L, d L D, res same, student
Taylor D L, son L D, res same, student
Taylor Jno W,* shoemaker, res 609 e Cabarrus
Taylor Jennie,* wife J W, washerwoman
Taylor Ella M,* d J W, res same, servant
Taylor Annie,* d J W, res same, student
Taylor Mary D,* d J W, res same, student
Taylor Lucy,* d J W, res same, student
Taylor Frank M,* son J W, res same
Taylor Lewis,* driver for Ferrall & Co, res 640 s McDowell
Taylor Willie,* son Lewis, res same, student
Taylor Lula,* d Lewis, res same, student

Taylor Thomas,* son Lewis, res same, student
Taylor Gabriel,* wood-cutter, res 742 s Person
Taylor Susan,* washerwoman, res Hayti
Taylor Archie,* son Susan, res same, lab
Taylor Robert,* lab, res 816 Manly
Taylor Mary,* wife Robt, washerwoman
Taylor Jennie,* d Robt, res same, student
Taylor Gertrude,* d Robt, res same, student
Taylor Alice,* washerwoman, res 315 e Lenoir
Taylor John,* son Alice, res same, farm hand
Taylor Alfred,* son Alice, res same, farm hand
Taylor Mary A.* cook, res 124 s Davie
Taylor Lydia,* washerwoman, res 712 s McDowell
Taylor Fred A,* son Lydia, res same, student
Taylor Wm A,* son Lydia, res same, student
Taylor John,* lab, res s e Davie
Taylor Mary,* g-d Isaac Clements, res same, student
Taylor Isaac,* g-s Isaac Clements, res same, student
Taylor Harmon,* painter, res 424 s Blount
Taylor Rena,* wife Harmon, washerwoman
Taylor Alice,* d Harmon, res same, cook
Taylor Mary,* d Harmon, res same, washerwoman
Taylor Sidney,* fireman S A L R R, res 117 w North
Taylor Mary,* wife Sidney, washerwoman
Taylor Susie,* d Sidney, res same, student
Taylor Thomas,* barber, 136 s Wilmington, res same
Taylor Ella,* wife Thomas, eating-house, 134 s Wilmington
Taylor Maggie,* cook for W W Smith, res on lot
Taylor Mary,* washerwoman, res 222 e Cabarrus
Taylor Rena,* washerwoman, res 424 s Blount
Taylor Mary,* d Rena, res same, washerwoman
Taylor Alice,* d Rena, res same, cook for C F Cook
Taylor Wm H,* fish dealer, res 511 s Blount
Taylor Kate,* wife Wm H
Taylor Mary A,* d Wm H, res same, washerwoman
Taylor Washington,* drayman, res 232 e South
Taylor Angeline,* wife Wash, cook colored Deaf and Dumb Asylum
Taylor Geo W,* son Wash, res same, clk James H Young
Taylor Jacob,* drayman, res e Davie, o s e
Taylor Emily,* wife Jacob, house work
Taylor Lucy,* d Jacob, res same, house work
Taylor Maggie,* d Jacob, res same, student
Taylor Ransom,* lab, res 712 s McDowell
Taylor Frances,* wife Ransom, washerwoman
Taylor Addie,* d Ransom, res same, student
Taylor Jessie,* d Ransom, res same, student
Taylor Jerry,* wks for city, res 562 Newbern ave

Tate James,* cook at Park Hotel, res 118 w Cabarrus
Tate Miss Bettie, house work, res 130 w Cabarrus
Tate Mrs Eliza, wid, res 214 w Cabarrus
Tate Walter, son Mrs Eliza, res same, wks Caraleigh mill
Tate Della,* washerwoman, res 118 w Davie
Tate Ceburn,* gardener, res 118 w Davie
TAYLOR W A, merchant tailor, 10 w Martin, res 116 Polk
Taylor Rose,* servant for M Bowes, res on lot
Taylor Charles,* carp, res 118 n Dawson
Taylor Lina,* wife Chas, washerwoman
Taylor Mary,* d Chas, res same, washerwoman
Taylor Cora,* d Chas, res same, washerwoman
Taylor Susan,* laundress, res 612 e Cabarrus
Taylor Carrie M,* d Susan, res same, servant
Taylor Jennie H,* d Susan, res same student
Taylor Susie A,* d Susan, res same, student
Taylor Reuben,* lab, res 710 s Saunders
Taylor Priscilla,* wife Reuben, house work
Taylor Daisy,* d Reuben, res same, student
Taylor Miss Emma, res with T B Womack
Taylor Ed L, mechanic, res n Salisbury
Taylor Mrs Dannie, wife Ed L
Taylor Miss Edna L, d Ed L, res same
Taylor Mrs R W, wid, res 558 Newbern ave
Taylor Miss Lula, d Mrs R W, res same, saleslady for W H & R S Tucker & Co
Taylor Angus, merchant tailor, res 116 Polk
Taylor Mrs Cornelia, wife Angus
Taylor W A, merchant tailor, res 116 Polk
TAYLOR WM T, tailor and grocer, Haywood, res e Hargett
Taylor Mrs Lanie, wife Wm T
Taylor Charles, son Wm T, res same, tailor app
Taylor Miss Mary, sister of Wm T, res same
Taylor John R, father of Wm T, res same, tailor
Taylor L D, merchant, 219 s Wilmington, res 313 s East
Taylor Mrs Rebecca J, wife L D
Taylor Miss Minnie L, d L D, res same, student
Taylor D L, son L D, res same, student
Taylor Jno W,* shoemaker, res 609 e Cabarrus
Taylor Jennie,* wife J W, washerwoman
Taylor Ella M,* d J W, res same, servant
Taylor Annie,* d J W, res same, student
Taylor Mary D,* d J W, res same, student
Taylor Lucy,* d J W, res same, student
Taylor Frank M,* son J W, res same
Taylor Lewis,* driver for Ferrall & Co, res 610 s McDowell
Taylor Willie,* son Lewis, res same, student
Taylor Lula,* d Lewis, res same, student

Taylor Thomas,* son Lewis, res same, student
Taylor Gabriel,* wood-cutter, res 742 s Person
Taylor Susan,* washerwoman, res Hayti
Taylor Archie,* son Susan, res same, lab
Taylor Robert,* lab, res 816 Manly
Taylor Mary,* wife Robt, washerwoman
Taylor Jennie,* d Robt, res same, student
Taylor Gertrude,* d Robt, res same, student
Taylor Alice,* washerwoman, res 315 e Lenoir
Taylor John,* son Alice, res same, farm hand
Taylor Alfred,* son Alice, res same, farm hand
Taylor Mary A,* cook, res 124 s Davie
Taylor Lydia,* washerwoman, res 712 s McDowell
Taylor Fred A,* son Lydia, res same, student
Taylor Wm A,* son Lydia, res same, student
Taylor John,* lab, res s e Davie
Taylor Mary,* g-d Isaac Clements, res same, student
Taylor Isaac,* g-s Isaac Clements, res same, student
Taylor Harmon,* painter, res 424 s Blount
Taylor Rena,* wife Harmon, washerwoman
Taylor Alice,* d Harmon, res same, cook
Taylor Mary,* d Harmon, res same, washerwoman
Taylor Sidney,* fireman S A L R R, res 117 w North
Taylor Mary,* wife Sidney, washerwoman
Taylor Susie,* d Sidney, res same, student
Taylor Thomas,* barber, 136 s Wilmington, res same
Taylor Ella,* wife Thomas, eating-house, 134 s Wilmington
Taylor Maggie,* cook for W W Smith, res on lot
Taylor Mary,* washerwoman, res 222 e Cabarrus
Taylor Rena,* washerwoman, res 424 s Blount
Taylor Mary,* d Rena, res same, washerwoman
Taylor Alice,* d Rena, res same, cook for C F Cook
Taylor Wm H,* fish dealer, res 511 s Blount
Taylor Kate,* wife Wm H
Taylor Mary A,* d Wm H, res same, washerwoman
Taylor Washington,* drayman, res 232 e South
Taylor Angeline,* wife Wash, cook colored Deaf and Dumb Asylum
Taylor Geo W,* son Wash, res same, clk James H Young
Taylor Jacob,* drayman, res e Davie, o s e
Taylor Emily,* wife Jacob, house work
Taylor Lucy,* d Jacob, res same, house work
Taylor Maggie,* d Jacob, res same, student
Taylor Ransom,* lab, res 712 s McDowell
Taylor Frances,* wife Ransom, washerwoman
Taylor Addie,* d Ransom, res same, student
Taylor Jessie,* d Ransom, res same, student
Taylor Jerry,* wks for city, res 562 Newbern ave

Taylor Jane,* wife Jerry, washerwoman
Taylor Roxanna,* d Jerry, res same, washerwoman
Taylor Clayton,* son Jerry, res same, shoemaker
Taylor Martha,* d Jerry, student
Taylor Mrs Eliza, wid, res with Mrs C F Lodge, 16 s Salisbury
Taylor Catherine,* cook for Mrs E C Jones, res same
Taylor James F, res with Charles M Busbee
Taylor Miss L N, lives with Charles M Busbee
Taylor Bettie,* washerwoman, res 423 n Salisbury
Taylor Ruflin,* porter for J P Wyatt & Co, bds Spencer Gill
Taylor Amanda,* washerwoman, res 563 e Cabarrus
Taylor Miss Annie, seamstress, res 534 e Cabarrus
Teachey J M, railroading, res 325 w Morgan
Teachey Mrs Carrie, wife J M
Teachey Miss Alma, d J M, res same, student
Teachey J M Jr, son J M, res same, student
Teachey J W, son J M, res same, student
Teasley Edward, cabinet-maker, res 119 s Dawson
Teasley Mrs Victoria, wife Edward, dressmaker
Teasley E E, clk, bds 326 Newbern ave
Tedder J L, machinist S A L R R, bds Exchange Hotel
Telfair Florence,* nurse, res Manly
Telfair Sam F, private sec to Gov of N C, bds 103 s McDowell
Telfair Mrs Mildred, wife Sam F
TEMPLE A H, gen mgr Glasgow Mantel and Tile Co, 122 Fayetteville, bds 109 s Blount
Temple Isham, cripple, res Fayetteville rd, o s s
Temple Leonard, son Isham, res same, wks Caraleigh cot mill
Temple Miss Alva, d Isham, res same, wks Caraleigh cot mill
Temple John, son Isham, res same, farm hand
Temple Miss Annie, d Isham, res same, hkpr
Temple Richard,* lab, res Martin, o s e
Temple Catherine,* washerwoman, res 406 w Edenton
Terrell S M, clk for Thos Pescud, res 514 e Hargett
Terrell Miss Linnie, d S M, res same, student
Terrell Miss Eldo, sister S M, res same

A. H. TEMPLE. A. F. TEMPLE.
GLASGOW MANTEL AND GRATE CO.,
MANUFACTURERS OF
SLATE, IRON and WOOD MANTELS and GRATES;
ALSO DEALERS IN
American and Imported Tiles for Floors, Vestibules, Hearths and Wainscoting.
FIRE-PLACE HEATERS A SPECIALTY.
GLASGOW, VA.
Branch House: Raleigh, N. C.

Terrell John R (Farker & Terrell), cot buyer, res 209 s Person
Terrell Miss Ida, sister John R, res same
Terrell Thos B, eng S A L, res 18 w Peace
Terrell Mrs Fannie L, wife T B
Terrell Thos F, son T B, res same, bkkpr
Terrell Miss Lizzie, d T B, res same, teacher
Terrell Miss Katie F, d T B, res same
Terrell Miss Fannie T, d T B, res same
Terrell Geo B, clk Agricultural dept, bds 207 n West
Terrell Mrs Fannie B, wife Geo B
Terrell Logan D, bds 207 n West
Terrell Mrs Mamie, wid, res 321 s Person
Terrell Miss Marjory, d Mrs Mamie, res same, student
Terrell Miss Marie, d Mrs Mamie, res same, student
Terrell Peter,* gardener, res 825 Manly
Terrell Edmund,* lab, res 806 Manly
Terrell Annie,* wife Edmund, washerwoman
Terrell Ora,* d Edmund, res same, washerwoman
Terrell Ralph,* lab, res 334 Cannon
Terrell Bettie,* wife Ralph, washerwoman
Terrell Millie,* d Ralph, res same, student
Terrell James,* son Ralph, res same, student
Terrell Jessie,* d Ralph, res same, student
Terrell Nellie, d Ralph, res same, student
Terrell Ada,* washerwoman, res 401 s Dawson
Terrell Annie,* washerwoman, res 728 e Davie, o s e
Terrell Eugene,* porter for J J Johnson, res 728 e Davie, o s e
Terrell W H,* blacksmith, res 612 s McDowell
Terrell Mary,* wife W H, house work
Terrell Lucy,* d W H, res same, student
Terrell Otis,* son W H, res same, student
Terrell Nancy,* washerwoman, res 726 Cannon
Terrell Wm D, wks Linnell laundry, res 125 e Hargett
Terry Mrs Julia A, wife Wm D
Terry Ashton, son Wm D, res same, student
Terry Miss Pearl, d Wm D, res same, student
Terry Turner, ins agt, res 413 s Blount
Terry Miss Kate M, sister Turner, res same, tailoress
Thacker Mrs Ann, saleslady W H & R S Tucker & Co, bds Yarboro' House
Thackston J W, gen mgr for the American Book Co, res cor Halifax and Franklin
Thackston Mrs A B, wife J W
Thackston Henry E, son J W, res same, student
Thackston James B, son J W, res same, student
Thackston Miss Roberta C, d J W, res same, student
Thackston John,* wks Caraleigh mill, res 825 Jenkins
Thackston Louise,* wife John

Thain A, inmate Soldiers' Home
Tharrington Benj,* porter Hicks & Rogers, res 110 e Lenoir
Tharrington Lucy,* wife Benj, dressmaker
THE ALLEN & CRAM MACHINE CO, machinists and founders, G M Allen, Mrs Helen Allen and W C Cram props
The A M E Church,* cor Edenton and n Harrington, Rev R H W Leak pastor
The Allen & Boyden Real Estate Agency, Pullen bldg
The Baptist Tabernacle, cor e Hargett and s Person, Rev Dr A M Simms pastor
The Biblical Recorder (weekly), organ of Baptist denomination, Edwards & Broughton owners, J W Bailey editor, 17 w Hargett
The Brooklin M E Church, northwest city limits, Rev R H Whitaker pastor
The Board of Missions and Baptist Book Store of the N C Baptist State Convention, Rev John E White cor sec, Rev B W Spillman Sunday-school missionary, 113 Fayetteville
The Blount-Street Baptist Church,* cor s Blount and Cabarrus, Rev Freeman Howell pastor
The Baltimore Immediate Benefit Association, 332 Fayetteville, S H Beam supt
The Capital Hose Company, w Morgan, W A Lineham foreman, Wm Allcott sec
The Central M E Church, cor Morgan and Person, Rev D H Tuttle pastor
The County Board of Health, Dr P E Hines pres
The Caraleigh Cotton Mill, South Raleigh, J J Thomas pres, Dr D E Everett vice-pres, F O Moring sec and treas, H C Butler supt
The Caraleigh Phosphate and Fertilizer Company, South Raleigh, J R Chamberlain pres, A Horne vice-pres, A L Chamberlain sec and treas, C H Kayler, supt
The City Hall, offices of the city, Fayetteville through to Wilmington
The Citizens National Bank, 239 Fayetteville, Jos G Brown pres, Henry E Litchford cashier, W W Robards teller
The City Shaving Saloon, 211 s Wilmington, Brittian Pierce proprietor
The Central Hotel, cor s Wilmington and e Hargett, H J Dowell proprietor
THE COMMERCIAL AND FARMERS BANK, cor e Martin and south Wilmington, J J Thomas pres, B S Jerman cashier, H W Jackson asst cashier and teller, capital stock $100,000
THE CITY LIVERY STABLES, e Morgan, near cor s Blount, E M Martin proprietor
The Centennial Graded School, cor Fayetteville and South, Prof Logan D Howell supt

The Christian Sun (weekly), organ of the Christian Church South, Emmett L Moffitt editor and prop
The City Market, City Hall bldg, on Fayetteville
The Christian Church,* old Fair Ground, o s e, Rev Wm Williams* pastor
THE CAPITAL PRINTING CO, Academy of Music bldg, w Martin, Guy V Barnes pres, R E Barnes vice-pres, Z P Smith sec & treas
The Christian Church, cor Hillsboro' and Dawson, Rev J L Foster pastor
The Caucasian (weekly newspaper), published by Caucasian Publishing Co, H W Ayer editor, office 334 Fayetteville
The Capital Club, Fayetteville, Henry bldg, Dr James McKee pres, Col A B Andrews vice-pres, S F Telfair sec, John A Duncan treas
The Davie-Street Presbyterian Church, Rev A G Davis* pastor
The Dawson-Street Baptist Church,* Wm Atwater deacon
The Edenton-Street Methodist Church, bet Dawson and McDowell near cor Dawson, Rev Dr W C Norman pastor
The East Martin Baptist Church,* Rev A R Price* pastor
The Farmers Warehouse, for sale of leaf tobacco, cor s Bloodworth and Davie, Williamson & Lea props
The First Baptist Church,* n Salisbury, Rev J J Worlds pastor
The Farina Roller Mills Company, near N C R R crossing, John A Mills pres, S A Johnson sec and treas
The First Baptist Church, cor Salisbury and Edenton, Rev Dr J W Carter pastor
The First Presbyterian Church, cor Morgan and Salisbury, Rev Dr Eugene Daniels pastor
The Governor's Guard (military) Armory, Brigg's building, Fred Woollcott captain, J F Jordan first lieutenant, A J Crawford second lieutenant
The Gazette newspaper (weekly), office over Jas I Johnson's drug store, Jas H Young* editor and proprietor
The Garfield Graded School,* Swain bet Davie and Martin, Chas N Hunter* prin
The Mechanics Dime Savings Bank, 117 Fayetteville, C E Johnson pres, B R Lacy cashier
The Murphy Graded School, cor Person and Polk, Logan D Howell supt, Miss Eliza Pool prin
THE MILLS MANUFACTURING CO, wagons, bldg material, &c, John A Mills pres, J A Jones sec and treas, shops Fayetteville-st crossing of N C R R
The Manly-Street Christian Church,* Rev Alex A Bright* pastor
The N C Department of Agriculture, offices in Agricultural building, cor Halifax and w Edenton, S L Patterson commissioner, T K Bruner sec
The N C Geological Survey, office in the Agricultural bldg, J A Holmes State geologist

The N C Board of R R Commissioners, office in Agricultural bldg, J W Wilson, E C Beddingfield and S Otho Wilson commissioners, Henry C Brown clk

The N C State Museum, in Agricultural bldg, H H Brimley curator

The N C Institution for the Blind, the block bet Jones, Lane, Dawson and McDowell, W J Young prin

THE N C HOME INS CO, office over Briggs & Sons' hardware store, W S Primrose pres, Chas Root sec and treas, P Cowper adjuster

The N C Agricultural Society, 6½ w Martin, John Nichols sec and treas

The N C Soldiers' Home, Newbern ave, Col A B Andrews pres, Wm C Stronach business mgr, Capt J H Fuller supt

The N C Deaf, Dumb and Blind Institution for the Colored, 605 s Bloodworth, Prof A W Pegues supervisor

THE N C BUILDING AND SUPPLY CO, builders and contractors, shops n West, W J Hicks pres, W J Ellington sec and treas

The N C Phosphate Co, wks at Castle Hayne, N C, office cor Fayetteville and e Davie, C M Hawkins pres, B S Jerman sec and treas

The N C Cotton-Oil and Fertilizer Co, mill cor Davie and Harrington, office 11 w Hargett, R F Monroe pres, Garland Jones sec and treas

The N C Insane Asylum, near city limits, Dr Geo L Kirby supt, Wm R Crawford Jr steward, Mrs M A Whitaker matron

The N C Penitentiary, near city limits, A Leazar mgr, Dr J W McGee Sr physician, Jos J Bernard clk

THE N C CAR CO, Franklin near r r, mfrs of iron castings and building material, R F Hoke pres, Jno Ward sec and treas, W E Ashley supt

The North State Trouser Co, mfrs, 216½ Fayetteville, Winston & Barbee props

THE NATIONAL BANK OF RALEIGH, cor w Hargett and Fayetteville, C H Belvin pres, C E Johnson vice-pres, F H

The following is our Line:

Gold Plating,   Brass Finishing,
  Silver Plating,   Burnishing,
   Nickel Plating,   Lacquering,
    Copper Plating,   Oxidizing.

All kinds of old work done over as good as new. Specialty of Re-plating Tableware, Bicycle work, Surgical Instruments, etc. We guarantee the best work that can be done. Send us your orders. Write us.

FOLSOM, FINGER & CO.,
Electro-Platers and Manufacturers of Highest-Grade Silver-Plated Ware,
SALISBURY, N. C.

Briggs cashier, Julian Timberlake teller, Charles D Jones collector

The New York Bazaar, dry goods, millinery, &c, 211 Fayetteville, I Rosenthal prop

The News and Observer (newspaper), office 413 Fayetteville, Josephus Daniels editor, W E Christian, J Wilbur Jenkins and F L Merritt asst editors, H B Hardy and W M Rogers trav agts

The News and Observer Publishing Co, 413 Fayetteville, Josephus Daniels pres, F B Arendell bus mgr, W P Whitaker cashier and bkkpr

The Outlook (newspaper), Rev R H W Leak* editor, office 16 s Salisbury

THE PARK HOTEL, w Martin, Brown & Crawford props

THE PEACE INSTITUTE (Presbyterian School), Prof James Dinwiddie pres and prin

The Postal Telegraph and Cable Co, 11 e Martin, W J Crews mgr

The Pilot Cotton Mill, North Raleigh, James N & W H Williamson owners

The Progressive Farmer (weekly newspaper), office Ral Savings Bank bldg, John L Ramsey editor

The Primitive Baptist Church, cor Morgan and Dawson

The Presbyterian Mission Room, cor North and McDowell

THE PRESS-VISITOR (afternoon daily), published by Press-Visitor Publishing Co, office 334 Fayetteville, Greek O Andrews editor, T J Pence city editor

The Peter Stumpf Brewing Co, bottlers, &c, 204 e Martin, W C Hudgins agt

The Raleigh Plate Ice Factory, s West, Jones & Powell props

The Raleigh Board of Health, Dr James McKee pres

The Raleigh Ice and Refrigerating Co, w Hargett

The Raleigh Gas Co, office 334 Fayetteville, B P Williamson pres

The Raleigh Cotton Mill, near Ral and Gaston R R shop, C G Latta pres, C E Johnson vice-pres, J S Wynne sec and treas, H B Greason supt

THE RALEIGH SAVINGS BANK, cor Fayetteville and e Hargett, W C Stronach pres, Jno T Pullen cashier, Jas O Litchford teller

The Raleigh Coffin Co, coffins and caskets, 128 s Wilmington, G A Strickland mgr

The Raleigh Water Co, office at water tower, 115 w Morgan, Julius Lewis pres, A A Thompson vice-pres, A M McPheeters Jr sec and Supt, F H Briggs treas

The Rescue Hose and Fire-Engine Co, Fayetteville, R E Lumsden foreman, W A Faucette sec

THE RALEIGH STATIONERY CO, 309 Fayetteville, mfg stationers, blank books, typewriters and supplies, W G Separk mgr

The Raleigh Male Academy, Morson & Denson principals
The Raleigh Electric Co, cor w Jones and n West, Alf A Thompson pres, Chas C Johnson sec and supt, F H Briggs treas
The Rex Hospital, 17 w South, Miss Maggie McLester matron
THE SHAW UNIVERSITY, cor s Wilmington and e South, Chas F Meserve, A M, pres, J Greenwood Snelling of New York treas, C W Jewett asst treas and sec
The St Paul A M E Church, n Harrington, Rev R H W Leak pastor
THE ST MARY'S SCHOOL, Rev Dr Bennett Smedes rector and prin
The Supreme Court of North Carolina, in Supreme Court bldg, cor w Edenton and n Salisbury, Wm T Faircloth chief-justice, A C Avery, Walter Clark, D M Furches and W A Montgomery associate justices, Thomas S Kenan clk
The Seaboard Air-Line Ticket Office, in Yarborough House bldg, H S Leard soliciting frt and passenger agt
The Southern Railway Office, Yarborough House bldg
The Yarborough House Saloon, Levy Walker proprietor
The Standard Oil Company, n Harrington, J A Hinnant agt
THE STAUNTON LIFE INSURANCE CO, of Staunton, Va, office over 304 Fayetteville, J J Hayes State agt
The Singer Sewing Machine Office, 115 Fayetteville, R L Green mgr
The U S Internal Revenue Service, offices in U S bldg, F M Simmons collector
The U S Circuit and District Court Room, U S bldg, A S Seymour district judge
The U S Post-Office, cor Fayetteville and e Martin, Chas M Busbee P M
The U S Marshal's Office, U S bldg, O J Carroll marshal of Eastern District of N C
The Victor Hose Company,* Salisbury and Davie, T B Burgess foreman, John Taylor sec
The Washington Graded School,* H S Christmas prin
The Walter R Womble Hook-and-Ladder Co, w Morgan, W W Parish foreman
The Western Union Tel Co, 328 Fayetteville, J A Egerton mgr
THE YARBOROUGH HOUSE, 319 Fayetteville, L T Brown proprietor
The Young Men's Christian Association, cor Fayetteville and Morgan, W H Overton sec
The Zion Methodist Church,* e Cabarrus, Rev H P Walker* pastor
Thiem Phil, accountant and bkkpr, res 311 w Jones
Thiem Mrs Annie, wife Phil
Thiem Miss Gertie, d Phil, res same
Thiem Edgar, son Phil, res same, clk Woollcott & Son
Thiem LeRoy, son Phil, res same, tel opr

Thiem John, son Phil, res same, student
Thiem James, son Phil, res same, student
Thiem Miss Erma, d Phil, res same
Thiem Phil Jr, clk for M Rosenthal, res 311 w Jones
Thomas Capt J J, cot broker, res cor Jones and McDowell
Thomas Mrs Lula, wife J J
Thomas Miss Evie B, d J J, res same
Thomas James, son J J, res same, student
THOMAS & MAXWELL, furniture dealers, 9 and 12 e Martin and 10 Exchange Place
Thomas Archie,* wks for Ral Gas Co, res cor West and Edenton
Thomas Lovie,* teacher, res cor n West and w Edenton
Thomas Iola, seamstress, res 213 e Cabarrus
Thomas Howard, bkkpr, res with sister, Mrs B T McAden
Thomas Judson,* wks Latta & Hunter, res e Jones, Idlewild
Thomas Eliza,* wife Judson, washerwoman
Thomas Renie,* son Judson, res same, student
Thomas Geo,* wks Ed Price, city market, res 513 Newbern ave
Thomas Burke,* butcher, wks W R Crawford & Son, r 513 Newbern ave
Thomas Mary,* wife Burke, nurse James A Briggs
Thomas Percy, brother of Mrs John A Duke, res same, student
Thomas Lena,* washerwoman, res 116 w South
Thomas Fannie,* house-servant, res 909 Manly
Thomas Beulah,* d Fannie, res same, student
Thomas Geo,* son Fannie, res same, student
Thomas Wiley,* lab, res 909 Manly
Thomas Sarah,* house-servant, res Whitaker ave
Thomas Wm, wks at Caraleigh mill, res 711 s West
Thomas Mrs Bettie, wife Wm, wks Caraleigh mill
Thomas Alice,* washerwoman, res 318 s Harrington
Thomas Louisa,* washerwoman, res 318 s Harrington
Thomas Robert,* son Alice, res same, student
Thomas A J (Darnell & Thomas), music dealer, res 318 s Dawson
Thomas Mrs Jessie, wife A J
Thomas Miss Louisa J, d A J, res same, student

A. S. THOMAS.   T. R. MAXWELL.   S. A. CAMPBELL.

GO TO The Double Stores,
Nos. 9 and 12 Martin Street,
THOMAS, MAXWELL & CO.,
———FOR ALL KINDS OF———
Furniture and House-Fitting Supplies.

The largest stock and the greatest variety at the lowest prices on easy terms. Stoves, Carpets, Mattings, Trunks, Clocks, Rugs, Lamps, Shades, etc., and everything kept in a first-class Furniture Store.

Thomas Shelburn, son A J, res same, student
Thomas S A, carp, res 720 s Saunders
Thomas Mrs Louisa B, wife S A
Thomas Miss Vela, d S A, res same, student
Thomas Frank L, son S A, res same, student
Thomas Miss Repsie R, d S A, res same, student
Thomas Ether, inmate Soldiers' Home
Thomas Alice,* chambermaid, res 726 Manly
Thomas Elias,* cook at Insane Asylum, res 521 Cannon
Thomas Martha,* wife Elias, house work
Thomas Mamie,* d Elias, res same, student
Thomas Mattie,* d Elias, res same, student
Thomas Annie,* d Elias, res same, student
Thomas Lizzie,* cook for C B Denson, res e Edenton
Thomas E B, bkkpr, res 102 w Lane
Thomas Mrs N R, wife B
Thomas Chas R, printer Edwards & Broughton, bds 426 s Wilmington
Thomason William, driver for Royall & Borden, bds 117 e Davie
Thomason James,* fireman S A L R R, bds 205 w North
Thomason Willie, clk for Royall & Borden, bds 110 n Saunders
Thomason Miss Annie, seamstress, res 545 e Martin
Thomason Miss Martha, seamstress, res 545 e Martin
Thomason Mrs Mary, wid, res 545 e Martin
Thompson R T, painter and moulder, res 554 e Davie
Thompson Mrs Winnie, wife R T
Thompson Frank L, son R T, res same, painter
Thompson John, son R T, res same, student
Thompson R T Jr, son R T, res same, student
Thompson Silvia,* washerwoman, res 526 e Martin
Thompson Ella,* d Silvia, res same, washerwoman
Thompson Fred,* son Silvia, res same, shoemaker
Thompson Alf A, cot broker, res 317 Newbern ave
Thompson Mrs Laura C, wife Alf A
Thompson Alfred M, son Alf A, res same, student
Thompson Robert, son Alf A, res same, student
Thompson Hugh A, son Alf A, res same, student
Thompson Miss Mary C, d Alf A, res same
Thompson William,* brick-mason, res bet Davie and Hargett, o s e
Thompson Penny,* wife Wm, laundress
Thompson Lillie,* d Wm, res same, student
Thompson Mrs Annie, seamstress, res 316 Cannon
Thompson Miss Bessie, d Mrs Annie, res same, student
Thompson Rev Z B,* Missionary Baptist minister, res 716 Fayetteville
Thompson Dora C,* wife Rev Z B, house work
Thompson Monroe, farmer, res Fayetteville, below R R
Thompson Mrs Nora, wife Monroe

Thompson Miss Columbia, d Monroe, res same, spinner
Thompson Miss Julia, d Monroe, res same, spinner
Thompson Willis, son Monroe, res same, student
Thompson Walter, son Monroe, res same, student
Thompson Mrs Susan, seamstress, res cor Davie and East
Thompson Miss Pattie, d Mrs Susan, res same
Thompson Miss Belle, seamstress, bds 520 s Harrington
Thompson Alfred,* wood-sawyer, res 836 s Wilmington
Thompson Rachel,* wife Alfred, washerwoman
Thompson John,* son Alfred, res same, lab
Thompson Gertrude,* d Alfred, res same, servant
Thompson William, inmate Soldiers' Home
Thompson Ella,* washerwoman, res 525 e Edenton
Thompson Moses,* shoemaker, s Wilmington, res e Hargett, o s e
Thompson Mary,* wife Moses, washerwoman
Thompson Manuel,* son Moses, res same, shoemaker
Thompson Joanna,* d Moses, res same, student
Thompson Mary E,* d Moses, res same, student
Thompson Anna,* d Moses, res same, student
Thompson William,* son Moses, res same, student
Thompson Geo W, cashier Commercial and Farmers Bank, res 116 w Martin
Thompson Mrs Rosa, wife Geo W
Thompson Steadman, son Geo W, res same
Thompson Miss Katherine, d Geo W, res same
Thompson Cornelius, machinist, res 410 w North
Thompson Miss Roena, sister Cornelius, res same
Thompson Jno W, trav salesman, res 424 Halifax
Thompson Mrs Sallie, wife Jno W
Thompson Miss Daisy, d Jno W, res same
Thompson Miss Lillian, d Jno W, res same
Thompson Herbert, son Jno W, res same, stenographer and typewriter
Thompson John, son Jno W, res same, clk for Eberhart & Baker
Thompson Frank, son Jno W, res same, student
Thompson Moses,* shoemaker, 103 s Wilmington
Thompson David,* driver for Dr P E Hines, res 106 e Cabarrus
Thompson Annie,* wife David, washerwoman
Thompson Martin, city policeman, res 306 n West
Thompson Mrs Emily, wife Martin
Thompson Miss Ella, d Martin, res same, saleslady for Barbee & Pope
Thompson Miss Bettie, d Martin, res same
Thompson Miss Beulah, d Martin, res same, wks for Smith, Faison & Co
Thompson Miss Emma, d Martin, res same
Thompson Miss Gertie, d Martin, res same, student
Thompson Miss May, d Martin, res same, student

Thompson Fred, shoemaker, 108½ e Hargett, res 526 e Martin
Thompson John D, blacksmith, res 218 s Bloodworth
Thompson Mrs Melissa C, wife John D
Thompson Charles,* cot worker, res 324 e Martin
Thompson Mary,* wife Charles, washerwoman
Thompson Florence,* d Charles, res same, student
Thompson Lizzie,* cook for Mrs L L Polk, res on lot
Thompson Robena,* servant at Mrs R S Tucker's, res on lot
Thornton Cato,* house-servant S A Ashe, res 106 e Cabarrus
Thornton Caroline,* wife Cato, cook for Dave Rosenthal
Thornton Willie,* son Cato, res same
Thornton Alonzo,* son Cato, res same, tobacco worker
Thornton Cato Jr,* tailor, res 106 e Cabarrus
Thornton Katie,* d Cato, res same, student
Thornton Thomas,* son Cato, res same, student
Thornton Bettie,* servant, res Idlewild
Thornton Wiley T, porter I Rosenthal, res Idlewild
Thorpe Charles,* tobacco worker, res Smith
Thorpe Maggie,* wife Charles, washerwoman
Thorpe Susan,* cook for A J Jones, res 314 n Dawson
Tighe Mrs Mary J, wid, res 803 n Dawson
Tighe Michael W, son Mrs Mary J, res same, eng S A L
Tighe Frank, son Mrs Mary J, res same, invalid
Tighe Miss Mary J, d Mrs Mary J, res same, dressmaker
Tighe Miss Maggie, d Mrs Mary J, res same, milliner
Tighe Miss Kate, d Mrs Mary J, res same
Tillinghast Thos H, teacher in Colored Deaf and Dumb Asylum
    res 426 n Bloodworth
Tillinghast Mrs Mary, wife T H
Tillinghast Miss Susie, d T H, res same, student
Tillman Miss Lovie, lives with Wm R Blake
Tilley James,* lab, res 225 e Lane
Tilley Albert,* lab, res 225 e Lane
Timberlake Capt J B, ticket agt S A L R R, res 116 w Jones
Timberlake Mrs J W, wife Capt J B
Timberlake Miss Susie, d Capt J B, res same
Timberlake Miss Mamie, d Capt J B, res same
Timberlake Miss Estelle, d Capt J B, res same
Timberlake J B Jr, teller of Nat'l Bank of Ral, r 113 n Blount
Timberlake Mrs Agnes, wife J B Jr
Todd Georgiana,* washerwoman, res Shaffer's field
Todd Nettie,* d Georgiana, res same, student
Tollith W R, clk to master mechanic S A L R R, bds 104 n
    McDowell
Tomlinson Hubert, step-son C J Hunter, res same, student
Toney Clara, seamstress, res Watson
Toney Nathan,* shoemaker, shop 318 s Salisbury, res 16 n East
Toney Lucy,* wife Nathan

Toney Charles,* shoemaker, res 16 n East
Toney Henry,* son Nathan, res same
Tonnoffski Geo L (C H Beine & Co), auctioneer, res 321 s Person
Tonnoffski Miss Lollie, d Geo L, res same, student
Tonnoffski Miss Mamie, d Geo L, res same, student
Tonnoffski Miss Josie, d Geo L, res same, student
Towles Miss Sallie, res with J M Monie
Townes Sam,* butler Dr T E Skinner, res e Lenoir
Townes Ida,* wife Sam
Townes Sallie,* d Sam, res same, student
Townes Frances,* seamstress, res 116 e Lenoir
Townes Silas,* mail-carrier, res s West
Townes Susan,* wife Silas
Townes Edward,* son Silas, res same, student
Townes Zach,* son Silas, res same, student
Trainer Lucy,* cook, rooms up-stairs 116 e Morgan
Trapier E S, wks S A L R R, res 120 n Saunders
Trapier Mrs Gertrude H, wife E S
Trapier Windham C, son E S, res same, student
Trapier Miss Margaret H, d E S, res same, student
Trapier Miss Jennie G, d E S, res same, student
Trapier Miss Elizabeth G, d E S, res same, student
Trice Martha,* cook, res 1 Johnson ave
Trice Ernest,* son Martha, res same, lab
Trice James,* son Martha, res same, lab
Trice Charles,* son Martha, res same, errand-boy
Trice Alfonzo,* son Martha, farm hand
Trice Roxie,* d Martha, res same, student
Trice Eliza,* sick-nurse, res 307 w Lenoir
Trimble Miss Mollie, res 522 e Davie
Trisband Eliza,* servant for Dr James McKee, res on lot
Tucker W H & R S, wholesale and retail dealers in dry goods, notions, carpets, &c, 123 and 125 Fayetteville, 124 and 126 s Wilmington
Tucker Mrs M E, wid, res cor Newbern ave and Person
Tucker Walter C, son Mrs M E, res same, trav salesman
Tucker C D, son Mrs M E, res same, clk for G S Tucker & Co
Tucker Garland S (G S Tucker & Co), furniture dealer, res cor Newbern ave and Person
Tucker Miss Minnie K, d Mrs M E, res same
Tucker Henry McKee, son Mrs M E, res same, medical student
Tucker Miss Lillie M, d Mrs M E, res same
Tucker Miss Susie, d Mrs M E, res same, student
Tucker Mrs R S, wid, res cor Hillsboro' and St Mary's
Tucker Miss Bessie, d Mrs R S, res same
Tucker Miss Sadie, d Mrs R S, res same
Tucker Miss Minnie F, d Mrs R S, res same, student
Tucker W T, paymaster S A L R R, res 519 n Blount

Tucker Mrs India V, wife W T
Tucker Miss Rebecca P, d W T, res same
Tucker J A, night clk Park Hotel, res same
Tucker G S & Co, furniture dealers, 128 e Martin
Tucker Eli,* lab, res old Fair Ground, o s e
Tucker Jennie,* d Eli, res same, washerwoman
Tucker Mary,* d Eli, res same, cook
Tucker Laura,* d Eli, res same, nurse
Tucker Emma,* d Eli, res same, student
Tucker Wm,* son Eli, res same, student
Tucker Richard,* son Eli, res same, student
Tucker Eli Jr,* son Eli, res same, student
Tucker Wm R, real est broker, office 226 Fayetteville, res 503 n Person
Tucker Mrs Gertrude, wife W R
Tucker Mary,* cook, res old Fair Ground, o s e
Tucker Lula,* d Mary, res same, cook
Tucker Van,* sexton Church of Good Shepherds, res 118 w Lenoir
Tucker Betsy,* wife Van, house work
Tucker Caroline,* house-servant for Mrs R B Haywood, res 112 n Swain
Tucker Hattie,* d Caroline, res same, servant
Tucker Claudia,* d Caroline, res same, student
Tucker William,* house servant for A B Andrews, res on lot
Tucker Robert,* servant for A B Andrews, res on lot
Tucker Armistead,* lab, res Martin, o s e
Tucker Mrs Chas J, wid, res with Wayne Allcott
Tucker Van,* servant at Rev Dr I McK Pittinger, res same
Tucker Wm W, conductor Ral street railway, res Hillsboro' rd
Tucker Mrs Ella, wife Wm W
Tucker Wm B, son Wm W, res same, student
Turbeville Graham J, printer, res 403 s Blount
Turbeville Mrs Susan, wife Graham J
Turner Dr V E, surg dentist, 107½ Fayetteville, res 210 n Person
Turner Mrs L G, wife Dr V E
Turner Chas R, son Dr V E, res same, dental student
Turner Miss Mary A, d Dr V E, res same, student
Turner Henry G, son Dr V E, res same, student
Turner J D, grocer, 447 Halifax, res same
Turner Alex,* wks for W C Stronach, res s Swain
Turner Ellen,* wife Alex, washerwoman
Turner Isabella,* d Alex, res same, cook
Turner Willie,* son Alex, res same, house-servant
Turner Ida,* d Alex, res same, student
Turner Mamie,* d Alex, res same, student
Turner Sophronia,* laundress, res 755 e Davie, o s e
Turner Jesse* lab, res 540 e Cabarrus
Turner Mary,* servant, res 224 Blount-st al

Turner Amanda,* chambermaid for Dr Hubert Haywood, res 551 e Edenton
Turner Chas,* waiter at Park Hotel, res 551 e Edenton
Turner Maggie,* nurse for Dr Hubert Haywood, r 551 e Edenton
Turner Edom,* adopted son Robert Hunter, res same
Turner Mrs R E, wid, res with W W Wynne
Turner Wm,* city hand, res 16 Fowle
Turner Henrietta,* wife Wm, house work
Turner Hattie,* d Wm, res same
Turner Adeline,* cook, res 523 Haywood
Turner Jennie,* cook, res 523 Haywood
Turner Bud,* son Adeline, res same, lab
Turner Pattie,* servant for C E Johnson, res on lot
Turner Lizzie,* servant for C E Johnson, res on lot
Turner W C, ins agt, bds 217 s West
Turner Phœbe,* carpet seamstress for W H & R S Tucker, res Cotton lane, o s e
Turner Manuel,* lab, res 414 e Martin
Turner Miss Carrie, attendant at Insane Asylum, res same
Turner Miss Mamie, attendant at Insane Asylum, res same
Turner Phœbe,* house-servant, res 418 e Martin
Turner James,* hackman, res 418 e Martin
Turner Eliza,* washerwoman, res e Davie
TUTTLE Rev D H, pastor Central Methodist church, res 221 e Morgan
Tuttle Mrs Ella, wife D H
Tuttle Miss Emeth, d Rev D H, res same, student
Tuttle Miss Cary, d Rev D H, res same
Tuttle Herndon W, son Rev D H, res same
Twitty Frank,* butler at Park Hotel, res 117 w Lenoir
Twitty Placide,* wife Frank, house work
Twitty Fannie,* nurse for Chn Lee, res 112 e Morgan
Tyler Helen,* cook for Jno A Bashford, res Idlewild
Tyler John,* son Helen, res same
Tyson W M, carp, res e Martin
Tyson Mrs Virginia, wife W M
Tyson Mrs Margaret, wid, res with Paul Lee

UELTSCHI Jacob, 2d asst boss Ral cot mill, r 715 n Salisbury
Ueltschi Mrs Lillie, wife Jacob
Underwood Jas E, eng at water-works, res 522 s Salisbury
Underwood Mrs Sallie, wife J E
Underwood Miss Placide H, d J E, res same, student
Underwood Miss Mary C, d J E, res same, student
Underwood Miss Myrtle A, d J E, res same, student
United States Court-House and Post-Office, cor Fayetteville and Martin, F M Simmons custodian, Chas M Busbee P M

Upchurch Mrs E M, wid, res 219 s McDowell
Upchurch Delmar D, son Mrs E M, res same, bkkpr at Ral Nat'l Bank
Upchurch Miss Belle W, d Mrs E M, res same
Upchurch W G, son Mrs E M, res same, clk for W C Stronach & Son
Upchurch Miss Eulah G, d Mrs E M, res same, student
Upchurch Miss Sadie R, d Mrs E M, res same, student
Upchurch Dr Harvey C, physician and surgeon, office and res 219 s McDowell
Upchurch Mrs Annie S, wife Dr H C
Upchurch W G, cot mill opr, res 532 n West
Upchurch Mrs Annie, wife W G
Upchurch Miss Candace, d W G, res same, wks Ral cot mill
Upchurch Miss Nelia, d W G, res same, wks Ral cot mill
Upchurch John, son W G, res same, wks Ral cot mill
Upchurch Ernest, son W G, res same, student
Upchurch Miss Retha, d W G, res same, student
Upchurch Miss Neva, d W G, res same, student
Upchurch Miss Nellie, d W G, res same, student
Upchurch Virginia,* washerwoman, res 407 w Edenton
Upchurch Lillie,* d Virginia, res same, washerwoman
Upchurch Frank,* son Virginia, res same, lab
Upchurch Mattie,* d Virginia, res same, servant
Upchurch Lovie,* d Virginia, res same, servant
Upchurch James, saloon clk, res 219 Smithfield
Upchurch Mrs Bettie, wife James
Upchurch Sallie,* cook for John W Brown, res e Hargett, o s c
Upchurch Beulah,* d Sallie, res same, student
Upchurch Charlie,* son Sallie, res same, student
Upchurch Minnie,* d Sallie, res same, student
Upchurch W D Jr, saloon, 215 s Wilmington, res 504 s Bloodworth
Upchurch William C, retired merchant, res 107 s Wilmington
Upchurch Vernon S, clk, res 107 s Wilmington
Upchurch John R, constable, res 319 e Cabarrus

UNIVERSITY PUBLISHING COMPANY,
43, 45, 47 East 10th Street, NEW YORK.

STANDARD SCHOOL-BOOKS. Holmes' Readers, Maury's Geographies, Sanford's Arithmetics, Fuiger's Civil Government, Hansell's (Chambers') Histories of U. S.

Write to W. B. KENDRICK, Gen'l Agent, Raleigh, N. C.

Upchurch Mrs Emma N, wife John R
Upchurch Miss Hallie E, d John R, res same, dressmaker
Upchurch Miss Nannie J, d John R, res same, student
Upchurch Ira G, son John R, res same, student
Upchurch Ada G, d John R, res same, student
Upchurch Alfred, wheelwright, res 320 e Hargett
Upchurch Mrs Ann E, wife Alfred
Upchurch Miss Placide, d Alfred, res same, student
Upchurch Mrs F J, wid, res 214 e Davie
Upchurch Robt G, son Mrs F J, res same, clk Royster candy factory
Upchurch Homer F, son Mrs F J, conductor Ral Elec Ry Co
Upchurch Miss B N, d Mrs F J, res same, seamstress
Upchurch Mrs C W, dressmaker, res 314 e Hargett
Upchurch C W, sewing machine agt, res 314 e Hargett
Upchurch Herman, pressman Edwards & Broughton, res 410 e Hargett
Upchurch Mrs Kate R, wife Herman
Upchurch Mrs A D, wid, res 717 n Person
Upchurch Walter, son Mrs A D, res same, farmer
Upchurch Julius, son Mrs A D, res same, spinner Ral cot mill
Upchurch Charles, son Mrs A D, res same, spinner Ral cot mill
Upchurch Nathan, tinner app, res 717 n Blount
Upchurch Mrs Annie, wife Nathan
Upchurch Mary,* washerwoman, res 406 w Jones
Upchurch Myra J,* d Mary, res same, washerwoman
Upchurch Ella M,* d Mary, res same, servant
Upchurch B W, grocer, 15 e Hargett, res 228 e Martin
Upchurch Mrs Mamie I, wife B W
Upchurch A P, cotton buyer for Ed H Lee, res 223 e Hargett
Upchurch Mrs Sarah M, wife A P
Upchurch Oris K, son A P, res same, clk for Sherwood & Co
Upchurch Miss Luta, d A P, res same, saleslady for Woollcott & Son
Upchurch Miss Iva, d A P, res same, student
Upchurch Miss Allie, d A P, res same, student
Upchurch Walter, son A P, res same, student
Upchurch Wm W, clk S A L, res 413 Oakwood ave
Upchurch Mrs Annie, wife W W
Upchurch Ed B, son W W, res same, moulder
Upchurch Miss Minnie A, d W W, res same
Upchurch Alfred H, son W W, messenger Postal Tel Co
Upchurch Miss Gertrude M, d W W, res same, student
Upchurch James N, son W W, res same, student
Upchurch W D, real estate, res 504 s Bloodworth
Upchurch Mrs Emily H, wife W D
Upchurch Mingo,* wks at ice factory, res rear 405 s Dawson
Upchurch Jennie,* wife Mingo, washerwoman

Upchurch Willie,* son Mingo, res same, student
Upchurch Geo C, city policeman, res 218 s Swain
Upchurch Mrs Virginia B, wife Geo C
Upperman Lizzie,* washerwoman, res 814 Manly
Upperman William,* son Lizzie, res same, student
Upperman Hilda,* laundress, res 308 w Lenoir
Upperman Julius,* son Hilda, res same, student
Upperman Marcellus,* carp, res 329 w South
Upperman Annie E,* wife M, house work
Upperman Sallie A,* d M, res same, teacher
Upperman Lewis M,* son M, res same, carp app
Upperman Annie R,* d M, res same, student
Upperman Arthur J,* son M, res same, student
Upperman Charity,* washerwoman, res 609 s Harrington
Upperman Albert,* son Charity, res same, dish-washer
Upperman Mary,* d Charity, res same, cook
Upperman Nancy,* d Charity, res same, cook
Upperman William,* carp, r 330 w South
Upperman Jane,* wife Wm, washerwoman
Utley W S, carp, res n Saunders
Utley Mrs Ella, wife W S
Utley Miss Minnie, d W S, res same
Utley Walter, son W S, res same, wks Ral cot mill
Utley Eugene, son W S, res same, messenger boy W U Tel Office
Utley Miss Nannie, d W S, res same, student
Utley J C, eng, res 320 e Cabarrus
Utley Mrs Della, wife J C
Utley Miss Clara, d J C, res same, dressmaker
Utley Clarence, son J C, res same, app blacksmith
Utley Miss Mary McK, d J C, res same, student
Utley W M, deputy sheriff, res 113 n Person
Utley Mrs M A, wife W M
Utley Clarence B, son W M, res same, student
Utley Miss Mattie, d W M, res same, student
Utley Philemon, son W M, res same, student
Utley W T, clk F A Watson, res 409 e Morgan

E. M. UZZELL.

Printer and Binder.

Cor. Wilmington and Martin Sts.,

RALEIGH, N. C.

FIRST-CLASS WORK AT BOTTOM PRICES.

Utley Florence, wife W T
Utley Miss Fannie, sister W T, res same
Utzman R M, grocer, 127 n Dawson, res same
Utzman Mrs M A, wife R M
UZZELL E M, printer and binder, cor s Wilmington and Martin, res 312 e Jones
Uzzell Mrs Isabella, wife E M
Uzzell Miss Helen M, d E M, res same
Uzzell Miss Nola C, d E M, res same, student
Uzzell Miss Jessie S, d E M, res same, student
Uzzell Miss Edwina H, d E M, res same
Uzzle W C, printer, res 230 n Saunders
Uzzle Mrs S I, wife W C
Uzzle W S, pianos and organs, res 217 s West
Uzzle Mrs Belle, wife W S
Uzzle Russell T, son W S, res same, student
Uzzle Miss Agnes E, d W S, res same, student
Uzzle Miss Virginia H, d W S, res same, student
Uzzle Carter C, son W S, res same, student
Uzzle Peyton R, mgr Wyatt & Co, res 18 Johnson
Uzzle Mrs Ailey, wife P R, dressmaker
Uzzle Harry, son P R, res same, moulder
Uzzle Archie B, son P R, res same, clk W H & R S Tucker & Co
Uzzle M P, son P R, res same, clk Charles W Young
Uzzle J E, huckster city market, bds 12 e Davie

VALENTINE Sam,* brakeman S A L R R, res 112 n West
Valentine Minnie,* wife Sam, washerwoman
Valentine D O, clk Central Hotel, res same
Van Horn Wm P, clk Frank Stronach, res 413 e Morgan
Van Horn Mrs Bettie E, wife Wm P
Vaughan Mrs Pal, dressmaker, res 227 e Davie
Vaughan Mrs R O, res 227 e Davie
Vaughan Miss Maud, saleslady at Woollcott & Son, r 227 e Davie
Vaughan Miss Mary, saleslady, res 227 e Davie
Vaughan Robt L, son Mrs R O, res same, student
Vaughan Edward, lab, res 19 Hayti
Vaughan Mrs Mary, wife Ed
Vaughan William,* farmer, res 422 s McDowell
Vaughan Ed, eng S A L, res Firwood ave, o s n
Vaughan Mrs Frankie, wife Ed
Vaughan Miss Etta, d Ed, res same, student
Vaughan George, son Ed, res same, student
Vass Maj W W, sec R & G R R, office S A L bldg, r 3 e Edenton
Vass Wm W Jr, son Maj W W, res same, lawyer
Vass Miss Eleanor N, d Maj W W, res same
Vass Miss Lilla M, d Maj W W, res same

Vass William,* lab, res 524 Yearby's lane
Vass Martha,* wife William
Vass William Jr,* son William Sr, res same, student
Vass Thomas,* son William, res same, student
Vass Mary,* cook for J R Barkley, res rear 128 n Wilmington
Venable Mrs Delia, wid, mother of Mrs T R Southerland, r same
Vestal Miss Ida, res with J H Robbins
Vick Miss Sallie, neice of Mrs J R Barkley, res same, student
Vincent Rev A B,* Baptist minister, res 618 s West
Vincent Cora P,* wife Rev A B
Vines Alex,* lab, res 109 w Lenoir
Vines Courtney,* wife Alex, house work
Vines Plummer,* son Alex, res same, student
Vines Mary,* laundress, res 246 w Cabarrus
Von Herrman C F, U S Weather Bureau, meteorologist, office Agricultural bldg, bds 118 n Wilmington
Von Herrman Mrs Evelina, wife C F
Voss John, carp, res 316 Cannon

WADDELL J W, grocer, 812 Fayetteville, res 22 McKee
Waddell Mrs Aithimitha, wife J W, dressmaker
Waddell J N, guard at penitentiary, res 748 Fayetteville
Waddell Mrs Pink, wife J N
Waddell Graham, son J N, res same, student
Waddell E M, inmate Soldiers' Home
Waddell Alfred, wks Edwards & Broughton, res 531 e Martin
Waddell Mack, lab, res 531 e Martin
Wade Phebe,* washerwoman, res s s Harrington
Wade Eliza,* nurse, res 116 w Lenoir
Wadford Miss Melissa, seamstress, res 307 w Morgan
Wadford A O, guard at penitentiary, res Avent Ferry rd, o s w
Wadford Mrs Arnetta, wife A O
Wadford Miss Geneva, niece A O, res same
Wahmann J H, clk at Raleigh Stationery Co, res 324 s Salisbury
Wahmann Mrs Dorah, wife J H
Waitt Mrs H V, wid, res 128 w Hargett
Waitt D S, son Mrs Hattie V, res same, student
Waitt Paul, son Mrs Hattie V, res same, clk for A Williams & Co
Waitt Miss Daisy B, d Mrs Hattie V, res same, teacher
Waitt Miss Ethel, d Mrs Hattie V, res same, student
Waitt Jos K, son Mrs Hattie V, res same
Waitt Robert C, son Mrs Hattie V, res same
Wait S D, gen agt Connecticut Mutual Life Ins Co, office and res 409 Fayetteville, bds Park Hotel
Walber Mrs Mary A, seamstress, res 327 s Bloodworth
Walker Wm H, clk in rev office, res 14 w Cabarrus
Walker Mrs Kate D, wife Wm H

Walker Alfonzo L, son Wm H, res same, student
Walker N L, son Wm H, res same, student
Walker Miss Emily H, d Wm H, res same, student
Walker Miss Kate D, d Wm H, res same, student
Walker S W, wks Supreme Court bldg, res 215 s Person
Walker Mrs S J, wife S W
Walker Miss Annie B, d S W, res same, milliner
Walker Miss Emma G, d S W, res same
Walker Miss Beulah B, d S W, res same, student
Walker John W, mgr N C Trouser Co, res 320 e Hargett
Walker Mrs Maggie M, wife John W
Walker John W, son John W, res same, student
Walker Miss Margarite, d John W, res same, student
Walker C A, barber, shop 112 e Hargett, res 225 e Cabarrus
Walker Sarah, wife C A
Walker Rev H P,* Methodist minister, res 423 Haywood
Walker Sarah J,* wife Rev H P, house work
Walker Nena L,* d Rev H P, res same, student
Walker W A, inmate Soldiers' Home
Walker Carter, inmate Soldiers' Home
Walker Grizzie,* house-servant, res 561 e Edenton
Walker Lewis,* farm hand, res 802 Manly
Walker Rosa,* wife Lewis, washerwoman
Walker Ida,* washerwoman, res 406 w Edenton
Walker W D, machinist, bds 314 Hillsboro
Walker Jane,* cook for Mrs W H Bagley, res 410 s Blount
Walker Levy J, propr Yarborough House Saloon, room Frap's bldg
Walker John,* brick-mason, res e Jones, Idlewild
Walker Henrietta,* wife John, cook and dining-room servant
Walker Jane,* cook for Thos H Briggs, res same
Walker Pauline,* washerwoman, res 524 s McDowell
Walker Mary,* washerwoman, res 524 s McDowell
Walker Thomas,* lab, res 122 w South
Walker Linnie,* wife Thos, house-servant
Walker Willie,* son Thos, res same, student
Walker Mabel,* d Thos, res same, student
Walker Jack,* well-digger, res 517 s Dawson
Wall Frank,* train hand Southern R R, res 120 w Peace
Wall Hester,* washerwoman, res e Edenton
Wallace Wm W, grocer, 745 s Blount, res e South
Wallace Augusta, wife Wm W, restaurant
Wallace Wm,* grocer, basement of 430 s Blount
Wallin Charles, eng at Institution for the Blind, res 316 w Jones
Wallin Mrs Emma, wife Charles
Wallin Alfred, son Chas, res same, student
Wallin Willie, son Chas, res same, student
WALTERS GEO N, merchant tailor, 234 Fayetteville, res 319 Newbern ave

Walters Mrs M K, wife Geo N
Walters Miss Vera N, d G N, res same, student
Walters Miss Edna E, d G N, res same, student
Walters Chas M, deputy sheriff, res 618 w Jones
Walters Mrs Columbia M, wife Chas M
Walters Archie D, son Chas M, res same, clk for L D Womble
Walters Fred M, son Chas M, res same, clk for W H & R S Tucker & Co
Walters Thos L, son Chas M, res same, app at Allen & Cram
Walters John C, son Chas M, res same, student
Walters B N, son Chas M, res same, student
Walters Arthur E, son Chas M, res same, student
Walters Lucinda,* cook, res Hayti
Walters Amos,* farm hand, res 207 s East
Walters Effie,* wife Amos, cook
Walton James H, clk for J E Walton, res w Edenton, rear First Baptist church
Walton Mrs Cora B, wife James H
Walton Wm,* lab, res e Davie, o s e
Walton J E, saloon, 235 s Wilmington, res 319 s Dawson
Walton Mrs Ella O, wife J E
Ward Wm,* corker for Ral Water Co, res 409 w Martin
Ward Annie M,* wife Wm, washerwoman
Ward Lena,* d Wm, res same, washerwoman
Ward Bessie,* d Wm, res same, house work
Ward Charles,* son Wm, res same, errand-boy
Ward Joseph,* son Wm, res same, student
Ward Eliza,* nurse, res rear 405 s Dawson
Ward Mary,* cook for L C Emmett, res on lot
Ward Miss Rose V, teacher in St Mary's School, res same
Ward Mrs Ann, wid, res 517 Halifax
Ward Frank T (Julius Lewis Hardware Co), hardware, res 517 Halifax
Ward John, sec and treas N C Car Co, res 517 Halifax
Ward Miss J E, d Mrs Ann, res same
Ward Miss M A, d Mrs Ann, res same
Wardrope Polly,* student, res 211 w South
Warren Henry, motorman, res Coxe ave, o s w
Warren Mrs Annie, wife Henry
Warren Miss Nellie G, d Henry, res same, student
Warren Miss Lillian E, d Henry, res same, student
Warren Robert A, son Henry, res same
Warren Miss Bertie L, d Henry, res same
Warren Miss Lina B, d Henry, res same
Warren H A, carp, res 615 e Davie
Warren Mrs Nannie, wife H A, house work
Warren Lawrence, salesman, res 615 e Davie
Warren Nathaniel, carp, res Smithfield

Warren Mrs Nancy, wid, res 516 Haywood
Warren Maria,* washerwoman, res 732 Fayetteville
Warren John,* lab, res 732 Fayetteville
Warren Charles,* lab, res 732 Fayetteville
Warren Matilda,* student, res 732 Fayetteville
Warren James M, bookbinder, res 738 e Davie, o s e
Warren Mrs Mary, wife James M
Warren Miss Minnie L, d Jas M, res same, student
Warren Harry L, son Jas M, res same, student
Warren Miss Nellie, d Jas M, res same, student
Warren Miss Jennie E, d Jas M, res same
Warren Mrs M E, wid, mother Mrs Blanche Bolton, res same, 505 n Wilmington
Washington George,* hostler for J B Batchelor, res 524 s Dawson
Washington Argo,* son Geo, res same, student
Washington Arthur,* son Geo, res same, student
Washington Oscar,* son Geo, res same, student
Washington Bessie,* d Geo, res same, student
Washington Henry,* wood-cutter and gardener, r Cotton lane, o s e
Washington Addie,* wife Henry, washerwoman
Washington John,* driver, res w Lenoir
Washington Polly,* cook, res w Lenoir
Washington Luvenia,* laundress for Dr James McKee, res on lot
Washington Ella,* cook, res 574 e Cabarrus
Washington Hattie,* washerwoman, res Cotton lane, o s e
Washington Millie,* cook for C W Bevers, res Cotton lane, o s e
Washington Dola,* d Hattie, res same, student
Washington Kittie,* washerwoman, res e Hargett, o s e
Washington Boyd,* driver for F A Watson, res e Hargett, o s e
Washington Bertha,* cook for Jno Robinson, res e Hargett, o s e
Washington Harriet,* laundress, res 30 Railroad
Washington Lizzie,* cook, res 613 e Cabarrus
Washington Duncan,* son Lizzie, res same, lab
Washington Harriet,* nurse for Mrs Sam B Norris, res same
Waters Mrs George, wid, res 501 n East
Watkins William, painter S A L shops, res 210 w North
Watkins Mrs Bettie, wife Wm
Watkins Norman, son Wm, res same, student
Watkins Miss Mattie D, d Wm, res same, student
Watkins Mrs S H, mother of Mrs A F Upchurch, res same
Watkins Jesse, blacksmith, res 312 St Mary's, o s w
Watkins Mrs Bettie, wife Jesse
Watkins Frank, son Jesse, res same, student
Watkins Charlie, son Jesse, res same, student
Watkins John, son Jesse, res same, student
Watkins Miss Matilda, bkpr Henry S Wilton, res same
Watkins Miss Mary, sister Miss Matilda, res same
Watkins John W, tel opr, res 416 s Wilmington

Watkins Mrs Laura, wife John W
Watkins Major,* lab, res 807 Jenkins
Watkins Sarah,* washerwoman, res 807 Jenkins
Watkins Peter, core-maker N C Car Co foundry, res 115 w Lane
Watkins Mrs Annie, wife Peter
Watkins James, son Peter, res same, app N C Car Co foundry
Watkins David, inmate Soldiers' Home
Watkins Jackson,* brick moulder, res Pugh
Watkins Luvinia,* wife Jackson, washerwoman
Watkins Sarah, washerwoman, res 911 Manly
Watkins Walter, son Sarah, res same
WATSON FRED A, picture and art store, 112 Fayetteville, res 414 n Person
Watson Mrs C E, wife F A
Watson Lea, son F A, res same, student
Watson Miss Edna, d F A, res same, student
Watson Charles, son F A, res same, student
Watson Miss Lotta, d F A, res same, student
Watson Emmett, son F A, res same
Watson Mrs A L, wid, res 413 n Saunders
Watson A L, son Mrs A L, res same, machinist
Watson J R, son Mrs A L, res same, student
Watson W M, son Mrs A L, res same, student
Watson W C, son Mrs A L, res same, student
Watson T I, son Mrs A L, res same, student
Watson T D, deputy U S marshal, res 310 Newbern ave
Watson Jos F, son T D, res same, clk Julius Lewis Hardware Co
Watson Miss Ellen, d T D, res same
Watson Miss Blanche, d T D, res same
Watson Miss Meta, d T D, res same, student
Watson James R, eng S A L, res 119 Firwood ave, o s n
Watson Mrs Lizzie O, wife Jas R
Watson James B, son Jas R, res same, student
Watson A S, son Jas R, res same, machinist S A L
Watson J H, son Jas R, res same, student
Watson Miss L C, d Jas R, res same, student
Watson J L, son Jas R, res same, student
Watson Henry L, clk in Baptist Supply Store, res 534 e Jones
Watson Mrs Annie, wife H L
Watson Walter L, son H L, res same, lawyer, office Fisher bldg
Watson Mrs Janet, wid, res 111 n Wilmington
Watson Miss Susie, d Mrs Janet, res same
Watson Miss Daisy, d Mrs Janet, res same, music student
Watson Robert,* driver for A B Stronach, res 102 n East
Watson Minnie,* wife Robt, washerwoman
Watson Isaac, inmate Soldiers' Home
Watson Mrs Lillie, wid, res 505 s Swain
Watson J W B, farmer, res 562 e Lenoir

Watson William,* brakeman S A L R R, res Fleming's lane
Watson Milliard,* stationary eng, res 517 s West
Watson John,* son Milliard, res same, farm hand
Watson Mary,* d Milliard, res same, cook
Watson Florence, d Milliard, res same, cook
Watson Joseph,* son Milliard, res same, produce pedler
Watson Bettie,* housekeeper for Milliard, res same
Watson Henry,* lab, res 507 s Dawson
Watson Mary,* wife Henry, washerwoman
Watson Mary A.* d Henry, res same, cook at Yarboro' House
Watson Effie,* d Henry, res same, house work
Watson Lustre,* d Henry, res same
Watson C P, attendant at Insane Asylum, res same
Watson Buck,* lab, rooms 407 s Dawson
Watts J T, accountant, res 113 Wilmington
Watts Mrs A E, wife J T, milliner
Watts Miss Margaret, d J T, res same, milliner
Watts Roderick, son J T, res same, wks Experimental station
Watts Maurice,* barber, 116 Fayetteville, res 509 s Person
Watts R E,* wife Maurice
Watts Mattie,* d Maurice, res same, student
Watts Katie D,* d Maurice, res same, student
Watts Evie V,* d Maurice, res same, student
Watts Mary,* washerwoman, res Pugh
Weathers Jos H, bkkpr, Ed H Lee, res 14 s Bloodworth
Weathers Mrs Ida, wife Jos H
Weathers Fab H, bkkpr for C E Johnson & Co, res 522 e Hargett
Weathers Mrs Ava D, wife Fab H
Weathers Miss Laura D, d Fab H, res same
Weathers H Carlisle, son Fab H, res same
Weathers J W, butcher, res 216 n Bloodworth
Weathers Mrs Delaney H, wife J W
Weathers L C, son J W, res same, paper-hanger and decorator
Weathers Wm C, son J W, res same, quiller at Caraleigh mill
Weathers W D, carp, res 110 s West
Weathers Mrs Mary, wife W D
Weathers Vernon, son W D, res same, student
Weathers Willer, son W D, res same, student
Weathers K R, father of Mrs E C Jones, res same
Weathers Mrs Mary A, wid, res 324 s Blount
Weathers Miss Minnie E, d Mrs Mary A, res same
Weathers Miss Rosa L, d Mrs Mary A, res same
Weathers Leon H, stenographer and typewriter, res 324 s Blount
Weathers Henry,* wks Insane Asylum, res 503 Smith
Weathers Emma,* wife Henry, cook
Weathers Prince,* lab, res old Fair Ground, o s e
Weathers Stella,* wife Prince, washerwoman
Weathers Anna,* d Prince, res same, cook

Weathers Farilla,* d Prince, res same, cook
Weathers Iola,* cook, res old Fair Ground, o s e
Weathers Myrtle,* d Prince, res same, invalid
Weathers Helen,* washerwoman, res 324 w Edenton
Weathers Alex,* wks for W C McMackin, res 324 w Edenton
Weathers Walter, wks Caraleigh mill, bds 744 Fayetteville
Weatherspoon Mrs Caroline, wid, res 723 s East
Weatherspoon W H, mgr city lamp-lighting department, res 723 s East
Weatherspoon Jackson,* lab, res 523 w South
Weatherspoon Susan,* wife Jackson, washerwoman
Weatherspoon Minnie,* d Jackson, res same, washerwoman
Weatherspoon Annie,* d Jackson, res same, student
Weatherspoon Thos Jr,* wks W R Blake, res 539 Newbern ave
Weatherspoon Thos,* restaurant cook, res 539 Newbern ave
Weaver Robert E, conductor Southern R R, res 605 Hillsboro'
Weaver Mrs Eliza N, wife Robert E
Weaver Mary,* nurse for Mrs Clem Carter, res same
Weaver Joseph,* porter Capital Club, res 224 Newbern ave
Weaver Annie,* wife Joseph
Webb Lizzie,* cook, res 749 s McDowell
Webb Miss Sarah, res with Rev J B Cheshire
Webb Sam J,* brick-mason, res Oberlin, o s w
Webster John, carp, res 315 s Bloodworth
Webster Mrs Bettie, wife John
Weddon & Francis, shoemakers, over 205 Fayetteville
Weddon J P, boot and shoemaker, res 212 n Harrington
Weddon Miss Rebecca C, res 212 n Harrington
Weddon Miss Nellie, res 212 n Harrington, stenographer and typewriter
WEIKEL C, tailor, shop up-stairs, 124 Fayetteville, res same
Weir Wm J, stone contractor, res 513 n Bloodworth
Weir Mrs Margaret, wife W J
Weir Miss May, d W J, res same
Weir Miss Hattie, d W J, res same, student
Weir Claude H, son W J, res same, traveling salesman

C. WEIKEL,
Artistic Tailoring,
124 Fayetteville St.
(UP-STAIRS)

Always on hand, a fine selection of Imported Woolens and latest styles.

Weir Harry H, son W J, res same, traveling salesman
Weir Fred B, g-s W J, res same, student
Weir Miss Margaret A, g-d of W J, res same, student
Welsh Mrs J W, wid, mother of Mrs F H Briggs, res same
West Miss Mabel, house work, bds 317 s East
West Miss Gracie, house work, bds 317 s East
West Nick W (Julius Lewis Hardware Co), hardware merchant, res 625 Hillsboro'
West Mrs Bessie, wife N W
West Miss Kate, d N W, res same
West Miss Maggie, d N W, res same
West John, son N W, res same, clk Southern R R office
West Thomas, son N W, res same, cot buyer for C E Johnson & Co
West Miss Lucy, d N W, res same
West Miss Ellen, d N W, res same, student
West Miss Julia, d Nick W, res same
West Nick W Jr, son Nick W, res same, student
West Julius, son Nick W, res same, student
West Raleigh Post-Office, B S Skinner P M
West William, clk for M T Norris & Bro, bds at Mrs M E Banks
Wharton Thos W, grocer, 806 s Wilmington, res same
Wharton Mrs Hibernia, wife Thos W
Wharton Thos W Jr, student, res 806 s Wilmington
Wharton Miss Elizabeth, d Thos W Sr, res same, student
Wharton Miss Ellen E, d Thos W Sr, res same, student
Wharton Hugh D, son Thos W Sr, res same, student
WHARTON C P, photographer, 119 Fayetteville, res 318 Oakwood ave
Wharton Mrs Eva L, wife C P
WHITAKER Rev R H, pastor Brooklyn M E church and Raleigh missions
Whitaker Mrs Fannie P, wife Rev R H
Whitaker Miss Sallie C, d Rev R H, res same, student
Whitaker Wesley, justice of the peace, office 119 e Martin, r 512 e Hargett
Whitaker Miss Neva E, d Wesley, res same
Whitaker James,* carp, res 517 Haywood
Whitaker Caroline,* wife James
Whitaker Walter B,* son James, res same, student
Whitaker Jas W,* son James, res same, student
Whitaker Violet,* servant, res Blount-st al
Whitaker Ben,* lab, res rear Colored Baptist church
Whitaker Bettie,* wife Ben, washerwoman
Whitaker Alice,* nurse for Thos Cook, res same
Whitaker W S, inmate Soldiers' Home
Whitaker William,* eng at Agricultural bldg, res 16 w Worth
Whitaker Mary,* wife Wm, house work

Whitaker Addie L,* d Wm, res same, house work
Whitaker Delno,* son Wm, res same, student
Whitaker Eleanor,* d Wm, res same, student
Whitaker Esther,* d Wm, res same, student
Whitaker Rufus,* farmer, res 685 Cannon
Whitaker Gracie,* wife Rufus, house work
Whitaker E S, tel opr, bds 507 s West
Whitaker Harriet,* cook, res 311 w Cabarrus
Whitaker W P, bkkpr for News & Observer Co, res 411 w Hargett
Whitaker Mrs Mamie, wife W P
Whitaker W P Jr, son W P, res same
Whitaker Mrs M E, matron N C Insane Asylum, res same
Whitaker Bert,* lab, res 515 Cannon
Whitaker Alice,* washerwoman, res Cannon
White Rev I A, Methodist minister, proprietor Branson House, 101½ and 103½ Fayetteville
White Mrs Johnnie L, wife Rev I A
White Lee L, son Rev I A, res same, student
White Miss Lucy N, d Rev I A, res same, student
White Ernest E, son Rev I A, res same, student
White Julian E, son Rev I A, res same, student
White Herbert, son Rev I A, res same, student
White Luther N, saloon, 231 s Wilmington, res 214 s Blount
White Mrs Blanche E, wife Luther N
White Wm C, son Luther N, res same
White Miss Bessie H, d Luther N, res same, student
White George L, son Luther N, res same, student
White John S, huckster, res 117 s West
White Mrs Corrie, wife John S
White Miss Mamie, d John S, res same
White Lewis W, son John S, res same
White Thomas,* lab S A L, res 318 s Bloodworth
White Penny,* wife Thos, washerwoman
White Eddie,* son Thos, res same, driver M Rosenthal
White Mrs Laura, wid, res 304 w Morgan
White Wm W, son Mrs Laura, app at moulding
White G H, son Mrs Laura, res same, app machinist
White A Wray, son Mrs Laura, res same, student
White Nancy,* cook for A C Lehman, res same
White Jno B,* wks cotton compress, res 823 Jenkins
White Matilda D,* wife Jno B, cook Branson House
White Walter J,* lab, res 823 Jenkins
White Bertha,* wife Walter J
White Mrs Mary E, wid, res 302 w Jones
White Chas W, son Mrs Mary E, res same, bkkpr for Wyatt & Co
White Edward L, son Mrs Mary E, r same, clk frt depot S A L R R
White W A, teacher of music Blind Institution, res same

White Luvenia,* house work, res Caswell lane
White Maggie,* house work, res Caswell lane
White Bettie,* washerwoman, res Fleming's lane
White Miss Mary, sister Mrs Lucy B Evans, res same
White H D, tel opr News and Observer, res 527 s Salisbury
White Mrs Elizabeth C, wife H D
White Miss S T, attendant at Insane Asylum, res same
White Jane,* washerwoman, res rear 407 s Dawson
White Lizzie,* cook, res 717 s McDowell
Whitehead Miss Minnie M, g-d Mrs J M Betts, res same
Whitehead Miss Jennie, g-d Mrs J M Betts, res same, student
Whitehead James, g-s Mrs J M Betts, res same, app boiler-maker
Whitehead Miss Katie, student, res with Wiley P Betts
Whitehead Mary,* cook for T R Purnell, res on lot
Whitehead W W, cotton broker, bds 118 n Wilmington
Whitehead Mrs Bessie, wife W W
Whitehead John J, clk frt office S A L, res 507 Halifax
Whitehead Mrs Annie C, wife Jno J
Whitehead John J Jr, son John J, res same, student
WHITELAW JOHN, stone-work contractor, res 201 w Martin
Whitelaw Mrs Esther V, wife John
Whitelaw Miss Octavia L, d John, res same, saleslady at W H & R S Tucker & Co
Whitelaw Miss Janet K, d John, res same, saleslady at J Hal Bobbitt
Whitelaw Miss Bettie A, d John, res same, student
Whitelaw Miss Mary A, d John, res same, student
Whitfield Geo,* carp, res 586 e Cabarrus
Whitfield Sallie,* wife Geo, washerwoman
Whitfield Georgiana,* d Geo, res same, cook
Whitfield Mary,* d Geo, res same, house-servant
Whitfield Kate,* d Geo, res same, student
Whitfield N G, clk for T H Briggs & Sons, res 108 w Edenton
Whitfield Mrs L S, wife N G
Whitfield Miss Lena, d N G, res same, student
Whitfield Alonzo,* servant for O J Carroll, res same
Whitfield Maria,* washerwoman, res rear 523 s Person
Whiting Bros, clothing, gent's furnishing goods, 10 e Martin
Whiting S W (Whiting Bros), merchant, res Saunders
Whiting Mrs Florence, wife S W
Whiting Geither, son S W, res same, student
Whiting Miss Carrie, d S W, res same, student
Whiting C G (Whiting Bros), merchant, bds n Saunders
Whiting Moses,* lab, res 20 Fowle
Whiting Sallie,* wife Moses, washerwoman
Whitley John, clk for Pool & Moring, res 122 Newbern ave
Whitley Mrs Pattie, wife John
Whitley Miss Leolia C, d John, res same

Whitley Miss Annie, d John, res same
Whitley Miss Pattie, d John, res same
Whitley Amanda,* cook for Mrs J M Betts, res on lot
Whitted James,* porter L N White, res 112 e Cabarrus
Whitted Sarah,* washerwoman, res 112 e Cabarrus
Whitted Chas S, conductor S A L R R, bds 40 e North
Whitted Arthur,* waiter Park Hotel, room 109 s Blount
Whittington Miss Alice, hkpr for Dan Hicks, res same
Wicker Robt D, printer, res 323 e Cabarrus
Wicker Mrs Alice, wife Robt D
Wicker Miss Carrie, d Robt D, res same, student
Wicker Robt D Jr, son Robt, res same, student
Wicker Mrs Emma J, wid, hkpr for J R Upchurch, res same
Wicker Miss Annie, washerwoman, res s Bloodworth
Wicker Miss Ella, wks Caraleigh mill, res s Bloodworth
Wicker E J, printer, res 323 e Cabarrus
Wiggins Jeff D, carp, res 407 n West
Wiggins Mrs Annie, wife Jeff D
Wiggins Thos, son Jeff D, res same, student
Wiggins Geo, son Jeff D, res same, student
Wiggins Miss Lula, d Jeff D, res same, student
Wiggins John, carp, res e Hargett, o s e
Wiggins Mrs Isabella, wife John, dressmaker
Wiggins Lonnie, son John, res same, student
Wiggins Mrs Mary L, mother Mrs Dannie Taylor, res same
Wiggins Eliza,* grocer, 581 e Cabarrus, res same
Wiggins Mary,* mother Eliza, res same
Wiggins Margaret,* d Mary, res same
Wiggins Mary,* seamstress, res 581 e Cabarrus
Wiggins Annie,* laundress, res 425 s Swain
Wiggins Ada,* house work, res 425 s Swain
Wiggins Ella,* nurse for Mrs C W Young, res on lot
Wiggins Judge,* farm hand, bds 581 e Cabarrus
Wilder Harry,* lab, res o s e
Wilder Hunter,* lab, res o s e
Wilder Haywood,* wks for Dr G W Blacknall, res same
Wilder Jane,* washerwoman, res old Fair Ground, o s e
Wilder Henry,* son Jane, res same, lab
Wilder Ella,* d Jane, res same, nurse
Wilder Laurine,* d Jane, res same, nurse
Wilder Amanda,* d Jane, res same, nurse
Wilder Shade,* son Jane, res same, lab
Wilder Manson,* lab, res East Raleigh
Wilder Nancy,* wife Manson
Wilder Harry,* son Manson, res same, lab
Wilder Manson Jr,* son Manson, res same, lab
Wilder Hunter,* son Manson, res same, lab
Wilder Adelaide,* d Manson, res same, servant

Wilder Hasty,* cook for J G Ball, res 2 Stronach ave
Wilder Annie,* sister Hasty, cook for H H Roberts
Wilder Hattie,* washerwoman, res 607 s McDowell
Wilder Chaney,* nurse, res 607 s McDowell
Wilder Carrie,* d Chaney, res same, nurse
Wilder Annie,* d Chaney, res same, cook
Wilder Maggie,* d Chaney, res same, cook
Wilder Romulus,* son Chaney, res same, student
Wilder William,* blacksmith, res 613 e Davie
Wilder Lucinda,* wife Wm, washerwoman
Wilder Amanda,* house servant for Dr T E Skinner, res Hargett, o s e
Wilder Lynn (Dewar & Wilder), grocer, 13 e Martin
WILDES CHAS D, stenographer, typewriter and notary public, office with Ernest Haywood, rooms 2 and 3 Bagley bldg, res 118 s Dawson
Wildes Mrs R D, wid, res 118 s Dawson
Wilker Miss Harriet, art teacher, res 605 Halifax
Wilkins Mrs Mary, wid, res cor Cabarrus and Harrington
Wilkins Miss Ida J, d Mrs Mary, res same, weaver
Wilkins Miss Mary R, d Mrs Mary, res same, weaver
Wilkins Wm H, son Mrs Mary, res same, weaver Caraleigh mill
Wilkins Miss Bessie, d Mrs Mary, res same, student
Wilkins Miss Eleanora, d Mrs Mary, res same, student
Wilkins Helen,* washerwoman, res 728 Fayetteville
Wilkinson Thos B, clk for W H & R S Tucker, res 528 e Jones
Wilkinson Mrs Katie, wife Thos B
Will Jno D, cot mill opr, res 717 n Person
Will Mrs Mary D, wife Jno D
Williams Henry, conductor S A L R R, bds 10 e North
Williams Julia,* servant, res Adams lane
Williams A & Co, books and stationery, 121 Fayetteville
Williams John T, druggist, res s Blount
Williams Mrs Lula, wife John T
Williams Mrs Caroline, wid, res with F L Bailey
Williams Mrs John G, wid, res with Mrs E R Stamps
Williams Mattie,* cook for A B Stronach, res on lot
Williams Hilliard,* lab, res old Fair Ground, o s e
Williams Lydia,* wife Hilliard, res same, washerwoman
Williams Mary,* washerwoman, res Hood's al
Williams Berta,* d Mary, res same, servant
Williams Mrs B L, mother of Mrs W J Ellington, res same
Williams Augustus,* stationary eng, res 6 Stronach ave
Williams Edith,* wife Augustus
Williams Henry,* son Augustus, res same, student
Williams Thomas,* son Augustus, res same, student
Williams Claude, harness-maker, res 308 s Bloodworth
Williams Lillie,* servant for B R Lacy, res on lot

Williams Wm., porter for John Y MacRae, res 414 s Swain
Williams Cherry,* wife Wm, washerwoman
Williams Richard B,* son Wm, res same, student
Williams Major,* wks Nixon & Johnson, res Townes al
Williams Phoebe,* wife Major
Williams Miss Louise, hkpr Mrs G S Barham, res same
Williams Peyton, carp, res 427 Halifax
Williams Fannie,* washerwoman, res 553 e Martin
Williams Margaret W,* seamstress, res 711 s East
Williams Rachel,* cook for Mrs L V Holden, res 805 Jenkins
Williams Lillie,* d Rachel, res same, servant
Williams Laura,* cook at restaurant, res 412 e Morgan
Williams Mrs Anna, milliner for W E Jones, res 224 w Hargett
Williams Tom,* train hand S A L, bds 435 n Salisbury
Williams Henry,* house-servant for Mrs Emma Swindell, res Idlewild
Williams Mary,* wife Henry
Williams Miss M V, attendant at Insane Asylum, res same
Williams W B, attendant at Insane Asylum, res same
Williams Polly,* cook, rooms at Nellie Wyche's
Williams Edna,* cook, rooms at Nellie Wyche's
Williams Timothy,* lab, res 310 Manly
Williams Eliza,* cook, res 324 Cannon
Williams Fannie,* d Eliza, res same, washerwoman
Williams Alice,* d Eliza, res same, student
Williams Thomas,* d Eliza, res same, student
Williams Joseph,* son Eliza, res same, student
Williams Brown,* lab, res 403 Cannon
Williams Clara,* wife Brown, washerwoman
Williams Willis,* son Brown, res same, driver for Express Co
Williams Maria,* d Brown, res same, house work
Williams Victoria,* d Brown, res same, student
Williams Julia,* d Brown, res same, student
Williams Matilda,* house-servant, res 407 w Martin
Williams Luke,* carp, res 218 w Lenoir
Williams Lethia,* wife Luke, washerwoman
Williams Beulah,* d Luke, res same, house-servant
Williams Annie,* nurse for J Schwartz, res same
Williams Narcissa,* cook, res 520 s Dawson
Williams J R, retired druggist, res 404 Fayetteville
Williams Geo H, res 404 Fayetteville
Williams Mrs Fannie M, wife Geo H, boarding-house
Williams Miss Laura W
Williams Geo H, son Geo H, res same, wks Caraleigh mill
Williams Robt I, druggist, bds 404 Fayetteville
Williams Caroline,* washerwoman, res 109 w Lenoir
Williams Judy,* d Caroline, res same, house-servant
Williams John,* son Caroline, res same, farm hand

Williams London,* gardener, res 109 w Lenoir
Williams Mary L* washerwoman, res 760 Fayetteville
Williams Ella F,* student, res 760 Fayetteville
Williams Miss Mary, res with John W Brown
Williams Peter,* lab, res 724 s Dawson
Williams Audney,* wife Peter, chambermaid
Williams Edward,* hackman, res 724 s Dawson
Williams Garfield,* son Peter, res same, student
Williams Lewis,* son Peter, res same, student
Williams Chas,* lab, res 724 s Dawson
Williams Jennie,* washerwoman, res 207 Cannon
Williams Ada,* d Jennie, res same, washerwoman
Williams Rosa,* d Jennie, res same, house work
Williams Dock,* lab, res Cannon
Williams Martha,* wife Dock, house work
Williams Alice,* d Dock, washerwoman
Williams Beattice,* d Dock, res same, house-servant
Williams Agnes,* washerwoman, res 513 w South
Williams Willie,* d Agnes, res same, student
Williams Mary,* d Agnes, res same, student
Williams Rosa,* washerwoman, res 710 s Dawson
Williams Bud,* d Rosa, res same, student
Williams Lillie,* cook, res 710 s Dawson
Williams Mary,* d Lillie, res same, student
Williams C B, student, bds Dr T D Martin
Williams Alex,* lab, res Avent Ferry rd, o s w
Williams Hannah,* wife Alex, house work
Williams Mary,* d Alex, res same
Williams James,* son Alex, res same
Williams Merritt,* cook, res 707 s Dawson
Williams Katie,* wife Merritt, laundress
Williams Lizzie,* laundress, res 712 s Saunders
Williams Rev Henry,* Congregational minister, r 134 w Cabarrus
Williams Mary,* wife Rev Henry
Williams Miss Annie, dressmaker, res 309 w Davie
Williams Miss Columbia, dressmaker, res 309 w Davie
Williams Alfred (A Williams & Co), bookseller, rooms 412 Fayetteville
Williams Mary,* laundress, res 201 Cannon
Williams Mark,* brick-mason, res 201 Cannon
Williams Lovie A,* d Mary, res same, house work
Williams Ed L,* son Mary, res same, student
Williams Willie F,* son Mary, res same, student
Williams Wm,* invalid, res rear 217 w South
Williams Lizzie,* wife Wm, cook
Williams Junius,* brakeman, res s Saunders
Williams Louisa,* wife Junius, house work
Williams David H, carp, res Hillsboro' rd, o s w

Williams Mrs Sallie W, wife D H, teacher at Blind Institution
Williams Hubert E, son D H, student
Williams Miss Eula V, d D H, res same, student
Williams David E, son D H, res same, student
Williams Mrs B E, wid, res 530 e Jones
Williams Miss Mary L, d Mrs B E, res same
Williams Walker A, son Mrs B E, res same, clk
Williams Ewan C, son Mrs B E, res same
Williams Miss Emma B, d Mrs B E, res same
Williams Lewis B, mechanic, res 224 w North
Williams Mrs Mattie E, wife Lewis B
Williams Alonzo, tinner S A L R R, res 224 w North
Williams Robert, son Alonzo, res same, wks Ral cot mill
Williams James, son Alonzo, res same, wks Ral cot mill
Williams Mack,* lab S A L R R, res 224 w North
Williams Rosa,* wife Mack
Williams Ann,* d Mack, res same, washerwoman
Williams Henry S,* son Mack, res same, lab
Williams Roger T,* son Mack, res same, lab
Williams Andrew J,* son Mack, res same, lab
Williams Robert M,* son Mack, res same, student
Williams Adeline,* d Mack, res same, student
Williams Laura J,* d Mack, res same, student
Williams John E, drug clk, bds 124 n Wilmington
Williams Laura,* house-servant Rev Dr M M Marshall, res rear 128 n Wilmington
Williams Theo,* cook for A Dughi, res 122 e Cabarrus
Williams Mamie,* wife Theo, cook for J A Egerton
Williams Sarena,* washerwoman, res 122 e Cabarrus
Williams Lula,* d Sarena, res same, student
Williams Henry,* son Sarena, res same, student
Williams John L, stationary engineer, res 522 n West
Williams Mrs Martha, wife John L
Williams Thomas, son John L, res same
Williams Miss May, d John L, res same, student
Williams Miss Agnes, d John L, res same, student
Williams Pat T, painter, res 110 s McDowell
Williams Mrs Susan C, wife Pat T, dressmaker
Williams Miss May, d Pat T, res same, dressmaker
Williams Wade, son Pat T, res same, printer at Caucasian office
Williams Charles, son Pat T, res same, painter
Williams Alice,* cook, res 720 Fayetteville
Williams Jerry,* lab, res 220 Blount-st al
Williams Penny,* wife Jerry, washerwoman
Williams Jerry Jr,* son Jerry, res same, lab
Williams George,* son Jerry, res same, farm hand
Williams Mary L,* d Jerry, res same, student
Williams Lula,* d Jerry, res same, student

Williams Frank,* son Jerry, res same, student
Williams Birdie,* d Jerry, res same, student
Williams Jas H, clothes dyer and cleaner, res 326 s Blount
Williams Mrs Mary H, wife Jas H
Williams Rev Wm M,* minister of Christian church, res 517 s Blount
Williams Jennie,* wife Rev W M
Williams Cleophas M, son Rev W M, res same, student
Williams Archie G,* son Rev W M, res same, student
Williams Bertie A,* d Rev W M, res same, student
Williams Lizzie O,* house-servant for Chas Root, res on lot
Williams Dora,* cook for J C S Lumsden, res 3 Stronach ave
Williams W A, wks in round-house S A L R R, res 324 w Lane
Williams Mrs Carcilla, wife W A, seamstress
Williams Miss Ellen, d W A, res same, seamstress
Williams Miss Emma, d W A, res same, seamstress
Williams Miss Roxie, d W A, res same
Williams Lazarus, son W A, res same
Williams Donnie, son W A, res same
Williams William, son W A, res same
Williams Eddie, son W A, res same
Williams Jno L, carp, res 324 w Lane
Williams Jno R, flagman S A L R R, res 324 w Lane
Williams Mrs Ella T, wid, res with father, W T Womble
Williams James, son Mrs Ella, res same
Williams Robert,* wks E B Barbee, res 316 s Bloodworth
Williams Mary,* wife Robert, washerwoman
Williams Maggie,* d Robert, res same, student
Williams Rodney,* wks N C Car Co, res 121 Smithfield
Williams Sallie,* wife Rodney, servant at C M Busbee
Williams John,* wks for city, res 121 Smithfield
Williams Sarah J,* d Rodney, res same, student
Williams Henry,* lab, res 748 s Person
Williams Laura,* wife Henry, washerwoman
Williams Martha,* cook for I Rosenthal, res 106 e Cabarrus
Williams Pattie,* washerwoman, res Smithfield al
Williams Lillie,* d Pattie, res same, student
Williams Blondie,* d Pattie, res same, student
Williams Sudie,* student, res Cotton lane, o s e
Williams Wiley,* carp, res 750 e Davie
Williams Annie,* wife Wiley
Williams Henderson,* son Wiley, res same, carp
Williams John L,* son Wiley, res same, carp
Williams Mary J,* d Wiley, res same, seamstress
Williams Adolphus,* son Wiley, res same, carp
Williams Josephine,* d Wiley, res same, house work
Williams Wm H,* son Wiley, res same, lab
Williams Haywood,* son Wiley, res same, student

Williams Eliza,* d Wiley, res same, student
Williams Louie B,* d Wiley, res same, student
Williams Henry M,* driver for J W Barber & Son, res 433 Smith
Williams Bettie,* wife H M, laundress
Williams Emma,* d H M, res same, cook for W H Lancaster
Williams Bettie,* d H M, res same, student
Williams Jas H,* son H M, res same, lab
Williams Thomas,* carpet-layer, res 816 s Blount
Williams Hodgie,* wife Thomas
Williams Marceletta,* d Thos, res same, student
Williams Geo J, gen merchandise, 401 s Blount, res 324 s Bloodworth
Williams Mrs Nellie D, wife Geo J
Williams Miss Georgiana, d Geo J, res same
Williams J R, painter, res 110 s McDowell
Williams Mrs Sallie, wife J R
Williams Squire,* shoemaker, res 509 Haywood
Williams Cora,* wife Squire, washerwoman
Williams Charles,* son Squire, res same, porter at Caucasian office
Williams Nelson,* gardener, res 419 Haywood
Williams Charles,* lab, res 411 Haywood
Williams Emma,* wife Chas, house work
Williams Dock,* servant at Institution for the Blind, r 516 Smith
Williams Helen,* wife Dock, laundress
Williams Edward,* lab, res 516 Smith
Williams Penny,* cook, res 428 Smith
Williams Mittie,* d Penny, res same, cook
Williams Ernest,* son Penny, res same, lab
Williams Eaton,* carp, res 424 Smith
Williams Mary,* wife Eaton, washerwoman
Williams Ida,* d Eaton, res same, servant
Williams Emma,* d Eaton, res same, student
Williams Eaton Jr,* son Eaton, res same, student
Williams Hilliard,* carp, res 102 n East
Williams Mary,* wife Hilliard, house work
Williams Wesley,* son Hilliard, res same, lab
Williams George,* lab, res 579 e Lenoir
Williams Haywood,* wood-cutter, res 16 Matthews' lane
Williams Angelina,* wife Haywood, cook for A W Shaffer
Williams Willie,* d Haywood, res same, servant for W H Hughes
Williams James, inmate Soldiers' Home
Williams Geo W,* carp, res 515 s Wilmington
Williams Bettie E,* wife Geo W, boarding-house
Williams Rosa,* d Geo W, res same, student
Williams Minnie L,* d Geo W, res same
Williams Mark,* driver for Deaf, Dumb and Blind Institution, res Hargett, o s e
Williams Stella,* wife Mark, washerwoman

Williams Sallie,* d Mark, res same, washerwoman
Williams Geo.* son Mark, res same, student
Williams Mary,* d Mark, res same, student
Williams Celia,* house-servant, res 518 e Martin
Williamson B P, farmer, res 122 w Hargett
Williamson Mrs Ella S, wife B P
Williamson Dr F P, son B P, res same, veterinary surgeon
Williamson Mial, son B P, res same, student
Williamson Herbert L, son B P, res same, student
Williamson Miss Rosalind, d B P, res same, student
Williamson Mrs Charlotte M, wid, res with mother, Mrs S H Montgomery
Williamson Miss Mary, bds Mrs M A Eatman
Williamson & Lea, props Farmers Warehouse, cor s Bloodworth and e Davie
Williamson Melissa,* washerwoman, res 324 w Edenton
Williamson Minnie,* d Melissa, res same, student
Williamson Jane,* nurse, res old Fair Ground, o s e
Williamson Ella,* d Jane, res same, cook
Willard W H, banker and mfr, res 628 Hillsboro'
Willis Wm W, brick-mason, res 514 s Person
Willis Mrs Nannie, wife Wm W
Willis Miss Claudia O, d W W, res same, student
Willis Miss Bertha M, d W W, res same, student
Willis Edgar H, son W W, res same, student
Willis Miss Essie A, d W W, res same, student
Willis Alfred, shoemaker, res 224 s Blount
Willis Mrs Susan P, wife Alfred, dressmaker
Willis Miss Effie A, d Alfred, res same
Willis Miss Hazel K, d Alfred, res same, student
Willoughby W J, carp, res 219 n West
Willoughby Mrs Harriet, wife W J
Wilson Thomas F, conductor S A L R'R, res 312 Oakwood ave
Wilson Mrs Blanche, wife Thomas F
Wilson Lillie, seamstress, res 517 e Martin
Wilson Annie,* servant of Rev J B Cheshire, res on lot
Wilson Mrs Janet, wid, mother of Mrs W A Montgomery, r same
Wilson W H, plumber, 219 s Wilmington, res 215 w Cabarrus
Wilson Mrs M E, wife W H
Wilson John H, son W H
Wilson Young V,* lab, res 335 w South
Wilson Mary E,* wife Young V, house work
Wilson Indiana L C,* house-servant, res 210 w Cabarrus
Wilson Mary,* cook, res 336 w South
Wilson Edward,* son Mary, res same, lab
Wilson Emeline,* cook, res old Fair Ground, o s e
Wilson Eliza,* d Emeline, res same, washerwoman
Wilson Quilly,* washerwoman, res 602 s Person

Willson Joel V, machinist, res 534 n West
Willson Mrs Mary L, wife Joel V
Willson Wm W, city auditor and bkkpr for John C Drewry, res 314 w Jones
Willson Mrs Alice W, wife Wm W
Willson Miss Lizzie V, d Wm W, res same, student
Willson Geo P, son Wm W, res same, student
Willson Miss Alice, d Wm W, res same, student
Wilton Henry S, car-trimmer, res 611 s Wilmington
Wimbush William,* grocer, cor Bloodworth and Edenton, res 521 Newbern ave
Wimbush Charity A,* wife William
Wimbush Esther,* d William, res same, student
Wimbush Peter,* carp, res 16 McKee
Wimbush Olivia,* wife Peter, house work
Winder Mrs J C, wid, res 504 n Person
Winder John H, railroading, res with Mrs R S Tucker
Winder Mrs Florence T, wife John H
Winslow Mary,* cook for Mrs C T Bailey, res on lot
Winslow J W,* restaurant cook
Winston John,* brakeman S A L, res 525 e Edenton
Winston Maggie,* wife John, washerwoman
Winston R T, clk Thomas & Maxwell, res Johnson
Winston Mrs Carrie, wife R T
Winters Harriet,* washerwoman, res 229 s East
Winters Frances,* d Harriet, res same, laundress
Winters Charles,* son Harriet, res same, lab
Winters Ida,* d Harriet, res same, servant
Wissner Miss H J, teacher in Peace Institute, res same
Withers W A, Prof of Chemistry and sec of A & M College, res n Blount
Withers Mrs Elizabeth W, wife W A
Womack T B, clk in revenue dept, res 507 n Blount
Womack Mrs Susie, wife T B
Womack Mrs J A, wid, res with son, T B Womack
Womack Mary,* farm hand, res rear 404 Fayetteville
Womack Virginia,* d Mary, res same, house servant
Womack Lizzie,* cook, res 728 Manly
Womble L D, general merchandise, 17 e Hargett, r 210 e Morgan
Womble Mrs Fannie, wife L D
Womble Miss Ada, d L D, res same
Womble Miss Ida, d L D, res same, teacher in Murphy School
Womble Miss Fannie, d L D, res same, student
Womble Albert, son L D, res same, machinist
Womble Louis, son L D, res same, student
Womble Herbert, clk, res 327 e Edenton
Womble Edgar, engraver, res 327 e Edenton
Womble Miss Carrie, sister of Herbert, res same, saleslady

Womble Miss Alice, sister of Herbert, res same
Womble Miss Agnes, sister of Herbert, res same
Womble Miss Jennie V, sister of Herbert, res same, saleslady
Womble Rufus, wks for J E Physioc, res 327 e Edenton
Womble W T, accountant and bkkpr, res 636 e Hargett
Womble Mrs O E, wife W T
Womble Mrs Martha A, d W T, res same
Womble Walter R, son W T, res same, printer
Womble Basil H, son W T, res same, pressman at E M Uzzell's
Womble Thomas R, son W T, res same, marble-cutter app
Womble John, dairyman Experimental farm, bds 209 w Morgan
Womble Mrs Bettie, wife John
Womble Miss Lillie, d John, res same, student
Womble Miss Bettie, d John, res same, student
Womble John, son John Sr, res same, student
Womble Thos,* wks for Ral Gas Co, res 325 w Edenton
Womble Louisa,* wife Thos
Womble Spencer,* son Thos, res same, student
Womble Cap,* son Thos, res same, driver
Womble Thomas, gardener, res 526 s Bloodworth
Womble Mrs Burline, wife Thos, seamstress
Womble Miss Alice, d Thos, res same, student
Womble Frank, artist, res 608 e Hargett
Womble Kittie,* dressmaker, room 6 Stronach ave
Womble Geo L, machinist, res 314 s Dawson
Womble Mrs Ava G, wife Geo L
Womble Miss Minnie L, d Geo L, res same
Womble Lewis,* porter Southern frt depot, res 221 w Cabarrus
Womble Ruthie,* wife Lewis, cook
Woodall L H, clk for W N Snelling, res 319 e Hargett
Woodall Mrs Cornelia, wife L H
Woodall Edwin, son L H, res same
Woodall Wm A, city policeman, res 102 n Saunders
Woodall Mrs Mildred M, wife Wm A
Woodall Mrs Sarah A, wid, res 413 s Blount
Woodall Miss Mabel N, d Mrs Sarah A, res same, student
Woodard M W, saloon, 316 w Cabarrus, res 522 s Harrington
Woodard Mrs Elizabeth, wife M W
Woodard Miss Lula, d M W, res same, student
Woodard Miss Bessie, d M W, res same, student
Woodard M W Jr, son M W, res same
Woodlief J W, painter, res Cox ave, o s w
Woodlief Mrs Zilphia, wife J W
Woodlief Miss Daisy, d J W, res same
Woodlief Miss Maud, d J W, res same
Woodlief George, son J W, res same
Woodlief Miss Lillie, d J W, res same
Woodlief Clarence, son J W, res same

Woodlief Miss Arma, d J W, res same
Woodruff Coit K, bds with Mrs R H Jones, 305 Hillsboro'
Woodruff Mrs Bettie, wife Coit K
Woods Mrs Annie, wid, res 119 e Davie
Woods Miss Mary, d Mrs Annie, res same, dressmaker
Woods Miss Lula, d Mrs Annie, res same, student
Woods Thomas, son Mrs Annie, res same, student
Woods Miss Bertha, d Mrs Annie, res same
Woods Wm A, son Mrs Annie, res same, printer
Woods Mrs Mary E, wife Wm A
Woods Samuel, salesman, res 407 Fayetteville
Woods Mrs Addie, wife Samuel, boarding-house
Woods Robert,* lab, res 208 w Lenoir
Woods Clara,* wife Robert, cook
Woods Wm,* farm hand, r Hargett, o s e
Woods Caroline,* wife Wm, washerwoman
Woods Bettie,* farm hand, res 583 e Lenoir
Woods Nancy,* washerwoman, res 583 e Lenoir
Woods Fannie,* farm hand, res 583 e Lenoir
Woods Richard,* gardener, res 579 e Lenoir
Woodson Mrs Nellie, lives at Rev Dr J B Bobbitt's
Woodson Fred,* waiter, res 318 w South
Woodson Martha,* wife Fred, washerwoman
Woodward Miss Imogene, periodical tickets, bds 404 Fayetteville
Woodward James L, clk for J D Riggan, res 545 e Jones
Woodward Mrs Emma J, wife J L
Woodward Miss Lillian, d J L, res same, student
Woodward Miss Maggie, d J L, res same, student
Woodward James L Jr, son J L, res same, student
Woodward Miss Julia, dry goods, notions, &c, 18 e Hargett, r 310 e Hargett
Woodward Charles W, clk for Miss Julia Woodward, res 310 e Hargett
Woodward Miss Em, clk for Miss Julia Woodward, res same
Woodward Miss Mattie, clk for Miss Julia Woodward, res same
Woodward Mrs M C, wid, res 220 e Martin

WE INVITE YOU TO INSPECT OUR
Shoe Department.

It is very large and prices are right.

WE KEEP ALL THE NEW STYLES IN MILLINERY.

Agents for Butterick Patterns. **WOOLLCOTT & SON,**
14 E. Martin St., RALEIGH, N. C.

Woodward Miss Mabel, d Mrs M C, res same
Woodward Miss Carrie, d Mrs M C, res same, student
Woodward Miss Valerie, d Mrs M C, res same
Woodward Miss Lotta, d Mrs M C, res same
Woodward, Miss Julia, seamstress, res 307 w Morgan
WOOLLCOTT & SON, dry goods, notions, shoes, &c, 14 e Martin
Woollcott Walter (Woollcott & Son), merchant, r 316 Newbern ave
Woollcott Mrs Lula, wife Walter
Woollcott Miss Alice, d Walter, res same
Woollcott Philip, son Walter, res same
Woollcott Wm (Woollcott & Son), merchant, res 127 Newbern ave
Woollcott Mrs Mary, wife Wm
Woollcott Miss Mary, d Wm, res same
WOOLLCOTT FRED, dry goods, notions, shoes, &c, 214 s Wilmington, res 127 Newbern ave
Woollcott Mrs Maud, wife Fred
Wooten Jos,* lab S A L shops, res 120 w Peace
Workman Miss Lillie, wks at Telephone Exchange, res 427 s Wilmington
Workman Fleming, student, res 427 s Wilmington
Workman Lalon, student, res 427 s Wilmington
Workman Colon, student, res 427 s Wilmington
Worlds Mrs Bettie, grocer, 530 s Bloodworth, res same
Worlds Rev J J,* Baptist minister, res 702 s West
Worlds Louisa J,* wife Rev J J
Worrell J R, bkkpr S A L R R, res 226 n Saunders
Worrell Mrs Nora, wife J R
Worrell Wm I, son J R, res same, machinist app
Worrell Miss Ethel, d J R, res same, student
Worrell Miss Lena, d J R, res same, student
Worrell Miss Bettie, d J R, res same, student
Worrell J H, grocer, 324 s East, res same
Worth Wm H, State Treasurer, office in Capitol, res 127 n McDowell
Worth Mrs Sallie M, wife Wm H
Worth Miss E L, d Wm H, res same, student
Worth Miss R M, d Wm H, res same, student
Worth Miss Annie, d Wm H, res same, student
Worth Rev V M,* Methodist minister, res 817 Manly
Worth Matilda,* wife Rev V M, house work
Worth James H,* son Rev V M, res same, lab
Worth Chas W,* son Rev V M, res same, student
Worth V M Jr,* son Rev V M, res same, student
Worth Alice,* cook, res 525 s Blount
Worth Zilphia,* cook for Mrs E E Moffitt, res 525 s Blount
Wortham Lizzie,* washerwoman, res 30 Fowle
Wortham Henry,* son Lizzie, res same, student
Wortham William,* son Lizzie, res same, student

Wortham James,* cook restaurant, rooms 108 e Hargett
Wortham Mary,* restaurant, 310 w Cabarrus, res same
Wortham Merrimon,* clk for M W Woodard, res 317 e Davie
Wortham Eliza M,* wife Merrimon
Wortham John T,* son M, res same, student
Wortham Walter W,* son M, res same, student
Wortham Edna L,* d M, res same, student
Wortham Jennie,* nurse, res 326 w Edenton
Wray J P, clk Cross & Linehan, bds 520 s West
Wray James,* wks Phosphate mill, bds 712 s Person
Wright Jas P, harness-maker, res 11 w South
Wright Mrs Carrie L, wife J P
Wright Miss Edna M, d J P, res same
Wright Wymdrom, son J P, res same, student
Wright William, son J P, res same, student
Wright Miss Jane E, d J P, res same, student
Wright Miss Alma E, d J P, res same, student
Wright Wiley,* lab, res 311 w Lenoir
Wright Matilda,* wife Wiley, washerwoman
Wright Fannie,* washerwoman, res room 2 Railroad al
Wright D K, eng S A L R R, bds 10 e North
Wright W E, electrician at Insane Asylum, res same
Wright C B (Latta & Wright), cotton broker, res 126 e Edenton
Wright Mrs Ella M, wife C B
Wright Miss Louise B, d C B, res same, student
Wright R B,* grocer, 612 s McDowell, res same
Wright J J,* lab, res 612 s McDowell
Wright Haywood,* drayman, res 612 s McDowell
Wright Della,* laundress, res 30 Railroad
Wright William A,* servant at Mrs Robt H Jones, res Idlewild
Wright Hattie E,* wife Wm A, washerwoman
Wright Mrs Frances, wid, seamstress, res Prairie bldg
Wyatt Job P & Bros, wholesale grocers and commission merchants, 15 e Martin, 16 Exchange Place
Wyatt Job P (J P Wyatt & Bros), merchant, res 113 n Dawson
Wyatt Willie, son Job P, res same, student
Wyatt Miss Louise, d Job P, res same, student
Wyatt Robert, son Job P, res same, student
Wyatt Miss Marion, d Job P, res same
Wyatt P T (J P Wyatt & Bros), merchant, res 211 e Morgan
Wyatt Mrs Rebecca, wife P T
Wyatt E F (E F Wyatt & Son), harness and saddles, res 218 n McDowell
Wyatt Mrs E A, wife E F
Wyatt E S (Wyatt Bros), grocer, res 218 n McDowell
Wyatt E F & Son, saddle and harness manufacturers, 109 e Martin
Wyatt W F (E F Wyatt & Son), harness and saddle mfr, res 511 e Jones

Wyatt Mrs Mary J, wife W F
Wyatt Miss Bessie, d W F, res same
Wyatt Miss Jessie, d W F, res same, student
Wyatt Henry E, son W F, res same, student
Wyatt Charles, son W F, res same, student
Wyatt & Co, grocers, cor Johnson and Salisbury
Wyche Miss M L, head nurse at Rex Hospital, res same
Wyche George,* lab, res Whitaker ave
Wyche Nellie,* wife Geo, washerwoman
Wyche Robert,* son Geo, res same, student
Wynne J S, sec and treas of Ral cot mill, res 408 Elm
Wynne Mrs Annie L, wife J S
Wynne Miss Lizzie L, d J S, res same, student
Wynne Robert W, son J S, res same, student
Wynne Wm H, son J S, res same
Wynne W W, farmer, res 404 Elm
Wynne Mrs Lucy E, wife W W
Wynne Miss Alma L, d W W, res same, organist at Edenton-St Methodist church
Wynne Mrs Addie, wid, dressmaker, res 411 e Morgan
Wynne Miss Clyde, d Mrs Addie, res same, dressmaker
Wynne John, son Mrs Addie, res same
Wynne Wm A, inventor of tel call bell, res Newbern ave, o s e
Wynne Mrs Mary, wife Wm A

YANCEY Thos B, carriage and buggy dealer, 130 e Morgan, res 250 Peace
Yancey Mrs E B, wife Thos B
Yancey Thomas B Jr, son Thos B, res same, clk in post-office
Yancey Miss Mary, d Thos B, res same, student
Yancey Miss Lola, d Thos B, res same, student
Yancey John,* driver for F L Bailey, res 421 s Blount
Yancey Mintree,* wife John, washerwoman
Yancey Peggie,* washerwoman, res rear Catholic church
Yancey Susan,* d Peggie, res same
Yancey Rosa,* d Peggie, res same, cook
Yancey Lucy,* house work, res 523 s Harrington
Yancey Millard,* student, res 523 s Harrington
Yancey Becky,* nurse, res e Hargett, o s e
Yancey Rosa,* cook for Chas Root, res on lot
Yancey Leah,* sick-nurse, res 728 Fayetteville
Yarboro Lee H, clk, res 105 Freeman, o s e
Yarboro Mrs Sue E, wife Lee H
Yarboro John,* blacksmith, res 513 s Blount
Yarboro Nancy,* wife John, washerwoman
Yarboro Ernest,* g-son John, res same, student
Yarboro Cooper,* lab, res o s e

Yarboro Emily,* cook for Dr R H Lewis, res 15 Stronach ave
Yarboro Lucy,* d Emily, res same, cook
Yates Alonzo C, yardmaster S A L, res 123 Firwood ave, o s n
Yates Mrs Mary, wife A C
Yates Robt V, son A C, res same
Yates Thomas, blacksmith, Morgan, rear Exchange Hotel
Yates Murphy, blacksmith, Morgan, rear Exchange Hotel
Yates Charles,* restaurant cook, res 215 w Lenoir
Yates Mrs Gabriella, wid, res with L G Rogers
Yates Robt E L, Adjunct Prof of Mathematics A & M College, res Maiden lane, o s w
Yates Mrs Minnie, wife Prof R E L
Yearby Wm, clk Levine & Brown, bds 426 s Wilmington
Yeargan Chaney,* nurse, res 114 w Cabarrus
Yeargan James,* painter, res 413 n Salisbury
Yeargan Fred,* carp, res 210 e Cabarrus
Yeargan Lizzie B,* d Fred, res same, seamstress
Yeargan Eliza,* d Fred, res same, servant
Yeargan John,* son Fred, res same, painter
Yeargan Fred Jr,* son Fred, res same, bell-boy Yarboro' House
Yeargan Thomas,* son Fred, res same, student
Yeargan George,* son Fred, res same, student
Yellowby Sam,* lab S A L R R, res 441 n Salisbury
Yellowby Jane,* wife Sam
Yellowby Florence,* d Sam, res same, washerwoman
Yellowby Peter,* lab, res 320 w South
Yellowby Mary,* washerwoman, res 320 w South
Yellowby William,* son Mary, res same, student
Yellowby Albert,* cook, res 320 w South
York Mrs Lula J, wid, res 211 Tucker
York Miss Minnie K, d Mrs Lula J, res same, wks Ral cot mill
York Chas W, son Mrs Lula J, res same, wks Ral cot mill
York Miss Rosa D, d Mrs Lula J, res same, wks Ral cot mill
York Geo H, son Mrs Lula J, res same, student
Younger Chas H, carp, res 707 n Bloodworth, o s n
Younger Mrs Lucy E, wife Chas H
Young Millie,* cook, res old Fair Ground, o s e
Young Alberta,* d Millie, res same, house servant
Young Hubert,* son Millie, res same, lab
Young Edmund,* farmer, res e Hargett, o s e
Young Jane,* wife Edmund, washerwoman
Young Rose,* d Edmund, res same, nurse
Young Esther,* d Edmund, res same, cook
Young Charles,* son Edmund, res same, lab
Young Sam,* student, res rear 527 Hillsboro'
Young Millie,* student, res rear 527 Hillsboro'
Young Willie,* student, res rear 527 Hillsboro'
Young Lillie,* student, res rear 527 Hillsboro'

Young Charles,* barber, res 12 n East
Young Florence,* wife Chas, house work
Young D F, lineman for W U Tel Co, res 320 s Dawson
Young Mrs Lucy, wife D F
Young Solomon,* gardener Park Hotel, res 723 s Dawson
Young Annie,* wife Solomon, house work
Young Sallie B,* d Solomon, res same, student
Young Lewis,* lab, res 714 s McDowell
Young Sallie,* wife Lewis, house work
Young Charles,* barber, s Wilmington
Young & Hughes, plumbers, steam and gas fitters, 2 Prairie bldg, Wilmington
Young Len,* well-digger, res 719 s Dawson
Young Mary,* wife Len, washerwoman
Young Mourning,* washerwoman, res 211 Cannon
Young Mary,* cook at Harrison House, room 114 e Lenoir
Young Effie,* d Mary, res same, student
Young Charles,* son Mary, res same, barber
Young J A,* clk for A T Mitchell, res same
Young Winnie,* cook for Dr H B Battle, res 5 Stronach ave
Young Nora,* washerwoman, res 5 Stronach ave
Young Maggie,* student, res 5 Stronach ave
Young Aaron,* shoemaker, res 817 s Wilmington
Young Dicey,* wife Aaron, washerwoman
Young Lewis,* son Aaron, res same, porter for C J Parker
Young Ben,* son Aaron, res same, student
Young Rufus,* son Aaron, res same, student
Young Lucinda,* cook, res 109 w Morgan
Young Bettie,* servant, res 109 w Morgan
Young Mary,* washerwoman, res 435 n Salisbury
Young Maggie,* d Affie Green, res Townes al
Young Men's Christian Association, cor Fayetteville and Morgan
Young Wm J, prin of Institution for the Blind, res at Institution
Young Miss Nellie, d W J, res same
Young Miss Daisy, d W J, res same
Young Miss Pattie, sister W J Young, res 206 w Lane
Young Wm J Jr (Young & Hughes), plumber, res 206 w Lane
Young Miss Laura, sister W J Jr, res same
Young Sam M, clk Julius Lewis Hardware Co, res 206 w Lane
YOUNG DANIEL H, clk Superior Court and Probate Judge of Wake co, res 116 w Edenton
Young Mrs Florentina, wife Dan H
Young Hubert, son Dan H, res same, student
Young Miss Alline, d Dan H, res same, student
Young Mrs Lovie G, wid, res 619 w Jones
Young J Benj, son Mrs Lovie G, res same, clk at W H & R S Tucker & Co
Young Miss Mamie, d Mrs Lovie G, res same

Young Henry J, bkkpr at Citizens National Bank, res 619 w Jones
Young Mrs Mary, wife Henry J
Young Geo P, guard at penitentiary, res 416 e Person
Young Mrs Arthelia, wife Geo P
Young Lela, d Geo P, res same, student
Young R Amos, son Geo P, res same, student
Young M F, boss carder Pilot cot mill, res Oakdale ave, o s n
Young Mrs A E, wife M F
Young Jas H,* editor Gazette, res 226 e Lenoir
Young Bettie,* wife Jas H
Young Maud,* d Jas H, res same, student
Young Isabella,* washerwoman, res Hood's al
Young Willie,* son Isabella, res same, student
Young Mary,* washerwoman, res Hood's al
Young Kate,* washerwoman, res Hood's al
Young Emma,* washerwoman, res Hood's al
Young Lizzie,* washerwoman, res Hood's al
Young Chas W, grocer, 11 e Hargett, res 515 Polk
Young Mrs Maggie C, wife C W
Young Miss Ethel W, d C W, res same, student
Young Miss Pauline, d C W, res same, student
Young Abram,* butcher, res 320 e Davie
Young Julia,* wife Abram

ZACHARY Henry C, contractor and builder, res 513 Polk
Zachary Mrs Mary, wife H C
Zachary Wm A, son H C, res same, conductor S A L
Zachary Miss Zettie H, d H C, res same
Zachary Miss Bessie C, d H C, res same, student
Zachary Miss Mary U, d H C, res same, student

Peace Institute,
Raleigh, N. C.

A Select School for Girls,

Complete in all its Appointments,

Thorough in Scholarship.

Principal, a M. A. of University of Virginia, with able Assistants under him.

Three Literary Courses, leading to the Degrees of B. L., B. S. and B. A.

Art Department
: is unsurpassed, and is in charge of an experienced Specialist, with one Assistant.

Music.
: There are two courses, leading to the Degrees Fellow of Music (F. Mus.) and Bachelor of Music (B. Music). The Music Faculty contains five (5) able and experienced teachers.

Health
: of our location proverbially good, and especial attention is paid to Hygiene and Physical Culture.

Terms
: very moderate for advantages offered.

Fare
: good and plenty of it.

For Catalogue and full information, address

JAS. DINWIDDIE,
Principal.

RALEIGH CLASSIFIED BUSINESS DIRECTORY.

1896-'97.

Agents.

Allcott Wayne, book and machinery, office Academy of Music bldg
Allen Chas S, S A L freight office
Bryan A P, Southern Express Co
Bunch T V, baggage at Union passenger station
Leard H S, passenger and soliciting for S A L R R, office 217 Fayetteville
Munson J B, Southern R R division, freight and passenger agt, office rear Citizens National Bank
Murray T H, S A L ticket agt at Union station
RALEIGH STATIONERY CO, Bar-Lock typewriters, 309 Fayetteville
Potts R L, Southern R R freight office

Almanacs.

North Carolina Almanac, Rev Levi Branson pubr
Turner's N C Almanac, James H Ennis pubr

Architects.

BAUER A G, 212 Fayetteville, up-stairs
CARPENTER & PEEBLES, cor Fayetteville and Martin, up-stairs
Hicks W J, 304 w Edenton
PEARSON CHARLES, Pullen bldg, up-stairs
Royster L H, res n Saunders

Art Studios.

JOHNSON T B, 113½ Fayetteville
Randall W G, cor Wilmington and Polk
WHARTON C P, 119½ Fayetteville

324

Artists.

Busbee J L, res 104 Hargett
Curtis Miss Minnie May, res 225 e Lenoir
Hicks Mrs Gertrude, res 513 n Salisbury
Johnson T B, 113½ Fayetteville
Randall W G, cor Wilmington and Polk
Wharton C P, 119½ Fayetteville
Womble B F, res 608 Hargett

Attendants at Insane Hospital.

Abernathy, W R
Austin, W E
Bell, Charles
Bell, Haywood
Bevers, J C
   Chief Attendant
Banks, T G
Broardhurst, R D
Bronson, Miss Lillie
Cotten, Miss Ag
Dupree, T M
Eagle, Miss Annie
Ferrall, W V
Fryar, Miss M V
Gardner, Miss A
Gilliam, Miss Lillie
Harris, J W
Hunnicutt, J D
Kelly, Miss Ada C
Kirby, Miss L M
Kirkland, J S
Kirkpatrick, Miss A B
Leggett, Miss A L
Monroe, Miss Janie
Moore, Miss A T
Newkirk, Miss M L
Pearce, Miss I O
Rhea, Miss Mary A
Shelton, Miss Rosa L
   Chief Lady Attendant
Smith, C N
Turner, Miss Carrie
Turner, Miss Mamie
Watson, C P
Williams, Miss M V
Williams, W B
White, Miss S T

Attorneys at Law.

Amis Moses N, office Central Hotel, res same
ANDREWS A B Jr, office 217 Fayetteville, res 407 n Blount
Argo & Snow, office 333 Fayetteville
Argo T M (Argo & Snow), res 12 n Person
Ashe S A, office 240 Fayetteville, up-stairs, res 628 Hillsboro'
BATCHELOR J B, office 333 Fayetteville, res 213 w Martin
Battle & Mordecai, office 240 Fayetteville, up-stairs
Battle R H (Battle & Mordecai), res 11 e Lane
Beckwith B C, office Commercial and Farmers Bank bldg, bds 118 n Wilmington
Bledsoe M A Sr, res cor Salisbury and South
Branch John H,* res 719 s Saunders
Burton R O Jr, office Pullen bldg, res cor Peace and Person
Busbee F H, office 217 Fayetteville, res 204 n Person
Busbee C M (Shepherd & Busbee), office Pullen bldg, res 104 w Hargett
Busbee Perrin, office Pullen bldg, res 104 w Hargett
Clarke Walter, Associate Justice Supreme Court, res 440 Halifax

Creech Joseph A, res 615 s Salisbury
Day W H (McRae & Day), res 120 Halifax
Devereux Thos P, office Commercial and Farmers Bank bldg
DOUGLASS W C, office 301½ Fayetteville
Fleming & Moffitt, office 12 w Martin
Fleming J H (Fleming & Moffitt), res outside city
Fuller Judge T C, U S Court of Land Claims, res 130 Hillsboro'
Gatling B M, office Pullen bldg
Gatling John, res 311 w Martin
GRAY ROBT T, office 16 w Martin, res 530 n Blount
Harris J C L, office Frap's bldg, res 213 e Hargett
HAYWOOD ERNEST, office 301½ Fayetteville, res 211 Newbern ave
HINSDALE JNO W, office 217 Fayetteville, res 330 Hillsboro'
Holding & Vass, office 6 w Martin
Holding J N (Holding & Vass), res 528 s Salisbury
Johnson E A,* res 519 s West
JONES W N, office 16 w Martin, res 522 Fayetteville
Jones Armistead, office Commercial and Farmers Bank bldg, res Hillsboro' near cor Dawson
Leary & Lane,* office cor Wilmington and Davie
Leary John S* (Leary & Lane), office Davie and Wilmington
Lane D P* (Leary & Lane), res Davie, o s e
MASSEY A P, office 217 Fayetteville, bds Park Hotel
Maynard E P (Peele & Maynard), res 120 n Person
McRae & Day, office 217 Fayetteville
McRae James C, bds 120 Halifax
Moffitt Elijah (Fleming & Moffitt), bds cor Hargett and McDowell
MONTAGUE B F, office Commercial and Farmers Bank bldg, res 313 Newbern ave
Montgomery W A, Associate Justice Supreme Court, res 529 n Person
Mordecai S F (Battle & Mordecai), res 303 n Boundary
Peele & Maynard, office 239½ s Wilmington
Peele W J (Peele & Maynard), bds 329 Hillsboro'
Purnell T R, office Mahler bldg, res 422 n Person
Ryan S G, office Pullen bldg, res 421 n Bloodworth
Shepherd & Busbee, office Pullen bldg
Shepherd James E (Shepherd & Busbee), bds Yarborough House
Smith E Chambers, office Pullen bldg, res 434 Halifax
Snow W B (Argo & Snow), res Boylan ave
Stronach Alexander, office Pullen bldg, res n Boundary
Strong & Strong, office 224½ Fayetteville
Strong Geo V (Strong & Strong), res 504 n Blount
Strong Robt C (Strong & Strong), res 410 n East
Vass Wm W Jr (Holding & Vass), res 3 e Edenton
Watson W L, office 217 Fayetteville, res 534 e Jones
Whitaker Spier, office Pullen bldg, res o s s

Auction Houses.

Beine C H & Co, 108-110 e Hargett
Stronach Frank, 319 s Wilmington

Auctioneers.

Stronach Frank, 319 s Wilmington
Thomason Edward, bds Central Hotel
Tonnoffski Geo L, 108 e Hargett

Bakers.

Bragassa J A, 306 s Salisbury
Bretsch Chas M, 103 Fayetteville
Jones E G,* 603 s McDowell

Banks and Bankers.

Citizens National Bank, cor Fayetteville and Martin
COMMERCIAL AND FARMERS BANK, cor Wilmington and Martin
Mechanics Dime Saving Bank, 117 Fayetteville
NATIONAL BANK OF RALEIGH, cor Fayetteville and w Hargett
RALEIGH SAVINGS BANK, cor Fayetteville and e Hargett

Barbers and Hair-Dressers.

City Shaving Saloon,* 211 s Wilmington
Collins Sarah,* 112 e Hargett
Davis & Dunston, 202½ Fayetteville
Dunston P B, Central Hotel
FAUST E G, Park Hotel
Hughes H I, 8 Exchange Place
Locklear Caswell, basement 224 Fayetteville
Moring J J,* Prairie building
OTEY W G, 215 Fayetteville
Taylor Thomas,* 136 s Wilmington
Watts Maurice, 216 Fayetteville

Beer Dealers—Wholesale.

Jones T R, 422 s Dawson
Stumpf Peter, 204 e Martin

Billiard Saloon.

Denton Ed V, 311-313 Fayetteville
Yarborough House, 317 Fayetteville

Bill-Posters.

Fowler Rod, r Fayetteville below R R

Blacksmiths and Wheelwrights.

Andrews R M, s Salisbury
Bowen T A, 130 w Morgan
Branch Frank,* 611 s Harrington
Evans J W, cor Morgan and Blount
Fowler W N, S A L R R shops
Godwin & Bashford, 133 s Wilmington
Green Austin,* res s East
Harris Walter,* s Wilmington
Hartsfield Henry,* res 536 e Lenoir
Haywood George,* s Wilmington
Hill Joseph & Son,* 126 s Blount
Holloway W H, 121 e Hargett
Horton Henry, S A L R R shops
Jordan John C, cor Morgan and Blount
King John C, at Allen & Cram Machine Co
Matthews Jonas, S A L R R shops
McDowell W F, S A L R R shops
Mitchell Henry, S A L R R shops
Pennington S P, cor Davie and Salisbury
Stewart Sam,* at N C Car Co
Watkins Jesse, S A L R R shops
Yates Thomas & Son,* w Morgan

Blank-Book Manufacturers.

CAPITAL PRINTING CO, Academy of Music bldg
Edwards & Broughton, cor Hargett and Salisbury
RALEIGH STATIONERY CO, 309 Fayetteville
UZZELL E M, cor Wilmington and Martin

Boiler-Makers.

Frost W A, S A L R R, res 108 n Saunders
Glenn Henry, S A L R R, res n Blount
Hamilton D S, res 225 w Martin
Lochrie William, S A L R R, res cor Jones and Dawson

Marcom Milton, wks Allen & Cram, res 416 e Hargett
Mitchell Charles, res 553 e Martin
Whitehead James, S A L R R, res n Harrington
Williams W A, S A L R R, res 324 w Lane

Bookbinderies.

CAPITAL PRINTING CO, Academy of Music bldg
Edwards & Broughton, cor Hargett and Salisbury
UZZELL E M, cor Wilmington and Martin

Bookbinders.

Bailey W E, res 305 s Person
Crabtree Richard, res 323 e Martin
Davis John F, res Elm
Edwards E W, res 323 s McDowell
Medlin Jno H, res 114 w Martin
Medlin J P, res 318 s Person
Miller W H, res 511 s Bloodworth
Norwood Geo T, bds 415 Elm
Warren James M, res 738 e Davie

Booksellers and Stationers.

N C BOOK COMPANY, 129 Fayetteville
RALEIGH STATIONERY COMPANY, 309 Fayetteville
Williams A & Co, 121 Fayetteville

Boarding-Houses.

Banks Mrs M E, 508 Fayetteville
Barkley J R, n Person
Blalock Mrs Tabitha, 224 e Martin
Branson House, 101½-103½ Fayetteville, Rev I A White propr
Dement A J, 215 e Davie
Dowell H J, cor Wilmington and Hargett
Edwards Mrs M J, 10 e North
Ellerbe Mrs M F, 213 w Martin
Evans Mrs L B, cor Edenton and McDowell
Germania House, N Deboy Sr propr, 109½ Fayetteville
Harris W S, 222 e Martin
Harris Mrs J M, 426 s Wilmington
Harrison House, cor Wilmington and Davie, Mrs E M Harrison
    propr
Hayes Mrs S A, 412 Fayetteville
Horton E G, cor Lane and Bloodworth
Hotel Florence, cor Fayetteville and Cabarrus, Mrs C R Lee propr

Johnson Mrs Albert, 329 Hillsboro'
Johnson R L, 421 s Wilmington
Jones Mrs R H, cor Hillsboro' and Dawson
King Mrs L M, 404 Hillsboro'
Koonce Richard, 314 Hillsboro'
Mansion House, 309 w Martin, R L Hedlin propr
Medlin J H, 114 w Martin
Millen Mrs Jennie, cor Newbern ave and Person
Moseley's Dining-Hall, 130 Fayetteville, N S Moseley propr
Myatt Mrs Emma, 109 s Blount
Parker Mrs C N, 117 Fayetteville
Ramsey Mrs M J, 119 w Martin
Ray Mrs A E, 11 s Wilmington
Richardson House, 120 e Hargett, Mrs S M Richardson propr
Smith Mrs R W, 213 Hillsboro'
Stother W H, cor Davie and Dawson
Siligson Ike, 114 s Blount
Taylor Ella,* 134 s Wilmington
White I A, propr Branson House, 101 Fayetteville
Willis Mrs S P, 224 s Blount

Board of Trades.

Raleigh Tobacco Board of Trade, E L Fleming pres

Boot and Shoe Dealers.

Heller Bros, 134 Fayetteville
Jones W E, 206 Fayetteville
Tucker W H & R S & Co, 123-125 Fayetteville
Whiting Bros, 10 e Martin
WOOLLCOTT & SON, 14 e Martin
WOOLLCOTT FRED, 214 s Wilmington

Boot and Shoemakers.

Abrams Charles, res Brooklyn, o s w
Barker S S,* 135 s Wilmington
Brown W D, res 123 w Cabarrus
Correll H A, 503 s Bloodworth
Dobbin Robert, basement 239 Fayetteville
Dunston M N,* 304 s Harrington
Earp H W, 539 e Martin
Evans Turner, 219 s Harrington
Francis Peter, Frap's bldg
Francis J E, Frap's building
Francis Bud, 205 Fayetteville
Haywood W C,* 407 Hillsboro'

Hunter J B,* 130 e Hargett
Jones D W, 219 s West
Jones W F,* cor McDowell and Morgan
Jones J M,* 539 Newbern ave
Jones S M & Bro,* 140 s Wilmington
Lewis J H,* 14 s Harrington
McKoy Neill,* cor Salisbury and Davie
Moore N H, e Martin
Moore W, basement 107 Fayetteville
Mullenix M S, e Martin
Smith George,* cor Wilmington and Cabarrus
Taylor Clayton,* cor Davie and Salisbury
Thompson Moses,* 104 s Wilmington
Tony N,* 318 s Salisbury
Weddon & Francis, 203½ Fayetteville
Weddon J P, 205 Fayetteville

Bottlers.

Jones T R, 422 s Dawson
Stumpf Peter, 204 e Martin

Bridge Builders.

Clifton W V, res 538 n Person

Brick-Masons and Plasterers.

Blackman J F,* res 110 w Cabarrus
Buffaloe W H, res Smithfield
Chavis Columbus,* res w South
Cook Edward,* res Oberlin, o s w
Dunston Sidney,* res Oberlin, o s w
Dunston Sylvester Sr,* res 520 s McDowell
Dunston Sylvester Jr,* res 520 s McDowell
Fann W E Sr, res 419 Cannon
Fann W E Jr, res 419 Cannon
Fann Walter, res 419 Cannon
Flagg John,* res Oberlin, o s w
Gant Emit,* res Fayetteville rd, o s s
Graves Willis M,* res Oberlin, o s w
Hall Isaac,* res 110 w South
Hamill & Hunnicutt, office s Salisbury
Hamill H J, res 559 e Martin
Harris George,* res 114 w Cabarrus
Hayes Wash,* res Hargett, o s e
Hayes Austin,* res 523 Smith
Haywood Henry,* res Hargett, o s e

Higgs Charles,* res Oberlin, o s w
Hunnicutt F W, res 230 s Swain
Hunnicutt W G, res Haywood
Hunnicutt F H, res 557 e Martin
Jeffreys Nortfleet,* res Oberlin, o s w
Lewis Charles W, res 326 n Saunders
Matthews W H,* res 211 w South
Matthews W J,* res w South
Matthews Robert,* res 211 w South
Mitchell James,* res 315 e Davie
Mitchell William,* res 315 e Davie
Perry C H, res 223 s Person
Phifer D P,* res 525 e Lenoir
Savage George, res Smithfield, o s s
Spencer T A,* res 409 Cannon
Thornton Charles,* res Oberlin, o s w
Williams Thomas,* res Oberlin, o s w
Williams George,* res Oberlin, o s w
Willis W W, res 514 s Person

Brokers—Cotton.

Barbee & Co, 305 s Wilmington
Cuthbert & Co, 305 s Wilmington
Johnson C E & Co, 303 s Wilmington
Latta & Wright, 317 s Wilmington
Lee Ed H, 307 s Wilmington
Parker M A, 312 s Wilmington

Brokers—Merchandise.

Duncan John A, 240 Fayetteville, up-stairs
Gattis W A, 239 s Wilmington, up-stairs
Grey J S, 120 Fayetteville
Harris E L, 107 Fayetteville
Hay O P, 218 Fayetteville
Johnson & Johnson, 109 Fayetteville

Building and Loan Associations.

MECHANICS AND INVESTORS UNION BUILDING AND LOAN CO, office in Pullen bldg
SOUTHERN BUILDING AND LOAN ASSOCIATION (Ral Branch), office 107 Fayetteville

Butchers.

Dancy William, stall 15, market
Donaldson Thos,* stall 2, market

Crawford W R & Sons, 230 Fayetteville
Jones J H, stall 18, market
Perry M M, stall 5, market
Perry C H,* stall 19, market
Sawyer William,* stall 6, market
Schwartz J, stall 1, market
Young Abram,* stall 22, market

Cabinet Makers.

Brown Ed S, res 311 w Morgan
Haynes M R, cor Morgan and Blount
Mitchell J E, 128 s Wilmington
Morris John T, cor Morgan and Wilmington
Teasley Edward, res 119 s Dawson

Cafes.

Denton's Cafe, 311 Fayetteville
DUGHI CAFE, 235 Fayetteville
Moseley Cafe, 130 Fayetteville

Candy Factories.

Barbee & Pope, 105 Fayetteville
Bretsch Chas, 103 Fayetteville
Royster A D & Bro, 207 Fayetteville

Carpenters.

Alford W H, res 213 n West
Aydlett Chas, res 709 n Salisbury
Beale Jesse, res 224 w Lane
Buck W A, wks N C Building & Supply Co
Bunch Thomas, res 415 n Salisbury
Burgess Wm,* res o s w
Burroughs Mike, wks S A L R R
Burwell M,* res 508 n Bloodworth
Busbee F M, res 522 n Person
Carroll James, res 207 n Harrington
Carroll John G, res 223 w Jones
Cawthorne J R, res cor Haywood and Davie
Collier J R, res 221 s West
Collins J W, res 329 Cannon
Ellison L S, res 415 n Salisbury
Emery L A, res Hargett, o s e
Falkner J F, res 9 Gatling's lane

Ford R J, res w North
Ford C T, res w North
Ford Wm, res w North
Grady C H, res 216 w Lane
Goodwin N M, wks S A L R R
Hall Lewis,* res 221 Bledsoe ave
Harper Jacob J, res 317 Polk
Harper Jas H, res 317 Polk
Hayes Richard,* res 822 s Blount
Horton W A, res 117 e Hargett
House J T, res 547 e Hargett
Hulin A D, res 315 s Harrington
Hunnicutt D O, res 412 e Morgan
Hunt J W, res 218 s Harrington
Hutchings I D, res 313 w Lane
Jackson A J, res 606 n Saunders
Jenkins Oscar,* 215 s Harrington
Jones A J, res s Blount
King C C, res 2 Franklin, o s n
Lamb Wm A, res 323 Pace
Lee C C, res 526 n Salisbury
Lindsey J M, res 110 s West
Miller Chris, wks N C Building and Supply Co
Mitchell H L, res 304 n Dawson
Neal L C, res n West near R R
Norman J R, res 536 e Jones
Parker J W, res 329 w Martin
Patterson S W, res 803 Jenkins
Peele B A, res 409 n Salisbury
Perry C H, res 223 s Person
Pool Jack,* res Martin, o s e
Potter Zach, res 402 w Morgan
Price John, wks S A L R R
Pulley R H, res Haywood
Riddle W L, res 404 w North
Riddle J S, res 215 n West
Riddle C A, res 210 n Harrington
Ruth H G, res 530 Hillsboro'
Ruth M F, res cor Hillsboro' and West
Ruth Geo H, res 517 Hicks lane
Ruth J O, res 108 Johnson
Ruth S L, res 302 St Mary's
Ruth Marvin, res 302 St Mary's
Sanders B W,* res 222 Smithfield
Smith Edward,* res old Fair Ground, o s e
Spiers L D, res 557 Newbern ave
Stewart Sam T,* res 806 s Blount
Strickland N B, res cor Dawson and Davie

Upperman Wm,* res 330 w South
Upperman M,* res 329 w South
Utley W S, res n Saunders
Waring Hubert, res 615 e Davie
Weathers W D, res 110 s West
Willoughby James, res 219 n West
Yeargan Fred,* res 210 e Cabarrus

Carriage Manufacturers and Dealers.

Evans J W, cor Morgan and Blount
Pace J M, 111 e Martin
Stronach Frank, 319 s Wilmington
Yancey T B, 130 e Morgan

Cashiers of Banks.

Briggs Fab H, cashier of the National Bank of Raleigh
Jerman B S, cashier of Commercial and Farmers Bank
Lacy B R, cashier of Mechanics Dime Savings Bank
Litchford H E, cashier of the Citizens National Bank
Pullen John T, cashier of Raleigh Savings Bank

Chamber of Commerce.

Raleigh Chamber of Commerce and Industry, Jos E Pogue pres

China, Glass and Queensware.

HUGHES W H, 127 Fayetteville

Cigar Manufacturers.

Norwood James M, 214 s Wilmington

Clergymen.

Atwater Wm,* pastor Dawson-Street Baptist church
Betts Alvin, Baptist, res cor Morgan and Person
Betts A L, city Baptist missionary, res 514 s Harrington
Bobbitt J B, D D, Methodist, res 129 s Dawson
Branson Levi, D D, Methodist, res Branson House
Bright A A, pastor Manly-Street Christian church, res Manly
Carter J W, D D, pastor First Baptist church, res 104 w Edenton
Cheshire Rt Rev J B Jr, Bishop of the Episcopal Diocese of N C,
    res cor Wilmington and North
Cobb Needham B, D D, Baptist, res 526 Polk

Crowder W J W, city missionary and colporter, r 115 s Harrington
Curtis A W, D D, pastor Congregational church, res 225 e Lenoir
Daniel Eugene, D D, pastor First Presbyterian church, res cor Hargett and Dawson
Davis A G,* pastor Davie-Street Presbyterian church
Foster James L, pastor Christian church, res 318 w Edenton
Hinton L B,* Methodist, res Oberlin, o s w
Howell Freeman,* Baptist, pastor Blount-Street church
Humphries L A,* pastor Cox Memorial Methodist church, res e Edenton
Hunter A B, Episcopal, prin St Augustine Normal School, r same
Johnson Cæsar,* Missionary Baptist, res 540 e Edenton
Leak R H W,* pastor St Paul A M E church, res 316 e Davie
Marshall M M, D D, rector of Christ Episcopal church, r 6 Newbern ave
Norman W C, D D, pastor Edenton-Street Methodist church, res cor Edenton and Dawson
Pegues A W,* Baptist, res D D & B Inst
Pettinger I McK, D D, rector of the Church of Good Shepherd, Episcopal, res cor Hillsboro' and McDowell
Prendergast Rev Father J M, pastor of the Church of Sacred Heart, Catholic, res 204 Hillsboro'
Price A R,* Baptist, res Martin, o s e
Roberts N F, D D,* Baptist, res Oberlin
Simms A M, D D, pastor Baptist Tabernacle, res cor Newbern ave and Bloodworth
Skinner Thomas E, D D, Baptist, r cor Wilmington and Edenton
Spillman B W, city Baptist S S missionary, res 312 Newbern ave
Smedes Bennett, D D, Episcopal, prin of St Mary's School, res at school
Tuttle D H, pastor Central Methodist church, res 221 e Morgan
Walker H P,* Methodist, res 423 Haywood
White I A, Methodist, res Branson House
Whitaker R H, D D, pastor City Missions, Methodist, res 509 n Person
Worlds J J,* pastor First Baptist church, res 702 s West

Clothing Dealers.

Berwanger S & D, 219 Fayetteville
Cross & Linehan, 210 Fayetteville
Whiting Bros, 10 e Martin
WOOLLCOTT & SON, 14 e Martin

Clubs.

Capital Club, Henry bldg, opp post-office

Coal and Wood Dealers.

EBERHARDT & BAKER, office 126 Fayetteville
Johnson & Johnson, 109 Fayetteville
JONES & POWELL, 107 Fayetteville

Commission Merchants.

Adams L H & Co, 310 s Wilmington
Crowder & Rand, 301 s Wilmington
Dewar & Wilder, 13 Martin and 14 Exchange Place
Johnson D T, agt, 16 e Hargett
Myatt & Hunter, 17 Martin and 18 Exchange Place
Norris M T & Bro, 239 s Wilmington
Parker & Terrell, 312 s Wilmington
Pool & Moring, 237 s Wilmington
Rogers W H, 12 Exchange Place
Snelling W N, 309 s Wilmington
Thomas J J & Co, 313-315 s Wilmington
Wyatt J P & Bros, 15 e Martin and 16 Exchange Place

Conductors—Railway.

Alderman J T, bds 204 Halifax
Bowen John, bds Halifax
Brown F F, res 110 s McDowell
Burroughs William, bds 105½ Fayetteville
Chavasse T H, bds Yarboro' House
Clements W P, bds 408 w Morgan
Faucette H M, res 223 n Harrington
Hogan J B, res Hicks' lane
Jones J C, bds Mrs A F Ray
Jones D B, bds Mrs A F Ray
Lassater G M, res 408 w Morgan
Martin T E, bds 10 e North
Maxwell Herbert, bds 105½ Fayetteville
Merritt J Mal, bds 10 e North
Stone E P, res 522 n Person
Weaver R E, res 605 Hillsboro'
Williams Henry, bds 10 e North
Wilson T F, res 312 Oakwood ave

Conductors—Street Railway.

Bashford A C, res Hillsboro' rd, o s w
Howell A A, res Hillsboro' rd, o s w
Royster F B, res 210 Newbern ave
Tucker W W, res Hillsboro' road, o s w
Upchurch H F, res 214 e Davie

Confectioners.

Barbee & Pope, 105 Fayetteville
Bretsch Charles, 103 Fayetteville
DUGHI A, 235 Fayetteville
Riggan J D, 132 Fayetteville
Royster A D & Bro, 207 Fayetteville

Contractors—Stone and Brick.

Hamill & Hunnicutt, office s Salisbury, rear T H Briggs & Sons
Linehan P & Son, office at Cross & Linehan, Fayetteville
N C BUILDING & SUPPLY CO, shops n West
Weir W J, n Bloodworth
Whitelaw John, cor McDowell and Martin

Contractors and Builders.

Briggs John D, 117 n Dawson
Cary Lumber Co, w Cabarrus
MILLS MFG CO, Fayetteville near r r crossing
N C BUILDING & SUPPLY CO, s West
N C CAR CO, Franklin

Cotton Buyers.

Barbee & Co, 305 s Wilmington
Johnson C E & Co, 303 s Wilmington
Latta & Wright, 317 s Wilmington
Lee Ed H, 307 s Wilmington
Parker M A, 312 s Wilmington

Cotton Compress Company.

Seaboard Air Line Railroad, at cot platform

Cotton Mills.

The Caraleigh Cotton Mill, South Raleigh
The Pilot Cotton Mill, North Raleigh
The Raleigh Cotton Mill, Firwood ave and r r crossing

Cotton Weighers.

Dowd P W, office Cotton Platform, res Hillsboro' rd
Dunn R G, office Cotton Platform, res outside city
Richardson T N, office Cotton Platform, res cor McDowell and Hargett
Stephenson W R, office Cotton Platform, res outside city

22

Dentists.

AYER J M, office 108 Fayetteville, up-stairs
CARROLL NORWOOD G, office cor Fayetteville and Hargett, up-stairs
CRAWFORD J H, office 116 Fayetteville, up-stairs
Everett D E, office 123½ Fayetteville, up-stairs
FLEMING J M, office 132½ Fayetteville, up-stairs
Turner V E, office 107½ Fayetteville, up-stairs

Dining-Hall.

Moseley's Dining-Hall, 130 Fayetteville

Dressmakers.

Bagwell Mrs A W, res 701 s Blount
Betts Mrs Mary L, res 112 Firwood ave
Boone Mrs Mary A, res 217 s East
Bolyn Mrs Clara, res 108 w Jones
Boyd Miss Lucy, res 121 n Wilmington
Bridgers Mrs M J, res 112 n East
Brogden Mrs O H, res Johnson
Brown Mrs Sallie D, res 121 w Cabarrus
Busbee Mrs Lizzie, res 226 w Hargett
Cheek Mrs Emeline, res 114 n Dawson
Cheek Miss Ida, res 114 n Dawson
Conn Miss Mary, res 104 w Jones
Crabtree Mrs Amy, res 205 n Salisbury
Debnam Miss L J, res 105 w Jones
Denton Miss Hattie M, res 117 s Bloodworth
Eatman Mrs W R, res 113 n Bloodworth
Glennan Mrs Fannie, res 119 w Morgan
Gruendler Mrs E V, res 314 s Blount
Hall Mollie,* res 511 n Salisbury
Hatton Mrs V F, res 600 n Salisbury
Hicks Mrs Gertrude, res 513 n Salisbury
Jolly Miss Bettie, res 116 s McDowell
Jones Mrs Jennie, res 219 s West
Jones Mrs Etta, res 110 s McDowell
Lewis Mrs Amanda, res 113 w Morgan
Little Mrs C M, cor Jones and Dawson
Lodge Mrs C F, res 14 s Salisbury
Moore Mrs Drusilla, res 129 e Hargett
Morris Mrs Solicitor, res 109 Grimes' al
Pope Mrs Martha, res 513 n Salisbury
Saintsing Mrs L A, res 118 Johnson
Schilling Mrs Eugene, res 101 Johnson

Smith Mrs Hattie, res 752 Fayetteville
Steine Miss Dixie, res 503 Newbern ave
Suggs Mrs Helen, res 808 s Wilmington
Teasley Mrs Victoria, res 119 s Dawson
Upchurch Mrs C W, res 314 e Hargett
Uzzle Mrs Ailey, res 18 Johnson
Williams Mrs Carcilla, res 324 w Lane
Williams Miss Annie, res 309 w Davie
Williams Miss Columbia, res 309 w Davie
Williams Mrs Susan, res 110 s McDowell

Druggists.

Bobbitt J Hal, 233 Fayetteville
HICKS & ROGERS, 101 Fayetteville
JOHNSON JAMES I, 304 Fayetteville
KING W H & CO, 201 Fayetteville
King O G, cor Wilmington and Hargett
MAC RAE JOHN Y, 19 e Martin and 20 Exchange Place
MAC RAE J Y (Branch Pharmacy), 240 Fayetteville
McKimmon James & Co, 133 Fayetteville
Park-Avenue Pharmacy, w Martin
Pescud John S, 118 Fayetteville
SIMPSON WM, 326 Fayetteville
Simpson Robert, corner Hillsboro' and Salisbury
WYNNE & BIRDSONG, Halifax near cor Johnson

Dry Goods, Notions, &c.

Crocker H H, 9 e Hargett
Jones W E, 206 Fayetteville
Lyon Racket Store, 16 e Martin
Moxie J M, 217 s Wilmington
Sherwood C A & Co, 203–205 Fayetteville
Stronach A B, 215 Fayetteville
Tucker W H & R S & Co, 123–125 Fayetteville
Woodward Miss Julia, 202 s Wilmington
WOOLLCOTT & SON, 14 e Martin
WOOLLCOTT FRED, 214 s Wilmington

Dyers and Scourers.

Harris D W C, 310 s Bloodworth
Kreth Alex, 122 s McDowell

Editors.

ANDREWS GREEK O, Press-Visitor, bds Yarboro' House
Ayer H W, The Caucasian, res cor Hargett and Salisbury
Bailey J W, Biblical Recorder, res 513 n Blount
Branson Levi, Almanac and State Directories, res Branson House

DANIELS JOSEPHUS, News and Observer, res 125 e South
Ennis James H, Turner's N C Almanac, res 117 n Salisbury
Leak R H W,* Outlook, res 316 e Davie
Merritt F L, North Carolinian, bds Park Hotel
Moffitt E L, Christian Sun, bds cor Hargett and McDowell
Ray M T, Sun Light, res 744 Fayetteville
Ramsey J L, Progressive Farmer, rooms cor Hillsboro' and Salisbury
Smith Z P, Lodge Weekly, res 404 Hillsboro'
Young James H,* Gazette, res 226 e Lenoir

Engineers—Locomotive.

Allen T W, res 203 Saunders
Allen J W, res 118 n Dawson
Atwood A C, res n Saunders
Beckham C H, res 229 n Dawson
Bishop W R, res 221 n Salisbury
Crone W H, res 214 n Harrington
Ennis T C, res 117 n Salisbury
Faison W A, res 617 w Jones
Fetner W H, res 313 w Jones
Harding W H, res cor Bloodworth and Oakdale ave
Heileg H J, res n Salisbury, o s n
Hicks Daniel, res 418 n Person
Hunnicutt C B, res 10 e North
Horton W T, res n Salisbury, o s n
Horton W A, res n Blount, o s n
Horton R H, res n Salisbury, o s n
Johnson J H, res o s n
King D M, res 224 n McDowell
Lacy B R, res 539 n Blount
Martin E M, res 215 w Jones
Neimeyer J C, res 118 Firwood ave, o s n
Nowell W L, res 120 Firwood ave, o s n
Pleasants T H, res 228 n Dawson
Robertson John, res 10 e North
Smith J O, res 409 Saunders
Smithurst W A, res 510 s Salisbury
Stone T S, res 12 e Johnson
Terrell T B, res 18 Peace
Tighe M W, res 801 Railroad ave
Vaughan E H, res Firwood ave, o s n
Watson J R, res 119 Firwood ave
Wright D K, res 10 e North

Embalmer and Funeral Director.

BROWN JOHN W, cor Salisbury and Hargett

Engineers—Civil.

Harris T C, res 14 n Saunders
Linehan W A, 210 Fayetteville
Massey C E, A & M College
Riddick W C, A & M College
Shaffer A W, cor Fayetteville and Lenoir

Engineers—Mechanical.

ANDREWS WM J, res 407 n Blount
Craighill N R, A & M College

Exchanges.

Raleigh Cotton and Grocers' Exchange, s Wilmington, Ed H Lee
    pres

Express Companies.

Southern Express Co, 108 Fayetteville, A P Bryan agt

Fertilizers.

The Caraleigh Phosphate and Fertilizer Co, South Raleigh
The N C Cotton-Oil and Fertilizer Co, cor Davie and Harrington

Fish Dealers.

Ives Geo N & Co, market, C D Arthur mgr
Smith W D, market, Fayetteville
Tate Jesse,* market, Fayetteville
Wallace C S,* market, Fayetteville

Florists.

STEINMETZ H, Halifax, o s n

Flour Mills.

The Farina Roller Flour Mills, Jenkins near N C R R

Founders and Machinists.

Allen & Cram Machine Co, cor West and Hargett
Gill J H, cor Davie and McDowell
N C Car Company, near Ral cot mill

Furniture Dealers.

Barber J W & Son, 110-112 e Martin
Ray J W & Co, 117 e Martin
ROYALL & BORDEN, 218 s Wilmington
THOMAS & MAXWELL, 9-12 e Martin and 10 Exchange Place
Tucker G S & Co, 128 e Martin

Furniture Manufacturers.

Roles Ruffin, w Jones near r r crossing

Gas and Electric Light Companies.

Raleigh Gas and Electric Light Co, wks cor Cabarrus and McDowell
Raleigh Electric Light Co, plant cor Jones and West

General Merchandise, Dry Goods, &c.

Heilig K, 209 s Wilmington
Levine & Brown, 208-216 and 220 s Wilmington
Morris A, 223 s Wilmington
Rosengarten J, 206 s Wilmington
Spence Co, 126 e Martin

Gentlemen's Furnishing Goods.

Berwanger S & D, 219 Fayetteville
Cross & Linehan, 210 Fayetteville
Jones W E, 206 Fayetteville
Whiting Bros, 10 e Martin
WOOLLCOTT & SON, 14 e Martin

Grocers—Wholesale.

Adams L H & Co, 310 s Wilmington
Crowder & Rand, 301 s Wilmington
Dewar & Wilder, 13 Martin and 14 Exchange Place
FERRALL JOHN R & CO, 222 Fayetteville
Johnson D T, agt, 16 e Hargett
Myatt & Hunter, 17 Martin and 18 Exchange Place
Norris M T & Bro, 239 s Wilmington
Parker & Terrell, 312 s Wilmington
PESCUD THOMAS, 214 Fayetteville
Pool & Moring, 237 s Wilmington
Rosenthal M, 136 Fayetteville
Snelling W N, 309 s Wilmington
Stronach & Sons, 213 Fayetteville
Wyatt J P & Bros, 15 Martin and 16 Exchange Place

Grocers—Retail.

Adams J G, 201 n Harrington
Adams L H & Co, 310 s Wilmington
Bailey F L, 233 s Wilmington
Baker James & Co,* cor Dawson and South
Ball Jesse G, 9 e Hargett
Barber J W & Son, 110 e Martin
Barham A A, 123 e Martin
Betts Bros, 12 e Hargett
Betts W A & Co, 14 e Hargett
Bledsoe M A Jr, cor Fayetteville and Davie
Braan Joseph,* Hargett, o s e
Branch D M, 401 w South
Broadwell D J, s Blount
CARROLL J D, 225 s Wilmington
Castlebury F D, 508 Hillsboro'
Cater Ben,* Hargett, o s e
Caudle & Ruth, cor Hillsboro' and West
Caudle W H T, cor Swain and Martin
Childress T W, 115 e Hargett
Cole Reuben,* 112½ e Hargett
Conn D G, 102 w Jones
Deboy N & Son, 13 Exchange Place
Dorsett Bros, cor Wilmington and Hargett
Duke J E, cor East and Davie
Ellis A J, Hillsboro' rd, o s w
Emery A V, cor Cabarrus and Dawson
FERRALL J R & CO, 222 Fayetteville
Gattis H O, Newbern ave, o s e
Gower W A, cor Harrington and South
Harris W N, 606 e Davie
Harris J J, 210 s Wilmington
Hornbuckle R T, 709 s Blount
Horton & Lee, cor Bloodworth and Lane
Jeffreys P J,* w South
Johnson D T, agt, 16 e Hargett
Johnson O H, cor Harrington and Hillsboro'
Johnson J J, Hargett, o s e
Kenneth Bros, cor Salisbury and Jones
King & Hales, 118 e Martin
Mann W B, 5 e Hargett
Matthews Frank, cor Blount and Lenoir
McIntosh J W, 122 e Martin
Moore Thomas E, 114 w Peace
Neal L C, n West near R R
Overby W H, cor Wilmington and Smithfield

Pace E R, 702 n Person
Pace R A, 713 n Person
Parker J W, cor Harrington and Martin
Parker Claude, cor Dawson and Martin
PESCUD THOMAS, 214 Fayetteville
Phillips & Co, 329 s Wilmington
Pool E N, e Davie, res 506 e Hargett
Pool Burborn, 121 w Morgan
Proctor C I,* 110 n Harrington
Ray Mrs Sallie, cor Haywood and Davie
Reavis W J, Hillsboro' rd, o s n
Renfrow Berry, cor Cabarrus and McDowell
Robinson B J,* 314 w Cabarrus
Rogers W H, 12 Exchange Place
Rogers W A, Prairie bldg
Rosenthal M, 136 Fayetteville
Sanderford W L, cor Blount and Smithfield
Sanderford J W, Hargett, o s e
Scarborough E F, 124 e Martin
Snelling W N, 309 s Wilmington
Stevens & Son, cor Salisbury and Martin
Stewart P M, 816 Fayetteville
Strickland H S,* 815 Fayetteville
Summerlin J J, cor Davie and East
Taylor L D, 219 s Wilmington
Turner J D, cor Halifax and Johnson
Upchurch B W, 15 e Hargett
Utzman R M, 127 n Dawson
Waddell Wm,* 745 s Blount
Williams Geo J, cor Blount and Davie
Wright J J,* cor Manly and Worth
Womble L D, 17 e Hargett
Worlds Mrs Bettie, s Bloodworth
Wyatt & Co, cor Salisbury and Johnson
Young C W, 11 e Hargett

Halls.

Academy of Music, cor Martin and Salisbury
A & M College, West Raleigh
Briggs Hall (Briggs Building)
Chapel Centennial Graded School
Chapel Murphy School
Chapel Peace Institute
Chapel Blind Institution
Commons Hall (State Building)
Court-House (County Building)
Knights of Honor

Knights of Pythias
Masonic (Holloman Building)
Metropolitan, over city market
Odd Fellows
Senate Hall (State Building)
Shaw University

Hardware and Cutlery.

BRIGGS THOS H & SONS, 220 Fayetteville
LEWIS JULIUS HARDWARE CO, 224 Fayetteville
Lumsden J C S, 226 Fayetteville
Womble L D, cor Hargett and Wilmington

Harness Makers and Saddlers.

Hinton L B,* 106 s Wilmington
Mitchell B N, 331 s Wilmington
Wyatt E F & Son, 109 e Martin

Hide and Fur Dealers.

Love E H, 118 e Hargett

Hospitals.

Leonard Hospital,* s Wilmington
Rex Hospital, 17 w South

Hotels.

Central Hotel, cor Wilmington and Hargett, H J Dowell proprietor
Exchange Hotel, Hillsboro', Mrs R W Smith proprietor
PARK HOTEL, cor McDowell and Martin, Brown & Crawford proprietors
YARBOROUGH HOTEL, Fayetteville, L T Brown proprietor

Hucksters.

Adams Jack L, stall 20, market
Fleming G W,* stall 9, market
Hiler Ben,* stall 8, market
Long Abe, stall 7, market
Marsh G W, stall 4, market
Patterson H A,* stall 16, market
Perry L H, stall 10, market
Pearce Brittian,* stall 21, market
White John, stall 23, market

Ice Dealers.

RALEIGH ICE & REFRIGERATING CO, w Hargett, T L Eberhardt pres
THE CRYSTAL ICE FACTORY, s West, Jones & Powell props

Insurance Agents—Life.

Beam S M, Baltimore Immediate-Payment Life, Pullen bldg
Burkhead & Farwell, Pullen bldg
Burkhead & Lindsey, Pullen bldg
Bonshall J D, Ætna Life, 113½ Fayetteville
Carpenter J C S, Pullen bldg
DREWRY JOHN C, Mutual Benefit of N J, 212 Fayetteville
Hay T T, Phœnix Life, 237 Fayetteville
HAYES J J, Staunton Life of Va, 301½ Fayetteville
Hollingsworth John R, Mutual Reserve Fund of N Y
HUNTER C J, Union Central Life, Com'l and Farmers Bk bldg
Johnson J R, Sun Life Assurance Co of Canada, 238 Fayetteville
RANEY R B, Penn Mutual, Yarborough House bldg
Rogers R W, Mass Mutual, 224½ Fayetteville
Russ Wm M, Mutual Life of Ky, City Hall bldg
Saunders Wm J, Mass Benefit, Commercial and Farmers Bk bldg
Waitt S D, Conn Mutual, Fayetteville

Insurance Agents—Fire.

ASHE S A & SON, 240 Fayetteville, up-stairs
BROUGHTON J M & CO, s w Martin
CAMERON & BATCHELOR, 238 Fayetteville
Carpenter J C S, Pullen bldg
Cowper B G, 240 Fayetteville, up-stairs
Dodd W H, 311 s Wilmington
Drewry & Gatling, 212 Fayetteville
HAY T T & BRO, 237 Fayetteville
Johnson & Johnson, 109 Fayetteville
KENNY JOHN B, Pullen bldg
PRIMROSE W S, 220 Fayetteville, up-stairs
PRIMROSE & ROOT, 220 Fayetteville, up-stairs
Smith W W, 217 Fayetteville
Thompson Geo W & Co, cor Wilmington and Martin
Wynne, Ellington & Co, 10 w Hargett

Jewelers.

BLAKE T W, 109 Fayetteville
Cole J W, 13 w Hargett
FASNACH EDWARD, 110 Fayetteville

JOLLY B R, 128 Fayetteville
Mahler's Sons H, 228 Fayetteville

Justices of the Peace.

WHITE.

Adams E A, 221 s Wilmington
Alford J H, 113 n Salisbury
Barbee M B, office 41⅛ s Wilmington
Beine C H, 108 e Hargett
Cheek E S, res 114 n Dawson
Hill J B, 220 Fayetteville
Marcom J C, office Central Hotel bldg
Martin W H, res Idlewild, o s e
Merritt K W, res 20 s Swain
Newsom J D, res 302 w Jones
Nichols John, office 6½ w Martin
ROBERTS H H, office Frap's bldg, e Davie
Russ Wm M, Mayor's office
Stewart P M, 816 Fayetteville
Whitaker Wesley, office 119 e Martin
Wynne W W, res cor Elm and Oakwood ave

COLORED.

Baker James, res 736 Fayetteville
Debnam W F, res 214 w Lenoir
Graves W M, res Oberlin, o s w
Hunter C N, res Cotten lane, o s e

Land Agents.

BROUGHTON J M & CO, s w Martin
Wynne, Ellington & Co, 10 w Hargett
Fort D I N Co, Commercial & Farmers Bank bldg

Laundries.

LINNELL STEAM LAUNDRY, 114 e Davie
OAK CITY STEAM LAUNDRY, 216 Fayetteville

Leather and Shoe Findings.

Womble L D, 17 e Hargett

Letter-Carriers.

Adams D T, superintendent, res 520 s Bloodworth
Brown W M Jr, res 304 e Morgan

Farmer J T, res 513 s West
Gorham A L,* res 114 e Lenoir
Hackney R H,* res 736 Fayetteville
Swain D Shelly, res 322 Oakwood ave
Pace R A, substitute, res 713 n Person
Perry Chas H,* substitute, res 402 e Davie

Libraries.

N C State Library, cor Edenton and Salisbury
Supreme Court Library, cor Edenton and Salisbury

Livery, Sale and Exchange Stables.

Barham A A, 121 e Martin
BLAKE'S LIVERY, cor Martin and Blount
Littlepage J W, s w cor Martin and Blount
Martin E M, 128 e Morgan
Nixon & Johnson, s Wilmington
O'Kelly Isaac,* 214 e Martin
Pace J M, 111 e Martin
Parham R E, 325 s Wilmington
Stronach Frank, 321 s Wilmington
Upchurch W A, 314 s Salisbury

Lock and Gunsmiths.

Brockwell T F, s Salisbury
Kenster A T, Academy of Music bldg

Lumber Dealers.

Cary Lumber Co, w Cabarrus
Mills Mfg Co, Fayetteville, near r r crossing
N C Building & Supply Co, n West
N C Car Co, Franklin near R R

Machinists.

Brinkley G W, S A L R R, res 114 Johnson
Clifton R V, S A L R R, res 714 n Person
Cole W H, S A L R R, res 124 Firwood ave
Cole H E, res 124 Firwood ave
Coley C H, S A L R R, res 523 Hicks' lane
Cram W C (Allen & Cram Machine Co), bds Park Hotel
Crawford A J, res 116 s McDowell
Cuthrell James, S A L R R, bds 10 e North
Dixon C N, S A L R R, res Franklin, o s n

Ellington R L, Allen & Cram, res 121 s West
Ellsworth C B, S A L R R, res 212 n Harrington
Engelhard Fred, res 313 e Martin
Fetner Frank, S A L R R, res 313 w Jones
Finnell Albert, wks J H Gill, res cor Cannon and West
Fraps J C, res cor Fayetteville and Davie
Gill Geo F, S A L R R, bds Exchange Hotel
Hanks W H, S A L R R, res 427 Halifax
Hatch F A, S A L R R, res 41 w Peace
Horton J W Jr, S A L R R, res 223 n Salisbury
Holtzman R L, wks at S A L R R
Jones Matthews, wks Ral Elec Co, res 122 n Dawson
Kaylor C H, wks Phosphate Co, res E Hargett
Kehoe R H, S A L R R, res Firwood ave
Larson A M, S A L R R, res 529 n Salisbury
Lyons James, S A L R R, res 415 n Wilmington
Maglenn James, master mechanic S A L R R, res Halifax
Massey C F, wks Ral cot mill, bds cor Halifax and Franklin
Mitchell Abe, wks Allen & Cram, res 604 e Davie
Mitchell Chas, wks Allen & Cram, res 553 e Martin
Mitchell W G, wks Allen & Cram, res 538 e Martin
Nottingham W G, S A L R R, res 218 n Harrington
Olmstead T C, res 602 e Davie
Pace E R, S A L R R, res Franklin, o s n
Park C B, instructor A & M College, res 314 Polk
Parish D B, S A L R R, res 109 Johnson
Partin Donald, res cor w Jones and St Mary's
Perkins T A, wks for S A L R R
Price T J, S A L R R, res 306 n Person
Price Sion D, S A L R R, res 306 n Person
Riggan J R, wks N C Car Co, res cor Hargett & West
Robbins W W, S A L R R, res 119 w Edenton
Shepherd Frank, foreman S A L R R, res 101 n McDowell
Shepherd W O, foreman N C Car Co, res 531 n Salisbury
Smith William Jr, S A L R R, res 427 Halifax
Smethurst W A, res 510 s Salisbury
Thompson C H, res 410 w North
Watson A L, S A L R R, res 413 n Saunders
Watson A S, S A L R R, res 119 Firwood ave
Willson J V, S A L R R, res 534 n West
Womble Geo L, res 314 s Dawson

Marble Works.

COOPER BROS, yard Fayetteville
Marks E T, yard w Martin

Mattress Makers.

N C Institution for the Blind, w Jones
ROYALL & BORDEN, 218 s Wilmington
THOMAS & MAXWELL, 9 e Martin, 10 Exchange Place

Mercantile Associations.

Raleigh Protective Mercantile Association, W C Stronach pres

Merchant Tailors.

Bridgers Bros, 218 Fayetteville
HERMAN FRANK, 14 w Hargett
PHYSIOC J E, 131 Fayetteville
Taylor W T, e Hargett, cor Haywood
TAYLOR W A, 10 w Martin
WALTERS GEO N, 234 Fayetteville
WEIKEL C, 124 Fayetteville

Millinery and Fancy Goods.

Besson Madame E, 111 Fayetteville
Jones W E, 206 Fayetteville
Lyon Racket Store, 16 e Martin
N Y Bazaar, 211 Fayetteville
Reese M, 209 Fayetteville
Woodward Miss Julia, 202 s Wilmington
WOOLLCOTT & SON, 14 e Martin

Motormen—Electric Railway.

Brown W D, res 121 w Cabarrus
Cooper W E, res Hillsboro' rd, o s w
Fender W A, bds Branson House
Harrison J B, bds w Morgan
Jones L, bds Branson House
Marcom E D, res 209 w Morgan
Warren H W, res Hillsboro' rd, o s w

Moulders—Brass.

Nottingham J T, res 220 n Salisbury
SEPARK CHAS A, 307 w Jones

Moulders—Iron.

Emery Edward, bds w Cabarrus
Gooch Charles, res 327 w South
Hunt J W Jr, 218 s Harrington
Jordan James F, res 565 e Hargett
King William S, res 402 e Hargett
Marcom Charles B, res 416 e Hargett
Morris Joseph, res 745 Fayetteville
Nottingham J T, res 220 n Salisbury
Pearce Jeff, res 214 w Cabarrus
Perry Henry, res cor West and Hargett
Riggan W H, res 412 e Hargett
Sadler Walter, res 132 w Cabarrus
Saintsing Atlas, res 559 Newbern ave
SEPARK CHAS A, 307 w Jones
Stranghan Wiley, res Brooklyn, o s w

Musical Instruments.

Cole J W, 13 w Hargett
Darnell & Thomas, 114 Fayetteville
Ludden & Bates, 332 Fayetteville
Royster A D & Bro, 207 Fayetteville

Newspapers.

Biblical Recorder The (weekly), organ of the Baptist denomination, J W Bailey editor, 17 w Hargett
Caucasian The (weekly), H W Ayer editor, 334 Fayetteville
Christian Sun The (weekly), organ of the Christian denomination, E L Moffit editor, 409 Fayetteville
Gazette The,* James H Young editor, over 301 Fayetteville
Lodge Weekly (Fraternal), Z P Smith editor, Academy of Music bldg
NEWS AND OBSERVER (Democratic daily), Josephus Daniels editor, 415 Fayetteville
North Carolinian The (Democratic weekly), Merritt editor, 415 Fayetteville
Outlook The,* R H W Leake editor, 16 s Salisbury
PRESS-VISITOR (Democratic daily), Greek O Andrews editor, 334 Fayetteville
Progressive Farmer The (weekly), organ of the State Farmers' Alliance, J L Ramsey editor, 135 Fayetteville
Sun Light (weekly), M T Ray editor

Notary Public.

Briggs F H, office Raleigh National Bank
BROUGHTON J M, office s w Martin
Crow E B, office Raleigh National Bank
Grandy Willis S, office 113 Fayetteville
Harris M F, office cor Halifax and North
Haywood F P Jr, office Citizens National Bank
Kenny Jno B, office Pullen bldg
Litchford H E, office Citizens National Bank
Litchford Jas O, office Raleigh Savings Bank
Marcom J C, office Central Hotel
Massey A P, office Fisher bldg
Miller H W, office Yarboro' House bldg
ROBERTS H H, office Frap's bldg
Smith W T, office Fisher bldg
Telfair S F, office Capitol bldg
Thompson Geo W, office Commercial and Farmers Bank
Upchurch D D, office Raleigh National Bank
Waitt S D, office Fayetteville
WILDES CHAS D, office over J I Johnson
Womble W T, office e Hargett

Oil Depots.

Standard Oil Co, n Harrington

Opticians.

FASNACH EDWARD, 110 Fayetteville
Mahler's Sons H, 228 Fayetteville

Oyster Dealers.

Carter W E, 120 Fayetteville
DUGHI A, 235 Fayetteville
Ives Geo N & Co, city market
Smith W D, city market

Painters—House and Sign.

BULLOCK CHAS F, basement Central Hotel
Cooper Walter, res 537 e Martin
Farnsworth H M, 112 w Jones
Glenn A E, res n Blount, o s n
Harrison Chas,* 16 s Salisbury
HOUSE S V, s Salisbury, rear T H Briggs & Sons

King W F, res Firwood ave, o s n
Klouse D B, res 229 w Cabarrus
Lancaster F S, res 217 n Harrington
Lancaster Robt E, res n Boylan ave
MACY W R, s Salisbury
Parish W W, 114 e Hargett
Parish Iowa S, res 547 e Jones
Peatross James, res Oberlin, o s w
Rogers Alvis, res 701 s Bloodworth
Taylor H B,* res 424 s Blount
Thompson R T, res 554 e Davie
Thompson Frank L, res 554 e Davie
Williams P J, res 110 s McDowell
Williams Jesse R, res 110 s McDowell
Williams Chas P, res 110 s McDowell
Woodlief J W, res Cox ave, o s w
Yeargan Jas,* res 413 n Salisbury

Paints, Oils and Glass.

BRIGGS THOMAS H & SONS, 220 Fayetteville
Lewis Hardware Co Julius, 224 Fayetteville

Paper Companies.

Raleigh Paper Co, 6 w Martin

Paper Hangers.

WATSON FRED A. 112 Fayetteville
Weathers L C, 113½ Fayetteville

Parks.

A & M College, West Raleigh
Brookside, n e city limits
Burke Square, n Blount
Moore Square, bet e Hargett and e Martin
Nash Square, bet w Hargett and w Martin
Pullen Park, West Raleigh
Union Square, centre of city

Pattern Makers.

Cooper J W, S A L R R, res Firwood ave, o s n
Haynes M R, cor Blount and Morgan
Kleuppelberg Charles, S A L R R, res 220 n Harrington
Rogers M F, wks Allen & Cram Machine Co, res Prairie bldg

Physicians and Surgeons.

Battle K P Jr (eye, ear, nose and throat), cor Lane and Wilmington
Bobbitt W H, office and res 222 w Hargett
Bowen M D,* office and res Shaw Institute
Buffaloe A J, office and res 312 w Edenton
Ellis R B, office and res 218 e Morgan
Faison J A, asst at Insane Asylum, res same
Goodwin A W, res 711 Hillsboro'
Haywood F J, office and res 126 Halifax
Haywood Hubert, office and res 218 Newbern ave
Hines P E, office and res 214 Newbern ave
Jones A O, office and res 118 n Person
Kirby Geo L, supt Insane Asylum, res same
Knox A W, office 133 Fayetteville, res 516 n Blount
Lewis R H (eye, ear, nose and throat), office 217 n Wilmington
McGeachy R S, asst Insane Asylum, res same
McGee J W Sr, office and res cor Edenton and Dawson
McGee J W Jr, office and res cor McDowell and Martin
McKee James, office and res cor Blount and Jones
Renn Geo A, office Park-Avenue Pharmacy
Rogers James R, office and res Park Hotel
Royster W I, office and res 323 w Morgan
Royster Hubert, office and res 323 w Morgan
Scruggs L A,* office and res 21 e Worth
Sexton J A, office and res 507 Fayetteville
Upchurch Harvey C, office and res 219 s McDowell

Photographers.

JOHNSON T B, 113½ Fayetteville
WHARTON C P, 119 Fayetteville, up-stairs

Pianos and Organs.

Cole J W, 13 w Hargett
Darnell & Thomas, 114 Fayetteville
Ludden & Bates, 332 Fayetteville

Picture Frames.

WATSON FRED A, 112 Fayetteville

Plumbers.

SPENCE PLUMBING CO, Academy of Music bldg
STEVENSON THOS S, 15 w Hargett
Young & Hughes, Prairie bldg, s Wilmington

Pool Rooms.

Denton Ed V, 311–313 Fayetteville
Yarborough House, 317 Fayetteville

Printers.

Adams T W, res 414 w Jones
Alford J H, res 113 n Salisbury
Alford L F, res 125 e South
Andrews D H, res 120 w Lane
Bailey O L, res 213 n Dawson
Betts C J, res 406 w Lane
Birdsong J C, res 306 e Hargett
Bogasse Samuel, res 315 e Martin
Brown C A, res 126 w Lane
Brown B B, res 118 s Person
Bynum R D, res 13 s East
Cheek E S, res 114 n Dawson
Collins J B, res 511 n Person
Collins Paul, res 511 n Person
Crabtree Otho, res 221 n West
Faison W E, res 8 s East
Faucette T O, res 510 s Salisbury
Faucette W A, res 228 n Saunders
Fulcher W A, res 521 s Bloodworth
Glenn F M, res 313 e Martin
Hampton J S, res 109 n Salisbury
Holder George, res 719 s East
Huggins H R, res 17 s East
Jones W A, res 519 s Bloodworth
Jones C H, res 213 Tucker
King J C, res 713 s Blount
Koonce C G, res 314 Hillsboro'
Koonce C F, res 204 e Lenoir
Lee R E, res 321 e Cabarrus
Lewis J J, res 113 w Morgan
Marcom John W, res 416 e Hargett
McGowan P W, res 328 s McDowell
McRary J N, res 309 w Davie
Mitchell G W, res 410 e Edenton
Nichols S L, res 408 n Bloodworth
Peddy D M, res 205 e Hargett
Pittman Jos C, res 543 e Hargett
Putney W A, res 205 Smithfield
Rivers R C, res cor Oakwood ave and Bloodworth
Royster W B, res 210 Newbern ave

Scarborough E F, res 212 e Davie
Scott W O, res Smithfield
Smith W O, res 323 s McDowell
Smith L W, res 308 n Dawson
Sutton J M, res cor Salisbury and North
Straughan T E, res Brooklyn, o s n
Turbeville G J, res 403 s Blount
Utley W M, res 113 n Person
Uzzle W C, res 23 n Saunders
Vaughan Pal, res 327 e Davie
Wicker R D, res 323 e Cabarrus
Wicker E J, res 323 e Cabarrus
Womble W L, res 636 e Hargett
Woods W A, res 119 e Davie

Printers—Book and Job.

CAPITAL PRINTING CO, Academy of Music bldg
Edwards & Broughton, cor Salisbury and Hargett
The Christian Sun Co, Fayetteville
UZZELL E M, cor Wilmington and Martin

Proof-Readers.

GORMAN MAXWELL J, res 408 n Person
Uzzell E M, res 312 e Jones

Railroad Depots and Offices.

Seaboard Air Line R R, office Yarboro' House bldg
Seaboard Air Line R R, freight office cor Halifax and Lane
Southern Railway, office of vice-president, Yarboro' House bldg
Southern Railway Division Office, rear Citizens National Bank
Southern Railway Freight Office, w Cabarrus
Union Depot Passenger Station, cor Martin and Dawson

Real Estate and Rental Offices.

ALLEN & BOYDEN CO, Pullen bldg
BROUGHTON J M & CO, s w Martin
Wynne, Ellington & Co, 10 w Hargett

Restaurants.

Brown A,* 113 e Hargett
Burns Tony,* 203 s Wilmington
Dunston Manda,* 229 s Wilmington
Johnson Martha,* 223 s Wilmington

Jones C C & Co,* 205½ s Wilmington
Page Hattie E,* 223 s Wilmington
Ray & Wallace,* 207½ Wilmington
Richardson James,* 205½ s Wilmington
Rochelle L S, 235 s Wilmington
Taylor Ella,* 134 s Wilmington

Stenographers and Typewriters.

Alderson Miss Mamie, res 212 n Harrington
Barnes R E, for R B Raney, res n East
Bauer Mrs Rachel, res 13 w Cabarrus
Birdsong Miss Mamie, res 306 e Hargett
Carroll J C, U S marshal's office, res 513 Fayetteville
Cobb N T, Southern Railway office, 607 n Person
Crabtree Walter, Raleigh Water Co, res 205 n Salisbury
Davis Miss Mary, for R T Gray, res 415 Elm
Fort Miss K W, for W H & R S Tucker & Co, res n Boundary
Harward Miss Addie, for J D Bushall, res 208 Newbern ave
Heartt T B, for Southern Railway, res 128 s Dawson
Hinsdale J W Jr, for J W Hinsdale Sr, res 330 Hillsboro'
Horton Miss Ina, for J C Drewry, res n Wilmington
Lee Miss Lizzie, teacher of stenography, res 220 Hillsboro'
Lindsey R L, res 110 s West
Massey A P, office 217 Fayetteville
Parkinson J L, for Southern Railway, bds Harrison House
Partin Miss L W, for Agricultural Dept, res cor East and Oakwood ave
Rivers Mrs R C, res cor Oakwood ave and Bloodworth
Rogers B W, for S A L R R, bds 112 w Edenton
Seawell J L, for Supreme Court, res cor Hargett and Swain
Smith W T, office 217 Fayetteville
Smith M M, office Y M C A bldg
Snow Geo H, res Boylan ave
Stunkel Miss M E, for J M Broughton & Co, res 603 n Saunders
Thompson Herbert, for W R Tucker, res 424 Halifax
Weathers L H, for C E Johnson & Co, res 324 s Blount
WILDES CHAS D, office 303 Fayetteville (upstairs), res 118 s Dawson

Saloons.

Adams E A, 221 s Wilmington
Bailey F L, 233 s Wilmington
CARROLL J D, 225 s Wilmington
Deboy N Jr, 15 Exchange Place
Denton E V, 311-313 Fayetteville
Freeman James, 13 e Hargett
Hamlin J E & Co,* 205 s Wilmington

Harris J S, 207 s Wilmington
Harris & Hill, 227 s Wilmington
Harris J J, 210 s Wilmington
Hoover C W,* 213 s Wilmington
Johnson J J, e Hargett, o s e
Mangum D C, s Blount
McClure William, 232 Fayetteville
Parham R E, 17 Exchange Place
Potter & Scott, 114 e Martin
Smith S T, 9 Exchange Place
Smith John U, 11 Exchange Place
Upchurch W D Jr, 215 s Wilmington
Walker L J, Yarborough House
Walton J E, 235 s Wilmington
White L N, 231 s Wilmington
Woodard M W, 316 w Cabarrus

Sash, Doors and Blinds.

N C BUILDING & SUPPLY CO, n West
N C CAR CO, Franklin

Sewing Machine Companies.

Singer Sewing Machine Company, 115 Fayetteville

Sign Writers.

BULLOCK CHAS F, shop basement Central Hotel
MACY W R, shop s Salisbury

Slate Roofers.

CLARK M S, res 319 e Jones

Steam and Gas Fitters.

ALLEN & CRAM MACHINE CO, cor Hargett and West
Raleigh Gas Co, cor McDowell and Cabarrus
SPENCE PLUMBING CO, Academy of Music bldg
STEVENSON THOS S, 15 w Hargett
Young & Hughes, Prairie bldg, s Wilmington

Ticket Agencies.

CAMERON & BATCHELOR, 228 Fayetteville

Telegraph Companies.

Postal Telegraph Company, 11 e Martin
Western Union Company, 328 Fayetteville

Telephone Companies.

Southern Bell Telephone Company, 110½ Fayetteville

Theatres and Places of Amusement.

Academy of Music, cor Salisbury and Martin
Metropolitan Hall, Fayetteville

Tin and Sheet Iron Workers.

Lewis Hardware Co Julins, 224 Fayetteville
Lumsden J C S, 226 Fayetteville
Lumsden Chas F, 108 s Wilmington

Tobacco Buyers—Leaf.

Fleming E L, res 516 s Salisbury
Johnson C E, res 120 Hillsboro
Lea C W, office Farmers Warehouse
Love T L, res 413 Newbern ave
McGhee Geo B, res 103 e Edenton
Moore Van B, res 311 w Martin
Pogue Jos E, 315 s Wilmington
Williamson R L, office Farmers Warehouse, res o s e

Tobacco Manufacturers—Chewing.

Pogue Jos E, 315 s Wilmington

Tobacco Manufacturers—Smoking.

Ball Jesse G, 118 e Hargett

Transfer Companies.

BLAKE JOSEPH, mgr, cor Martin and Blount
CAMERON & BATCHELOR, 228 Fayetteville
Martin E M, e Morgan
Upchurch W A, s Salisbury

Traveling Salesmen.

Bagwell L C, res 701 s Blount
Bailey C Tom, res 513 n Blount
Baker Charles C, res 529 s Salisbury
Barkley J R, res n Person
Blake H D, res 231 w Morgan
Gulley J P, res 425 s Wilmington
Habel F W, res 327 w Jones
Hamlet J T, res 119 s Blount
Higgs James A, res 417 n Blount
Kendrick W B, res 435 Halifax
King R O, res 713 s Blount
King A J, res 402 e Hargett
Levy Emmett E, res Smithfield
Miller Henry, bds cor Newbern ave and Person
Pegram L B, res 622 w Jones
Sanders J A, res 328 w Jones
Southerland T R, bds Park Place, n Blount
Thaxton J W, res cor Halifax and Franklin
Thompson John W, res 424 Halifax
Tucker W C, res cor Newbern ave and Person

Typewriter Agents.

Cobb N T (Remington), Yarborough House bldg
Lewis Hardware Co (Hammond), 124 Fayetteville
RALEIGH STATIONERY CO (Bar-Lock), 309 Fayetteville

Typewriter Supplies.

RALEIGH STATIONERY CO, 309 Fayetteville

Undertakers.

Brown John W, cor Salisbury and Hargett
Strickland G A, 128 s Wilmington

Veterinary Surgeons.

Williamson Dr Frank P, res 122 w Hargett

Wagon Manufacturers.

Bowen T A, 130 e Morgan
Evans J W, cor Morgan and Blount
Holloway W H, 123 e Hargett
MILLS MFG CO, Fayetteville, near R R

Warehouses—Tobacco.

Farmers Warehouse, cor Davie and Bloodworth
Jones Warehouse, cor Blount and Davie

Watchmakers and Repairers.

BLAKE T W, 109 Fayetteville
Cole J W, 13 w Hargett
Crawford John W, 128 Fayetteville
FASNACH EDWARD, 110 Fayetteville
JOLLY B R, 128 Fayetteville
Mahler H Sons, 228 Fayetteville
Mahler L A, 228 Fayetteville
Koehler H R, with H Mahler's Sons

Wines and Liquors—Wholesale.

FERRALL JOHN R & CO, 222 Fayetteville
PESCUD THOMAS, 214 Fayetteville
Rosenthal M, 136 Fayetteville

Yeast Dealers.

Fleischmann & Co, 240 Fayetteville, up-stairs, H D Bunch agt

Read

THE PRESS-VISITOR

Every Day for all the News.

RALEIGH'S LEADING DAILY.

Has triple the circulation in the City of any Daily Paper ever Published in Raleigh.

Publishes full Associated Press dispatches every day, giving all the news of the world up to the hour of going to press; also full Market Reports, giving the New York and Liverpool Cotton quotations, New York Stocks, Chicago Grain and Provisions, and daily Commercial and Financial Gossip from all trade centres.

The local news of Raleigh is published more fully in THE PRESS-VISITOR than in any other Raleigh paper.

The Best Advertising Medium.

THE PRESS-VISITOR goes to every family in Raleigh, and is read every day by the entire population of this city. Your advertisement in THE PRESS-VISITOR is read by every man, woman and child in Raleigh.

CIRCULATION INCREASING DAILY.

Subscription Price: $3.00 per year; 25 cents per month.

GREEK O. ANDREWS,
EDITOR AND MANAGER.

G. C. ROYALL. J. L. BORDEN.

ROYALL & BORDEN,

DEALERS IN   **TERMS EASY.**

Lamps, Stoves,

Trunks, Clocks,

PRICES LOW.   Crockery, Shades,

218 S. Wilmington Street,

Stronach Building,

Front Entrance through Stronach Store,

RALEIGH, N. C.

NORTH CAROLINA BOOK CO., 129 Fayetteville St., RALEIGH, N. C.

E. G. HARRELL, Manager.

WE CAN SUPPLY ALL YOUR WANTS.

OUR SPECIALTIES:

Law Books, School Books, Sunday-School Books, Stationery, and all Supplies for the School-Room and Business Office.

North Carolina Headquarters for Public School Books.

SEND FOR CATALOGUES.

SHAW UNIVERSITY, RALEIGH, N. C.

Established at Raleigh, N. C., December 1, 1865, was a pioneer in the education of colored young men and young women. Its Young Ladies' Department, formerly known as Estey Seminary, was the first of its kind ever established.

ALL DEPARTMENTS

have grown better with age, and parents can feel that SHAW is a safe place for their sons and daughters. While a high degree of scholarship is maintained by her students, solid character is insisted upon, and all unwilling to comply with rules and regulations necessary to this end will not find here a congenial atmosphere.

There are Departments of

**LAW, MEDICINE, PHARMACY, MUSIC,
MISSIONARY TRAINING and THEOLOGY,**

AS WELL AS **NORMAL, SCIENTIFIC and COLLEGE COURSES OF STUDY.**

A corps of thirty-two Professors, Teachers and Employés is in charge of the various Departments. Excellent opportunities for acquiring a solid education at a trifling cost are presented.

For Catalogues and other information, address **THE PRESIDENT,**
Shaw University, RALEIGH, N. C.